100 Most Popular
Nonfiction Authors

Recent Titles in the Popular Authors Series

The 100 Most Popular Young Adult Authors: Biographical Sketches and Bibliographies, Revised First Edition
Bernard A. Drew

Popular Nonfiction Authors for Children: A Biographical and Thematic Guide
Flora R. Wyatt, Margaret Coggins, and Jane Hunter Imber

100 Most Popular Children's Authors: Biographical Sketches and Bibliographies
Sharron McElmeel

100 Most Popular Picture Book Authors and Illustrators: Biographical Sketches and Bibliographies
Sharron McElmeel

100 More Popular Young Adult Authors: Biographical Sketches and Bibliographies
Bernard A. Drew

Winning Authors: Profiles of the Newbery Medalists
Kathleen L. Bostrom

Children's Authors and Illustrators Too Good to Miss: Biographical Sketches and Bibliographies
Sharron McElmeel

100 Most Popular Genre Fiction Authors: Biographical Sketches and Bibliographies
Bernard A. Drew

100 Most Popular African American Authors: Biographical Sketches and Bibliographies
Bernard A. Drew

100 Most Popular
Nonfiction Authors

Biographical Sketches and Bibliographies

Bernard A. Drew

Popular Authors Series

LIBRARIES
UNLIMITED
A Member of the Greenwood Publishing Group

Westport, Connecticut • London

Library of Congress Cataloging-in-Publication Data

Drew, Bernard A. (Bernard Alger), 1950–
  100 most popular nonfiction authors : biographical sketches and bibliographies / Bernard A. Drew.
    p. cm. — (Popular authors series)
  Includes bibliographical references and indexes.
  ISBN 978–1–59158–487–2 (alk. paper)
  1. American prose literature—20th century—Bio-bibliography—Dictionaries. 2. Popular literature—United States—Bio-bibliography—Dictionaries. I. Title.
PS369.D74 2008
813'.54—dc22   2007019949

British Library Cataloguing in Publication Data is available.

Library of Congress Catalog Card Number: 2007019949
ISBN: 978–1–59158–487–2

First published in 2008

Libraries Unlimited, 88 Post Road West, Westport, CT 06881
A Member of the Greenwood Publishing Group, Inc.
www.lu.com

Printed in the United States of America

The paper used in this book complies with the Permanent Paper Standard issued by the National Information Standards Organization (Z39.48–1984).

10 9 8 7 6 5 4 3 2 1

Contents

Introduction

Readers have an insatiable appetite to learn more about the world around them, and nonfiction authors have an insatiable yearning to share what they've learned or experienced. *100 Most Popular Nonfiction Authors*, the latest volume in Libraries Unlimited's Popular Author reference series, is a companion to the earlier *100 Most Popular Genre Fiction Authors*. It surveys a range of writers, most of whom specialize in a given area, many of whom rove among nonfiction's genres and writing styles. Yes, nonfiction has genres, and the authors represented here fall into diverse categories. They are environmental writing (ecology, outdoor living, animals), true adventure (survival stories, treks), travel narratives (sampling other cultures through journeys or relocation), life stories (memoirs, biography, and autobiography, including food and sports memoirs), true crime, science, and history. In addition, various writing styles are covered, in particular, investigative writing (political, social, race, and consumer issues) and humor. Not covered are authors who specialize in academic books, cookbooks, puzzle books, how-to books, religious tracts, and political satire.

Genres should not be confused with writing styles. Within genres such as adventure and biography, writers employ traditional narrative, investigative journalism, New Journalism, and New New Journalism. Nonfiction writers also distinguish themselves by style. Investigative reporters, for example, ferret out sources and lock their jaws on a topic. Participatory writers immerse themselves in their subjects and report firsthand. Narrative historians, on the other hand, burrow into archival sources and interview knowledgeable subjects. There have been several waves of investigative writing, dating back at least to Ida Tarbell a century ago. Tom Wolfe and a wave of 1960s writers established a new generation of investigative writers, sometimes called "New New Journalists." New New Journalists active today prefer the term "creative nonfiction" to describe their use of literary techniques.

Authors covered in this volume have been selected, in consultation with librarians, to represent the various genres. The authors also represent "the most popular" within their genre or style—for example, among environmental writers, among sports writers. Each entry comprises an 850-word or so biography with personal and professional information, critical views from published sources, descriptions of writings, and pertinent comments from the authors about their craft. Bibliographies of the authors' works and further sources of information round out the entries.

This guide concentrates on contemporary authors, often ones not covered in large biographical databases and guides—those who have made their mark in the past half century, and particularly on durable writers who are actively writing and are at or nearing their best. The writers included here are best known for their nonfiction; thus, some popular fiction writers who have only occasionally written nonfiction have been excluded. A dozen of the writers included are now gone, among them Henry David Thoreau, but their influence is still felt, by both readers and later writers. Another dozen writers are rising stars. They may have only produced a couple of books so far, but those books show enormous spark and promise. Typical of these dynamic authors is Laura Hillenbrand, who has made her mark with stories of racehorses.

Nonfiction authors have not generally enjoyed the glamour and celebrity of fiction authors, but the rise in popularity of recreational or creative nonfiction means increased interest in these authors. The purpose of this guide is to provide librarians and other users with background information about popular, contemporary, nonfiction authors. The information can be used for selection and collection development to meet reader interest (particularly for male readers) and to compile reading lists for nonfiction fans. Book club leaders might draw upon this information in book club preparation. Likewise, secondary students and other readers will find this a handy reference for research and reports on their favorite nonfiction authors. However it is used, it is hoped that these profiles will increase reading and enjoyment of some of our best and most popular nonfiction.

— Bernard A. Drew

Edward Abbey

Environment, Politics, Travel

Benchmark Title: *Desert Solitaire*

Home, Pennsylvania

1927–1989

About the Author and the Author's Writing

As you motor north on Route 119 in the small Pennsylvania town of Home, in the Laurel Highlands west of Pittsburgh, you'll pass a state historical marker. Installed in 1996, at the urging of a legion of readers and fans, including actor Robert Redford, the sign proclaims the community as the birthplace of Edward Abbey, "Author and defender of wilderness." Interestingly, although one of Abbey's books, the autobiographical *Fool's Progress,* is about his native Indiana County, most of his writing centers on the American West, where Abbey settled permanently in 1948.

Born in 1927, the son of Paul Revere and Mildred Postewaite Abbey, Edward frequently hiked and camped in an old forest area in the Chambersville section of his hometown as a boy. When he was seventeen, he hitchhiked through the Rocky Mountains. The exposure turned him into a committed westerner. He moved to Albuquerque and entered the University of New Mexico, where he earned a bachelor of arts degree in 1951, and a master's degree five years later. He also attended the University of Edinburgh in Scotland. He performed odd jobs and did seasonal work as a park ranger and fire spotter in Utah.

His first nonfiction book, *Desert Solitaire,* described his months alone in the wild and gave voice to a nascent environmental movement that emerged with the rapid growth in the Southwest. Abbey nurtured his persona as "Cactus Ed," an outspoken, at times cranky, champion of untrammeled wilderness, opposed to loggers and dam builders, miners, cattle ranchers, and housing developers.

"Though in many ways he was a quiet scholar and fine craftsman as a writer, he recreated himself as a brawling revolutionary, shocking conservative audiences and frustrating environmental allies by throwing beer cans out the window as he drove at high speed through the desert he assailed others for despoiling," Don Weiss wrote on an Ecology Hall of Fame Web page.

Sierra magazine summed up Abbey's philosophy in quoting him in 2001: "A venturesome minority will always be eager to set off on their own, and no obstacles should be placed in their path; let them take risks, for Godsake, let them get lost, sunburnt, stranded, drowned, eaten by bears, buried alive under avalanches—that is the right and privilege of any free American."

Abbey also adopted Walt Whitman's adage "Resist much, obey little" and found comfort in Henry David Thoreau's anthem to independent ethics, "On Civil Disobedience." Although he participated in anarchic acts against machines, Abbey was not necessarily a Luddite, although it's sometimes hard to tell. Abbey praised the marvel of the electric refrigerator in *Desert Solitaire* and had his main character blast a Coldspot with a shotgun in *The Fool's Progress.* Equally contrarily, he owned both a utilitarian pickup truck and an ark of a 1975 Cadillac Eldorado (a vehicle that later owner Luis Alberto Urrea found haunted by Abbey's ghost; he wrote about it for *Tucson Weekly*).

Abbey's early fiction reflected his academic studies. His second novel, a Western called *The Brave Cowboy,* attracted Hollywood attention. It was made into a film starring Kirk Douglas. Perhaps more influential than *Desert Solitaire* was the author's novel *The Monkey Wrench Gang.* Under continuous studio option since before it appeared in print, it has never been filmed, the topic too touchy for the establishment, no less so in the post–September 11 era.

Abbey wrote *The Monkey Wrench Gang* after he witnessed the destruction in 1962 of Glen Canyon, its grottos flooded, its Anasazi rock art submerged following completion of a federally funded dam. Although shelved with fiction, the work doesn't roam too far from fact. It is about George Washington Hayduke and his mates, who sabotage bulldozers to discourage what they see as rampant and overly destructive "progress." Together they plot to blow up the Glen Canyon Dam. Abbey based the character of Hayduke on his close friend Doug Peacock; Seldom Seen Smith on Ken Slight; Bonnie Abbzug on a Bronx girlfriend named Ingrid; and Doc Sarvis on a mix of friends Al Sarvis, Brendan Phibbs, and others. How much monkey-wrenching these friends did in real life goes unsaid, but Abbey himself wasn't averse to anarchic behavior, according to Douglas Carithers, who describes what he calls the Great Goliath Fiasco on the AbbeyWeb Web site. After *Monkey Wrench*'s publication, there emerged Earth First!, a radical environmental group with a reputation for spiking trees and pouring sugar in heavy equipment gas tanks.

James M. Cahalan rejects any attempts to label Abbey an "eco-terrorist." "Abbey's rejection of violence and clear definition of sabotage as focused on machines, not people, remained part of his principles of monkeywrenching," the biographer wrote in *Infonews* for the British Columbia Environmental Network. Abbey advocated a civil disobedience; his homage to Thoreau is clear in *Down the River,* his 1982 account of a down-river, up-mountain trek.

The unconventional author distrusted organized religion. But as his friend Peacock explained in an article for *Outside* magazine, "he nevertheless believed there were observable guidelines for living, an accessible wisdom that resided in the land. He called the Taoist philosopher Chaung-tzu—who viewed government as deadly not only to mankind but to all of creation—the first anarchist."

Abbey's message is as strong today as when he wrote it. When asked about the future of environmentalism, he told interviewer Eric Temple, "Well I think that it has a very good future. The worse the environment gets, the more popular environmentalism becomes."

Burgeoning population figures as much in Abbey's assessment of nature's loss as technology does. "And we should revise the taxation system to penalize big families and reward single people or childless couples," he told *Mother Earth News* interviewer Dave Petersen. "There are far too many of us here already."

Of course, ever contradictory, Abbey was five times married (Jean Schmechalon in 1950; Rita Deanin in 1952; Judith Pepper in 1965; Renee Dowling in 1974; and Clarke Cartwright in 1982) and was five times a father (with his second, third and fifth wives). Three marriages ended in divorce, one in the wife's death, the last in his own death.

Abbey outlined his mission in the essay "A Writer's Credo" from *One Life at a Time, Please*: "I write to record the truth of our time as best I can see it.... I write to oppose injustice, to defy power, and to speak for the voiceless. I write to make a difference."

Although the place of Abbey's birth is well marked, his grave is not. After he died of internal bleeding at home in Oracle, Arizona, in 1989, Peacock and other friends wrapped his body in a sleeping bag and conveyed it into his beloved desert. "There is no describing what any of us felt," Jack Loeffler wrote in *Adventures With Ed*. "We made final ablutions as we saw fit. We poured beer on his grave in a final toast. Then we left our friend to become one with the desert."

Works by the Author

Desert Solitaire: A Season in the Wilderness (1968), reprinted as *Desert Solitaire* (1988)

Appalachian Wilderness: The Great Smoky Mountains (1970)

Slickrock: The Canyon Country of Southeast Utah, with Philip Hyde (1971)

The Journey Home: Some Words in Defense of the American West (1977)

Back Roads of Arizona (1978), reissued as *Arizona's Scenic Byways* (1992)

The Hidden Canyon: A River Journey (1978)

Desert Images: An American Landscape, with David Muench (1979)

Abbey's Road: Take the Other (1979)

Down the River (1982)

In Praise of Mountain Lions, with John Nichols (1984)

Beyond the Wall: Essays from the Outside (1984)

Slumgullion Stew: An Edward Abbey Reader (1984), reprinted as *The Best of Edward Abbey* (1988)

Confessions of a Barbarian (1986), revised as *Confessions of a Barbarian: Selections from the Journals of Edward Abbey, 1951–1989,* edited by David Petersen (1994)

One Life at a Time, Please (1988) (older bibliographies list this by the author's working title, *Rock Salt & Cherry Pie*)

Vox Clamentis in Deserto: Some Notes from a Secret Journal (1989), reprinted as *A Voice Crying in the Wilderness: Essays from a Secret Journal* (1990)

Desert Skin, edited by Thomas Miller (1994)

The Serpents of Paradise: A Reader (1995)

Postcards from Ed: Dispatches and Salvos from an American Iconoclast, edited by Terry Tempest Williams and David Petersen (2006)

Contributor

Cactus Country (1973)

Utah Wilderness Photography: An Exhibition (1978)

Images from the Great West, edited by Marnie Walker Gaede (1990)

Late Harvest: Rural American Writing, edited by David R. Pichaske (1991)

The Best of Outside: The First 20 Years (1998)

Introductions

Walden by Henry David Thoreau (1981)

Ecodefense: A Field Guide to Monkeywrenching, edited by Dave Foreman (1987)

The Land of Little Rain, by Mary Austin (1988)

Wilderness on the Rocks, by Howie Wolke (1991)

Fiction

Jonathan Troy (1956)

The Brave Cowboy (1958), reprinted as *The Brave Cowboy: An Old Tale in a New Time* (1977)

Fire on the Mountain (1962)

Black Sun (1971), in England as *Sunset Canyon* (1972)

The Monkey Wrench Gang (1975), a new edition illustrated by Robert Crumb contains an additional chapter (1985)

Good News (1980)

The Fool's Progress (1988)

Hayduke Lives! (1990), sequel to *The Monkey Wrench Gang*

Poetry

Earth Apples: The Poetry of Edward Abbey (1994)

Film Adaptations and Documentaries

Lonely Are the Brave (1962), based on *The Brave Cowboy*

Fire on the Mountain (1981)

Edward Abbey's Road (1983, PBS documentary)

Edward Abbey: A Voice in the Wilderness (1993 documentary)

For Further Information

Abbey, Edward, "Last Words," *Sierra,* March 2002.

Bishop, James Jr., *Epitaph for a Desert Anarchist: The Life and Legacy of Edward Abbey.* New York: Atheneum, 1994.

Cahalan, James M. *Edward Abbey: A Life.* Tucson: University of Arizona Press, 2001.

Cahalan, James M., "Was Ed Abbey an 'Ecoterrorist'?" "Infonews," British Columbia Environmental Network Web site. http://www.ecobc.org/NewsToday/2005/10/TodaysNews1069/index.cfm (viewed May 9, 2006).

Carithers, Douglas, "Abbey's Boots" (unpublished, 1998), AbbeyWeb. http://www.abbeyweb/net/articles/boots/index.html (viewed May 15, 2006).

Duryea, Kent, "Edward Abbey: A Man Hard to Talk About," *New Dimensions,* Albertus Magnus College. http://www.desertusa.com/mag00/nov/papr/abbey.html (viewed May 9, 2006).

Edward Abbey entry, Contemporary Authors Online, Gale, 2006. Reproduced in Biography Resource Center. Farmington Hills, MI: Tomson Gale, 2006. http://galenet.galegroup.com/servlet/BioRC.

Edward Abbey Historical Marker, ExplorePAhistory.com. http://www.explorepahistory.com/hmarker/phpo?markerId=515 (viewed May 9, 2006).

Hepworth, James, and Gregory McNamee, editors. *Resist Much, Obey Little: Remembering Ed Abbey.* San Francisco: Sierra Club Books for Children, 1996.

Loeffler, Jack. *Adventures with Ed: A Portrait of Abbey.* Albuquerque: University of New Mexico Press, 2002.

Peacock, Doug, "Chasing Abbey," *Outside*, August 1997. http://outside.away.com/magazine/0897/9708abbey.html (viewed May 15, 2006).

Petersen, Dave, "Edward Abbey: Slowing the Industrialization of Planet Earth," Plowboy interview, *Mother Earth News*, May/June 1984. http://www.motherearthnews.com/library.1984_May_June/The_Plowboy_Interview_Edward_Abbey_ (viewed May 9, 2006).

Philippon, Daniel J., Edward Abbey entry, *The Scribner Encyclopedia of American Lives, Volume 2: 1986–1990.* New York: Charles Scribner's Sons, 1999.

Quigley, Peter, editor. *Coyote in the Maze: Tracking Edward Abbey in the World of Words.* Salt Lake City: University of Utah Press, 1998.

Temple, Eric, "An Interview with Edward Abbey . . .," KAET-TV. http://www.canyoncountryzephyr.com/archives/abbey-interview.html (viewed May 9, 2006).

Urrea, Luis Alberto, "Dead Reckoning," *Tucson Weekly*, November 30, 1995.

Weiss, Don, Edward Abbey page, Ecology Hall of Fame. http://www.ecotopia.org/ehof/abbey/index.html (viewed May 9, 2006).

Williamson, Chilton, Jr., *One Life at a Time, Please* review, *National Review*, February 5, 1988.

Diane Ackerman

Adventure, Environment, Memoir, Science

Benchmark Title: *A Natural History of the Senses*

Waukegan, Illinois

1948–

Photo courtesy the author

About the Author and the Author's Writing

Diane Ackerman is an avocational gardener, so it's little surprise she took her well-honed investigative prowess, and her philosophical empathy, into her backyard in *Cultivating Delight* (2004) to expound on the virtues of lopping dead blossoms, nurturing rose bushes, and interacting with a frenetic hummingbird. Her vivid vocabulary shines as she writes of trees that "wear gray-green pantaloons of lichen."

"Complexity excites the mind," Ackerman said on her HarperCollins Web page, "and order rewards it. In the garden, one finds both, including vanishingly small orders too complex to spot, and orders so vast the mind struggles to embrace them. An orderly garden is always on the brink of chaos, and that's part of its charm, I think."

A naturalist and poet, Ackerman is the daughter of restaurant owner Sam Ackerman and his wife, Marcia Tischler Fink Ackerman. She was born in 1948 in Waukegan, Illinois. She first felt an urge to write when she was twelve and attempted an espionage novel. "I understood that it had to have a lot of kissing in it and romance and stuff and violence and all that," she told *January Magazine*'s Linda L. Richards. "But I didn't know anything about any of those worlds. So it was just hopeless." Instead, she started another book about more familiar topics: a girl and a horse.

The author attended Boston University in 1966 and 1967, and received her bachelor of arts degree from Pennsylvania State University in 1970. She received a master of fine arts in 1973, a master's in 1976, and a Ph.D. in 1978, all from Cornell University. Married to fiction writer Paul West, she has worked at various times as a social worker, a government researcher, an editor, an English professor, and a visiting professor or writer in residence for several universities. Her writing career is equally varied. She was a staff writer for *New Yorker* magazine from 1988 to 1994; and she has contributed to *Parade, National Geographic,* and other periodicals, as well as writing poetry, memoirs, and other nonfiction books. For her work, she has received critical recognition and numerous awards and prizes, including a Guggenheim Fellowship, a John Burroughs Nature Award, and a Lavan Poetry Prize. The New York Public Library considers Ackerman one of its Literary Lions. She was a semifinalist in the Journalist-in-Space project.

Ackerman's first nonfiction book was a memoir, *Twilight of the Tenderfoot,* about her experiences in New Mexico where she had gone to enjoy horses and riding. She ended up staying for a year and experiencing cattle ranch life. Her next memoir, *On Extended Wings,* was about her experiences learning to fly an airplane. *A Slender Thread* presents her experiences as a counselor for a crisis hotline, about which she told *U.S. News & World Report* a sense of community is a hallmark of civilization. "Our ancestors were terrified of being outside the group. It could mean their death. We still feel rejection at a hideous event even though we can feed and house ourselves."

A Natural History of the Senses was her first major seller. It discusses all five human senses through a spectrum of subjects, from kisses to tattoos to music. "One of the real tests of writers is how well they write about smells," Ackerman writes in the book. "If they can't describe the scent of sanctity in a church, can you trust them to describe the suburbs of the heart?"

The Moon by Whale Light finds the naturalist waddling with penguins, wading with alligators and basking with whales in a book *Publishers Weekly* described as "popular natural-history writing at its most persuasive." Her examination of unusual ecosystems, *The Rarest of the Rare,* includes a disheartening overview of the annual flight of the monarch butterfly. *Publishers Weekly* called it "a sparkling combination of natural history, travel and adventure."

A Natural History of Love, a follow-up to *Senses,* looks at the emotion's evolution from ancient Egypt to modern marriage rites. Naturally, it examines the fascinating differences between men and women.

In her recent *An Alchemy of the Mind,* Ackerman incorporates the latest neuroscience to craft, as *Booklist* described it, an "agile, uniquely poetic, and insightful inquiry into 'how the brain becomes the mind.'" *The Zookeeper's Wife* is about the wrenching World War II experiences of Warsaw Zoo director Jan Zabinski and his wife, Antonia, who sheltered Jews and Polish resistance members from the Nazis.

Ackerman brought her first poetry into publication in a three-author collection in 1973. Her first independent collection of poetry, *The Planets: A Cosmic Pastoral,* is a comic exploration with scientific accuracy, composed before the *Voyager* spacecraft widened the public's vision of space. She was still a graduate student when the book was published. Throughout her career, she has alternated verse with nonfiction and has often looked at the same subjects in her poetry as in her prose. For instance, she brings her naturalist's eye to *Jaguar of Sweet Laughter,* while *I Praise My Destroyer* uses the author's strong sense of language and imagery to explore and honor all manner of life. The latest volume of poems for adults is *Origami Bridges: Poems of Psychoanalysis and Fire* (2002).

"It's hard for me to keep science out of my writing," Ackerman told interviewer Dulcy Brainard for *Publishers Weekly.* "A critic once said that airfoils, quasars, corpuscles aren't the proper form of art. But to agree ignores much of life's fascination and variety. Writing, which is my form of celebration and prayer, is also my way of inquiry."

Works by the Author

Twilight of the Tenderfoot: A Western Memoir (1980)

On Extended Wings (1985), reprinted as *On Extended Wings: An Adventure in Flight* (1987)

A Natural History of the Senses (1990)

The Moon by Whale Light: And Other Adventures among Bats, Penguins, Crocodilians and Whales (1991)

A Natural History of Love (1994)

The Rarest of the Rare: Vanishing Animals, Timeless Worlds (1995)

A Slender Thread: Crisis, Healing, and Nature (1997)

Deep Play (1999)

Cultivating Delight: A Natural History of My Garden (2001)

An Alchemy of the Mind: The Marvel and Mystery of the Brain (2004)

The Zookeeper's Wife: A War Story (2007)

Juvenile

Monk Seal Hideaway (1995)

Bats: Shadows in the Night (1997)

Poetry

Poems: Ackerman, Bolz, and Steele, with Jody Bolz and Nancy Steele (1973)

The Planets: A Cosmic Pastoral (1976)

Wife of Light (1978)

Reverse Thunder: A Dramatic Poem (1982)

Lady Faustus (1983)

Jaguar of Sweet Laughter: New and Selected Poems (1991)

I Praise My Destroyer (1998)

The Senses of Animals (2000)

Origami Bridges: Poems of Psychoanalysis and Fire (2002)

Animal Sense (2003) (juvenile)

Editor

The Book of Love, with Jeanne Macklin (1998)

Documentaries

Ideas (1990)

Mystery of the Senses (PBS, 1995)

Recordings

The Naturalists (1992) (producer)

A Natural History of Love (1994) (producer)

For Further Information

Alchemy of the Mind review, *Booklist,* January 1, 2005.

"An Interview with Diane Ackerman," HarperCollins Web site. http://www.harpercollins.com/global_scripts/product_catalog/book_xml.asp?isbn=0060505362&tc=ai (viewed May 3, 2006).

Brainard, Dulcy, "Diane Ackerman: A Poet and Naturalist Writer Reports on Adventures with Unusual Animals in Essays Distinguished by Sensory Detail," *Publishers Weekly*, November 1, 1991.

Diane Ackerman biography, Diane Ackerman Web page. http://www.dianeackerman.com (viewed May 3, 2006).

Diane Ackerman entry, Contemporary Authors Online, Gale, 2006. Reproduced in Biography Resource Center. Farmington Hills, MI: Tomson Gale, 2006. http://galenet.galegroup.com/servlet/BioRC.

Moon by Whale Light review, *Publishers Weekly*, September 6, 1991.

Rarest of the Rare review, *Publishers Weekly*, September 11, 1995.

Richards, Linda, "At Play with Diane Ackerman," *January Magazine,* August 1999. http://www.januarymagazine.com/profiles/ackerman.html (viewed May 3, 2006).

"Tea, Sympathy, and Superheroes," *U.S. News & World Report,* February 10, 1997.

Caroline Alexander

Adventure, History, Sports, Survival, Travel

Benchmark Title: *The Endurance*

Gainesville, Florida

1956–

About the Author and the Author's Writing

Writer Caroline Alexander thrives on a good story, but even more so on the interplay of individuals. "The historical details in Alexander's gripping books are surpassed only by her vivid descriptions of the actions of people caught in dire straights," suggests critic Sarah Statz Cords in *The Real Story*.

Alexander was born in Gainesville, Florida, in 1956. She received her bachelor's and master's degrees from Somerville College, Oxford, England, in 1977 and 1980, respectively. She went on to complete requirements for a master's degree in philosophy from Columbia University in 1987. She received a Ph.D. from the same institution. From 1982 to 1985, she lectured in classics at the University of Malawi, Zomba, Malawi, then became a professional writer.

Her first book, *One Dry Season,* published in 1990, traces the steps of Mary Kingsley, who in 1895 wrote a journal, *Travels in West Africa,* about the former French colony of Gabon in West Africa. With thorough research and great detail, Alexander compares yesterday and today. She interviews missionaries and natives—as Kingsley had done—and forges a literary bond with her historical predecessor.

The author channeled another adventurer with her next book, *The Way to Xanadu* in which she searches for specific sites and likely inspirations for images depicted in Samuel Taylor Coleridge's poem "Kubla Khan." Clues of Coleridge's real travels are found in his notebooks. "Alexander began her literal quest on the undulating grasslands of Inner Mongolia, where she made her way to the ruins of Shangdu (or Xanadu)," according to journalist Donna Seamon in *Booklist*. She continued to violent but exotic Vale of Kashmir and Ethiopia, "sharing her candid and illuminating observations of each realm while simultaneously linking them back to Coleridge and his 'dream.'"

"Anderson's next journey was one of time rather than location. Florida State University's Doak Campbell Stadium wasn't far from where she attended college in Tallahassee, and she tutored freshmen football players in 1981 to hone their writing skills. More than a decade later, she sought out those seven players and interviewed them to craft a fascinating story of what they had become." "What she found, as revealed in this book, should chill the hearts of those who hold fast to the belief that the good spawned by college athletics outweighs the bad," suggests reviewer Steve Gtietschier in *Sporting News.* Two of the freshmen had played football professionally. Others ended up working for a bank, in mosquito control, in the court system, or in the prison system. Two were confined in that prison system.

The author returned to her adventurer theme with an unlikely story of Mrs. Chippy, a cat that accompanied Sir Ernest Shackleton's grueling Antarctic expedition in 1914. That was only a prelude to Anderson's full-blown saga of the trek, *The Endurance,* which gave full life to the twenty months seamen were stranded after their ship was trapped by ice floes miles from shore. Shackleton had hoped to be the first to cross the continent on foot. The book, which incorporates material not previously available, is a testimonial to human courage. "Anderson's recounting of the subsequent (and miraculously successful) voyage made by Shackleton and five of his crew, will leave you feeling cold, damp and seasick for days afterward," suggests Salon Books' Scott Sutherland.

The Endurance contains fascinating juxtaposition with today's adventurers—who enjoy the benefits of satellite communications, GPS, Gore-Tex garments, freeze-dried foods and more." "In a crisp narrative lushly decorated with original photographs [from glass-plate negatives and Kodak roll film by Australian Frank Hurley, one of the crew], she captures the spirit of Shackleton's merry band with an intimate, occasionally claustrophobic portrait of the untamed forces that raged against them," according to a reviewer in *U.S. Catholic.* Anderson cowrote the screenplay for a documentary film of the Shackleton experience in 2001.

For her next examination of sea adventure and leadership fallacy, Anderson went back another century. *The Bounty* gives a richer take on Fletcher Christian's revolt against Captain William Bligh on the British vessel in 1789." "In this detailed, balanced and fascinating study of the mutiny, its origins, history and consequences, the author shows that, like so much Hollywood history, the story people know is a travesty of the truth," points out *Contemporary Review.* Among the myths she debunks are that Bligh was a despicable tyrant, that the sailors were abused, and that Christian was a hero. Christian was, in fact, intoxicated and a victim of his own pride. Bligh, who was set adrift with eighteen other sailors, survived a four-thousand-mile ocean jaunt, returned to service, and rose to the rank of admiral.

Anderson told a Borders interviewer that she saw many similarities between Shackleton and Bligh, and also some differences. Surprisingly, she found Bligh more appealing. "For Bligh any feat he performed was solely in the line of his professional duty," she said." "This makes for a less glamorous, but more practical kind of hero."

◥ Works by the Author

One Dry Season: In the Footsteps of Mary Kingsley (1990)

The Way to Xanadu (1994)

Battle's End: A Seminole Football Team Revisited (1995)

Mrs. Chippy's Last Expedition: The Remarkable Journal of Shackleton's Polar-Bound Cat (1997)

The Endurance: Shackleton's Legendary Antarctic Expedition (1998)

The Bounty: The True Story of the Bounty (2003)

Screenplay

The Endurance: Shackleton's Legendary Antarctic Expedition, with Joseph Dorman (2001)

For Further Information

Bounty review, *Contemporary Review*, May 2004.

Caroline Alexander entry, Contemporary Authors Online, Gale, 2006. Reproduced in Biography Resource Center. Farmington Hills, MI: Thomson Gale, 2006. http://galenet.galegroup.com/servlet/BioRC.

Caroline Alexander interview, Borders Web site. http://www.bordersstores.com/features/feature.jsp?file=alexandercaroline (viewed May 1, 2006).

Caroline Alexander interview, "Curator Interview" Peabody Essex Museum Web site. http://www.pem.org/endurance/curator.html (viewed May 9, 2006).

Cords, Sarah Statz, edited by Robert Burgin, *The Real Story: A Guide to Nonfiction Reading Interests*. Westport, CT: Libraries Unlimited, 2006.

Endurance review, *U.S. Catholic,* April 2000.

Gietschier, Steve, "Battle's End: A Seminole Football Team Revisited," *Sporting News*, February 19, 1996.

Seaman, Donna, "The Way to Xanadu," *Booklist,* June 1, 1994.

Sutherland, Scott, *The Endurance* review, "Salon Books," salon.com. http://www.salon.com/books/sneaks/1998/12/03sneaks.html (viewed May 19, 2006).

Stephen E. Ambrose

Adventure, Biography, History

Benchmark Title: *Band of Brothers*

Decatur, Illinois

1936–2002

About the Author and the Author's Writing

Stephen Ambrose was an explorer-in-residence for the National Geographic Society; founder and president of the National D-Day Museum in New Orleans; recipient of the Teddy Roosevelt, Will Rogers Memorial, Bob Hope, and other awards; and consultant to directors Steven Spielberg (for the 1998 motion picture *Saving Private Ryan*) and Ken Burns (for *Lewis & Clark*). On top of all these achievements, he organized Stephen Ambrose Historical Tours—and somehow found time to write.

Stephen Edward Ambrose, the middle of three children of Stephen Hedges Ambrose and Rosepha Trippe Ambrose, grew up in Whitewater, Wisconsin, where his father was a small-town physician in general practice. Ambrose first became hooked on history while in high school and read biographies and campaign accounts of Napoleon Bonaparte. He attended the University of Wisconsin and joined the ROTC. He began premed studies, but when he took an eye-opening course with historian William B. Hesseltine, he changed his major. Hasseltine instilled in his students the need to undertake original research from primary sources. That became Ambrose's career.

In 1957, Ambrose married Judith Dorlester. After her death in 1966, he married Moira Buckley. There were two natural children and three adopted children from the first marriage.

Ambrose received a bachelor of science degree in 1957 and a doctorate in 1963, securing in between a master's degree from Louisiana State University. An associate professor of history at Johns Hopkins University from 1964 to 1969, Ambrose also taught at the University of New Orleans, where he was the Boyd Professor of History from 1989 until he retired in 1995. In later years, he lived in Helena, Montana.

The author's writing career began early. Ambrose published his first book while completing doctoral work. It was about General Henry Halleck, Abraham Lincoln's chief of staff. President Dwight D. Eisenhower read that book and enjoyed it; he contacted Ambrose when the author was an assistant professor at Louisiana State University, involved in study of the Civil War. Eisenhower asked Ambrose to help with his biography. The author went to work on Eisenhower's papers and on his biography. Ambrose eventually wrote six books about Eisenhower. He also wrote a book about

Eisenhower's brother Milton. And he wrote three books about Eisenhower's vice president, Richard M. Nixon, who eventually rose to the chief executive's office himself.

Although his first biographies showed Ambrose's research tenacity and *Eisenhower: Soldier, General of the Army, President-Elect, 1890–1952* won him the Freedom Foundation's National Book Award, critics decried a lack of perspective on his subjects. Popular notice came with *Band of Brothers,* an account of the exploits of parachutists during World War II, based on interviews with surviving members. Those parachutists captured Hitler's Eagle Nest retreat. "What made them special even among those who were already self-selected special, was their leadership," Ambrose said in a BBC interview, "and how well it held together. And it got tested severely on several occasions. Not all elite units had such luck in their leaders, and that's the difference." A *Publishers Weekly* reviewer noted that "The book is enlivened with pertinent comments by veterans of 'Easy Company,' who recall not only the combat action but their relations with their officers ... and their impressions of the countries through which they campaigned."

Ambrose delved further into World War II with *D-Day, June 6, 1944,* again based on oral histories and interviews. "I was ten years old when the war ended," Ambrose is quoted in a National Geographic News obituary. "I thought the returning veterans were giants who had saved the world from barbarism. I still think so. I remain a hero-worshipper."

Although he wasn't yet through with World War II, Ambrose for a time turned his attention to early American history and an idea that grew from numerous family vacations. During summer travels, he and his family sometimes followed the course of Lewis and Clark; Ambrose read from their journals. He persuaded his editor that he should write about Meriwether Lewis and William Clark and their 1804–1806 safari. The result, *Lewis & Clark: Voyage of Discovery*, was a best seller. Ambrose reshaped the material for young adults in *This Vast Land: A Young Man's Journal of the Lewis and Clark Expedition.* Ambrose next wrote a history of expansionism and construction of a rail line across the American continent.

In *The Wild Blue,* Ambrose attempted to do for the U.S. Air Force what *Band of Brothers* did for the infantry, although it centers on one pilot, former Senator George McGovern. Ambrose broadened his approach, and as reviewer Robert Freeman Smith in *The Historian* noted, "One finds important and interesting material on such topics as the role of the Tuskegee Airmen who flew fighter escorts for the bombers; the attempts to knock out the oil refineries at Picesti, Romania; the difficulties of flying the B-24; and the questions of bombing strategy."

Ten months before his death from lung cancer in October 2002, journalists and fellow historians found that four of Ambrose's works—*Citizen Soldiers, Nixon: Ruin and Recovery 1973–1990, Crazy Horse and Custer,* and *The Wild Blue*—contained material from works written by others.

Working under a double cloud of a dark medical prognosis and the criticism of his peers, Ambrose's last book, *To America: Personal Reflections of an Historian,* was a memoir in which he set out, as he told CBS News in May 2002, to "correct all the mistakes I made ... when I would tell my history classes that dropping the bomb on Hiroshima was a crime, that the Mexican-American War was nothing but a land grab and that people like Henry Ford and J.D. Rockefeller got into philanthropy to buy their way into heaven." He told of his personal transformation from a political liberal to a conservative.

In an interview for the Academy of Achievement, the author explained his historian's itch and writing process. Often he began writing before his research was finished. "You learn what the gaps in your knowledge are by starting to tell the story. So the act of writing becomes the act of learning.... There's got to be a flow between, and the writing guiding the research, or at least for me. That's the only way I can do it."

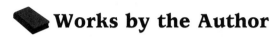 **Works by the Author**

Halleck: Lincoln's Chief of Staff (1962)

Upton and the Army (1964)

Duty, Honor, and Country: A History of West Point (1966)

Eisenhower and Berlin, 1945: The Decision to Halt at the Elbe (1967)

The Supreme Commander: The War Years of General Dwight D. Eisenhower (1970)

Rise to Globalism: American Foreign Policy since 1938 (1971)

Crazy Horse and Custer: The Parallel Lives of Two American Warriors (1975)

Ike's Spies: Eisenhower and the Espionage Establishment, with Richard H. Immerman (1981)

Milton S. Eisenhower: Educational Statesman, with Richard H. Immerman (1983)

Eisenhower: Soldier, General of the Army, President-Elect, 1890–1952 (1983)

Eisenhower: The President (1984)

Pegasus Bridge: 6 June 1944 (1985)

Nixon: The Education of a Politician, 1913–1962 (1987)

Nixon: The Triumph of a Politician, 1962–1972 (1989)

Eisenhower: Soldier and President (1990), condensed version of *Eisenhower: Soldier, General of the Army, President-Elect, 1890–1952* and *Eisenhower: The President*

Nixon: The Ruin and Recovery of a Politician, 1973–1990 (1991)

Band of Brothers: E Company, 506th Regiment, 101st Airborne, from Normandy to Hitler's Eagle's Nest (1991)

D-Day, June 6, 1944: The Climactic Battle of World War II (1994)

Undaunted Courage: Meriwether Lewis, Thomas Jefferson, and the Opening of the American West (1996)

Americans at War (1997)

Citizen Soldiers: The U.S. Army from the Normandy Beaches to the Bulge to the Surrender of Germany (1997)

The Victors: Eisenhower and His Boys—The Men of World War II (1998)

Lewis & Clark: Voyage of Discovery (1998)

Comrades, Brothers, Fathers, Heroes, Sons, Pals (1999)

Nothing Like It in the World: The Men Who Built the Transcontinental Railroad, 1863–1869 (2000)

The Good Fight: How World War II Was Won (2001)

The Wild Blue: The Men and Boys Who Flew the B-24s over Germany (2001)

To America: Personal Reflections of an Historian (2002)

The Mississippi and the Making of a Nation: From the Louisiana Purchase to Today, with Douglas E. Brinkley (2002)

Editor

A Wisconsin Boy in Dixie (1961)

Institutions in Modern America: Innovation in Structure and Process (1967)

The Military and American Society, with James A. Barber Jr. (1972)

The Wisdom of Dwight D. Eisenhower: Quotations from Ike's Speeches and Writings, 1939–1969 (1990)

Eisenhower and the German POWs: Facts against Falsehood, with Gunter Bishof (1992)

American Heritage New History of World War II, revised edition, with C. Sulzberger (1998)

Witness to America: An Illustrated Documentary History of the United States from the Revolution to Today (1999)

Assistant Editor

The Papers of Dwight David Eisenhower: The War Years, five volumes edited by Alfred Chandler (1972)

Contributor

The Harry S Truman Encyclopedia, edited by Richard S. Kirkendall (1989)

What If? The World's Foremost Military Historians Imagine What Might Have Been: Essays, edited by Robert Cowley (1999)

No End Save Victory: Perspectives on World War II, edited by Robert Cowley (2001)

Young Adult

General Ike: Abilene to Berlin (1973)

This Vast Land: A Young Man's Journal of the Lewis and Clark Expedition (2003)

Documentary

Eisenhower: Supreme Commander (BBC, 1973)

Television Mini-Series Based on the Author's Work

The Band of Brothers (2001)

For Further Information

Band of Brothers review, *Publishers Weekly,* May 4, 1992.

"Conversation with Stephen Ambrose," McNeil/Lehrer Productions. http://www.pbs.org/newshour/gergen/ambrose_book_6-20.html (viewed May 9, 2006).

Gray, Paul, "Other People's Words," *Smithsonian*, March 2002.

"Historian Steven [sic] Ambrose Dead at 66," National Geographic News, Oct. 15, 2002. http://news.nationalgeographic.com/news/2002/10/1015_021015 _ambrose.html (viewed May 9, 2006).

Kirkpatrick, David, "As Historian's Fame Grows, So Do Questions on Methods," *New York Times*, Jan. 11, 2002.

Lewis, Mark, "More Controversy for Stephen Ambrose," Forbes.com. http://www.forbes.com/2002/01/09/0109ambrose.html (viewed May 9, 2006).

Morris, Edward, "Stephen Ambrose; A Guide for Appreciating Our History," BookPage. http://www.bookpage.com/0009bp/stephen_ambrose.html (viewed May 9, 2006).

Plotz, David, "Why Stephen Ambrose Is a Vampire," Slate.com http://www. slate.com/id/2060618 (viewed May 9, 2006).

Rosenblatt, Roger, "When the Hero Takes a Fall," *Time*, January 21, 2002.

Smith, Robert Freeman, *Wild Blue* review, *Historian,* Summer 2003.

Stephen Ambrose Historical Tours Web site. http://www.stephenambrosetours. com/ (viewed May 9, 2006).

Stephen E. Ambrose entry, *Authors and Artists for Young Adults*, Volume 44. Detroit: Gale, 2002.

Stephen E(dward) Ambrose entry, Contemporary Authors Online. Reproduced in Biography Resource Center. Farmington Hills, MI: Thomson Gale, 2006. http://galenet.galegroup.com/servlet/BioRC.

Stephen E. Ambrose interview, Academy of Achievement. http://www.achievement. org/autodoc/printmember/amb0int-1 (viewed May 9, 2006).

Stephen E. Ambrose interview, BBC. http://www.bbc.co./uk/drama/ bandofbrothers/features/stephen_ambrose.shtml (viewed May 9, 2006).

"Stephen Ambrose's Last Book," CBS News, May 23, 2002. http://www. cbsnews.com/stories/2002/05/23/print/main509976.shtml (viewed May 9, 2006).

Vast Land review, *Booklist*, September 1, 2003.

Maya Angelou

Fiction, Memoir, Poetry

Benchmark Title: *I Know Why the Caged Bird Sings*

St. Louis, Missouri

1928–

About the Author and the Author's Writing

"[Maya] Angelou's writings have altered society for the better," proclaims the National Women's Hall of Fame Web page for the author and poet, "bringing greater diversity into the theater and literature. Her autobiographical works provide powerful insights into the evolution of black women in the 20th century."

The acclaimed author's insights are large—her screenplay *Georgia, Georgia* was the first produced by a black woman, as she describes in one of her memoirs—and small—she recreates the bygone bustle in her mother's kitchen in her first cookbook, *Hallelujah! The Welcome Table.*

Angelou has had a wide-ranging career in the performing arts and literature. She has sung, danced, and acted on stage. She has directed, produced, and crafted dramas and screenplays. A writer, editor, and civil rights activist, she was invited to read her own poem "On the Pulse of Morning" at Bill Clinton's inauguration in 1993. A few years later, the president presented her with the National Medal of Arts. With a deep memory, a keen eye for detail, and a way with words, she has written poetry that is accessible to younger readers. And she has compiled six volumes of rich memoir beginning in 1970 with *I Know Why the Caged Bird Sings.*

One of the great voices in African American literature, Angelou struggled long against adversity—as is evocatively described in her reminiscences. "Her work reads like a novel because of her ability to craft language in prose that reads easily in paragraph form yet often sounds like poetry," in the view of critic Joyce L. Graham. "For example, early in *I Know Why the Caged Bird Sings,* Angelou confronts her own realization that only blond-haired, blue-eyed white girls are regarded as beautiful and that being black brings many apparent limitations to her life."

Graham gives as an example of Angelou's rich language this sentence from *I Know Why the Caged Bird Sings*: "If growing up is painful for the Southern Black girl, being aware of her displacement is the rust on the razor that threatens the throat."

The author was born Marguerite Annie Johnson in St. Louis, Missouri, in 1928. Her father was a cook for the navy, her mother a nurse and real estate agent. Her parents divorced when she was three. She and a brother were raised by a grandmother in Stamps, Arkansas. Maya attended public schools in Arkansas and California and later

18

went back to live with her mother in St. Louis. Raped by her mother's boyfriend, the author remained virtually mute for five years. She returned to her grandmother's home and, with the help of a woman named Mrs. Flowers, gradually regained her speech, her dignity, and her self-confidence. Finding life with her mother one of turmoil, she ran away to stay with her father and his girlfriend. But his trailer-park life was one of destitution, so she went back to living at times with her mother, at times with her grandmother.

These years of overcoming her dysfunctional upbringing and breaking through the walls of white oppression are documented in her autobiographical books. The first, *I Know Why the Caged Bird Sings,* takes its title from a poem by poet Paul Laurence Dunbar and looks at her earliest years. The second, *Gather Together in My Name,* follows the author as she and her brother move from their grandmother's home in her late teen years, when she served cocktails, tap danced, cooked Creole, and worked as a prostitute. At age sixteen, Angelou had a son out of wedlock.

Singin' and Swingin' and Gettin' Merry Like Christmas is about Angelou's early twenties, when she was married to a white man and former sailor, Tosh Angelou. Although there were a few years of stability for the author and her child, the Angelous divorced after five years, and she again became a dancer, joining a production of *Porgy and Bess* and touring Europe and Africa. During this time, Angelou felt great guilt at neglecting her son. *The Heart of a Woman* finds Angelou active in the civil rights movement, married again (although she eventually also divorced Paul Du Feu), and still feeling guilty about her son.

All God's Children Need Traveling Shoes, the fifth book in the series, expresses Angelou's enthusiasm for the African country of Ghana, which she adopted as her homeland. By this time, Angelou had traveled widely, worked as a journalist and writer as well as entertainer, and attained a degree of success.

"The life and work of Maya Angelou are fully intertwined," according to a *Women Writers of Color* essay. "Angelou's poetry and personal narratives form a larger picture wherein the symbolic Maya Angelou rises to become a point of consciousness for African American people, and especially for black women seeking to survive masculine prejudice, white illogical hate, and Black lack of power. *I Know Why the Caged Bird Sings* has generated a wealth of critical literature as well as solid recognition for Maya Angelou."

"Maya Angelou's stories are aptly called testimonials. She 'testifies' not only for herself but also for her community," said Lyman B. Hagen in *Twentieth-Century Young Adult Writers.* "She seems to speak for black consciousness. Her voice as a writer is the voice of her people. What her community endures, she endures. She writes about what she knows: the black experience. The universals contained in her work serve to underscore her frequently expressed thesis: that as people, we are more alike than unalike."

Angelou's 2002 work, *A Song Flung Up to Heaven,* brings her life story up to the 1960s and her experiences of racism and her discovery and loss of close friends Malcolm X and Martin Luther King Jr. As she has aged, she has come to believe there are evil people in the world. Nevertheless, the author told John Holden for *Pages* that she is optimistic that "the majority of human beings have within us—and I put myself in that majority—the ability and the desire to do the right thing."

Works by the Author

Memoir

I Know Why the Caged Bird Sings (1970)
Gather Together in My Name (1974)
Singin' and Swingin' and Gettin' Merry Like Christmas (1976)
The Heart of a Woman (1981)
All God's Children Need Traveling Shoes (1986)
A Song Flung Up to Heaven (2002)
The Collected Autobiographies of Maya Angelou (2004), omnibus

Cookbook

Hallelujah! The Welcome Table: A Lifetime of Memories with Recipes (2004)

Inspirational

Amazing Peace (2006)

Poetry

Just Give Me a Cool Drink of Water 'fore I Diiie (1971)
Oh Pray My Wings Are Gonna Fit Me Well (1975)
And Still I Rise (1978)
Shaker, Why Don't You Sing? (1983)
Poems: Maya Angelou (1986)
Life Doesn't Frighten Me (1993)
On the Pulse of Morning (1993)
Soul Looks Back in Wonder (1994)
Complete Collected Poems of Maya Angelou (1994)
Phenomenal Woman: Four Poems Celebrating Women (1994)
Celebrations: Rituals of Peace and Prayer (2006)
Mother, a Cradle to Hold Me (2006)

Drama

Cabaret for Freedom (musical revue written with Godfrey Cambridge) (1960)
The Least of These   (1966)
The Clawing Within (1966)
Adjoa Amissah (1967)
Encounters (1973)
Sophocles, Ajax (adaptation) (1974)
And Still I Rise (1976)

Screenplays and Teleplays

Blacks, Blues, Black (1968)

Georgia, Georgia (1972)

All Day Long (1974)

I Know Why the Caged Bird Sings (adaptation of autobiography, written with Leona Thuna and Ralph B. Woolsey) (1979)

Sister, Sister (1982)

Brewster Place (1990)

Juvenile

Mrs. Flowers: A Moment of Friendship (1986)

Now Sheba Sings the Song (1987)

I Shall Not Be Moved (1990)

Lessons in Living (1993)

Wouldn't Take Nothing for My Journey Now (1993)

My Painted House, My Friendly Chicken, and Me (1994)

A Brave and Startling Truth (1995)

Kofi and His Magic (1996)

Even the Stars Look Lonesome (1997)

Maya's World: Angelina of Italy (2004)

Maya's World: Mikale of Hawaii (2004)

Maya's World: Renee Marie of France (2004)

Maya's World: Izak of Lapland (2004)

For Further Information

Angaza, Maitefa, "A Precious Prism: Maya," *Black Issues Book Review,* March-April 2001.

Baum, Joan, "An Interview with Poet Maya Angelou," *Education Update,* February 2005.

Buck, Claire, editor. *Bloomsbury Guide to Women's Literature.* New York: Prentice Hall General Reference, 1992.

Frost, David, "An Interview with Maya Angelou," The New Sun Web site. http://www.newsun.com/angelou.html (viewed April 5, 2001).

Garcia-Johnson, Ronie-Richele, Maya Angelou entry, *Authors & Artists for Young Adults*, Volume 20, edited by Thomas McMahon. Detroit, MI: Gale, 1997.

Graham, Joyce L., Maya Angelou entry, *Writers for Young Adults,* edited by Ted Hipple. New York: Scribner's, 1997.

Hagen, Lyman B., Maya Angelou entry, *Twentieth-Century Young Adult Writers,* edited by Laura Standley Berger. Detroit, MI: St. James Press, 1994.

Hogan, John, "A Conversation with Maya Angelou," *Pages,* March/April 2002.

Lim, Grace, "Spotlight on . . . Maya Angelou," *People Weekly*, January 25, 1999.

"Maya Angelou," *Current Biography*, February 1994.

Maya Angelou entry, *Contemporary Authors, New Revision Series*, Volume 65. Detroit, MI: Gale, 1998.

Maya Angelou: The Official Web site. *http://www.mayaangelou.com* (viewed October 14, 2001).

Maya Angelou Web page, National Women's Hall of Fame. http://www. greatwomen.org/women.php?/action=viewone&id=11 (viewed May 19, 2006).

Meroney, Maya, "The Real Maya Angelou," *American Spectator,* March 1993.

Sylvester, William, Maya Angelou entry, *Contemporary Women Poets,* edited by Pamela L. Shelton. Detroit, MI: St. James Press, 1998.

"Voices from the Gaps: Maya Angelou," Women Writers of Color. http://voices. cla.umn.edu/authors/MayaAngelou.html (viewed April 5, 2001).

Dave Barry

Humor, Memoir

Benchmark Title: *Dave Barry Hits
below the Beltway*

Armonk, New York

1947–

Photo courtesy Dave Barry

About the Author and the Author's Writing

"I finally finished the script for the sequel to the movie *Titanic*," syndicated *Miami Herald* columnist Dave Barry wrote in his May 31, 1998, essay. "I am calling it—and let the legal record show that I thought of this first—*Titanic II: The Sequel*."

That's as amusing as any introduction to Barry's twist-and-poke style of social commentary. Further hint of his humor comes from the titles of some of his books: *Dave Barry's Money Secrets: Like, Why Is There a Giant Eyeball on the Dollar* and *Boogers Are My Beat*.

No topic is safe from the Barry wit.

The author was born in Armonk, New York, in 1947, the son of David W. and Marion Barry, and by all accounts he had a normal childhood. As reviewer Alison Teal put it in the *New York Times Book Review,* he "grew up in an all-WASP upper-middle-class neighborhood, played Little League baseball, mowed [his] parents lawn and . . . attended the Episcopal Church." In 1969, he received a bachelor of arts degree from Haverford College, where he has admitted he took greater interest in his rock 'n' roll band Federal Duck than in English literature textbooks. He has been married twice, to Elizabeth Lenox Pyle in 1975, then, after a divorce, to Michelle Kaufman. They have a son and a daughter.

Barry was a reporter for the *Daily Local News* in West Chester, Pennsylvania, from 1971 to 1975, covering subdivision hearings and sign permit validations. As he wrote for his alumni magazine, one of the rules of journalism he learned is, "Reporters never really hear what a source is saying, because they're frantically trying to write down what the source just said." He went to work for the Associated Press in Philadelphia for a year. Then he ran seminars for business people, in the employ of R.S. Burger Associates, 1975 to 1983, teaching participants how to write. Gene Weingarten, editor of the *Miami Herald*'s Sunday magazine, took an interest in his freelance satirical column—which he had begun in 1980—and hired Barry in 1983. A few years later, he moved to Florida. Barry's first book, *The Taming of the Screw,* came out in 1983. The publisher, Rodale Press, interestingly, specialized in gardening books but made an exception for Barry's work.

Barry has said his humor was inspired by the essayist Robert Benchley and by his mother. As *Miami Herald* magazine editor Weingarten told Slate.com columnist Bryan Curtis, Barry's rules of comedic writing include the following: "Put the funniest word at the end of a sentence," and "Put the funniest sentence at the beginning of the story."

There's no typical Barry passage, but consider this example from his March 7, 1999, column, "On History's Cutting Edge," in which he describes a visit to a Renaissance fair whose participants "were leaping around, swinging large, realistic swords at each other and yelling Renaissance insults such as—this is an actual insult they yelled—'You snotmuffin!' "

The writer's syndicated column eventually appeared in five hundred newspapers. He made fun of everyone from telemarketers to Barry Manilow fans. The public loved the comic riffs, the author's ability to give a humorous take to the most ordinary of objects or experiences.

Barry's interest in music continued; he played in an oldies rock band with fellow writers Stephen King, Amy Tan, and others. The Rock Bottom Remainders, as they called themselves, appeared at several bookseller conventions.

Barry published two dozen books, some of them collections of columns, some of new takes on topics ranging from American history to Japanese travel to home maintenance to politics. In 1988, he received a Pulitzer Prize for Commentary.

Then in 2005 Barry quit writing the column. With his typical tongue in cheek humor, he told Jeff Chu for *Time* magazine, "I don't think I'm ever going back to writing weekly columns. It was clear early on—like with my second column—that I had nothing to say. Thirty years was a long time to write with nothing to say."

Barry's first novel, a less-than-serious thriller, *Big Trouble,* came out in 1999 and was made into a movie with Tim Allen. In a half-hour television sitcom, *Dave's World,* on CBS, Harry Anderson played the author, with some liberties. Barry teamed with Ridley Pearson to write a series for younger readers, for Walt Disney, based on J. M. Barrie's *Peter Pan.*

In whatever genre he's writing, Barry's advice to writers, as he gave in *The Writer* magazine, holds for himself as well: "Don't be boring. Don't assume every thought you have is fascinating to others. Your job is to give people a reason to keep reading."

◆ Works by the Author

The Taming of the Screw: Several Million Homeowners' Problems Sidestepped (1983)

Babies and Other Hazards of Sex: How to Make a Tiny Person in Only Nine Months, with Tools You Probably Have around the Home (1984)

Bad Habits: A 100-Percent Fact-Free Book (1985)

Stay Fit and Healthy Until You're Dead (1985)

Claw Your Way to the Top: How to Become the Head of a Major Corporation in Roughly a Week (1986)

Dave Barry's Guide to Marriage and/or Sex (1987)

Dave Barry's Greatest Hits (1988)

Homes and Other Black Holes: The Happy Homeowner's Guide (1988)

Dave Barry Slept Here: A Sort of History of the United States (1989)

Dave Barry Turns Forty (1990)

Dave Barry Talks Back (1991)

Dave Barry's Guide to Life (1991)

Dave Barry's Only Travel Guide You'll Ever Need (1991)

Dave Barry Does Japan (1992)

Dave Barry Is Not Making This Up (1994)

Dave Barry's Gift Guide to End All Gift Guides (1994)

The World According to Dave Barry (1994)

Dave Barry's Complete Guide to Guys: A Fairly Short Book (1995)

Dave Barry in Cyberspace (1996)

A Golf Handbook: All I Ever Learned I Forgot by the Third Fairway, with Jeff MacNelly (1997)

Dave Barry Is from Mars AND Venus (1997)

Dave Barry's Book of Bad Songs (1997)

Dave Barry Turns Fifty (1998)

Dave Barry Is Not Taking This Sitting Down! (2000)

Dave Barry Hits below the Beltway: A Vicious and Unprovoked Attack on Our Most Cherished Political Institutions (2001)

The Greatest Invention in the History of Mankind Is Beer, and Other Manly Insights from Dave Barry (2001)

"My Teenage Son's Goal in Life Is to Make Me Feel 3,500 Years Old" and Other Thoughts on Parenting from Dave Barry (2001)

Boogers Are My Beat: More Lies, but Some Actual Journalism (2002)

Dave Barry's Money Secrets: Like, Why Is There a Giant Eyeball on the Dollar? (2006)

Dave Barry on Dads (2007)

Dave Barry's History of the Millennium (So Far) (2007)

Contributor

Not So Funny When It Happened: The Best of Travel Humor and Misadventure, edited by Tim Cahill (2000)

Fiction

Big Trouble (1999)

Tricky Business (2002)

The Shepherd, the Angel, and Walter the Christmas Miracle Dog (2006)

Young Adult

Neverland Adventures written with Ridley Pearson

Peter and the Starcatchers (2004)

Peter and the Shadow Thieves (2006)
Escape from the Carnivale (2006)
Cave of the Dark Wind (2006)

Film Adaptation

Big Trouble (2001)

Television Adaptation

Dave's World (CBS, 1993–1997)

For Further Information

Barry, Dave, "How I Write," *The Writer,* May 2003.

Barry, Dave, "On History's Cutting Edge," syndicated column, March 7, 1999.

Barry, Dave, "My Newspaper Career, *Haverford Alumni Magazine*, 2003.

Chu, Jeff, "10 Questions for Dave Barry," *Time*, January 16, 2006.

Curtis, Bryan, "Elegy for the Humorist," Slate.com, January 12, 2005. http://www.slate.com/id/2112218 (viewed May 20, 2006).

Dave Barry biography, DaveBarry.com, the Unofficial Dave Barry Web site. http://www.davebarry.com/about.html (viewed May 9, 2006).

Dave Barry entry, Authors and Artists for Young Adults, Gale, Volume 14, 1995. Reproduced in Biography Resource Center. Farmington Hills, MI: Thompson Gale, 2006. http://galenet.galegroup.com/servlet/BioRC.

Dave Barry entry, Contemporary Authors Online, Gale, 2006. Reproduced in Biography Resource Center. Farmington Hills, MI: Thomson Gale, 2006. http://galenet.galegroup.com/servlet/BioRC.

"Dave Barry: Killer Wit," *Book,* November-December 2002.

Johnson, Mclain, "The Life of Dave Barry." http://mcclain.johnson. googlepages.com/dave.barry.html (viewed August 27, 2007).

Taylor, Jeff, "There's Big Trouble ahead for Dave Barry," *BookPage.* http://www.bookpage.com/9909bp/dave_barry.html (viewed May 9, 2006).

Welch, Dave, "Dave Barry and Ridley Pearson Will Never Grow Up," Powells.com. http://wwwpowells.com/authors/barry.html (viewed May 9, 2006).

Rick Bass

Adventure, Environment, Fiction

Benchmark Title: *The Ninemile Wolves*

Fort Worth, Texas

1958–

Photo by Nicole Blaisdell

About the Author and the Author's Writing

Less strident than Edward Abbey, more lyrical than John McPhee, but no less passionate in his beliefs than either, environmental writer Rick Bass has brought to focus the pressures that could destroy the fragility of the great outdoors.

Bass was born in 1958 in Fort Worth, Texas, the son of C. R. and Lucy Robson Bass. His father was a geologist, his mother an English teacher. As a boy, Rick hunted deer with his grandfather in Texas (as he describes in his first book, *The Deer Pasture*). In 1979, Bass received a bachelor of science degree from Utah State University. He married artist Elizabeth Hughes, and they have two children.

From 1979 to 1987, the author worked as a petroleum geologist in Mississippi, searching for likely new oil wells, as he describes in *Oil Notes*. Of this book, *New York* magazine reviewer Rhoda Koenig commented that Bass comes across "as a very gentle, indeed mild-mannered knight, someone whom homeless and repulsive dogs know as a soft touch, and someone who is rather worryingly accident-prone for a man whose occupation is dealing with flammable substances."

Eventually, Bass became a full-time writer and continued to hone his authorial voice and presentation of character. He contributes regularly to periodicals including the *New York Times, Esquire, GQ,* and the *Paris Review*. The Basses live in Montana (a state that figures in several of the author's books).

After four collections of columns and essays, Bass published *The Ninemile Wolves* in 1992. It is an examination of the fate of wildlife in a state—Montana—populated by disparate neo-hippie ex-urbanites and retro ranchers. To control a burgeoning elk herd, Yellowstone Park officials considered importing a wolf herd. The hunters panic. Bass relates what happens to a black-furred she-wolf as she produces litters in 1989 and 1990 to, as an *Economist* reviewer noted, provide "an intriguing glimpse of

27

the battle of man against man over the wolf." Bass revisits the subject in *The New Wolves*, about the release of a dozen Mexican wolves in Arizona's Blue Mountains. "Bass' involving descriptions of the lobos and their home in the mountains explain the interaction between species preservation and ecological recovery," reviewer Mary Carroll said in *Booklist*.

In *The Lost Grizzlies: A Search for Survivors in the Wilderness of Colorado,* Bass made the case that another large predator should be given a new chance to roam freely. The author describes treks into the mountains with biologist Dennis Sisemore and bear expert Doug Peacock and "conveys in freewheeling style his appreciation of the wilderness and a strong sense of camaraderie," according to a *Publishers Weekly*'s reviewer. *Caribou Rising* ventures out of usual Bass territory to the Arctic Circle to look at the Gwich-'ins Indian tribe and the severe changes brought to their area, and specifically to a caribou birthing area, by oil exploration.

Bass's German shorthaired pointer is a frequent character in the author's essays and earns his own book, *Colter: The True Story of the Best Dog I Ever Had,* which contrary to what you might surmise from the title, delves into environmental issues.

What is Bass reaching for, in his environmental essays and books? When Weber Studies interviewer Scott Slovic asked if it might have to do with the search for happiness, he responded, "You know, if you can give that up and learn to look at the smaller things and things other than yourself, I think some growth and happiness will come out of that. And I think you'll treat things better, treat the land better, treat each other better."

Bass also writes fiction. His first short story collection, *The Watch,* brought him the 1988 PEN/Nelson Algren Award. *The Hermit's Story,* which has also enjoyed a young adult audience, brought this comment from *Booklist* reviewer Donna Seaman: "Beautiful in their magical imagery, dramatic in their situations, and exquisitely poignant in their insights, these stories of awe and loss are quite astonishing in their mythic use of place and the elements of earth, air, fire, and water."

Bass's environmental interests have taken him beyond writing to political involvement, such as preserving the Yaak Valley that surrounds his home. "I'm putting in eight hours a day easy on the computer or in lobbying, educating and running different organizations," he told *BookPage*'s Alden Mudge. "That means that fiction takes a back seat to family and activism. The good news is that I've got a chance to effect change, permanent change on a landscape. I'd be a fool to complain."

Works by the Author

The Deer Pasture (1985), essays
Wild to the Heart (1987), essays
Oil Notes (1988), essays
Winter: Notes from Montana (1991)
The Ninemile Wolves (1992)
The Lost Grizzlies: A Search for Survivors in the Wilderness of Colorado (1995)
The Book of Yaak (1996)
The New Wolves (1998)

Brown Dog of the Yaak: Essays on Art and Activism (1999)
Colter: The True Story of the Best Dog I Ever Had (2000)
The Roadless Yaak: Reflections and Observations about One of Our Last Great Wild Places (2002)
Caribou Rising: Defending the Porcupine Herd, Gwich'in Culture, and the Arctic National Wildlife Refuge (2004)

Contributor

Tales from Gray's: Selections from Gray's Sporting Journal, 1975–1985, edited by Ed Gray (1985)
The Pushcart Prize XIII, edited by Bill Henderson (1988)

Fiction

The Watch (1988), stories
Platte River (1994), stories
In the Loyal Mountains (1995), stories
The Sky, The Stars, The Wilderness (1997), novellas
Fiber (1998)
Where the Sea Used to Be (1998)
The Hermit's Story (2002), stories
The Diezmo (2005)
The Lives of Rocks (2006), stories

Fiction, Contributor

New Stories from the South: The Year's Best, edited by Shannon Revenel (1989)
The O. Henry Awards (1998)
Best American Short Stories 1999, edited by Amy Tan (1999)

For Further Information

Hutchinson, Alvin, *Caribou Rising* review, *Library Journal,* October 1, 2004.
Koenig, Rhoda, *Oil Notes* review, *New York*, July 17, 1989.
Last Grizzlies review, *Publishers Weekly*, October 2, 1995.
Mudge, Alden, "Champion of the Wilderness: Acclaimed Writer Rick Bass Blends Art and Activism," *BookPage.* http://www.bookpage.com/0207bp/rick_bass.html (viewed May 9, 2006).
New Wolves review, *Booklist*, October 15, 1998.
Ninemile Wolves review, *Economist*, June 20, 1992.
O'Grady, Brian, and Rob Sumner, "A Conversation with Rick Bass, October 24, 2003," *Willow Springs,* 2004.
"Rick Bass," Mississippi Writers Page. http://www.olemiss.edu/depts/english/ms-writers/dir/bass_rick (viewed May 9, 2006).
Rick Bass entry, Contemporary Authors Online. Reproduced in Biography Resource Center. Farmington Hills, MI: Tomson Gale, 2006. http://galenet.galegroup.com/servlet/BioRC.

Rick Bass entry, *Environmental Encyclopedia,* 3rd ed. Detroit, MI: Gale, 2003.

Seaman, Donna, *The Hermit's Story* review, *Booklist,* May 1, 2002.

Shea, Mike, *The Diezmo* review, *Texas Monthly,* May 2005.

Slovic, Scott, "A Paint Brush in One Hand and a Bucket of Water in the Other: Nature Writing and the Politics of Wilderness, An Interview with Rick Bass," *Weber Studies,* fall 1994. http://weberstudies.weber/edu/archive/ archive%20B%20Vol.%2011-16.1/Vol.%2011.3/11.3BassIterview.htm (viewed May 9, 2006).

Wendell Berry

Environment, Memoir, Social Reportage

Benchmark Title: *The Unsettling of America*

Henry County, Kentucky

1934–

Photo courtesy Shoemaker & Hoard

About the Author and the Author's Writing

Wendell Berry's views on personal computers are as succinct a way as any to introduce this author. He doesn't own one, and probably never will. "I would hate to think that my work as a writer could not be done without a direct dependence on strip-mined coal. How could I write conscientiously against the rape of nature if I were, in the act of writing, implicated in the rape?" he wrote in a piece published in *New England Review and Bread Loaf Quarterly,* later reprinted in *Harper's.*

Wendell Berry is strongly Thoreauvian, sympathetically Luddite, anachronistically Shaker, charmingly eloquent, disturbingly pointed, presciently concerned. That is, he loves the outdoors, is suspicious of modern technology, prefers simplicity, is articulate, aggressive, and cares greatly about people and the environment. Wal-Mart is a tool to destroy small towns. A global economy is an action plan for disaster, he suggests, a means of making money at the expense of entire countries. Modest local sustainability is the way we must prepare for the future. These and similar pronouncements shine through the author's essays and books.

Berry has not strayed far from his Henry County, Kentucky, roots. Born there in 1934, the oldest of John and Virginia Berry's four children, he and his wife, Tanya (Amyx), today own a 125-acre homestead in Lane's Landing, just down the road from his parents' place. His father grew tobacco and practiced law. After he attended Millersburg Military Institute, Wendell earned bachelor's and master's degrees in English from the University of Kentucky in Lexington. A year after his marriage in 1957, Berry, through a Wallace Stegner Fellowship, attended Stanford University's program for creative writing. In 1961, he and his family (two children) went to Italy and France, thanks to a Guggenheim Foundation Fellowship. He taught at New York University's University College from 1962 to 1964, then left to teach creative writing at the University of Kentucky for more than a decade. He has written fiction, poetry, technical articles and essays—produced, as he has said, at his farmhouse, his wife typing his manuscripts on a Royal Standard typewriter and suggesting changes here and there.

The Berrys live as independently as they can. They raise vegetables, some market grains, and tobacco. They cut their own firewood and graze sheep in their pastures. As a high school student, Wendell didn't imagine his future rural lifestyle. Young people in those days, and yet today, found opportunity elsewhere. "When I decided to come back here, a lot of people I respected thought I was deliberately achieving my ruin," he told *Smithsonian*'s Paul Trachtman. "I realize every day how extremely fortunate I've been as a writer to live where my imagination took root."

Berry's imagination shines in verse: "Berry's poetry is lucid, elegiac, rooted in deep lace and slow time," an article in *The Writer* noted in singling him out as an author who has made a difference.

His imagination also shines in his prose: "As this telling of a farm woman's life in her voice continues—and voice it seems more than writing, so spontaneously speechlike are its cadences and the simple accuracy of its diction—it feels ever more poetic. Not gnomic and surrealist, like prose poetry, but flowing and long breathed, like epic poetry," reviewer Ray Olson remarked in *Booklist* of Berry's novel *Hannah Coulter*.

And his imagination shines in his essays: "One of Berry's fundamental concerns is working out a basis for living a principled life," Charles Hudson wrote in *Georgia Review*. "And like Thoreau, in his quest for principles Berry has chosen to simplify his life, and much of what he writes about is what has attended this simplification, as well as criticism of modern society from the standpoint of this simplicity."

The same themes weave in and through all of Berry's work. "One of Berry's most consistent themes through 30 years of writing has been the practicality of virtue," Lionel Basney said in *Christian Century*, meaning an orderly, traditional, caring life. "Because these virtues make community possible, they enable us to look after people and places in a way that promises health and security."

Berry displays a reverence for the natural world in essays included in *The Art of the Commonplace* (2002). "If we take care of the world of the present, the world will have received full justice from us," he writes. In *Life Is a Miracle* (2000), he suggests we must overcome our materialism if we're to resolve ecological, economic, and political problems. As much as Berry preaches community-supported agriculture and mom-and-pop retail, and rejects science and technology as saviors of our future, he also sees the large picture. He doesn't shy from pondering post–September 11 America. Among his "Thoughts in the Presence of Fear" essay for *Orion* magazine, he stated: "One of the gravest dangers to us now, second only to further terrorist attacks against our people, is that we will attempt to go on as before with the corporate program of global 'free trade,' whatever the cost in freedom and civil rights, without self-questioning or self-criticism or public debate."

Although the author might have hoped change would sap the message of his *The Unsettling of America*, "it's more relevant now than it ever was," he said in a conversation with Rose Marie Berger, an interviewer for *Sojourners*. "I don't think that national security can be achieved the way we're trying to achieve it. I don't think that being the strongest country in the world can necessarily make us the most secure country. And the fact remains that we're destroying our country ourselves."

Works by the Author

The Rise (1968)

The Long-Legged House (1969), portions reprinted as *A Native Hill* (1976)

The Hidden Wound (1970)

Ralph Eugene Meatyard, with Ralph Eugene Meatyard and A. Gassan (1970)

The Unforeseen Wilderness: An Essay on Kentucky's Red River Gorge (1971), revised and expanded as *The Unforeseen Wilderness: Kentucky's Red River Gorge* (1991)

A Continuous Harmony: Essays Cultural and Agricultural (1972)

Civilizing the Cumberland: A Commentary (1972)

The Unsettling of America: Culture and Agriculture (1977)

Recollected Essays, 1965–1980 (1981)

The Gift of Good Land; Further Essays, Cultural and Agricultural (1981)

Standing by Words: Essays (1983)

Home Economics: Fourteen Essays (1987)

The Landscape of Harmony (1987)

Traveling at Home (1988)

Harland Hubbard: Life and Work (1990)

What Are People For? Essays (1990)

Standing on Earth (1991)

Sex, Economy, Freedom, and Community: Eight Essays (1993)

Another Turn of the Crank (1995)

A World Lost (1996)

Waste Land: Meditations on a Ravaged Landscape, with William Kittredge, Susan Griffin, Peter Montague, and Mark Dowie (1997)

Life Is a Miracle: An Essay against Modern Superstition (2000)

Citizenship Papers (2003)

Tobacco Harvest: An Elegy (2004)

The Way of Ignorance, and Other Essays (2005)

Editor

Meeting the Expectations of the Land: Essays in Sustainable Agriculture and Stewardship, with Wes Jackson and Bruce Colman (1984)

Blessed Are the Peacemakers: Christ's Teachings of Love, Compassion, and Forgiveness (2005)

Contributor

The Blue Grass Region of Kentucky, and Other Kentucky Articles, edited by James Lane Allen (1972)

Fiction

Nathan Coulter (1960/revised 1985)

A Place on Earth (1967/revised 1983)

The Memory of Old Jack (1974)

The Wild Birds: Six Stories of the Port William Membership (1986)

Remembering (1988)

Fidelity: Five Stories (1992)

Watch With Me: And Six Other Stories of the Yet-Remembered Ptolemy Proudfoot and His Wife, Miss Minnie, née Quinch (1994)

Two More Stories of the Port William Membership (1997)

Jayber Crow: The Life Story of Jayber Crow, Barber, of the Port William Membership as Written by Himself (2000)

That Distant Land: The Collected Stories of Wendell Berry (2002)

Three Short Novels (2002), contains *Nathan Coulter, Remembering*, and *A World Lost*

Hanna Coulter (2004)

Andy Catlett: Early Travels (2006)

Poetry

November Twenty-Six Nineteen Hundred Sixty-Three (1964)

The Broken Ground (1964)

Openings: Poems (1968)

Findings (1969)

Farming: A Handbook (1970)

The Country of Marriage (1973)

An Eastward Look (1974)

Reverdure: A Poem (1974)

Horses (1975)

To What Listens (1975)

Sayings and Doings (1975)

The Kentucky River: Two Poems (1976)

There Is Singing around Me (1976)

Clearing (1977)

Three Memorial Poems (1977)

The Gift of Gravity (1979)

A Part (1980)

The Salad (1980)

The Wheel (1982)

Collected Poems, 1957–1982 (1985)

Sabbaths (1987)

Sayings and Doings/An Eastward Look (1990)

Entries: Poems (1994)

The Farm (1995)

The Selected Poems of Wendell Berry (1998)

A Timbered Choir: The Sabbath Poems, 1979–1997 (1998)

The Art of the Commonplace: The Agrarian Essays of Wendell Berry (2003)

Given: New Poems (2005)

Recording

Wendell Berry Reading His Poems (1980)

For Further Information

Basney, Lionen, *Another Turn of the Crank* review, *Christian Century*, June 19, 1996.

Berger, Rose Marie, Wendell Berry interview, *Sojourners,* July 2004. http://www.sojo.net/index.cfm?action=magazine.article&issue=soj0407& article=040710 (viewed September 7, 2006).

Berry, Wendell, "Thoughts in the Presence of Fear," *Orion.* http://www. orionsociety.org/pages/oo/sidebars/America/Berry.html (viewed September 5, 2006).

Berry, Wendell, "Why I Am *Not* Going to Buy a Computer." http://www. tipiglen.dircon.co/uk/berrynot.html (viewed September 5, 2006).

"An Exchange with Wendell Berry," *Preservation*, March/April 2005.

Fisher-Smith, Jordan, "Field Observations: An Interview with Wendell Berry," Envirolink.org. http://arts.envirolink.org/interviews_and_conversations/ WendellBerry.html (viewed September 5, 2006).

Heidmann, Ilse, *Art of the Commonplace* review, *Library Journal,* May 1, 2002.

Hudson, Charles, *Recollected Essays* review, *Georgia Review,* Spring 1982.

Life Is a Miracle review, *Publishers Weekly,* May 22, 2000.

Olson, Ray, *Hannah Coulter* review, *Booklist,* November 15, 2004.

Trachtman, Paul, "Wendell Berry: A Kentucky Poet Draws Inspiration from the Land That Sustains Him," *Smithsonian,* November 2005.

Wendell Berry Web page, University of Louisville. http://library.louisville. edu/government/states/kentucky/kylit/berry.html (viewed September 5, 2006).

Wendell (Erdman) Berry entry, Contemporary Authors Online. Reproduced in Biography Resource Center. Farmington Hills, MI: Thomson Gale, 2005. http://galenet.galegroup.com/servlet/BioRC.

"Writers Who Make a Difference," *The Writer,* January 2004.

Mark Bowden

Adventure, Sports, True Crime

Benchmark Title: *Black Hawk Down*

St. Louis, Missouri

1951–

About the Author and the Author's Writing

Seventy feet above a marketplace street in Mogadishu, tethered to a hovering Blackhawk helicopter, Staff Sgt. Matt Eversmann was about to join his squad when he spotted one of his men, prone and unmoving. "He felt a stab of despair. Somebody's been shot already! He gripped the rope hard to keep from landing on top of the guy. It was Pvt. Todd Blackburn, at 18 the youngest Ranger in his Chalk, a kid just months out of a Florida high school. He was unconscious and bleeding from the nose and ears."

That's how investigative journalist Mark Bowden began his report that was serialized in twenty-nine issues of the *Philadelphia Inquirer* beginning November 16, 1997. The newspaper ran the series on the Internet, enhanced with documents and audio clips, and Bowden received feedback on early chapters even as he polished later ones. Feedback—as in as many as 46,000 hits on the site a day. He incorporated new information. He made corrections. It was living, breathing journalism. "This greatly enhanced the account's credibility. Instead of dealing with the reporter as a distant 'expert,' and speculating on the reasons for mistakes or omissions, readers saw my own eagerness to simply get the story right, something which in my experience is the primary motivation of most reporters," the author related in *Nieman Reports*.

Subsequently published as a book, Bowden's *Black Hawk Down* recounted the unnerving October 3, 1993, raid in Somalia that was part of an undeclared war against warlord Mohamed Farrah Aidid. U.S. Rangers and Delta Force members captured two of Aidid's senior lieutenants, but before they could evacuate, militiamen brought down two American helicopters, *Super Six One* and *Super Six Four,* and some 140 soldiers were trapped, isolated in a firefight for fifteen hours. Suffering from poor morale, inadequate reconnaissance, no night-vision goggles, little ammunition, 18 Americans died, and as many as 500 Somalis, militiamen, and civilians died as well.

As a boy, Bowden had come to appreciate the dramatic impact of military victory and defeat as he devoured Martin Caidin and Saburo Sakai's World War II work *Samurai,* about a Japanese fighter plane pilot. Bowden said *Hiroshima* author John Hersey was his greatest writing influence for *Black Hawk Down,* although in general he takes inspiration from George Orwell, John McPhee, and Peter Matthiessen. "I'm a writer; I look for good stories," he related in an interview with *Bookreporter.* "When I read initial newspaper accounts of this battle … I thought what an amazing story it would be if I could talk to those men who were in that situation and write about that experience."

Born in St. Louis, Missouri, in 1951, the son of Richard H. and Rita Lois Keane Bowden, Mark grew up in suburbs of Chicago, New York, and Baltimore. "I was raised without ethnicity," he told *Contemporary Authors.* "You grow up like that and your goal is to find trouble, find experience, wallow in it, and (for me) write it down. Writing is my way of making sense of what happens to me, and of somehow keeping it." He devoured comic books, and eventually the highly charged 1960s new journalism of Tom Wolfe, Norman Mailer, and Gay Talese.

In 1973, the journalist-author graduated with a bachelor of arts degree from Loyola College of Maryland. He was a staff writer for the *Baltimore News American* from 1973 to 1979. Then he joined the *Inquirer,* where he has been a staff writer since. He and his wife, Gail McLaughlin, have four children and live in New London, Pennsylvania.

It is Bowden's muckraker tenacity that brought him the *Black Hawk Down* details. As he related in conversation with Bookreporter, he sought out soldiers who had been in Mogadishu through Special Forces Operations Command's media office. Once he found one Delta Force veteran who would speak on the record, he uncovered written reports by others, chased military commanders and American politicians, and even found some Somali fighters. "This relentlessly paced reconstruction of the 1993 Battle of Mogadishu in Somalia exposes in horrifying detail the murkiness of war and the dangers of reliance on fragile military technology," a *Booklist* reviewer said. John Carver Edwards, writing for *Library Journal,* said the author "succeeds in giving both the U.S. and Somalia perspectives, blending the human element with a political and military overview." Producer Jerry Bruckheimer turned the book into a film in 2002.

Bowden had three earlier books under his belt. The first, *Doctor Dealer,* was about a dentist-turned-drug lord, Larry Lavin, who long eluded authorities. *Bringing the Heat* relates Bowden's experiences over the course of the year 1992, which he spent with the National Football League's Philadelphia Eagles. *Killing Pablo* follows the rise and demise of a Colombian street criminal. "I was interested to know how Pablo Escobar wound up dead on a rooftop in Medellín. I wanted to know to what extent the United States was responsible for that," Bowden told Seth Clark Walker for *Etude.* "The quest of the book is to understand what happened, why it happened and how it happened."

Ever alert to misadventure, Bowden profiled another criminal, a longshoreman, in *Finders Keepers.* It is about the inept attempts of Joey Coyle, who with two buddies one day in the 1980s in Philadelphia happened on more than $1 million in unmarked bills that had fallen from an armored Purolator transport vehicle to launder the money. "Bowden's intense story is like a joyride in print," *Library Journal* observed. The author said in *Creative Nonfiction* that he found "the story of Joey Coyle was a parable of addiction, of how hopeless and empty it is to assume success and happiness can be scooped up off the street or administered through a needle."

Again venturing overseas, Bowden brought enormous detail to an account of the 1979 occupation by Iranians of the U.S. Embassy in Tehran—a fifteen-month hostage crisis that saw eight elite Delta Force soldiers die in an ill-conceived rescue attempt and a weakened Jimmy Carter lose the presidency. As the author points out, the crisis was "the first battle in America's war against militant Islam." Twenty-six years later, said *Time* writer Richard Lacayo, "the passions of the moment still reverberate. In Bowden's book, you can feel them on every page."

 Works by the Author

Doctor Dealer (1987)

Pitt Rivers: The Life and Archaeological Work of Lieutenant-General Augustus Henry Lane Fox Pitt Rivers, DCL, FRS, FSA (1991)

Bringing the Heat: A Pro Football Team's Quest for Glory, Fame, Immortality, and a Bigger Piece of the Action (1994)

Black Hawk Down: A Story of Modern War (1999)

Killing Pablo: The Hunt for the World's Greatest Outlaw (2001)

Our Finest Day: D-Day, June 6, 1944 (2002)

Finders Keepers: The Story of a Man Who Found $1 Million (2002)

Road Work: Among Tyrants, Heroes, Rogues, and Beasts (2004) essays

Guests of the Ayatollah: The First Battle in America's War with Militant Islam (2006)

Film Adaptations

Money for Nothing (1993), based on Bowden's newspaper articles that became the book *Finders Keepers*

Black Hawk Down (2002)

The True Story of Killing Pablo (History Channel, 2003)

For Further Information

Bedway, Barbara, "Bowden's Pen Now Down," *Editor & Publisher*, November 4, 2002.

Black Hawk Down review, *Booklist,* March 15, 2000.

Bowden, Mark, "Narrative Journalism Goes Multimedia," *Nieman Reports,* Nieman Foundation for Journalism at Harvard University, Fall 2000. http://www.nieman.harvard.edu/reports/00-3NRfall/Goes-Multimedia.html (viewed May 14, 2006).

Collins, Rachel, *Finders Keepers* review, *Library Journal,* September 15, 2002.

Edwards, John Carver, *Black Hawk Down* review, *Library Journal,* January 1999.

Lacayo, Richard, "The First Strike: How the 1979 Takeover of the U.S. Embassy in Tehran Prefigured Sept. 11," *Time,* May 29, 2006.

Mark Bowden entry, Contemporary Authors Online. Reproduced in Biography Resource Center. Farmington Hills, MI: Thomson Gale, 2006. http://galenet.galegroup.com/servlet/BioRC.

Mark Bowden interview, Bookreporter.com, November 12, 1999. http://www.bookreporter.com/authors/au-bowden-mark.asp (viewed May 14, 2006).

Mark Bowden interview, *Creative Nonfiction,* No. 7. http://www. creativenonfiction.org/thejournal/articles/issue07/07bowden_ai.htm (viewed April 22, 2006).

Moores, Alan, *Road Work* review, *Booklist,* October 15, 2004.

Walker, Seth Clark, Mark Bowden Q&A, *Etude: New Voices in Literary Nonfiction.* http://etude.uoregon.edu/summer2005/bowden/index.html (viewed May 14, 2006).

Taylor Branch

Photo © J. Brough Schamp

Biography, History, True Crime

Benchmark Title: *At Canaan's Edge*

Atlanta, Georgia

1947–

About the Author and the Author's Writing

Yes, he's been pretty much a one-topic historian. But Taylor Branch must be forgiven for taking more than two decades to masterfully pull together a mountain of material for a three-volume biography of one of the most defining figures of the modern civil rights movement in America, Martin Luther King Jr.

"Almost as color defines vision itself—race shapes the cultural eye—what we do and do not notice, the reach of empathy and the alignment of response," the author states in the preface to *Parting the Waters: America in the King Years, 1954–1963.* The first volume of his epic biography trilogy, the book won him the Pulitzer Prize for History in 1988.

Born in Atlanta in 1947, Taylor Branch is the son of dry cleaning plant proprietor Franklin T. Branch, and his wife, Jane Worthington Branch. After earning an A.B. from the University of North Carolina at Chapel Hill in 1968, the author did graduate studies at Princeton University for two years. He was on the staff of *Washington Monthly* from 1970 to 1973, then *Harper's* from 1973 to 1975 and *Esquire* from 1975 to 1976. Since then he has been a full-time writer. Besides books, he has contributed to *New England Monthly, New Republic,* and the *New York Times.* He and his wife, speechwriter Christina Macy, have two children.

Growing up in an apolitical household, Branch's eyes were opened by the violent response of police to the 1963 peace marches. In 1969, he worked for the Voter Education Project in rural Georgia. He had the idea for the King study several years before he felt he had the skill to take it on. The material waited for him. "There are a lot of people who say, well, this is over and done with and we don't want to worry about it any more," says Branch, quoted on a Howard County Poetry and Literature Society Web page. "That attitude is very, very common, very modern, and to me kind of frightening because it's basically people who will eventually re-create the problems that we're trying to solve."

Branch's first book, *Blowing the Whistle: Dissent in the Public Interest*, reflected his realm of interest, and established him as an authority within it. He helped basketball star Bill Russell craft a memoir, *Second Wind*; ghostwrote a book for presidential advisor John Dean, *Blind Ambition*, about Watergate; and shaped a novel, *The Empire Blues*, that involved drug dealers and intelligence agents. *Labyrinth* is an investigative work about the car-bomb slaying of Chilean ambassador Orlando Letelier in 1976, following the 1976 assassination from an explosion on a Washington street to the FBI and Justice Department investigation to the identification of the Cuban and Chilean perpetrators. Coauthor Eugene M. Propper was head prosecutor when the case came to trial.

Branch, now living in Baltimore, took six years to research and write his first King biography. It was more daunting than he'd anticipated. "In December of 1981 I signed on for a three-year project to write a book about America in the King years," he said in a 2006 interview with Jack Rightmyer of *Daily Gazette*. "I wanted it to be a narrative history of the United States from the 1950s through the late 1960s. My original manuscript for the first book, *Parting the Waters*, was over 1900 pages, and I had only gotten up to 1963."

Branch was true to his promise in exploring the 1960s civil rights movement in context. He found, for example, that President John F. Kennedy's White House was skittish about Martin Luther King Jr. and secretly hoped he would go away. Yet the two men had similarities. "Both King and JFK were closet smokers, quick catnappers and skirt chasers," he told Alvin Sanoff for *U.S. News & World Report* in 1989, "and both had overbearing fathers whose politics were sharply at odds with their own." King in his lifetime made nearly everyone feel threatened, from redneck segregationists who were taunted for their racism to white-color liberals, who were made to feel they were shunning their obligations.

"I wanted to do something different as an historian," Branch told the *Santa Monica Mirror*. "Instead of the usual analysis, I wanted to tell an epic story. I wanted to provide a narrative of absolutely everything that happened. I feel that we learn through stories, not through the abstractions and analysis present in most historical texts."

Branch's writing, particularly his ability to present dozens of multifaceted characters, shines. "His book is rich with a fascinating array of actors: the movement's idealistic leaders, driven to mad and saintly heroics; the women who quietly orchestrated the daily life of the movement (to whom Mr. Branch gives their long-neglected due)," said a reviewer in *The Economist*.

Branch's *Pillar of Fire: America in the King Years, 1963–1965* deals with only three years—but they are fiery years. The author, as reviewer Andrew E. Kersten noted in *The Historian*, examines other national figures including Malcolm X and Lyndon B. Johnson but also regional activists. "Branch uses these grassroots histories to demonstrate how King's actions aided local activities. For instance, although King's 1964 visit to St. Augustine [Florida] was not a complete success, it nonetheless attracted national press attention to the struggles in Florida, which in turn reminded the nation of the need for the proposed 1964 Civil Rights Bill."

LBJ takes center stage in Branch's *At Canaan's Edge: America in the King Years, 1965–1968*, and we glimpse Martin Luther King Jr.'s chess plays with Chicago Major Richard Daley, who held true to a promise to raze slums and fund antipoverty programs. "But Daley also held his ground, insisting just as vehemently that he would not alienate his white constituents by taking legislative measures to pry open middle-class white neighborhoods to blacks, calling King a troublemaker, and asking him to leave," Benjamin Wallace-Wells noted in his review of the book for *Washington Monthly*.

Branch met a major challenge in examining all sides to his story. "It was difficult to get some people to talk," he said in a *Time* interview in 2006, "just because a lot of people think that the realities of the movement are so far removed from whatever the myth was, that it's not worth talking [about]." In the end, he persuaded key members of the movement to speak openly about King.

Task completed, Branch told *Publishers Weekly*'s Sarah F. Gold, "I think this book reflects my conviction that it's not just dusty history, that it's contemporary, that these are the same issues that still define our politics about how you create freedom."

◣ Works by the Author

Blowing the Whistle: Dissent in the Public Interest, editor with Charles Peters and contributor (1972)
Blind Ambition by John Dean (ghostwriter) (1979)
Second Wind: The Memoirs of an Opinionated Man, with Bill Russell (1979)
Labyrinth, with Eugene M. Propper (1982)

Martin Luther King Jr. Trilogy

Parting the Waters: America in the King Years, 1954–1963 (1988)
Pillar of Fire: America in the King Years, 1963–1965 (1997)
At Canaan's Edge: America in the King Years, 1965–1968 (2006)

Fiction

The Empire Blues (1981)

For Further Information

Gold, Sarah F., "The End of the Saga: Moses Needed Five Books to Tell of the Jews' Journey to Freedom, Taylor Branch Needed Only Three for African-Americans', Ending with *At Canaan's Edge*," *Publishers Weekly,* January 9, 2006.
Kersten, Andrew E., *Pillar of Fire* review, *The Historian*, Winter 2000.
Morris, Edward, Taylor Branch interview, *BookPage.* http://www.bookpage.com/0602bp/taylor_branch.html (viewed May 10, 2006).
Parting the Waters review, *The Economist,* May 6, 1989.
Pillar of Fire review, Powells.com. http://www.powells.com/biblio/16-0684808196-2 (viewed May 10, 2006).
Rightmyer, Jack, "An Interview with Taylor Branch," *Daily Gazette,* March 26, 2006. http://www.albany.edu/writers-inst/gaz_branch_taylor.html (viewed May 10, 2006).

Sanoff, Alvin P., "The Greening of a Martyr," *U.S. News & World Report*, January 23, 1989.

Taylor Branch biography, Howard County Poetry and Literature Society. http://www.hocopolitso.org/Artist_Biographies/Taylor_Branch.html (viewed May 10, 2006).

Taylor Branch entry, Contemporary Authors Online. Reproduced in Biography Resource Center. Farmington Hills, MI: Thomson Gale, 2006. http://galenet.galegroup.com/servlet/BioRC.

"Taylor Branch: His Book on MLK Attracts Notice of *Time & Newsweek*," History News Network, January 10, 2006. http://hnn.us/roundup/entries/20325.html (viewed May 10, 2006).

Wallace-Wells, Benjamin, "Down from the Mountain: Taylor Branch Shows How the End of Martin Luther King Jr.'s Civil Rights Movement Marked the Beginning of Liberalism's Crack-Up," *Washington Monthly*, March 2006.

Bill Bryson

Adventure, Humor, Memoir, Travel

Benchmark Title: *A Walk in the Woods*

Des Moines, Iowa

1951–

Photo by Julian James

About the Author and the Author's Writing

A peripatetic, ursine-phobic, etymological island hopper is one way to describe American wordsmith Bill Bryson. Another is to say he is a wandering, pig-fearing, language-loving traveler, who became known in England for his madcap travelogues, and recrossed the ocean to secure renown in the United States for his wacky word probing. His experiences hiking the Georgia-to-Maine Appalachian Trail brought him back to the land of the Union Jack, all the while demonstrating his expertise in nearly everything he wrote about.

Born in Des Moines, Iowa, in 1951, the son of sports columnist William Bryson, the author attended Drake University. While vacationing in England in 1973, he met his future wife, Cynthia, a nurse, and decided to stay. Living in North Yorkshire, he worked as a copy editor with and wrote travel articles for the *Times* and the *Independent*. He assembled his own personal style book, and it became the basis of his *Dictionary of Troublesome Words,* now in its third edition.

His first travel book, *The Palace under the Alps*, sold few copies. But another publisher accepted his idea for a land-cruise book based on his native country. Bryson quit his day job. His road-trip experiences across small-town America, recounted in *The Lost Continent,* did not meet his stated expectations, which were derivative of 1950s movies he'd viewed as a youth, as he says in the book, "Bing Crosby would be the priest, Jimmy Stewart the mayor, Fred MacMurray the high school principal, Henry Fonda a Quaker farmer. Walter Brennan would run the gas station, a boyish Mickey Rooney would deliver the groceries, and somewhere, at an open window, Deanna Durbin would sing."

That's a rather gentle example of Bryson's humor, which can be biting. "Jack Kerouac, of all people, thought that Iowa women were the prettiest in the country," he wrote, "but I don't think he ever went to Merle Hay Mall on a Saturday."

When *Lost Continent* met a receptive audience, Bryson followed with a humorous European sojourn in the company of his childhood friend Stephen Katz, *Neither Here nor There,* and then a report on the country that he had adopted for two decades, Great Britain, in *Notes from a Small Island.* It received some critical attention. "Interweaving descriptions of landscapes and everyday encounters with shopkeepers, pub customers and fellow travelers, Bryson shares what he loves best about the idiosyncrasies of everyday English life in this immensely entertaining travel memoir," a *Publishers Weekly* reviewer said of *Notes.*

For *In a Sunburned Country,* Bryson toured the land of kangaroos and boomerangs, for what *Booklist*'s Mary Frances Wilkens noted was "loaded with descriptions of unusual characters and odd meals encountered along the way." Underlying Bryson's pokes and prods is an affection for his subjects. "Everything I discovered was new to me. It's just like when you hear a great story in a bar, an anecdote that you want to rush right home and relate to other people. You want to spread the word," he told Dave Welch for Powells.com.

In 1995, Bryson relocated with his wife and four children to the collegiate town of Hanover in New Hampshire. Even though they lived within a stone's throw of the 2,174-mile Appalachian Trail, the author noticed his neighbors didn't hike extensively. As he told *People Weekly,* "You'll see people out sort of walking with little dumbbells. But if you have an errand to run, you grab the car keys." He decided to take a crack at a through-hike. Although he abandoned the effort after 870 miles, he returned with a backpack full of anecdotes for *A Walk in the Woods,* which became Bryson's breakthrough book in the United States. On foot, in the forest, he found a different angle on America than he had in a car.

Bryson never got over the fear of bears that emerged on that amble. Any unusual sound could trigger his paranoia. One night in the tent: "I sat bolt upright. Instantly every neuron in my brain was awake and dashing around frantically, like ants when you disturb their nest. I reached instinctively for my knife, then I realized I had left it in my pack, just outside the tent."

His friend Stephen refused to be roused by the noise.

" 'It sounded big,' " Bryson said.

" 'Everything sounds big in the woods.' "

The author's travel writing contains generous dollops of humor, although he's at times had to struggle with the differences in what amuses British and American readers. "There's a greater element of cynicism in British life, generally," he told *Publishers Weekly* in 1998. Brits, he added, exhibit "a natural gift for making excellent, uttered jokes about authority without ever challenging it."

But, he found, one has to be careful of spontaneous remarks in America, particularly these days. "Once I was going through customs and immigration in Boston, and the guy said as I went past, 'Any fruit or vegetables?' and I said, 'OK, I'll have four pounds of potatoes if they are fresh' and it was like he was going to take me off and pin me to the floor," he told interviewer Douglas Schatz for *Stanfords.*

In between traveling and travel writing, Bryson wrote books about language and usage in *The Mother Tongue* and the differences between American and British words in *Made in America.* "One of the abiding glories of English," the author had earlier said in *Bryson Dictionary of Troublesome Words,* "is that it has no governing authority, no group of august worthies empowered to decree how words may be spelled and deployed. We are a messy democracy."

Why diverging topics? "I don't have any ambition to make great literature," the author told *Guardian Online*, tongue-in-cheek. "I'll do anything to keep my kids in Reeboks."

That includes taking a stab at science and an attempt to explain the utterly complex in *A Short History of Nearly Everything*. As he researched for that book, Bryson found himself dismayed that things he'd learned in high school, including misrepresentations of plate tectonics or the reasons marsupials populated South America and Australia, had turned out to be wrong. He initially pictured the book as containing more interviews and interactions with scientists. "It didn't end up like that because I wasn't able to prepare myself well enough," he told *New Scientist*. "It was almost impossible to talk to these scientists in a way that wasn't wasting their time.... It almost was not possible to know less in these fields than I did."

When *U.S. News & World Report* asked with which one he would most like to have dinner, Bryson named Isaac Newton "because he is the most enigmatic and would most benefit from having someone sit down with him." Less intimidating, though, would be physicist Niels Bohr. "I think he was a nice human being as well as one of the great scientists of the 20th century."

Everything was published about the time the author moved his family back to England and set to work writing *The Life and Times of the Thunderbolt Kid*, a Jean Shepardesque reminiscence of his childhood in Des Moines, Iowa, in the 1950s—and of course, it's humorous.

Recognizing a cultural asset when it saw one, the government of England bestowed an honorary Order of the British Empire on Bryson in December 2006, declaring him one of the country's best-loved authors.

Works by the Author

The Facts on File Dictionary of Troublesome Words (1984), as *Penguin Dictionary of Troublesome Words* (1988), and as *Bryson's Dictionary of Troublesome Words* (2002)

The Palace under the Alps, and Over Two Hundred Other Unusual, Unspoiled, and Infrequently Visited Spots in Sixteen European Countries (1985) (as William Bryson)

The Lost Continent: Travels in Small-Town America (1989)

The Mother Tongue: English and How It Got That Way (1990)

Neither Here nor There: Travels in Europe (1991)

The Penguin Dictionary for Writers and Editors (1992)

Made in America: An Informal History of the English Language in the United States (1994)

Notes from a Small Island: An Affectionate Portrait of Britain (1995)

A Walk in the Woods: Rediscovering America on the Appalachian Trail (1998)

I'm a Stranger Here Myself: Notes on Returning to America after Twenty Years Away (1999), in Great Britain as *Notes from a Big Country* (1999)

In a Sunburned Country (2000), in Great Britain as *Down Under* (2000)

The English Landscape: Its Character and Diversity (2001)

Bill Bryson's African Diary (2002)

A Short History of Nearly Everything (2004)

The Life and Times of the Thunderbolt Kid (2006)

Editor

The Best American Travel Writing 2000, with Jason Wilson (2000)

Contributor

Not So Funny When It Happened: The Best of Travel Humor and Misadventure, edited by Tim Cahill (2000)

For Further Information

"Accolades for Bryson," *Albany (N.Y.) Times-Union* (AP), December 16, 2006.

Bill Bryson entry, Contemporary Authors Online. Reproduced in Biography Resource Center. Farmington Hills, MI: Thomson Gale, 2006. http://galenet.galegroup.com/servlet/BioRC.

Bill Bryson profile, *Guardian Unlimited.* http://books.guardian.co.uk/authors/author/0,,-27,00.html (viewed May 10, 2006).

Bill Bryson Web page, Random House. http://www.randomhouse.com/features/billbryson/flat/about.php (viewed May 10, 2006).

Hunt, George W., "Made in America: An Informal History of the English Language in the United States," *America*, November 25, 1995.

Leddy, Chuck, "Bryson Offers a Pithy, Common-Sense Guide to Usage," *The Writer,* July 2003.

"Longest Journey," Bill Bryson interview, *New Scientist,* May 31, 2003.

"Notes from a Small Island," *Publishers Weekly*, March 4, 1996.

Oder, Norman, "Bill Bryson: An Ex-Expat Traveling Light," *Publishers Weekly*, May 4, 1998.

Orme, Marianne, *Bryson's Dictionary of Troublesome Words* review, *Library Journal*, July 2002.

Ott, Bill, "Traveling with Bill Bryson," *Booklist*, September 15, 2003.

Pethokoukis, James M., "Across the Universe and Back Home with Bill Bryson," *U.S. News & World Report,* June 26, 2003.

Schatz, Douglas, Bill Bryson interview, *Stanfords Newsletter.* http://www.stanfords.co.uk/articles/interviews/the-bill-bryson-interview,57,AR.html (viewed May 10, 2006).

"Talk with Bill Bryson," "Wanderlust," salon.com. http://www.salon.com/wlust/feature/1998/05/20feature.html (viewed May 10, 2006).

"Talking with . . . Bill Bryson," *People Weekly*, August 3, 1998.

Tierney, Bruce, "Back to School with Bill Bryson," *BookPage,* May 2003. http://www.bookpage.com/0305bp/bill_bryson.html (viewed May 10, 2006).

Trefil, James S., "Know It All," *American Scientist*, January-February 2004.

Welch, Dave, "Bill Bryson Is More Popular Than the Beatles," Powells.com. http://www.powells.ocm/authors/bryson.html (viewed May 10,1 2006).

Wilkens, Mary Frances, *In a Sunburned Country* review, *Booklist,* September 15, 2000.

Tim Cahill

Adventure, Travel, True Crime

Benchmark Title: *Jaguars Ripped My Flesh*

Nashville, Tennessee

1944–

Photo courtesy Crown Publishing

About the Author and the Author's Writing

They're climbing El Capitan, the magnificent wall cliff in Yosemite National Park, nearly three thousand feet of unbroken vertical surface. Tim Cahill is suspended from ropes six hundred feet above the scree when his climbing partner "Nick" Nichols advises that he needs relief. "At this point, in this exceedingly inconvenient situation, six hundred feet above the rocks (and two feet above me), Nick needed a men's room."

Cahill's reaction? "That was the first time I thought, What am I doing here? I mean, really, what's wrong with me?"

Adventure (truly, contained misadventure) is writer Cahill's trademark. As evidenced from that opening cliff scene in a San Francisco *Examiner* essay "Rope Tricks," which is included in *Pecked to Death by Ducks,* he is adept at dramatizing, and humanizing, encounters with the unexpected—at everywhere from deep caves to ocean depths to dense jungles and with everything from stalking jaguars to snarling wolverines to snapping ducks. In 2006, *Men's Journal* ranked him among its twenty-five favorite adventure writers, "the one with whom you'd most want to grab a beer."

Born in Nashville, Tennessee, in 1944, Tim Cahill grew up in Waukesha, Washington. In his teens, while his male friends might be sneaking a look at *Stag,* he secretly bought copies of *Writer's Digest* and dreamed of becoming a writer. He earned a bachelor of arts degree in European intellectual history from the University of Wisconsin, abandoned an attempt to study law, then completed requirements for a master's degree in creative writing from San Francisco State University. To cover tuition costs, he worked variously as a longshoreman, a lifeguard, and a warehouseman. In 1971, he joined the staff of *Rolling Stone* magazine. "I wrote about rock-and-roll and politics and the like," he said in a *Mother Jones* interview. "At the time, I really didn't know what I wanted to write and I did a bunch of investigative journalism."

When *Rolling Stone* established an exploring-and-adventure offshoot, *Outside,* in 1976, Cahill became a founding editor. He has been a contributor and freelance writer for that publication and others since.

48

Although he made his name in writing about rock music and outdoor adventure, Cahill's first book was true crime, *Buried Dreams,* a profile of notorious 1970s serial killer John Wayne Gacy. The book sold a lot of copies but discouraged him on the genre because he detested having to invest so much in the sick killer's mind.

Cahill embraced the great outdoors as he wrote about it. *Jaguars Ripped My Flesh* and subsequent collections showcase Cahill's great talent at bringing an everyman's sense of discovery to all manner of places and creatures. "I seem to do my best work when stimulated by vaguely threatening situations," the author told *Bloomsbury* interviewer David Petersen. In *Please Pass the Butterworms,* Cahill typically demonstrates his mild ineptness at horseback riding and sea kayaking. He self-deprecatingly owns up to singing "Tea for Two" in a Donald Duck voice to villagers in one exotic land. *In Pecked to Death by Ducks,* he sleeps with grizzly bears in Yellowstone Park and gropes the depths of Lechiguilla Cave. Wherever he roams, he ably creates the environment on paper—he engages his readers, bringing them with him on his encounters.

Cahill says he is willing to give most any place a serious try. But he won't be a tourist. "When I read about how 200 people died on a polar expedition, I wonder why they didn't get to know the Inuit people who were around and presumably know something about surviving in the Arctic after living there for thousands of years. Talking to people is a survival mechanism," he said in an interview on his Random House Web page.

Nothing in Cahill's writing is haphazard. He admits to having a poor sense of direction. He's been known to fall. But some of his naiveté in print is simply a persona. Cahill keeps a journal of all his travels. "One way to write is to simply chronicle events," he explained in an interview with Rolf Potts for *Vagabonding.* "This sometimes constitutes a failure of imagination. The events will work themselves into a story if you think about them enough. It is like holding a prism to the sun: turn it just the right way and a rainbow of light pours through."

Cahill considers his work to be directly linked to the writing of James Fenimore Cooper, Mark Twain, and Ernest Hemingway in which the outdoors is as important as the characters or story. He lists as influences or favorite writers Twain and Tom Wolfe, Elmore Leonard and Edward Abbey, along with Bill Bryson, Paul Theroux, Dianne Ackerman, and Tony Horwitz.

Over the years, Cahill has felt a growing maturity in his craft. "I know tricks now to make it smooth," he said in an interview with "WanderLust" on salon.com. "I know tricks to make the structure work. I know that if I am having a real hard time writing a part, maybe the part doesn't even belong in the piece. But I also try to keep elements from my earlier writing alive—like the sense of amazement—and that is an adolescent thing."

Since 1978, Cahill has lived in Livingston, Montana, with his companion Linnea Larson, where he hikes, fishes and explores the Yellowstone River, volunteers with Big Brothers/Big Sisters, serves on the community search-and-rescue team, and once in a while dresses as Santa Claus at Christmas. Cahill has lost some of his urge to travel and has come to enjoy his own immediate environment. That's expressed in the title of a recent book, *Lost in My Own Backyard: A Walk in Yellowstone National Park,* in which he admits that proximity does not always bring familiarity with, in his case, geysers and moonbows and microbes. "I've spent entire afternoons not knowing exactly where I was, which is to say, I was lost in my own backyard," he says in the book.

In a conversation found on the *Outside* magazine Web site, Cahill summed up his approach to writing, "I have a theory that as human beings we see our lives through the lenses of stories. Stories are the way we organize the complete chaos of our existence into something that we can understand. And that's what I try to do—I try to tell stories that allow us to make sense of things."

Works by the Author

Buried Dreams: Inside the Mind of a Serial Killer (1987)
Jaguars Ripped My Flesh: Adventure Is a Risky Business (1987), essays
A Wolverine Is Eating My Leg (1989), essays
Road Fever: A High-Speed Travelogue (1991)
Pecked to Death by Ducks (1993), essays
Pass the Butterworms: Remote Journeys Oddly Rendered (1997), essays
Dolphins, with Jean-Michel Cousteau (2000)
Silence & Solitude: Yellowstone's Winter Wilderness, with Tom Murphy (2001)
Hold the Enlightenment (2003)
Lost in My Own Backyard: A Walk in Yellowstone National Park (2004)

Editor

Wild Places: Twenty Journeys into the North American Outdoors (1996) (and contributor)
Not So Funny When It Happened: The Best of Travel Humor and Misadventure (2000)
The Best Travel Writing of 2006, with Jason Wilson (2006)

Contributor

In Search of Adventure: A Wild Travel Anthology (1999), edited by Bruce Northam and Brad Olsen
Muses in Arcadia (2000)
Hidden Coast: Coastal Adventures from Alaska to Mexico (2000)
When In Doubt, Go Higher: A Mountain Gazette Anthology (2002)
Everest: Mountain without Mercy (2003)
Hyenas Laughed at Me and Now I Know Why: The Best of Travel Humor and Misadventure (2003)
Lonely Planet: Yellowstone & Grand Teton National Parks (2003)
The Mammoth Book of Wild Journeys: 30 First-Hand Heart-Racing Accounts of Travel in Remote Places (2005)
Top Trails: Yellowstone & Grand Teton National Parks: Must-Do Hikes for Everyone (2005)

Screenplay

Everest, with Stephen Judson (1998)

For Further Information

"Conversation with Tim Cahill," Tim Cahill Web page, Random House. http://www.randomhouse.com/boldtype/0902/cahill/interview.html (viewed April 18, 2006).

George, Don, "An Interview with Tim Cahill," *WanderLust.* http://www.salon.com/march97/wanderlust/cahill970325.html (viewed April 18, 2006).

Kancler, Erik, "Wild Life: An Interview with Tim Cahill," *Mother Jones,* March 2005.

Miles, Jonathan, "25 Best Adventure Authors," *Men's Journal,* May 2006.

Petersen, David, "Road Fever: Tim Cahill Has It," *Bloomsbury Review,* September 1991.

Potts, Rolf, Tim Cahill interview, *Vagabonding.* http://www.rolfpotts.com/writers/cahill.php (viewed April 18, 2006).

"Q&A: Tim Cahill," Outside Online. http://outside.away.com/outside/news/cahill.html (viewed April 18, 2006).

Tim Cahill entry, Contemporary Authors Online. Reproduced in Biography Resource Center. Farmington Hills, MI: Thomson Gale, 2006. http://galenet.galegroup.com/servlet/BioRC.

Vestal, Shawn, "For On-the-Edge Traveler Cahill, the Adventure Is in the Telling," *Bozeman Daily Chronicle*, April 3, 1997.

Truman Capote

Fiction, True Crime

Benchmark Title: *In Cold Blood*

New Orleans, Louisiana

1924–1984

About the Author and the Author's Writing

Truman Capote, the fiction writer who turned journalism on its ear, experienced the lows of childhood poverty and family dysfunction, and the highs of best-sellerdom and fame. In the soaring journey from one extreme to the other, he became a celebrity of great controversy, both fawned over and disdained.

Truman Streckfus Persons was born in New Orleans in 1924, the son of salesman and steamship company clerk Archulus Persons and his sixteen-year-old bride, Lillie Mae Faulk, a former Miss Alabama. When the marriage fell apart, Truman at age four was sent to live with relatives in Monroeville, Alabama, one of whom, his aunt, Sook Faulk, inspired spinster characters in the author's later writings including *A Christmas Memory*. As a boy, Truman was mostly left to his own devices. "I began writing really sort of seriously when I was about eleven," he's quoted on an American Masters Web page. "I say seriously in the sense that like other kids go home and practice the violin or the piano or whatever, I used to go home from school every day and I would write for about three hours. I was obsessed by it."

His mother divorced and remarried. Truman rejoined her and his stepfather, Joseph Capote, in New York City in 1929. Two years later, his name changed through adoption. He attended Trinity School and St. John's Academy, as well as also public schools in Greenwich, Connecticut. He joined the staff of the *New Yorker* at age seventeen.

Capote gradually sold stories to that periodical and others. He won an O. Henry award in 1946 for a story called "Miriam," published in *Mademoiselle*. Publisher Bennett Cerf signed the author to Random House, where his first novel was *Other Voices, Other Rooms,* published in 1948. The book, in something of a Southern gothic style, was about alienated youth. It discussed homosexuality.

In 1948, Capote, who was openly gay, befriended Jack Dunphy, a former Broadway dancer. They traveled together to Europe in 1949. Capote began to sell stories to Hollywood. He met Marilyn Monroe through his friendship with director John Huston, with whom he would collaborate on the script of *Beat the Devil* in 1954. Capote drifted into New York's social scene, where he became a literary celebrity. His *Breakfast at Tiffany's* (1958), about sprightly, sexually adventurous Holly Golightly (played by Audrey Hepburn in the film version), solidified Capote's stature with upper social circles.

In spite of his early successes, Capote yearned to push literary boundaries. "Magazine reportage was bread and butter for Capote, until he saw its possibilities for yielding a piece de resistance," according to Thomas Mallon in The *New Yorker*. "In the late fifties, he began applying innovative techniques to both a profile of Marlon Brando and the articles in 'The Muses Are Heard,' a tag-along chronicle of an American theatre troupe performing *Porgy and Bess* in Soviet Russia."

When he read a newspaper account in 1959 of the brutal killing of four members of a rural Kansas ranch family, Capote persuaded the *New Yorker*'s editor William Shawn to assign him to the story. He was intrigued by what drew together an unassuming Midwestern family and a pair of hardened criminals.

Capote went to the small town of Holcomb and began his research. Serendipitously, the alleged killers were tracked down and arrested in Las Vegas while the author was still collecting material. They were eventually brought to trial, convicted, and sentenced to death. This gave Capote opportunity that he exploited fully. He squeezed information from the Kansas Bureau of Investigation (although agent Harold "Nappy" Nye long kept his distance) and nudged details from family and friends. The author smartly took a friend with him. As a boy in Alabama, the author had chummed with Nelle Harper Lee. He based a character in *Other Voices, Other Rooms* on her. Lee, in turn, portrayed Capote as the character Dill in her Pulitzer Prize–winning novel *To Kill a Mockingbird* (1960). Lee's pleasant approach in Kansas opened many farmhouse doors. Capote was short; had an abrasive, screeching voice; and spoke with exaggerated mannerisms, all traits that turned off the conservative Kansans.

Capote befriended the killers, Richard Hickock and, particularly, Perry Smith, toward whom he came to feel some empathy, even infatuation. He went to Switzerland to begin his book, but as he wrote in a letter to Kansas lawman Alvin Dewey, who had apprehended Smith and Hickock, "The problem is, I have reached a point in my book where I must know how the book ends.... The book is going to be a masterpiece."

Tiffany's came out as a movie. Lee's *Mockingbird* was published. And Capote assisted with the Smith's and Hickock's appeals. Six years after the murders, both men were executed by hanging in April 1965. Capote witnessed their deaths. When he finished *In Cold Blood*, the *New Yorker* serialized it, and it appeared in bookstores in early 1966.

David Bowman in *Book* suggests that *In Cold Blood* had an automatic appeal in its grisly subject. "[B]ut the book was a curiosity in and of itself, a new type of literature altogether. Capote was a novelist, and he wrote *In Cold Blood* with plenty of imaginative flair. The final product was an oxymoron: a nonfiction novel."

Capote summarized his technique to George Plimpton, who wrote in the *New York Times* in 1966: "[A]bove all, the reporter must be able to empathize with personalities outside his usual imaginative range, mentalities unlike his own, kinds of people he would never have written about had he not been forced to by encountering them inside the journalistic situation. This last is what first attracted me to the notion of narrative reportage."

The book was an enormous critical success and a best seller. Capote moved into United Nations Plaza where celebrity neighbors included talk-show host Johnny Carson and dancer Katharine Graham. He threw his black-and-white ball at the Plaza Hotel to celebrate *Blood's* publication. Richard Brooks directed the 1967 motion picture version of *In Cold Blood* featuring Robert Blake and Scott Wilson as the killers.

After the success of *In Cold Blood,* Capote's writing tapered off severely. Royalties made him wealthy. He collected old stories and wrote a few new ones, but little of major substance. He appeared on television talk shows, perpetuating the exaggerated mien of gays. His romps at the nightclubs Studio 54 or The Anvil peppered tabloid gossip columns. He began work on *Answered Prayers,* a novel closely based on the social circles in which he moved. When samples appeared in *Esquire* in 1975, their uncomfortable accuracy so revolted Capote's friends that they would have no more to do with him. Gore Vidal, once a friend, sued him and won. Capote never completed the work.

Capote died in 1984, his last years wracked by alcoholism and drug abuse. His notoriety has lingered. Robert Morse played Capote in a Broadway play, *Tru* (1990). Actor Philip Seymour Hoffman won a best actor Academy Award for his portrayal of the author in Bennett Miller's biopic *Capote* (2005), based on Gerald Clarke's biography, *Capote: A Life.* The film's popularity promoted Vintage to print 130,000 new copies of *In Cold Blood* for a new audience. Toby Jones took the Capote part in another film, based on Plimpton's book *Truman Capote, Infamous* (2006).

With this kind of myth-making, Capote won't quickly be forgotten.

 # Works by the Author

Local Color (1950), sketches
The Muses Are Heard: An Account (1956)
Selected Writings (1963)
In Cold Blood: A True Account of a Multiple Murder and Its Consequences (1966), described as nonfiction novel
The Dogs Bark: *Public People and Private Places* (1973)
Conversations with Capote (1985)
Marilyn Monroe: Photographs 1945–1962 (1994)
Too Brief a Treat: The Letters of Truman Capote (2004)

Contributor

Observations, with Richard Avedon (1959)
Five Modern American Short Stories (1962), edited by Helmut Tischler and M. Diesterweg
Then It All Came Down: Criminal Justice Today Discussed by Police, Criminals, and Correction Officers, with Comments by Truman Capote (1976)
Marlon Brando: Portraits and Film Stills 1946–1995 (1996), edited by Lothar Schirmer

Fiction

Other Voices, Other Rooms (1948)
A Tree of Night and Other Stories (1949)

The Grass Harp (1951), included in *The Grass Harp* and *A Tree of Night, and Other Stories* (1956)

Breakfast at Tiffany's (1958)

A Christmas Memory (1966)

The Thanksgiving Visitor (1968), included in *The Thanksgiving Visitor, One Christmas,* and *A Christmas Memory* (1996)

House of Flowers (1968)

Then It All Came Down (1976)

Music for Chameleons: New Writings (1980)

One Christmas (1982)

Answered Prayers: The Unfinished Novel (1986)

I Remember Grandpa (1987)

A Capote Reader (1987)

A House on the Heights (2002)

The Complete Stories of Truman Capote (2004)

Summer's Crossing (2005)

Stage Plays

The Grass Harp (1952)

The House of Flowers, with Harold Arlen (1954)

Screenplays or Teleplays

Beat the Devil, with John Huston (1954)

The Innocents, with William Archibald and John Mortimer (1961), based on Henry James's *The Turn of the Screw*

A Christmas Memory (1966)

Among the Paths to Eden (1967)

The Thanksgiving Visitor (1968)

Laura (1968)

Trilogy, with Eleanor Perry (1969), adapted from Capote's stories "Miriam," "Among the Paths to Eden," and *A Christmas Memory*

Behind Prison Walls (1972)

The Glass House, with Tracy Keenan Wynn and Wyatt Cooper (1972)

Crimewatch (1973)

Film and Television Adaptations

Breakfast at Tiffany's (1961)

In Cold Blood (1966)

A Christmas Memory (1966)

Among the Paths to Eden (1967)

The Thanksgiving Visitor (1968)

The Grass Harp (1996)

In Cold Blood (1996), television miniseries

For Further Information

Bowman, David, "A Murder in Middle America: Truman Capote's Killer Instincts and the Making of the Sensational *In Cold Blood,*" *Book,* November-December 2002.

Clarke, Gerald, *Truman Capote: A Biography.* New York: Simon & Schuster, 1986.

Goldfarb, Brad, "Conversations with Capote," *Interview,* December 1997.

Grobel, Lawrence, *Conversations with Capote.* New York: New American Library, 1985.

Malin, Irving, editor *Truman Capote's* In Cold Blood: *A Critical Handbook.* Belmont, CA: Wadsworth, 1968.

Mallon, Thomas, "Golden Boy," *New Yorker,* September 13, 2004.

Plimpton, George, "Capote's Long Ride," *New Yorker*, October 13, 1997.

Plimpton, George, "The Story behind a Nonfiction Novel," *New York Times*, January 16, 1966.

Plimpton, George, *Truman Capote: In Which Various Friends, Enemies, Acquaintances, and Detractors Recall His Turbulent Career.* New York: Doubleday, 1997.

Shields, Charles J., *Mockingbird.* New York: Henry Holt, 2006.

Truman Capote entry, *Authors and Artists for Young Adults,* Vol. 61. Detroit, MI: Thomson Gale.

Truman Capote entry, Contemporary Authors Online. Reproduced in Biography Resource Center. Farmington Hills, MI: Thomson Gale, 2006. http://galenet.galegroup.com/servlet/BioRC.

Truman Capote Web page, *American Masters.* http://www.pbs.org/wnet/americanmasters/database/capote_t.html (viewed May 16, 2006).

Truman Capote Web page, *Knitting Circle: Literature.* http://myweb/lsbu.ac/auk/stafflag/trumancapote.html (viewed May 16, 2006).

Truman Capote Web page. http://www.kirjasto.sci.fi/capote.htm (viewed May 16, 206).

Weiss, Irving and Anne D., editors *Thesaurus of Book Digests 1950–1980.* New York: Crown, 1981.

Wiebe, Crystal K., " 'To Kill a Mockingbird' Author Helped Truman Capote Break the Ice in Kansas," Lawrence *Journal-World,* April 3, 2005.

Rachel Carson

Environment, Science

Benchmark Title: *Silent Spring*

Springdale, Pennsylvania

1907–1964

Photo by Harris & Ewing, courtesy of the
Lear/Carson Collection, Connecticut College

About the Author and the Author's Writing

The Ninth Street Bridge in Pittsburgh, which spans the Allegheny River near where Rachel Carson played as a child, was renamed the Rachel Carson Bridge on Earth Day 2006. That's only the latest honor for a scientist who is celebrated as one of the most influential women of the twentieth century.

Even so, five decades after her death in 1964 of breast cancer, the author of *Silent Spring,* the book that launched the environmental movement in America, remains a controversial scientist and writer.

Rachel Carson was born in 1907 on a small farm about forty miles north of Pittsburgh, the youngest of three children of Robert Warden Carson and Maria McLean Carson. Her mother, the daughter of a Presbyterian minister, encouraged Rachel's early interest in the outdoors and in the arts. She sent nature essays to *St. Nicholas Magazine,* and it published one of her stories when she was ten years old.

Rachel graduated from Parnassus High School in 1925 and magnum cum laude from Pennsylvania College for Women (now Chatham College) four years later. While at the school, she changed her major from English to zoology. With a growing interest in marine biology, she was a summer fellow at the Marine Biology Laboratory at Woods Hole in Massachusetts. She earned a master's degree in zoology and genetics from Johns Hopkins University in 1932 and later taught there and at the University of Maryland at College Park.

Her father's death in 1935, during the height of the Great Depression, put enormous financial burden on Carson. The family had already sold the farm and moved to Maryland. Her sister, Marian Williams, died in 1937, saddling Carson and her mother with the responsibility for two younger children, Marjorie and Virginia.

For sixteen years Carson worked for the United States Bureau of Fisheries. She passed a rigorous civil service exam to become only the second woman hired by the agency. As an information specialist, she wrote text for technical brochures, several of them about fish as a food source, and radio scripts. One of those scripts, rejected by her boss as too involved, found a home as an essay, "Undersea," in a 1937 issue of *Atlantic Monthly*. After World War II, Carson rose to be biologist and editor-in-chief of publications for what became known as the U.S. Fish and Wildlife Service.

Her first book came out in 1941. Titled *Under the Sea Wind,* it was an expansion of the *Atlantic* essay. It sold modestly. But Carson had at hand new and newly declassified government research material, some of which she herself had obtained in the field in the Florida Everglades and Chesapeake Bay. It was the basis of her next work, *The Sea around Us,* published in 1951. The book found a wide audience and earned Carson a National Book Award for Nonfiction in 1952, and a John Burroughs Medal. She resigned her government job to write full time. In 1955, *The Edge of the Sea* became another award winner.

Carson built a Maine retreat in 1952. Four years later, she adopted Roger, the son of her late niece Marjorie. She built a new home in Silver Springs, Maryland. And she began work on her next endeavor. A Boston newspaper reporter, Olga Owens Huckins, had written Carson to complain that pesticides were wiping out birds that once flocked to Massachusetts. Carson queried *Reader's Digest* about writing such an article, and ultimately, through essayist E. B. White, she approached *New Yorker* editor William Shawn, who encouraged her to write a book. After four years of collecting material; speaking with biologists, entomologists, and pathologists; and studying scientific studies and reports, she wrote *Silent Spring*. In 1962, the *New Yorker* serialized it.

The work, which posited that more controls were needed on the use of DDT and other pesticides, ignited a firestorm. Scientists hailed it as a major achievement.

"Carson's work on behalf of biological preservation served as the foundation for the environmental movement of the last half of the 20th century," according to an entry in *Feminist Writers*.

Chemical company executives charged that it was the contrivance of a "hysterical woman." Carson had done her research well, however, and supported all of her assertions with scientific sources, explains the Natural Resources Defense Council Silent Spring Web page. "Many eminent scientists rose to her defense, and when President John F. Kennedy ordered the President's Science Advisory Committee to examine the issues the book raised, its report thoroughly vindicated both *Silent Spring* and its author."

Although her health had begun to decline, Carson accepted numerous invitations to speak. She addressed the U.S. Senate's Ribicoff Committee, which was looking into environmental hazards. The book was translated into thirty languages. The United States banned the use of DDT in 1968.

Its thorough documentation hasn't stopped the undermining of *Silent Spring*. Entomologist J. Gordon Edwards in *21st Century Science & Technology Magazine* in 1992 complained that "each reference was cited separately each time it appeared in the book, thus producing an impressive array of 'references' even though not many different sources were actually cited." He then proceeded to enumerate more specific complaints about Carson's text.

On the other hand, the effects of the legislation the book induced were undeniable: "bald eagles that were once threatened with extinction in the contiguous forty-eight states have increased from roughly 400 nesting pairs in 1963 to more than 5,700 pairs today. As a result, the federal government in July [1999] formally proposed removing them from the country's Endangered Species List," *National Wildlife* reported in 1999.

In 2004, charges emerged that African babies were dying in enormous numbers because of the unavailability of DDT—one of nine pesticides banned by ninety-one countries by international treaty in 2001—mosquitoes continued to spread malaria in underdeveloped nations.

Obviously the debate continues. In 2003, *Time* magazine selected Carson and her book among "80 Days That Changed the World" and quoted the author as saying the book was "something I believed in so deeply that there was no other course; nothing that ever happened made me ever consider turning back."

"True, the damage being done by poison chemicals today is far worse than it was when she wrote the book," in the opinion of Peter Matthiessen in *Time* in 1999. "Yet one shudders to imagine how much more impoverished our habitat would be had *Silent Spring* not sounded the alarm.. . . . Even if she had not inspired a generation of activists, Carson would prevail as one of the greatest nature writers in American letters."

Carson's writing tapered off after *Silent Spring*. *The Sense of Wonder* was a *Woman's Home Companion* essay paired with photographs by Nick Kelsh. *The Rocky Coast* was an essay and photo journey along the northern New England coast. Following her death, besides two posthumous collections of her writings, the Rachel Carson National Wildlife Refuge was established in her memory on the southern Maine coast in 1966. Further assuring her legacy, she was elected to the National Women's Hall of Fame in 1973. The Rachel Carson Homestead Association formed in 1975 to preserve her birthplace home in Springdale, Pennsylvania. She received the Presidential Medal of Freedom in 1980. A year later, she appeared on a seventeen-cent United States postage stamp. She was also installed in the Ecology Hall of Fame in 1992.

Works by the Author

Under the Sea-Wind: A Naturalist's Pictures of Ocean Life (1941)
Food from Home Waters: Fishes of the Middle West (1943)
Food from the Sea: Fish and Shellfish of New England (1943)
Fish and Shellfish of the South Atlantic and Gulf Coasts (1944)
Fish and Shellfish of the Middle Atlantic Coast (1945)
The Sea around Us (1951), selections in *Life under the Sea* (1968)
The Edge of the Sea (1955)
Silent Spring (1962)
The Sense of Wonder (1965)
The Rocky Coast (1971)
Always Rachel: The Letters of Rachel Carson and Dorothy Freeman, 1952–1964 (1995)
Lost Woods: The Discovered Writings of Rachel Carson (1998)

Scripts

Omnibus television episode "Something about the Sky," 1955.

Film Adaptations

The Sea around Us (1951)

For Further Information

"Bridge to Be Re-Named in Honor of Rachel Carson," PR Newswire, April 21, 2006.

Brooks, Paul, editor. *The House of Life: Rachel Carson at Work.* Boston: Houghton Mifflin, 1972.

Edwards, J. Gordon, "The Lies of Rachel Carson," *21st Century Science & Technology Magazine.* http://www.21stcenturyscientcetech.com/articles/ summ02/ Carson.html (viewed May 16, 2006).

Karaim, Reed, "Not So Fast with the DDT: Rachel Carson's Warnings Still Apply," *American Scholar,* Summer 2005.

Lear, Linda J., *Rachel Carson: Witness for Nature.* New York: Henry Holt, 1997.

Lipske, Michael, "How Rachel Carson Helped Save the Brown Pelican: One of America's Most Charismatic Coastal Birds Is Thriving Again, Thanks in Part to a Biologist-Turned-Author," *National Wildlife*, December-January 1999.

Marco, Gino J., Robert M. Hollingworth, and William Durham, editors *Silent Spring Revisited.* Washington, DC: American Chemical Society, 1987.

Matthiessen, Peter, "Environmentalist: Rachel Carson—Before There Was an Environmental Movement, There Was One Brave Woman and Her Very Brave Book," *Time*, March 29, 1999.

Rachel Carson entry, *Authors and Artists for Young Adults,* Vol. 49. Detroit: Thomson Gale, 2003.

Rachel Carson entry, *Feminist Writers.* Chicago: St. James Press, 1996.

Rachel Carson Homestead Web page, Rachel Carson Homestead Association. http://www.rachelcarsonhomestead/org/ (viewed May 16, 2006).

Rachel Carson National Wildlife Refuge Web page, U.S. Fish & Wildlife Service. http://www.fws.gov/northeast/rachelcarson/ (viewed May 16, 2006).

Rachel Carson postage stamp, NNDB. http://www.nndb.com/people/843/ 000031750 (viewed June 2, 2006).

Rachel Carson Web page, Ecology Hall of Fame. http://www.ecotopia. org/ehof/carson/bio.yhtml (viewed May 16, 2006).

Sterling, Philip, *Sea and Earth: The Life of Rachel Carson.* New York: Crowell, 1970.

"Story of Silent Spring," National Resources Defense Council. http://www.nrdc. iorg/health/pesticides/hcarson.asp (viewed May 16, 2006).

Watson, Bruce, "Sounding the Alarm: Forty Years Ago, Rachel Carson's *Silent Spring* Forever Changed Our View of the Environment," *Smithsonian*, September 2002.

Jung Chang

Biography, Memoirs

Benchmark Title: *Wild Swans*

Yibin, Sichuan Province, China

1952–

Courtesy Knopf Publicity
Chang is shown here with her husband and
coauthor Jon Halliday.

About the Author and the Author's Writing

"Mao Tse-tung, who for decades held absolute power over the lives of one quarter of the world's population," begins Jung Chang's *Mao: The Unknown Story,* "was responsible for well over 70 million deaths in peacetime, more than any other twentieth-century leader."

The provocative seven-hundred-page biography, which Chang cowrote with her husband, Jon Halliday, "boasts a monumental marshaling of detail and historiographically overturning revelations," said *Booklist* reviewer Brad Hooper. "It takes time to get through and more time to digest, but there is no time when its value is not apparent."

It took Jung Chang and Jon Halliday a decade to research and write *Mao*—a luxury afforded by the 10 million copies sold in fifteen languages of Chang's earlier memoir, *Wild Swans: Three Daughters of China.*

Chang was born in Yibin, Sichuan Province, China, in 1952. Her parents, Shou-Yu Chang and De-Hong Xia, were both Communist party officials, and Chang herself was briefly, at age fourteen, a member of the Red Guard. She was a "barefoot doctor," a steelworker, and an electrician before she became a student of the English language. From 1973 to 1977, she was an assistant lecturer at Sichuan University. She was allowed to travel to Great Britain in 1978, and when she received her Ph.D. in linguistics in 1982 at York University, she became the first from her country to earn such a high degree in England.

Chang married writer Jon Halliday. She and her husband first collaborated on a biography of Madame Sun Yat-Sen, wife of the Chinese revolutionary and political leader, in 1986.

The basis of the author's first book was the difficult experiences of her family living in China under Mao's rule. Chang's father died without medical treatment after he suffered a mental breakdown following his imprisonment for questioning Mao's policies. Jung Chang's mother was also questioned, imprisoned, and tortured, but she survived. She visited her daughter in London in 1988 and made some sixty hours of audio recordings that provided material for her family memoir, *Wild Swans*. Intense research filled in the details for the story of three generations of Chinese women—Chang, her mother, and her grandmother, a warlord's concubine in the 1920s who managed to escape and marry a physician. Judith Shapiro in *Washington Post Book World* found the book "an unfailingly gripping tale of abuse and suffering, broken by moving accounts of family loyalty in the face of tremendous pressure."

If *Wild Swans* told the personal side, *Mao* related the political and historical detail of the Communist chairman's reign. "I decided to write about Mao because he is one of the major historical figures of the last century," Chang said in a Radio Free Asia interview. "Because I think that most people in the world, including Chinese people, actually don't know very much about him."

What Chang and Halliday presented was quite a different picture of Mao and his policies and achievements than was painted—or propagandized, as Chang said—in China and abroad. "We bent over backward to be fair to him," Chang told *Time Asia*. "But we could find nothing nice to say. He was completely immoral, and yet also very smart. He could rise from seemingly impossible situations. We were constantly impressed."

Chang's allegations are strong. "He was as evil as Hitler or Stalin, and did as much damage to mankind as they did. Yet the world knows astonishingly little about him," Chang said in a feature for ABC Queensland.

In their research, the authors interviewed two hundred international figures in all, including former President George H. W. Bush, former Secretary of State Henry Kissinger, the Dalai Lama, and Imelda Marcos. Chang also interviewed people who had been active in Mao's regime, despite warnings from the present Chinese government. "People were dying to say things," Chang said in an interview with Lisa Allardice for the *Guardian*. "They realized that if the government was that bothered, their story was going to be heard."

The author these days travels widely to speak—for example, to the University of York and the London School of Economics—or appear on television programs to discuss her work, which found an enormously interested audience.

Works by the Author

Madame Sun Yat-Sen: Soong Ching-Ling, with Jon Halliday (1986)
Wild Swans: Three Daughters of China (1991)
Mao: The Unknown Story, with Jon Halliday (2005)

For Further Information

Allardice, Lisa, "This Book Will Shake the World," *Guardian Unlimited,* May 26, 2005. http://books.guardian.co.uk/departments/biography/story/0,6000, 1492173,00.html (viewed May 2, 2006).

Austin, Steve, and Geoff Shang, "Authors Jung Chang and Jon Halliday," ABC Queensland, July 22, 2005. http://www.abc.net.au/queensland/stories/ s1420192.htm (viewed May 2, 2006).

Hooper, Brad, *Mao: The Unknown Story* review, *Booklist,* September 1, 2005.

Jung Chang entry, Contemporary Authors Online. Reproduced in Biography Resource Center. Farmington Hills, MI: Thomson Gale, 2006. http://galenet.galegroup.com/servlet/BioRC.

Morrison, Donald, "Mao Didn't Care," *Time Asia,* June 6, 2006.

Shapiro, Judith, *Wild Swans* review, *Washington Post Book World,* September 8, 1991.

" 'Wild Swans' Author Rushes to Produce Mao Book in Chinese," Radio Free Asia, October 12, 2005. http://www.rfa.org/english/news/arts/2005/10/12/china_mao/ (viewed May 2, 2006).

Deepak Chopra

Autobiography, Health, Spirituality

Benchmark Title: *Creating Health*

New Delhi, India

1946—

About the Author and the Author's Writing

A guru of alternative medicine, Deepak Chopra is a vibrant speaker and prolific writer about Ayurvedic medicine, an ancient Indian method of healing. Chopra believes meditation, controlled diet, and personal expression can lead to a healthier and longer life, and he brings this message to a wide audience through his speaking and his books.

Born in New Delhi, India, in 1946, the son of Dr. Kishan, Deepak Chopra earned his medical degree at All India Institute of Medical Science. He came to the United States in 1970 to complete residency requirements, then entered private medical practice. He was chief of staff for the New England Memorial Hospital and taught at Tufts University and Boston University, but he stopped seeing patients in the mid-1980s as he became more involved in his writing and lecturing.

Disturbed by what he perceived as an overreliance on prescription drugs as solutions for medical problems, Chopra gravitated to Maharishi Mahesh Yogi, the Indian spiritual teacher favored by the Beatles and other celebrities in the 1960s. Chopra adopted transcendental meditation and the holistic approach of Ayurvedic medicine. In 1985, he established the Maharishi Ayur-Veda Health Center for Behavioral Medicine and Stress Management, a facility that offered both Ayurvedic and Western avenues of treatment. Since 1995, he has been chief executive officer of the Chopra Center for Well Being in La Jolla, California.

Chopra's first book, *Creating Health,* came out in 1987 and has been followed by two dozen other popular works. He wrote about his journey to enlightenment in an autobiography, *Return of the Rishi.* His *Perfect Health* stresses looking at the whole body, not just that part affected by a particular ailment, in searching for a cure. *Ageless Body, Timeless Mind,* published in 1993, suggests the body needn't be on a relentless path of deterioration as one grows older. Chopra takes his self-help message to teenage readers in *Fire in the Heart,* in which he creates the character of a wise old man who poses to the author questions such as, "Do wishes come true?" and "Is there a supreme being?"

"Most people think that aging is irreversible and we know that there are mechanisms even in the human machinery that allow for the reversal of aging, through correction of diet, through anti-oxidants, through removal of toxins from the body, through exercise, through yoga and breathing techniques, and through meditation," the physician told journalist Veronica M. Hay in an interview in 2006.

Chopra's beliefs have not gone unchallenged; some in the medical community have questioned his assertions, particularly those about transcendental meditation, and suggest there is little empirical proof of its physical benefits.

In 2006, Chopra told interviewer Daniel Redwood that contemporary lifestyles are not conducive to good health. "The most harmful [aspect] is the loss of simplicity, and the loss of trust. The experience of alienation, fragmentation, isolation . . . this ultimately leads to all of the problems, like contamination of our environment, hostility towards each other, poor nutrition, and hard work, too much work."

He went on to explain the critical value of spiritual awareness in an interview with *Share International Magazine*: "Spiritual awareness is the only way that healing can occur."

Chopra's teachings challenge certain traditions, both religious and medical. "If you're a fundamentalist, it doesn't matter what religion you are, Hindu or Buddhist or Christian or Muslim, you're tied to a literal interpretation of the scripture," he said in an interview with Dave Weich of Powells.com. "Some of these ideas would be considered blasphemous if you get stuck with just one aspect." He went on to point out what he calls the seven biological responses—fight/flight, reactive, restful awareness, intuitive, creative, visionary and sacred—have parallels in the Bible. The intuitive response is seen, as an example, in Jesus Christ's admonition, "Ask and you shall receive; seek and you shall find; knock and it shall be open unto you."

Chopra said illness can be eliminated in two ways. One way is, for instance, not to smoke cigarettes. Another is broader and requires everyone's participation. Using the example of a teenager who experiences leukemia through no direct action of his own but perhaps through a bad gene, he said in a *Psychology Today* interview with James Mauro, "Every stress that I inherit is genetically there because it is the end-product of how my ancestors metabolized their own experience. And if we gain self-knowledge and change our behavior now we can affect future generations. If we don't then we share the responsibility for it."

Chopra is a busy writer. He has produced thirty-five books, some with narrow perspectives: *Golf for Enlightenment* links the sport with a happier life; *Restful Sleep* offers tips to insomniacs; *Fire in the Heart* addresses an audience just developing a body and spirit awareness. He has also written four novels and participated in several audio recordings. In summer 2005 his Deepak Chopra's Wellness Radio began over Sirius satellite radio. "With Sirius I hope to reach a critical mass of people with a message of self development and personal and social transformation," He told PR Newswire. "I will be focusing on four areas—success; love, sexuality and relationships; well being; and spirituality. My hope is to develop a more personal relationship" with listeners. How does Chopra see his mission? "My attempt is to bridge the scientific insights of today with the spiritual yearnings that we all have," he said in a *Time* interview with Andrea Sachs. "I'm writing because I find that my insights are very empowering to me and I want to share them.. . . I'm just singing in the bathroom, and if anyone wants to listen, they're welcome."

Works by the Author

Creating Health: The Psychophysiological Connection (1985), reprinted as *Creating Health: Beyond Prevention, Toward Perfection* (1987), revised as *Creating Health: How to Wake Up the Body's Intelligence* (1991)

Return of the Rishi: A Doctor's Search for the Ultimate Healer (1988), revised as *Return of the Rishi: A Doctor's Story of Spiritual Transformation and Ayurvedic Healing* (1991)

Quantum Healing; Exploring the Frontiers of Mind/Body Medicine (1989)

Perfect Health: Maharishi Ayurveda, the Mind/Body Program for Total Well-Being, with Richard Averbach and Stuart Rothenberg (1990)

Perfect Health: The Complete Mind/Body Guide (1991)

Unconditional Life: Mastering the Forces That Shape Personal Reality (1991), reprinted as *Unconditional Life: Discovering the Power to Fulfill Your Dreams* (1992)

Creating Affluence: Wealth Consciousness in the Field of All Possibilities (1993), revised as *The A-to-Z Steps to a Richer Life* (1994), revised as *The Seven Spiritual Laws of Success: A Practical Guide to the Fulfillment of Your Dreams* (1994)

Ageless Body, Timeless Mind: The Quantum Alternative to Growing Old (1993)

Restful Sleep: The Complete Mind/Body Program for Overcoming Insomnia (1994)

Journey into Healing: Awakening the Wisdom Within You (1994), reprinted as *Journey into Healing: A Step-by-Step Personal Guide Compiled from the Timeless Wisdom of Deepak Chopra, N.D.* (1994)

Perfect Digestion: The Key to Balanced Living (1995)

Living without Limits (1995)

Boundless Energy: The Complete Mind/Body Program for Overcoming Chronic Fatigue (1995)

The Way of the Wizard: Twenty Spiritual Lessons for Creating the Life You Want (1995)

The Path to Love: Renewing the Power of Spirit in Your Life (1997), reprinted as *The Path to Love: Spiritual Strategies for Healing* (1998)

Overcoming Addictions: The Spiritual Solution (1997)

Healing the Heart: A Spiritual Approach to Reversing Coronary Artery Disease (1998)

World of Infinite Possibilities (1998), reprinted as *A Deepak Chopra Companion: Illuminations on Health and Human Consciousness,* edited by Leon Nacson (1999)

Everyday Immortality: A Concise Course in Spiritual Transformation (1999)

How to Know God: The Soul's Journey into the Mystery of Mysteries (2000)

The Chopra Center Herbal Handbook: Natural Prescriptions for Perfect Health, with David Simon (2000)

Grow Younger, Live Longer; Ten Steps to Reversing Aging, with David Simon (2001)

The Deeper Wound: Preserving Your Soul in the Face of Fear and Tragedy (2001)

Chopra Center Cookbook: A Nutritional Guide to Renewal/Nourishing Body and Soul, with David Simon and Leanne Backer (2002)

Golf for Enlightenment: The Seven Lessons for the Game of Life (2003)

The Spontaneous Fulfillment of Desire: Harnessing the Infinite Power of Coincidence (2003)

The Seven Spiritual Laws of Success (2003)

The Book of Secrets: Unlocking the Hidden Dimensions of Your Life (2004)

Power, Freedom, and Grace: Living from the Source of Lasting Happiness (2006)

Deepak Chopra: Kama Sutra (2006)

The Seven Spiritual Laws for Parents: Guiding Your Children to Success and Fulfillment (2006)

Teens Ask Deepak: All the Right Questions (2006)

Life after Death: The Burden of Proof (2006)

Buddha: A Story of Enlightenment (2007)

Contributor

Hot Chocolate for the Mystical Lover; 101 True Stories of Soul Mates Brought Together by Divine Intervention, edited by Arielle Ford (2000)

Sound Recordings

Total Health: The Rediscovery of Ayurveda (1986)

A Gift of Love (1998), participants read poetry by Jalal-al-din Rumi

Secrets of Inner Power: A Profile in Courage with Rosa Parks (1999)

Grow Younger, Live Longer, with the Eurythmics (2001)

Fiction

The Return of Merlin (1995)

The Lords of Light, with Martin Greenberg (1999)

The Angel Is Near, with Martin Greenberg (2000)

Soulmates (2001)

The Daughters of Joy: An Adventure of the Heart (2002)

Editor

The Love Poems by Maulana Jalal al-din-Rumi (1998) and translator, with Fereydoun Kia

On the Shores of Eternity: Poems from Tagore on Death and Immortality by Rabindranath Tagore (1999)

For Further Information

Brunner, Rob, "Deepak Thoughts," *Entertainment Weekly*, November 20, 1998.

Cooper, Ilene, *Fire in the Heart* review, *Booklist,* May 15, 2004.

Deepak Chopra entry, Contemporary Authors Online. Reproduced in Biography Resource Center. Farmington Hills, MI: Thomson Gale, 2006. http://galenet.galegroup.com/servlet/BioRC.

Deepak Chopra entry, *Gale Encyclopedia of Medicine*, 2nd ed. Detroit, MI: Gale Group, 2002.

Deepak Chopra interview, *Share International Magazine.* http://www.spiritual.com/au/articles/healing/interviewdeepak_mleach.htm (viewed May 17, 2006).

Deepak Chopra profile. *Religious Movements.* http://religiousmovements.lib/virginia/edu/nrms/Chopra.html (viewed May 17, 2006).

"Deepak Chopra, World Renowned Mind and Body Expert and Author, to Host Show on SIRIUS Satellite radio," PR Newswire, May 4, 2006.

Devereaux, Elizabeth, *Finding the Sacred* review, *Publishers Weekly,* April 26, 2004.

Golf for Enlightenment review, *Publishers Weekly,* January 20, 2003.

Goodman, Sandra, and Mike Howell, Deepak Chopra interview, *Positive Health.* http://www.positivehealth.com/permit/Articles/Interviews/chopra.htm (viewed May 17, 2006).

Hay, Veronica M., Deepak Chopra interview, *In Touch Magazine.* http://www.intouchmag.com/chpra.html (viewed May 17, 2006).

Leland, John, Carla Power, and Larry Reibstein, "Deepak's Instant Karma," *Newsweek*, October 20, 1997.

Lord, Douglas C., *The Book of Secrets* review, *Library Journal,* October 1, 2004.

Mauro, James, "From Here and Not to Eternity," *Psychology Today,* November-December 1993.

Redwood, Daniel, "Quantum Healing," *Health World Online.* http://www.healthy.net/asp/template/interview.asp?PageType=Interview&Id=167 (viewed May 17, 2006).

Sachs, Andrea, "10 Questions for Deepak Chopra," *Time,* January 24, 2005.

Weich, Dave, Deepak Chopra interview, Powells.com. http://www.powells.com/author/chopra.html (viewed May 17, 2006).

Ted Conover

Adventure, True Crime

Benchmark Title: *Newjack*

Okinawa, Japan

1958–

Photo courtesy the author

About the Author and the Author's Writing

Ted Conover is drawn to the lesser known, the scruff of American society. He's curious about the tenuous lives of illegal Mexican immigrants who dream of green cards, rail-riding hobos who heat stew over an open fire, and guards in pressure-cooker prisons who itch to meet menace with menace. The author fully immerses himself in his subjects' lives—something Robert S. Boynton in *The New New Journalism* calls "participatory journalism." When describing his work, Conover prefers the term "narrative nonfiction," and he explains to Boynton that he was drawn to it through his anthropology studies in college. "I sometimes think of what I do as a kind of a guerrilla action. I try to find people and groups who have *not* been heard from. I depend on the *newness* of this information to keep my audience interested in my writing."

Frederick King "Ted" Conover III was born in 1958 in Okinawa, Japan, where his father was barracked as a U.S. Navy pilot. The oldest of four children of Frederick King Conover II, who later became a lawyer, and Kathryn Beim Conover, he grew up in Denver, Colorado, traveling to Spain and Mexico during the summers. In 1981, he graduated summa cum laude from Amherst College, and from 1982 to 1984, he did graduate work at Cambridge University as a Marshall Scholar. He and his wife, Margo, have two children.

Conover's career spans a broad range, from VISTA volunteer in Dallas, Texas, to writer-in-residence at Aspen Writers Conference and Bread Loaf Writers Conference. In 2000 and 2001, he was a visiting fellow at Harvard University's Institute of Politics. He has written for the *New Yorker, Travel & Leisure, Outside,* and other periodicals.

Conover quickly dispelled the myths of the world-wise hobo when, as a student at Amherst, he took time off to write his anthropology thesis. He traveled to St. Louis, hooked a train, and began a four-month journey that took him to El Paso, Seattle, and places in between. He learned that his traveling companions were, for various reasons, incapable of making ties—to permanent jobs, to stable families. He wrote his college paper, turned in an article for the alumni magazine, and then shaped his experiences into a book, *Rolling Nowhere.*

"I like writing where the writer has something at stake; . . . [where he] has had time to think and research and transform himself into an expert; where his caring and the urgency of the subject can transform the writing into something that matters, an act of witnessing," the author says on his Web site.

During his travels, Conover had met an illegal alien, and their conversation gave him an idea for his next subject and book, *Coyotes: A Journey through the Secret World of America's Illegal Aliens.* Fluent in Spanish, he joined a group of Mexican immigrants as they sought temporary jobs at citrus orchards—never losing the hope for permanence and legitimacy in the United States.

Conover told *Contemporary Authors,* "I am fascinated by the differences between cultures; I love adventure; I think some things need to be changed in the world. Somehow these three parts of myself have been able to find a kind of unified expression in my books."

For a change of pace, the author sought out the deluxe lifestyle of the flourishing and irresponsible in Aspen, Colorado. Driving a cab, writing for a local newspaper, instructing novice skiers, and crashing parties, Conover explored the city's excessive 1980s culture, and he wrote about it in *Whiteout.*

Not long after *Whiteout* was published, Conover became embroiled in another project. When the New York State corrections system refused Conover's request to shadow a recruit as he went through training as a guard for a high-security prison, the author applied to become a guard himself and went through nine months of training for a posting at Sing Sing, for his next book, *Newjack.*

One of Conover's goals in writing the book was to learn more about what it took to be a prison guard—were certain types of people drawn to the job, or did the job shape people? He found the latter was the case. "It's a soul-shrinking job. It's a job that can easily get the better of you and you have to be a strong person to do the work and stay whole.. . . That said, most people in corrections are good people," the author said in a Blue Dog Press interview.

"[H]e appears to have identified completely with the persona of a prison guard," notes reviewer Frances Sandiford. "He braces himself to walk the galleries amid catcalls and threats of violence and tries to keep on top of the games inmates play."

Conover said corrections officers are essentially keepers at a zoo. "Prison is full of frustration, and very little catharsis," he asserted in an article by Julian E. Barnes in the *New York Times Book Review.* "The use of force is one of the few catharses there is, and the more I did the job, the more I longed for a use of force.. . . You come home having done things that don't come from the better part of you and you feel dirty."

Prisoners, particularly ones held in isolation in the new generation of high-security or "supermax" facilities, have no freedom, no hope. There's virtually no rehabilitation in the prison system—inmates have no chance to receive even a modicum of education which might help them break out of the cycle once they're back on the outside. Conover found Islam the most popular of religions adopted by prisoners. "I think in most cases that's really a positive thing," he told Paula Zahn for CNN's *American Morning* in 2002. "You can ask any officer, and they'll tell you that inmates who are involved in religion have more discipline in their lives, they cause you less trouble. You know, they have got something they are working for."

The author explained his writing craft to *Publishers Weekly*'s Norman Oder: "First-person nonfiction is tricky. It's a combination of the voice you use, the self-revelation you offer, and the more discursive material that's important."

He amplified on this, in a question-and-answer session with *Etude*'s Rita Radostitz: "The stories materialize along the way when you find a person who can be a character in the narrative, and then you watch what the person is trying to do, and you go with them, often sort of complicating the plot. So I'm a character as well, but generally, I'm a minor one...."

The author has earned wide recognition. The *New York Times* named *Coyotes, Whiteout* and *Newjack* among its Notable Books; and *Newjack* earned the National Book Critics Circle Award in General Nonfiction in 2000 and was a finalist for the Pulitzer Prize.

Works by the Author

Rolling Nowhere: A Young Man's Adventures Riding the Rails with America's Hoboes (1983)
Coyotes: A Journey through the Secret World of America's Illegal Aliens (1987)
Whiteout: Lost in Aspen (1991)
Newjack: Guarding Sing Sing (2000)

Contributor

The Sparkling-Eyed Boy: A Memoir of Love, Grown Up (2004)

For Further Information

Barnes, Julian E., "Life As a Jailer," *New York Times Book Review*, May 14, 2000.

Boynton, Robert S., *The New New Journalism: Conversations with America's Best Nonfiction Writers on Their Craft.* New York: Vintage Books, 2005.

Oder, Norman, "In the Belly of the Beast: Ted Conover," *Publishers Weekly*, May 8, 2000.

Radostitz, Rita, Ted Conover interview, *Etude,* autumn 2003. http://etude/ uoregon.edu/autumn2003/conover/index.html (viewed April 25, 2006).

Saniford, Frances, *Newjack* review, *Library Journal,* June 1, 2000.

Ted Conover entry, Contemporary Authors Online. Reproduced in Biography Resource Center. Farmington Hills, MI: Thomson Gale, 2006. http:// galenet.galegroup.com/servlet/BioRC.

Ted Conover interview, with Paula Zahn, June 12, 2002. CNN.com. http:transcripts. cnn.com/TRANSCRIPTS/0206/12/ltm.o2.html (viewed April 25, 2006).

Ted Conover Web site. http://www.tedconover.com (viewed April 25, 2006).

"Wasted Lives: An Interview with Ted Conover," *Blue Dog Press*, July 18, 2001.

Richard Dawkins

Science

Benchmark Title: *The Selfish Gene*

Malawi, Kenya

1941–

Photo by Lalla Ward

About the Author and the Author's Writing

Richard Dawkins staked out his ultra-Darwinian ground in 1976 with *The Selfish Gene,* a book in which he argues evolution was dominated by the gene. "We, and all other animals, are machines created by our genes," he wrote. It goes without saying, Dawkins upset the creationists. But even fellow Darwinists disagreed with him, believing rather that organisms made some decisions about evolution.

One critic, Robert J. Richards, in *American Scientist* commented, "In his disturbing book *The Selfish Gene,* Dawkins portrays biological individuals as being merely vehicles driven from below by genes fixed on their own perpetuation. Human beings are not merely chained to their genomes, they are hollow men whose slightest feelings, passing notions and stumbling actions are cranked out by evolutionary machinery put in place long ago by natural selection."

Despite the complexity of his subject, Dawkins captivated readers. "Dawkins is far more potent than your everyday populariser. The book's polemic spiel is mesmeric: the prose compels not only your attention, but also your acceptance. It is little wonder that *Selfish Gene* changed the way people think. It even changed many lives," said *Guardian* journalist Colin Hughes.

Dawkins was born in Kenya in 1941. His grandfather had been a colonial forestry officer in Burma, and his father was an administrator in Nyasaland (now Malawi) before the family relocated to Nairobi during World War II. They returned to England to live on a farm when Richard was eight years old. His parents were orthodox Anglicans, and he was confirmed at age thirteen, although he says he can remember only going to church at Christmas. He graduated from Oxford University in 1962 with a bachelor's degree in zoology then continued his graduate studies at Oxford University, leading to master's, doctor of science, and doctor of philosophy degrees. From 1967 to 1969, Dawkins worked as an assistant professor of zoology at the University of California at Berkeley. He was a lecturer in zoology at Oxford and a fellow of its New College in 1970. In 1995, he was appointed to the Charles Simonyi Chair of Public Understanding of Science at Oxford University. Two years later, he was elected a fellow of the

Royal Society of Literature. Dawkins was married to and later divorced from Marian Stamp and Eve Barham (with whom he had a daughter). His third wife, actress Lalla Ward (*Doctor Who*), illustrated two of his books.

Danish biologist Niko Tinbergen, Dawkins's doctoral supervisor, and theoretical biologist Bill Hamilton guided the author to ethology—explaining the behavior of animals through an understanding of biology, psychology, physiology, ecology, taxonomy, and evolution. "I was particularly taken with two phrases of his—*behavior machinery* and *equipment for survival*," Dawkins said in an interview with *Wired* magazine. "When I came to write my first book, I combined them into the brief phrase *survival machine*."

In a nutshell, "Dawkins speculates in this best-selling popular science title that all human activity, sexual or otherwise, is driven by our genes' 'selfish' need to preserve themselves, combined with their surprisingly subtle drive toward altruism meant primarily to help themselves while superficially helping others," explains scholar Sarah Statz Cords in *The Real Story*. Further, they're memes, or "units of culture spread by imitation and 'natural selection' within society."

Although Dawkins has carried the evolutionary debate well beyond Darwin's theory, he remains very respectful of that earlier scientist. He once appeared on television with an actor playing Darwin, and he told reporter Simon Hattenstone that he "felt daunted in the presence of genius. 'Darwin was not only the founding father of my subject, he was terribly gentle and self-effacing'." Dawkins, on the other hand, is frequently characterized as self-assured and intolerant.

Dawkins is unsympathetic to those who would reconcile natural selection and random mutation with faith. "If it's true that it causes people to feel despair, that's tough," he said in a Beliefnet interview with Laura Sheahen. "The universe doesn't owe us condolence or consolation; it doesn't owe us a nice warm feeling inside. If it's true, it's true, and you'd better live with it."

Some in the scientific community charge that Dawkins tries to make things too simple, to which Tufts University philosophy professor Daniel C. Dennett on the Edge Web page responds: "Some people object to Dawkins as being what I now call a greedy reductionist—that is, they think he's vastly oversimplifying, trying to get the job done with too few levels of explanation. Even though some version of that objection maybe true, it's not a big deal. The algorithmic approach as Dawkins represents it is deliberately oversimple."

Dawkins condenses his theory for younger readers in *River Out of Eden*. In *Climbing Mount Improbable,* the scientist explains the beauty of the spider's web or the sea creature's shell through Darwinism that he describes in the book as "not a theory of random chance. It is a theory of random mutation plus non-random cumulative natural selection."

In *Unweaving the Rainbow* (published in 1998), the author posits that art and beauty are enhanced by scientific truth. He employs a Chaucerian framework in *The Ancestor's Tale* to examine and discuss the evolution of evolutionary thought. *A Devil's Chaplain,* Dawkins's 2003 book, is a collection of thoughts and pieces that, according to *American Scientist* reviewer Michael Ruse, preaches against the existence of God but fails to make a fully persuasive case. "Perhaps one agrees that traditional religions—Christianity specifically—do not offer the full answers. But what is to stop a nonbeliever like myself from saying that the Christians are asking important questions and that they are right to have a little humility before the unknown?" In *The God*

Delusion from 2006, the author again argues against there being a God and posits that atheists can be happy, fulfilled, upright people. The book reached the number two spot on Amazon.com's best-seller list.

Dawkins, in response to a question from reporter Doug Brown, said if he were to invite five interesting historical figures for a meal, he would settle on Darwin, Shakespeare, "possibly Jesus, Newton, I guess. Maybe Lucy."

Works by the Author

The Selfish Gene (1976/1989)
The Extended Phenotype: The Long Reach of the Gene (1982)
The Blind Watchmaker: Why the Evidence of Evolution Reveals a Universe without Design (1986)
River Out of Eden: A Darwinian View of Life (1995)
Climbing Mount Improbable (1996)
Unweaving the Rainbow: Science, Delusion and the Appetite for Wonder (1998)
A Devil's Chaplain: Reflections on Hope, Lies, Science, and Love (2003)
The Ancestor's Tale: A Pilgrimage to the Dawn of Evolution (2005)
The God Delusion (2006)

Contributor

Not One More Death (2006)

Television Adaptation of the Author's Work

Horizon ("The Blind Watchmaker" episode, BBC production, 1987)

For Further Information

Blume, Harvey, "The Origin of Specious: And Why Reductionists Are Winning the Darwin Wars,' *American Prospect*, September 23, 2002.

Brown, Doug, "Richard Dawkins: The Biologist's Tale" [author interview], Powells.com. http://www.powells.com/authors/dawkins.html (viewed May 23, 2006).

Dawkins, Richard, curriculum vitae, Simonyi Professorship Web page, Oxford University. http://www.simonyi.ox.ac.uk/dawkins/CV.shtml (viewed March 15, 2007).

Eldredge, Niles, *Why We Do It: Rethinking Sex and the Selfish Gene*. New York: W.W. Norton, 2004.

Grafen, Alan, and Mark Ridley, editors. *Richard Dawkins: How a Scientist Changed the Way We Think: Reflections by Scientists, Writers, and Philosophers*. New York: Oxford University Press, 2006.

Hattenstone, Simon, "Darwin's Child," *Guardian*, February 10, 2003.

Hughes, Colin, "Richard Dawkins: The Man Who Knows the Meaning of Life," *Guardian*, October 3, 1998.

Nash, David, "Arguing by Design," *History Today,* March 1997.

"Revolutionary Evolutionist," *Wired*, July 1995.

Richard Dawkins entry, *The Real Story: A Guide to Nonfiction Reading Interests,* by Sarah Statz Cords. Westport, CT: Libraries Unlimited, 2006.

Richard Dawkins interview, BBC, April 2004. http://www.bbc.co.uk/religion/religions/atheism/features/dawkins (viewed June 5, 2006).

Richard Dawkins interview, Counterbalance Interactive Library. http://www.meta-library.net/transcript/dawk-body.html (viewed May 23, 2006).

Richards, Robert J., "And gladly wolde he lerne and gladly teche," *American Scientist,* March-April 2005.

Riddell, Mary, "The Taboo against Cannibalism Is the Strongest We Have—but Even That Needs to Be Looked At," *New Statesman,* March 26, 1996.

Ruse, Michael, "Through a Glass, Darkly," *American Scientist,* November-December 2003.

Seaman, Donna, *Climbing Mount Improbable* review, *Booklist,* September 15, 1996.

Seaman, Donna, *Unweaving the Rainbow* review, *Booklist,* December 1, 1998.

Sheahen, Laura, "The Problem with God: Interview with Richard Dawkins," beliefnet. http://www.beliefnet.com/story/178/story_17889_1.html (viewed May 23, 2006).

Taylor, Gilbert, *River Out of Eden* review, *Booklist,* February 15, 1995.

World of Richard Dawkins Web page. http://www.simonyi.ox.ac.uk/dawkins/WorldOfDawkins-archive/index.shtml (viewed June 5, 2006).

Jared Diamond

Environment, Science

Benchmark Title: *Guns, Germs and Steel*

Boston, Massachusetts

1937–

Photo by K. David Bishop

About the Author and the Author's Writing

Why did Western culture of Europe and North America rise to dominance when societies in Africa, Asia, and South America did not? That weighty topic did not daunt a scientist and academic whose previous works were about birds. Why did Jared Diamond make the jump? The acclaimed author of *Guns, Germs and Steel* told *Publishers Weekly* in 2004 that he was long curious about the Easter Island statues and ancient Mayan ruins. "I was turned on by the mystery—why did these people build these monuments, how did they maintain this civilization and why did these civilizations collapse? . . . [recent archaeological studies made clear] that many of these mystery collapses involved a component of environmental damage."

Jared Mason Diamond was born in Boston in 1937, the son of Louis K. and Flora K. Diamond. In 1958, he received a bachelor of arts degree from Harvard University. He was a fellow with the National Science Foundation from 1958 to 1961, the year he received a Ph.D. from Cambridge University. From 1961 to 1965, he was a fellow in physiology at Trinity College, Cambridge, and a junior fellow with Harvard University's Society of Fellows from 1962 to 1965.

As a physiologist and ecologist, Diamond is intensely interested in evolutionary biology. He has extensively studied birds in New Guinea and other Pacific islands. More specifically, he has become expert in bird ecology and membrane physiology—topics not closely related. He was an associate professor in biophysics at Harvard Medical School from 1965 to 1966, then an associate professor of physiology at University of California Medical School from 1966 to 1968, when he was promoted to full professorship. He became a research associate with the American Museum of Natural History's ornithology department in 1973 and assumed a similar post with the Los Angeles County Museum of Natural History in 1985. He and his wife, Marie M. Cohen, have two children.

Beyond the world of academic papers, Diamond produced his first book, *Avifauna of the Eastern Highlands of New Guinea,* a study of New Guinea birds, in 1972 and followed that effort with a second islands book seven years later. That he was

76

able to change course and had the necessary time to pursue complex study was due to the receipt in 1985 of a ten-year MacArthur Foundation "genius grant." He now had the ease to satisfy his curiosity, to answer some of the questions everyone has. "Why is it that there are these ethnic differences in the United States? Why were Africans being brought here as slaves instead of Europeans being brought as slaves to Aboriginal Australia? They're the most obvious things in life, but when you get into the details of them—the details!—they're just fascinating," he said in an interview with Judith Lewis for *LA Weekly*.

His book *The Third Chimpanzee* looks at human prehistory, human sexuality, human language and behavior, and human destructiveness. Noting that humans and chimps share all but 2 percent of their genetic heritage, he elaborates on how critical that small difference is to the way the species developed.

Whereas *Chimpanzee* was an ambitious attempt at assembling and digesting a lot of material, *Guns, Germs, and Steel* was an even more intense investigation that brought the author a 1998 Pulitzer Prize in nonfiction. Searching for clues as to why Western Europe came to dominate the modern world's politics and economics, Diamond concluded that no one race had an advantage over another.

"All the interesting stuff like technology, writing, and empires requires a productive economy that is producing enough food to feed technological experts, bureaucrats, kings, and scribes," the author said in a *National Geographic News* interview. "Hunter-gatherer societies don't produce enough food surpluses to support those extra people. Agriculture does."

Diamond followed *Guns* with *Why Did Human History Unfold Differently on Different Continents for the Last 13,000 Years?* and *Collapse: How Societies Choose to Fail or Succeed,* something of a sequel to *Guns* in which the author looks at places such as the remote Easter Islands in which society totally disappeared after inhabitants chopped down all of the palm trees—eliminating wood with which to make boats, root systems with which to prevent soil erosion. He asserts that reasons for societal collapses vary from the environmental (climate changes) to the political (aggressive, militaristic neighbors) to the ecological. In the Bitterroot Valley of Montana, the potential for collapse exists today. "The economy of Montana was founded in part on copper mines, and the arsenic and cadmium and copper and acid that's coming out of those mines will come out forever, and it has already cost Montanans $2 billion of tax money [for environmental cleanup]," he said in an interview with Amos Esty of *American Scientist*. Environmentally ravaged Hudson River and Chesapeake Bay suffer similar threats, he suggests.

Societies, Diamond points out, can be stubborn about change. The European Christians who populated Greenland refused to give up their dairying society or change their diets or deal with the Inuit, whom they despised as pagans. They, as the Easter Islanders, leveled the forests, and thus removed potential fuel for their forges. After 450 years there, their society withered. The author believes the United States needs to grapple with its inbred sense of infinite resources and entitlement as well. "The United States has long thought of itself as the land of infinite plenty," he said in a *Sierra Magazine* interview, "and historically we did have abundant resources. But now we are gradually exhausting our fisheries, our topsoil, our water. On top of that, we're coming to the end of the world resources." Furthermore, the United States, he suggests, particularly since September 11, should realize it cannot function in isolation, it cannot lead the world without alliances, compromises.

Diamond dispels old myths, such as Africans as a race are unable to help themselves, and he vehemently challenges racism: "It's dead wrong because it explains the grand pattern of history by assumptions about differences among people, assumptions for which there's no evidence in favor, lots of evidence against."

Diamond is not without optimism. "Despite all the devastation, there are hopeful messages in *Collapse*," notes *Time* magazine's Lev Grossman. "In most cases, the problems those extinct peoples faced weren't insoluble; they just couldn't spot the difficulties in time, whether because of cultural blind spots, scientific ignorance or sheer pigheadedness."

As Diamond writes in *Collapse*, "We don't need new technologies to solve our problems, we 'just' need the political will to apply solutions already available."

Works by the Author

Avifauna of the Eastern Highlands of New Guinea (1972)

Birds of Karkar and Bagabag Islands, New Guinea, with Mary Lecroy (1979)

The Third Chimpanzee: The Evolution and Future of the Human Animal (1992), released in Great Britain as *The Rise and Fall of the Third Chimpanzee* (1992)

Guns, Germs, and Steel: The Fates of Human Societies (1997)

Why Is Sex Fun? The Evolution of Human Sexuality (1997)

The Birds of Northern Melanesia: Speciation, Dispersal, and Ecology, with Ernst Mayr (2001)

Why Did Human History Unfold Differently on Different Continents for the Last 13,000 Years? (2001)

Collapse: How Societies Choose to Fail or Succeed (2004)

Editor

Ecology and Evolution of Communities, with Martin L. Cody (1975)

Community Ecology, with Ted J. Case (1986)

Contributor

Evolutionary Physiology, edited by D. Noble and C. A. R. Boyd (1993)

Television Adaptation

Guns, Germs and Steel (2005)

For Further Information

Boisvert, Will, "Apocalypse Then," *Publishers Weekly,* November 15, 2004.

Esty, Amos, "The Bookshelf Talks with Jared Diamond," *American Scientist* online. http://www.americanscientist.org/template/InterviewTypeDetail/assetid/40344;jessionid-aaa4KxL1uKYE6 (viewed May 17, 2006).

Grossman, Lev, "When Things Fall Apart: The Author of *Guns, Germs, and Steel* Asks, Why Do Some Civilizations Die Out While Others Survive?, *Time,* February 14, 2005.

Jared Diamond interview, PBS. http://www.pbs.org/gunsgermssteel/about/interview.html (viewed May 1, 2006).

Jared (Mason) Diamond entry, Contemporary Authors Online. Reproduced in Biography Resource Center. Farmington Hills, MI: Thomson Gale, 2006. http://galenet.galegroup.com/servlet/BioRC.

Joseph, Pat, "Societies Choose to Fail or Succeed," *Sierra*, May/June 2005.

Lewis, Judith, "What Did the Last Easter Islander Say As He Chopped Down the Last Tree?" *LA Weekly,* February 17, 2005.

Lovgren, Stefan, " 'Guns, Germs and Steel': Jared Diamond on Geography as Power," *National Geographic* News, July 6, 2005. http://news.nationalgeographic.com/news/2005/07/0706_050706_diamond.html (viewed May 17, 2006).

Marcus, Mary Brophy, "The Fun of Sex," *U.S. News & World Report,* August 4, 1997.

Maxwell, Gloria, *Guns, Germs, and Steel* review, *Library Journal,* February 15, 1997.

Joan Didion

Fiction, Memoir, Politics

Benchmark Title: *The Year of Magical Thinking*

Sacramento, California

1934—

About the Author and the Author's Writing

"Life changes fast. Life changes in the instant. You sit down to dinner and life as you know it ends." Thus begins Joan Didion's precise, wrenching, touching memoir of death and endurance and survival, *The Year of Magical Thinking*. Didion and her husband, John Gregory Dunne, married for four decades, came back to their Manhattan apartment from a visit to the hospital where their only child, Quintana Roo Dunne Michael, was in septic shock and coma. Didion and Dunne were writers with numerous novels, nonfiction works and screenplays to their single and joint credit. The two sat down to dinner, and Dunne slumped forward at the table, suddenly dead of a massive coronary attack.

It should be no surprise that Didion experienced severe anguish, but she managed to pull herself together after that tragic day in 2003 and regain a modicum of control through her writing. The result was a memoir that struck a chord with the reading public and that she reshaped into a one-woman play—a very personal play, with her friend, actress Vanessa Redgrave, to play the part. The book earned the author a National Book Award for nonfiction in 2005 and nomination for a Pulitzer Prize in biography in 2006.

Memoirs and remembrances of people gone are not unusual in the publishing field or on best-seller lists. What distinguishes Didion's work is her experience and her supreme skill as a writer. "[B]y continuing to utilize [a] declarative, reserved tone to convey moments of extreme anguish, Didion makes her book nearly moan with loneliness," observes Drew Limsky in *Poets & Writers*. "Her sentences prove that form indeed makes the meaning. In straightforward yet subtle prose, she creates something searing and indelible."

"Didion's intricate narrative moves forward, circles back, pauses to describe a memory with Dunne—a long-ago swim in a coastal cave, a rain-soaked walk in Paris—or to recall a fragment of a poem or a clue in a crossword puzzle. Then it dives down again to grasp a deeper meaning," said Cathleen McGuigan in *Newsweek*.

"Her writing—especially her essays, for which she is best known and which drew the crowd to the store—is elegant, refined and personal. Nobody dresses a sentence in precise detail the way this author does," said reviewer Bill Gunlocke in *America*.

80

Joan Didion was born in Sacramento, California, in 1934, the daughter of Frank Reese Didion, a U.S. Army finance officer, and his wife, Eduene Jerrett Didion. She received a bachelor of arts degree from the University of California at Berkeley in 1956, her graduation requirements only met at the last moment with hasty study of Milton to fulfill an English obligation. She joined the staff of *Vogue* and remained with that periodical (becoming associate feature editor) until 1963. By this time she had begun her first novel, *Run River,* which is about the offspring of two prosperous California families who marry and eventually suffer a fractured union.

In 1964, she married John Gregory Dunne, and they moved back to the West Coast. She was a visiting regents lecturer for her university's English department in 1976. Apart from that, she made her living as a freelance writer. Her regular assignment included columns for the *Saturday Evening Post.* Her pieces, including, for example, examination of the hippie culture in San Francisco, were collected in *Slouching toward Bethlehem,* published in 1968, and received wide critical approval. Her novel *Play It as It Lays* was nominated for a National Book Award. Her second compilation of essays, *The White Album* (1979), was solidly popular.

Salvador, initially published in the *New York Review of Books* and released in book form in 1983, was nominated for a Pulitzer. *Salvador* described a visit by Didion and Dunne to the small republic that was then in the vice-grip of a military leadership.

"My interest in El Salvador came from the fact that the United States was down there playing some kind of role nobody seemed to understand," the author told *Interview*'s Mark Marvel. "[My husband] and I just decided to go down, and it was much more interesting than I had imagined from reading the *Los Angeles Times.*"

In the novel *Democracy,* Didion looked at America's colonial roots. She returned to nonfiction, and wrote about the Cuban exile population in Florida in *Miami,* then tackled political and other issues in *After Henry.* Between books, she and Dunne accepted screenwriting assignments, most of them based on their or others' books, but also a new version of *A Star Is Born* for Barbra Streisand and a Robert Redford vehicle, *Up Close and Personal.*

Didion and Dunne had a close professional relationship. "He reads everything I write. I read everything he writes," she said in a 1999 interview for *The Writer.* "We might make suggestions of where something could go."

Sporadically, Didion returned to fiction, as with *The Last Thing He Wanted,* which involves political intrigue and Nicaraguan contras. Politics still interested the author when she assembled recent literary essays from the *New York Review of Books,* titled *Political Fictions,* in 2001. Didion described her home state in a family history/ social investigation *Where I Was From* in 2003—some of the luster had worn off. "I was really just trying to investigate for myself why California's idea of itself was so different from the reality," she told Joel Hirschhorn of *Publishers Weekly.* By that time she and Dunne were again living in New York—during the September 11 attack—and she wrote about that in *Fixed Ideas: America since 9.11.*

Didion has described her views on writing bluntly: "In many ways writing is the act of saying I, of imposing oneself upon other people, of saying listen to me, see it my way, change your mind. Its an aggressive, even a hostile act," she said in *New York Times Magazine* in 1976. "You can disguise its aggressiveness all you want with veils of subordinate clauses and qualifiers and tentative subjunctives... but there's no getting around the fact that setting words on paper is the tactic of a secret bully."

Despite her lauded, and often award-winning, body of work, Didion has remained unpretentious: "I never felt particularly successful," she told Dave Eggers in a salon.com interview. "I always feel like I've not quite done it right, that I ought to be doing better or something."

After her husband's death, Didion initially stopped writing and concentrated on learning more about her daughter's affliction. She found she had to write her way through her grief and produced her memoir. "Crying all the time. That's now what happens. You become crazy. I found quotes from Freud and Melanie Klein where they call grief a form of psychosis we don't treat. We let it run its course," she said in an interview for *O, The Oprah Magazine.*

Didion's daughter, Quintana, died in August 2005, at age thirty-nine, after the book was completed. "It's a different process," the author said of her daughter's death in a December 2005 interview with Emma Brockes of *The Guardian,* "because the relationship to a child is at once more fundamental and less intimate. Because a grown child has his or her own life and isn't part of your daily life. And you might talk on the phone once a day, but that's not every breath you take. Which someone you live with is."

Works by the Author

Slouching toward Bethlehem: Essays (1968)
The White Album (1979)
Salvador (1983)
Joan Didion: Essays and Conversations (1984)
Miami (1987)
Robert Graham: The Duke Ellington Memorial in Progress (1988)
After Henry (1992), published in England as *Sentimental Journeys* (1993)
Political Fictions (2001)
Where I Was From (2003)
Fixed Ideas: America since 9.11 (2003)
Vintage Didion (2004)
The Year of Magical Thinking (2005)
We Tell Ourselves Stories in Order to Live: Collected Nonfiction (2006)

Fiction

Run River (1963)
Play It as It Lays (1970)
A Book of Common Prayer (1977)
Democracy (1984)
The Last Thing He Wanted (1996)

Screenplays with John Gregory Dunne

Panic in Needle Park (1971), based on James Mills's novel
Play It as It Lays (1972), based on Joan Didion's novel
A Star Is Born, with others (1976)

True Confessions (1981), based on John Gregory Dunne's novel
Hills Like White Elephants (1990), based on Ernest Hemingway short story
Broken Trust (1995), based on William Wood's novel
Up Close and Personal (1996)

Drama

The Year of Magical Thinking: The Play (2007)

For Further Information

Brockes, Emma, "Interview: Joan Didion," *Guardian Unlimited,* December 16, 2005. http://books.guardian.co.uk/print/0,3858,5357320-99942,00.html (viewed May 24, 2006).

Didion, Joan, "Why I Write," *New York Times Magazine,* December 5, 1976.

Eggers, Dave, Joan Didion interview, salon.com. http://www.salon.com/oct96/didion961028.html (viewed May 24, 2006).

Frumkes, Lewis Burke, "A Conversation with . . . Joan Didion," *The Writer,* March 1999.

Gunlocke, Bill, "In Widow's Weeds," *America,* February 13, 2006.

Hirschhorn, Joel, "The Golden State Loses Its Luster," *Publishers Weekly,* June 30, 2003.

Joan Didion entry, Contemporary Authors Online. Reproduced in Biography Resource Center. Farmington Hills, MI: Thomson Gale, 2006. http://galenet.galegroup.com/servlet/BioRC.

Joan Didion interview, *Paris Review,* Spring 2006.

Limsky, Drew, "The Art of Reading Joan Didion," *Poets & Writers,* May-June 2006.

Marvel, Mark, Joan Didion, *Interview,* September 1996.

McGuigan, Cathleen, "Alone with Her Words; Joan Didion's Spare, Stunning Memoir of Loss and Grief," *Newsweek,* October 10, 2005.

McGuigan, Cathleen, "Death Becomes Her," *Newsweek,* March 26, 2007.

Patterson, Troy, "Where I Was From," *Entertainment Weekly,* October 3, 2003.

"Play It as It Lays," *O, The Oprah Magazine*, November 2005.

Porterfield, Christopher, "Dire State: Joan Didion Revisits Her Native California. Ouch!" *Time,* October 27, 2003.

Robertson, Campbell, "Being Joan Didion," *New York Times,* May 26, 2006.

Spindler, Amy, "Joan Didion: The Writer Who Can Capture America Like No One Else," *Interview*, November 2001.

Young, Josh, "Almost Golden," *Esquire,* March 1996.

Annie Dillard

Environment, Memoir, Outdoors, Politics

Benchmark Title: *Pilgrim at Tinker Creek*

Pittsburgh, Pennsylvania

1945–

Photo courtesy Phyllis Rose

About the Author and the Author's Writing

> *I propose to keep here what Thoreau called "a meteorological journal of the mind," telling some tales and describing some of the sights of this rather tamed valley, and exploring, in fear and trembling, some of the unmapped dim reaches and unholy fastnesses to which those tales and sights so dizzyingly lead.*
>
> —Annie Dillard, *Pilgrim at Tinker Creek*

In writing this, Dillard paid homage to America's genius of a century before, and her book, written with such stylist flair, her first prose work, garnered a Pulitzer Prize for nonfiction.

Annie Dillard is widely hailed for her fine writing—whether in magazine essays or in memoirs, in verse or short fiction. She discerns the hand of a higher being in her investigations of the natural world—and thus she enjoys a strong Christian readership. Raised a Presbyterian, as a teenager she rebelled at what she saw as the church's hypocrisy. Temporarily lured back when her minister interested her in the works of C. S. Lewis, she went on to explore a range of religions from Buddhism to Sufism to Hassidic Judaism before she joined the Catholic church. She places herself firmly in the Christian mystical writing tradition in many of her works including *Holy the Firm* (1977). "Her razor-sharp lyricism hones this mind-expanding existential scrapbook, which is imbued with the same spiritual yearning, moral urgency and reverence for nature that has informed nearly all of her nonfiction since the 1975 Pulitzer Prize–winning *Pilgrim at Tinker Creek*," a *Publishers Weekly* reviewer ventured of *For the Time Being* in 1999.

Dillard has commented on her spirituality. "I say God has one hand tied behind his back," she told *U.S. Catholic* interviewer Maureen Abood. "If you deal with the problem of evil in an honest way, it seems to me that eventually you will have to tinker with the doctrine of God's omnipotence, which in no way diminishes the power and the holiness of God. And it saves the doctrine that God is always merciful."

Dillard's career has not been without controversy. The California State Board of Education removed an excerpt from *An American Childhood* from its statewide public schools examination in 1994 after they were assailed by a conservative Christian group. She declined a California literary award, and then-state Governor Pete Wilson apologized for the incident.

The author was born Meta Ann Doak in 1945 in Pittsburgh, the first of three daughters of industrial businessman Frank Doak and Pam Lambert Doak. She grew up in the Eisenhower 1950s when most mothers were homemakers. Given general free rein by her well-to-do parents, Annie developed an early fascination with her environment, spurred by an accumulation of interesting rock and insect specimens. She has called her father a dreamer, her mother a thinker and "wildcard." About her mother, she wrote in *Inventing the Truth*. "She regarded even tiny babies as straight men, and liked to step on the drawstring of a crawling baby's gown, so that the baby crawled and crawled and never got anywhere except into a little ball at the top of the gown."

The author acknowledges her family gave her a sense of presentation: "The straight man's was an honorable calling, a bit like that of the rodeo clown; despised by the ignorant masses, perhaps, but revered among experts who understood the skills required and the risks run," she wrote in *An American Childhood*.

In 1968, Dillard earned a master of arts degree from Hollins College in Virginia —her thesis topic, *Walden*. She had been sent to the all-female Hollins purposely to calm her rebellious impulses, though she wrote in her memoir that she "had high hopes for my rough edges. I wanted to use them as a can opener, to cut myself a hole in the world's surface, and exit through it."

She married one of her instructors, poet Richard Dillard, in 1964. They eventually divorced. In 1980, she married writer Gary Clevidence. He had two children by a previous marriage; they had one together, a daughter. After they divorced, she married educator and writer Robert D. Richardson Jr. in 1988 and moved to Connecticut. He is the author of *Henry Thoreau: A Life of the Mind* (1986). They met after she read the book and penned a fan letter.

While in high school, Dillard had taken an interest in Thoreau's fellow Concordian Ralph Waldo Emerson, and her first husband nurtured her poetry. Her first book was a collection, *Tickets for a Prayer Wheel. Pilgrim* came out the same year, based on journals she kept during a year's seclusion near Tinker Creek, following a near-fatal bout of pneumonia in 1971. After that, "So absorbed did she later become, in developing her various notes into a book, that she began writing 16 hours a day, living on coffee and Coca-Cola, and sometimes going without sleep," according to NNCB's Dillard Web page.

Applause for *Pilgrim* in the literary world startled Dillard, who took temporary refuge on a Puget Sound island from 1975 to 1979. She wrote a novel, *The Living,* which she left behind as a work in progress, about families living in the region. "It took three years altogether to write and I spent 16 months in just pure research," she said in a BookPage interview. "I decided early on to write it as if it were a 19th-century novel, as if Thomas Hardy wrote it. So it's a completely old-fashioned novel, and the language is old-fashioned."

Her writing has prompted considerable literary and scholarly interest. Pamela A. Smith in "The Ecotheology of Annie Dillard," for instance, sees in Dillard an ambivalence toward God and nature because of her understanding of the Big Bang, evolution, and quantum physics. "The law of nature for Dillard is not survival of the fittest," the writer says. "It is more a matter of the survival of those who circumstantially survive. Accident, luck, unpredictability, nonsense, murder, and default all come into play. These all go on with senseless abandon, with nature's own bizarre brand of happenstance and freedom."

Journalist Michael Joseph Gross observed that since *Pilgrim*, "Dillard has frequently and fearlessly explored the most flagrant brutalities of the natural world, and she has never given up her project of questioning what place such brutality might have in the grand scheme of things."

Scholar Sandra Stahlman comments in "The Mysticism of Annie Dillard's *Pilgrim at Tinker Creek*, "Her wavering faith in light of the horrors of the world—horrors that spring from that same Divine she adores—is not unusual. On the contrary, she precisely conveys universal questions and doubts about the existence and nature of God."

From 1973 to 1985, Dillard worked as an editor for *Harper's Magazine*. She has been scholar-in-residence at Western Washington University, Bellingham, and visiting professor, adjunct professor, and writer-in-residence at Wesleyan University. In 1982, she became a member of the U.S. cultural delegation to China. She has written for *Atlantic Monthly, Living Wilderness, American Scholar, New York Times Magazine, Chicago Review,* and other periodicals, and has been a member of *American Heritage Dictionary*'s usage panel. A member of the Academy of Arts and Letters, the author has received fellowships from the Guggenheim Foundation and the National Endowment for the Arts.

Dillard is a painstaking craftsman. Composition, she said in *The Writing Life,* "grows cell to cell, bole to bough to twig to leaf; any careful word may suggest a route, may begin a strand of metaphor or event out of which much, or all, will develop."

A voracious reader, Dillard offered words of wisdom to aspiring writers, in an *@Herald* interview with Grace Suh: "You have enough experience by the time you're five years old. What you need is the library. What you have to learn is the best of what is being thought and said. If you had a choice between spending a summer in Nepal and spending a summer in the library, go to the library."

Works by the Author

Pilgrim at Tinker Creek (1974)
Holy the Firm (1977)
The Weasel (1981), chapbook
Living by Fiction (1982)
Teaching a Stone to Talk: Expeditions and Encounters (1982)
Encounters with Chinese Writers (1984)
An American Childhood (1987)

The Annie Dillard Library (1989), includes *Living by Fiction, An American Childhood, Holy the Firm, Pilgrim at Tinker Creek,* and *Teaching a Stone to Talk*

The Writing Life (1989)

Three by Dillard (1990), includes *Pilgrim at Tinker Creek, An American Childhood,* and *The Writing Life*

The Annie Dillard Reader (1994)

For the Time Being (1999)

Editor

Best American Essays of 1988, with Robert Atwan (1988)

Modern American Memoirs, with Cort Conley (1995)

Contributor (Selected)

Inventing the Truth: The Art and Craft of Memoir, edited by William Zinsser (1987)

Best American Essays, edited by Geoffrey Wolff and Robert Atwan (1989)

Late Harvest: Rural American Writing (1996)

The Fourth Genre: Contemporary Writers of/on Creative Nonfiction, edited by Robert L. Root Jr. and Michael Steinberg (2002)

Fiction

The Living (1992)

The Maytrees (2007)

Poetry

Tickets for a Prayer Wheel (1974)

Mornings Like This: Found Poems (1995)

For Further Information

Abood, Maureen, "Natural Wonders," *U.S. Catholic*, November 1999.

Annie Dillard entry, *Authors and Artists for Young Adults,* Vol. 43. Detroit, MI: Thomson Gale, 2002.

Annie Dillard entry, Contemporary Authors Online. Reproduced in Biography Resource Center. Farmington Hills, MI: Thomson Gale, 2006. http://galenet.galegroup.com/servlet/BioRC.

Annie Dillard entry, *Environmental Encyclopedia,* third edition. Detroit, MI: Gale, 2003.

Annie Dillard Web page, NNDB. http://www.nndb.com/people/102/000084847 (viewed May 24, 2006).

Annie Dillard Web site. http://anniedillard.com (viewed May 24, 2006).

Gross, Michael Joseph, "Apparent Contradictions: By Keeping Her Private Life Under Wraps, Personal Essayist Annie Dillard Has Created a Writing Life of Uncommon Integrity," *Boston Phoenix,* June 24, 1999.

Langstaff, Peggy, "When the West Was New: Annie Dillard's 'The Living,' " *BookPage.* http://www.bookpage.com/BPinterviews/dillard492.html (viewed May 24, 2006).

McCormick, Patrick, "Is There Anybody Out There?" *U.S. Catholic*, September 1999.

"NCIBA to Distribute Copies of Barred Walker, Dillard stories," *Publishers Weekly,* April 4, 1994.

Pettingell, Phoebe, An American Childhood review, *New Leader,* November 2, 1987.

Smith, Pamela A., "The Ecotheology of Annie Dillard: A Study in Ambivalence," *Crosscurrents.* http://www.crosscurrents.org/dillard.htm (viewed May 24, 2006).

Suh, Grace, "Ideas Are Tough; Irony Is Easy," *@Herald.* http://www.yaleherald.com/archive/xxii/10.4.96/ae/dillard.html (viewed May 24, 2006).

Torrens, James S., "Of Many Things," *America,* November 19, 1994.

W.E.B. Du Bois

Biography, History, Investigative Reporting, Memoir

Benchmark Title: *The Souls of Black Folk*

Great Barrington, Massachusetts

1868–1963

Photo courtesy Special Collections, W.E.B. Du Bois Library, University of Massachusetts, Amherst

About the Author and the Author's Writing

Henry Louis Gates Jr., chairman of Harvard University's Afro-American Studies Department, nominated W.E.B. Du Bois (pronounced Doo-boys) as one of *Time* magazine's 100 most influential people of the millennium: "Who could have done more than he to redefine American democracy over 60 years of the 20th century?" he asked.

William Edward Du Bois was born in Great Barrington, Massachusetts, in 1868, the son of French-Haitian barber Alfred Du Bois and African American domestic and laundress Mary Burghardt Du Bois. When he was in college, William added his mother's maiden name to his own—and came to prefer it: Burghardt Du Bois. His mother encouraged his education and a sympathetic high school principal, Frank Hosmer, saw that he had adequate Greek and other texts so that he was prepared to enter Fisk University. While he would rather have gone directly to Harvard, in later years Du Bois wrote that his time in Atlanta both opened his eyes to racial injustice and forced him to isolate himself and develop a hard shell—which served him well when he did reach the Cambridge, Massachusetts, university and became the first of African descent to earn a Ph.D. there.

Du Bois's first writing of note was a high school graduation essay about abolitionist Wendell Phillips in 1885 when he was sixteen. His last writing, unfinished at his death in 1963, when he was ninety-five, was *Encyclopedia Africana*. In the eight decades between, he wrote almost continuously—a list of his myriad book publications fails to catalog his thousands of letters, newspaper articles, speeches, editorials, and magazine essays. It's no wonder Langston R. Hughes, who dedicated his poem "The Negro Speaks of Rivers" to Du Bois, once remarked that when he was growing up, the words with which he was most familiar "were those of W.E.B. Du Bois and the Bible."

Du Bois taught at the University of Pennsylvania, where he completed his landmark anthropological work, *The Philadelphia Negro*. At Wilberforce University in Ohio, he met his future wife, Nina Gomer. They married in 1896 and had two children, a son who died in childhood, and daughter who survived into adulthood. After Nina Du Bois's death in 1950, Du Bois married Shirley Graham. Her son by her first marriage, David Graham, took the Du Bois name.

From 1897 to 1910, Du Bois taught at Atlanta University. During this time, he put together his best-known work. Ghanaian biographer Daniel Agbeyebiawo noted that the Chicago publisher McClurg had a tight deadline when it asked Du Bois to assemble *The Souls of Black Folk*. "He needed more time but the publishers would not wait. Du Bois complained, 'I am sure that with more time and thought I could do a better job; in so many respect[s] this is incomplete and unsatisfactory.' "

The seminal work in black literature soared higher than Booker T. Washington's *Up from Slavery,* Frederick Douglass's *Narrative,* or Malcolm X's *Autobiography*. Historian Henry Marable is of the view, "Few books make history, and fewer still become foundational texts for the movements and struggles of an entire people. *The Souls of Black Folk* occupies this rare position. It helped to create the intellectual argument for the black freedom struggle in the twentieth century." The book, which influenced succeeding generations of black scholars and writers, defined clearly and for the first time issues of race and racism in the modern political era. It explained exactly what it meant to be black, to have overcome slavery and lived through the disappointment of emancipation. "The problem of the Twentieth Century is the problem of the color-line," he wrote. Many would argue it remains the problem of the twenty-first century as well.

Du Bois was a dynamo. He was founder and general secretary of the Niagara Movement, 1905 to 1909—precursor to modern-day civil rights activist organizations. From 1910 to 1934, he was director of publicity and research and a director of the National Association for the Advancement of Colored People (NAACP) and during that time founded and edited its monthly magazine, *The Crisis*. He urged a Pan-African Congress in Paris to examine issues in Africa under the influence of European colonizers. He received the NAACP's Spingarn Medal for outstanding achievement by a black American.

In spite of his numerous accomplishments, Du Bois was also accustomed to failure. He resigned from the NAACP in 1934 over internal political issues and returned to Atlanta University to teach and write for a decade. While at the university, he read and increasingly absorbed the teachings of Karl Marx, which ultimately ended in battles with the U.S. State Department and FBI. In the 1950s, the State Department took his passport, although it was restored when he filed an appeal with the Supreme Court. In 1961, after joining the American Communist Party, he thumbed his nose at the United States and left the country to accept an invitation of President Kwame Nkrumah to relocate to Ghana to work on a comprehensive encyclopedia of African people. Despite what many have written, Du Bois never renounced his American citizenship. As scholar Mike Forrest Keen has discovered through governmental documents, the State Department had just instigated action to take away his citizenship when Du Bois died in 1963, on the eve of the Civil Rights March on Washington. NAACP President Roy Wilkins announced Du Bois's death to the throng, and its irony was well appreciated.

Works by the Author

The Suppression of the African Slave Trade to the United States of America, 1638–1870 (1896)

The Conservation of Races (1897)

The Philadelphia Negro: A Special Study (1899)

The Souls of Black Folk: Essays and Sketches (1903)

The Negro in the South: His Economic Progress in Relation to His Moral and Religious Development, with Booker T. Washington (1907)

John Brown (1909)

The Negro (1915)

Darkwater: Voices from within the Veil (1920)

The Gift of Black Folk: The Negroes in the Making of America (1924)

Africa: Its Geography, People, and Products (1930)

Africa: Its Place in Modern History (1930), reprinted with *Africa: Its Geography, People and Products* (1977)

Black Reconstruction: An Essay toward a History of the Part Which Black Folk Played in the Attempt to Reconstruct Democracy in America, 1860–1880 (1935), reprinted as *Black Reconstruction in America, 1860–1880* (1969)

Black Folk, Then and Now: An Essay in the History and Sociology of the Negro Race (1939)

Color and Democracy: Colonies and Peace (1945)

The World and Africa: An Inquiry into the Part Which Africa Has Played in World History (1947; revised 1965)

In Battle for Peace: The Story of My 83rd Birthday (1962)

An ABC of Color: Selections from Over Half a Century of the Writings of W.E.B. Du Bois (1963)

Three Negro Classics, edited by John H. Franklin (1965)

The Autobiography of W.E. Burghardt Du Bois: A Soliloquy on Viewing My Life from the Last Decade of Its First Century, edited by Herbert Aptheker (1968)

Black North in 1901: A Social Study (1970)

W.E.B. Du Bois Speaks: Speeches and Addresses, edited by Philip S. Foner (1970)

The Selected Writings of W.E.B. Du Bois, edited by Walter Wilson (1970)

W.E.B. Du Bois: A Reader, edited by Meyer Weinberg (1970)

The Seventh Son: The Thought and Writings of W.E.B. Du Bois, edited by Julius Lester (1971)

A W.E.B. Du Bois Reader, edited by Andrew G. Pascal (1971)

W.E.B. Du Bois: The Crisis Writings, edited by Daniel Walden (1972)

The Emerging Thought of W.E.B. Du Bois: Essays and Editorials from 'The Crisis', edited by Harvey Lee Moon (1972)

The Correspondence of W.E.B. Du Bois, three volumes edited by Herbert Aptheker (1973)

The Education of Black People: Ten Critiques, 1906–1960, edited by Herbert Aptheker (1973)

The Writings of W.E.B. Du Bois, edited by Virginia Hamilton (1975)

Book Reviews, edited by Herbert Aptheker (1977)

Prayers for Dark People, edited by Herbert Aptheker (1980)

Writings in Periodicals (1985)

Creative Writings by W.E.B. Du Bois: A Pageant, Poems, Short Stories and Playlets (1985)

Pamphlets and Leaflets by W.E.B. Du Bois (1985)

Against Racism: Unpublished Essays, Papers, Addresses, 1887–1961, edited by Herbert Aptheker (1985)

W.E.B. Du Bois on Sociology and the Black Community, edited by Dan S. Greene and Edwin D. Driver (1987)

W.E.B. Du Bois Writings (1987)

W.E.B. Du Bois: A Reader, edited by David Levering Lewis (1995)

The Oxford W.E.B. Du Bois Reader (1996)

The Selected Speeches of W.E.B. Du Bois (1996)

Editor

Mortality Among Negroes in Cities (1896)

Social and Physical Condition of Negroes in Cities (1897)

Some Efforts of American Negroes for Their Own Social Benefit (1898)

The Negro in Business (1899)

The Negro Common School (1901)

A Select Bibliography of the American Negro: For General Readers (1901)

The Negro Artisan (1902)

The Negro Church (1903)

Some Notes on Negro Crime, Particularly in Georgia (1904)

A Select Bibliography of the Negro American (1905)

The Health and Physique of the Negro American (1906)

Economic Co-operation Among Negro Americans (1907)

The Negro American Family (1908)

Efforts for Social Betterment among Negro Americans (1909)

The College-Bred Negro American, with Augustus Granville Dill (1910)

The Common School and the Negro American, with Augustus Granville Dill (1911)

The Negro American Artisan, with Augustus Granville Dill (1912)

Morals and Manners Among Negro Americans, with Augustus Granville Dill (1914)

An Appeal to the World: A Statement on the Denial of Human Rights to Minorities in the Case of Citizens of Negro Descent in the United States of America and an Appeal to the United Nations for Redress (1947)

Atlanta University Publications (1968)

Fiction

The Quest of the Silver Fleece (1911)
Dark Princess: A Romance (1928)

Mansart Trilogy

The Ordeal of Mansart (1957)
Mansart Builds a School (1959)
Worlds of Color (1961)
The Black Flame (1976), includes all three novels

Anthologies

"The Comet" in *Dark Matter: The Anthology of Science Fiction, Fantasy and Speculative Fiction by Black Writers,* edited by Sheree R. Thomas (2000)
"Jesus Christ in Texas," in *Dark Matter: Reading the Bones,* edited by Sheree R. Thomas (2004)

Poetry

Selected Poems (1964)

Drama

"Haiti" in *Federal Theatre Plays,* edited by Pierre de Rohan (1938)

For Further Information

Agbeyebiawo, Daniel, *The Life and Works of W.E.B. Du Bois.* Accra, Ghana: author, 2003.

Asch, Moses, *W.E.B. DuBois/a recorded autobiography.* New York: Folkways, 1961.

Buckley, Kerry W., *W.E.B. Du Bois: An Exhibit of Materials from the Collected Papers of W.E.B. Du Bois.* Amherst: University of Massachusetts, undated.

Drew, Bernard A., *Dr. Du Bois Rebuilds His Dream House.* Great Barrington, MA: Attic Revivals Press, 2006.

Drew, Bernard A., *Fifty Sites in Great Barrington, Massachusetts, Associated with the Civil Rights Activist W.E.B. Du Bois.* Great Barrington, MA: Great Barrington Land Conservancy & Great Barrington Historical Society with support of the National Park Service, 2002.

Du Bois, David Graham, "Remembering W.E.B. Du Bois," *Essence,* February 1996.

Du Bois, Shirley Graham, *Du Bois: A Pictorial Biography.* Chicago: Johnson Publishing, 1978.

Du Bois, Shirley Graham, *His Day Is Marching On.* New York: J.B. Lippincott, 1971.

Keen, Mike Forrest, "Stalking the Sociological Imagination: J. Edgar Hoover's FBI Surveillance of American Sociology," *Contributions in Sociology,* No. 126. Westport, CT: Greenwood Press, 1999.

Lewis, David Levering, *W.E.B. Du Bois: Biography of a Race, 1868–1919.* New York: Henry Holt, 1993.

Lewis, David Levering, *W.E.B. Du Bois: The Fight for Equality and the American Century, 1919–1963.* New York: Henry Holt, 2000.

Marable, Manning, *Living Black History: How Reimagining the African-American Past Can Remake America's Racial Future.* New York: Basic Books, 2006.

Moon, Henry Lee, "History of the Crisis," *Crisis,* November 1970.

Partington, Paul G. *W.E.B. Du Bois: A Bibliography of His Published Writings.* Whittier, CA: author, 1979, and *Supplement,* 1984.

W.E.B. Du Bois entry, *Authors and Artists for Young Adults,* Vol. 40. Detroit, MI: Gale, 2001.

"W.E.B. DuBois Declassified FBI Files," undated, Innovations USA.

Pete Earley

Adventure, Investigative Reporting, True Crime

Benchmark Title: *Family of Spies*

Douglas, Arizona

1951–

Photo by Patti Luzi-Earley

About the Author and the Author's Writing

In his gripping *Crazy: A Father's Search through America's Mental Health Madness,* Pete Earley tells the story not only of his own experience with his son Mike's psychotic episodes but also of Florida resident Alice Ann Collyer and her arrest, incarceration, trial, and ordeal as the result of her mental illness.

Likening mental illness to heart disease, Earley, in an interview with *Washingtonian* Online, said those with psychoses should no more be held to blame than those who have had a heart attack. "The big three mental illnesses have been shown to be chemical malfunctions that can happen to anyone. We don't know what causes them. They simply happen. If it happened to my son, it could happen to yours. That's why it is so important that we discuss what to do to reform our system."

Peter Earley was born in 1951 in Douglas, Arizona. He graduated from Phillips University in Enid, Oklahoma, in 1973 with a bachelor of science degree in business and mass communication.

From 1972 to 1986, he worked as a reporter with the *Enid Morning News and Daily Eagle*, the *Emporia [Kansas] Gazette*, and the *Tulsa [Oklahoma] Tribune*, and, since 1980, he has worked with the *Washington Post*.

Since leaving the *Post*'s magazine staff in 1986, he has written books. "For me, there is no purer form of journalism than a book," he explains on his Web site, petearley.com. "A journalist doesn't have to worry about 'sacred cows' or partisan politics. If you can find a publisher willing to finance your idea, you can write about any topic that you wish without pulling punches."

Family of Spies, Earley's first book, is about John Walker, the naval officer who, along with family members, peddled governmental secrets to the Soviets—not for political reasons but just for the money. *New York Times Book Review*'s Lucinda Franks found the thoroughly researched book "paced and organized as seamlessly as a novel."

The journalist delved into a second infamous spy in *Confessions of a Spy,* about Aldrich Ames, the CIA insider who revealed the identities of American agents to the Soviets. "The author's impeccable research includes uncensored interviews with Ames and his KGB handlers in Moscow as well as the victims' families," noted James Dudley in a review for *Library Journal.*

Earley spent a fair amount of time behind bars—unlike the prisoners, he could go home at night—for *Hot House: Life inside Leavenworth Prison.* As research, he interviewed the warden and many of the prisoners, all the way down to the lifers, "many of whom are imprisoned for shocking crimes," said *Publishers Weekly* in its review. "[T]he author takes readers into the mind of the recidivist criminal to show an egoistic, violent nature locked into a code of behavior with elements of machismo, hyper-sensitivity to slights and the conviction that informing is the greatest crime of all."

In Circumstantial Evidence (1992), Earley followed a particular drug dealer, Walter McMillan, through his trial and sentencing in small-town Monroeville, Alabama. McMillan, an African American, was convicted of killing a white female store clerk. Trial evidence was inconsistent, testimony perjured. Earley uncovered information held back by the police. The CBS news program *60 Minutes* ran a segment about his case. As the result of a new investigation, McMillan was set free.

"I wanted to show just how difficult it can be in a death penalty case to discover the truth," Earley said in the book, which *Publishers Weekly* described as "a memorable tale of the many points where investigations are fallible." Not least of which is racism's dirty hand.

The book earned the author the Robert F. Kennedy Book Award for Social Justice and an Edgar Fact-Crime Award.

Earley continued his insider accounts with *Super Casino* (2000), a sojourn to neon Las Vegas and the rise of the luxury Luxor casino, and then with *WITSEC*, a rigorously fair overview of the federal witness protection program, cowritten with Gerald Shur, the prosecutor who organized the system to ensure protection, particularly for gangsters who turned state's evidence.

For a change of pace, Earley has turned his attention to writing novels, beginning with the political thriller *The Big Secret* (2006). The book received positive reviews, and it stirred interest inside the Washington Beltway when the *New York Post* reported there was a grudge between Earley and Bob Woodward of the *Washington Post.* It was hinted that the main character, Nick LeRue, a Senate Judiciary Committee investigator, was modeled on, and took a swipe at, Woodward.

The newsroom, obviously, has its politics.

Works by the Author

Family of Spies: Inside the John Walker Spy Ring (1988)
Today's Best Nonfiction, Vol. 6, includes *Family of Spies* (1989)
Prophet of Death; The Mormon Blood-Atonement Killings (1991)
The Hot House; Life inside Leavenworth Prison (1992)
Circumstantial Evidence: Death, Life, and Justice in a Southern Town (1995)
Confessions of a Spy: The Real Story of Aldrich Ames (1996)

Super Casino: Inside the "New" Las Vegas (2000)

WITSEC: Inside the Federal Witness Protection Program, with Gerald Shur (2002)

Crazy: A Father's Search through America's Mental Health Madness (2006)

Comrade J: The Untold Secrets of Russia's Master Spy in America after the End of the Cold War (2008)

Fiction

The Big Secret (2004)

Lethal Secrets (2005)

The Apocalypse Stone (2006)

Television Adaptations

The Hot House (CBS, 1993)

For Further Information

Anderson, Patrick, "Grudge Report," *Washington Post,* June 14, 2004.

Apocalypse Stone review, *Publishers Weekly,* April 17, 2006.

Circumstantial Evidence review, *Publishers Weekly*, June 26, 1995.

Dudley, James, *Confessions of a Spy* review, *Library Journal,* August 1999.

Franks, Lucinda, *Family of Spies* review, *New York Times Book Review,* January 8, 1989.

Hot House review, *Publishers Weekly,* December 20, 1991.

Lundy, Allan, "How Legal System Fails the Nation's Mentally Ill," *Philadelphia Inquirer,* May 8, 2006.

Maxwell, Lynne, *Crazy* review, *Library Journal,* March 15, 2006.

Peter Earley interview, *Washingtonian Online*, April 18, 2006. http://www.washingtonian.com/chats/earley.html (viewed May 23, 2006).

Pete Earley Web site. http://www.peteearley.com/bio/index.html (viewed May 23, 2006).

Root, Deirdre, *WITSEC* review, *Library Journal,* February 1, 2002.

Super Casino review, *Publishers Weekly,* November 22, 1999.

Barbara Ehrenreich

Health, Investigative Reporting

Benchmark Title: *Nickel and Dimed*

Butte, Montana

1941–

Photo by Sigrid Estrada

About the Author and the Author's Writing

Barbara Ehrenreich got a job—several jobs, in fact—to write *Nickel and Dimed,* her book describing the trials of those barely getting by in America. These weren't just any jobs. The idea came about, she explained in *Columbia Journalism Review,* over lunch with her editor at *Harper's* magazine. She had an idea for a book about sports fandom but discussion turned to welfare reform and the myth that minimum-wage work would lift people out of poverty. " 'Someone,' she averred, 'ought to do the old-fashioned kind of journalism—you know, go out there and try it for themselves.' " Her editor, Lewis Lapham, didn't miss a beat when he responded: " 'You.' "

Ehrenreich abandoned her then-home in Key West, Florida, to follow George Orwell and Jacob A. Riis and other pioneer journalists, not into the coal mines or slums, but into American trailer parks.

The author, a feminist and social activist, was born Barbara Alexander in Butte, Montana, in 1941, the daughter of Ben Howes Ehrenreich, a copper miner who attended night school and eventually became a Gillette executive, and Isabelle Oxley Isely Alexander, a warehouse worker. Both were New Deal Democrats. In 1963, she earned a bachelor of arts degree from Reed College, and she was awarded a Ph.D. in biology from Rockefeller University five years later. Barbara married John Ehrenreich in 1966 and, after that marriage ended, Gary Stevenson in 1983. She has two children from her first marriage.

After brief stints with the Health Policy Advisory Center in New York City and the health sciences department at State University of New York College, Ehrenreich became a full-time writer and editor. She has been a columnist with *Mother Jones, Time,* and the London *Guardian* and a contributor to *Nation, Esquire, Vogue, New*

York Times Magazine, and *Ms.* In 1980, she became a fellow with the New York Institute for the Humanities, and she joined the Institute for Policy Studies in 1982. In 1983, she was named cochair of the Democratic Socialists of America.

Ehrenreich's writing career grew out of her work in the health field. *Complaints and Disorders,* which she cowrote with Dierdre English, examined the way health care for women is a means of male social control. Next she tackled an array of feminist issues in *The Hearts of Men.* In *Re-making Love,* Ehrenreich and her two coauthors, Elizabeth Hess and Gloria Jacobs, gave a positive overview of the sexual revolution of the 1970s and 1980s.

The author shifted her attention to other social issues with *Fear of Falling,* an examination of those who have entered successful fields such as medicine or law, yet cannot ensure their success for their children. "Doctors can't pass on their medical licenses to their children. All they can hope to transmit is the same orientation toward achievement that boosted them over the top," explains reviewer Katherine Newman in *Psychology Today.* "And yet, the security and affluence their status affords may dampen the very desires that are critical to their children's educational and professional success." Parents raised in the post–World War II 1950s, Ehrenreich gives as an example, were shocked at their flower children of the 1960s, who rebelled at social expectations and constraints.

The Worst Years of Our Lives, The Snarling Citizen, and *Maid to Order* collect Ehrenreich's essays on a range of issues from consumerism to class arrogance to political ennui. The author notes the rise of a working-class, conservative electorate. "I think the root cause of the anger is economic insecurity," she said in an interview with *The Progressive*'s Ruth Conniff in 1995. "[We no longer have] a political culture in which you can criticize employers, much less 'Big Business.' We have a political culture in which the happy myth is that employers are philanthropists because they've given you a job—not that you give them your labor power and don't get paid enough for it, but that they have given you a job, how kind of them." That $25,000 or $30,000 a year, however, isn't enough to support a family.

Ehrenreich preaches social activism. Discussing *Nickel and Dimed* with Powells.com's Jill Owens, she said, "Coming together to work for change helps overcome fear. When you see that other people have the same problems, you feel that kind of strength that comes from mutual support."

She advocates unionism. "I have to laugh when people talk about 'big labor.' Where is big labor? It's so tiny, unfortunately, compared to what it's up against."

She also supports participatory journalism. "When you interview people," she told a *BuzzFlash* interviewer, "they'll say, yeah, the job was hard, or something like that. But I actually put myself in that situation and found how difficult it was for me to learn to do the work, and how difficult it was physically to keep up, even though I'm a very strong person. That comes through, by this type of investigating. I could only find out by entering into this world in my actual body."

To research *Nickel and Dimed,* Ehrenreich lived in trailers. She cleaned motel rooms. She assisted Wal-Mart shoppers find bargains. She waited on tables. Although she began her research in good health, white, able to speak English, with a college degree, as *Humanist* reviewer Joni Scott notes, she "exposes the anti-America of flophouses, multiple house sharing, employees sleeping in cars, and the homeless who work forty hours or more weekly. Those who used to be middle class, despite often working two jobs, now endure a daily scramble to prioritize such needs as food, housing, child care and health care." While repulsed by dining room patrons who didn't tip and Christian revivalists who distorted Jesus' message, Ehrenreich did find stories of caring and thoughtfulness and optimism.

In *Bait and Switch,* the author looks at people who are talented, have college degrees, are in the workforce, yet have not found happiness, security, or true success. She again assumes a journalistic identity, an unemployed white-collar worker who wants a public relations position. "Despite a carefully crafted CV, though, and a willingness to go anywhere for a job or even an interview, none was forthcoming," *New Statesman's* Kira Cochran said in a review. "Ehrenreich spent the entire period searching, finding herself in a nether world of life coaches, idiotic self-help speak, shady Christian meetings and image consultants."

She failed to secure a job. "She concludes without bitterness but without much hope that what 'the unemployed and anxiously employed' need is 'not a winning attitude' but 'courage to come together and work for change,' " notes *Library Journal's* Jack Forman.

Works by the Author

Long March, Short Spring: The Student Uprising at Home and Abroad, with John Ehrenreich (1969)

The American Health Empire; Power, Profits, and Politics, with John Ehrenreich (1971)

Witches, Midwives, and Nurses: A History of Women Healers, with Deirdre English (1972)

Complaints and Disorders: The Sexual Politics of Sickness, with Deirdre English (1977)

Poverty in the American Dream: Women and Children First, with others (1983)

Women in the Global Factory, with Annette Fuentes (1983)

The Hearts of Men: American Dreams and the Flight from Commitment (1987)

The Mean Season: An Attack on the Welfare State, with Fred Block, Richard Cloward, and Frances Fox Piven (1987)

Re-Making Love: The Feminization of Sex, with Elizabeth Hess and Gloria Jacobs (1987)

For Her Own Good: 150 Years of the Experts' Advice to Women, with Deirdre English (1989)

Fear of Falling: The Inner Life of the Middle Class (1990)

Worst Years of Our Lives (1990)

The Snarling Citizen: Essays (1995)

Blood Rites: Origins and History of the Passions of War (1997)

Nickel and Dimed: On (Not) Getting By in America (2001)

Bait and Switch: The (Futile) Pursuit of the American Dream (2005)

For Her Own Good: Two Centuries of the Experts' Advice to Women (2005)

Dancing in the Streets: A History of Collective Joy (2007)

Editor

Global Woman: Nannies, Maids, and Sex Workers in the New Economy, with Arlie Russell Hochschild (2004)

Novel

Kipper's Game (1993)

Stage Adaptation

Nickel and Dimed, by Joan Holden (2002)

For Further Information

"Barbara Ehrenreich Brings You Life without Safety Nets—the Growing Reality for Everyday Americans," *BuzzFlash.* http://www.buzzflash.com/interviews/05/04/int05015.html (viewed May 30, 2006).

Barbara Ehrenreich entry, Contemporary Authors Online. Reproduced in Biography Resource Center. Farmington Hills, MI: Thomson Gale, 2006. http://galenet.galegroup.com/servlet/BioRC.

Barbara Ehrenreich Web site. http://www.barbaraehrenreich.com/books/htm (viewed May 30, 2006).

Birnbaum, Robert, Barbara Ehrenreich interview, *Identity Theory.* http://www.identitytheory.com/people/birnbaum21.html (viewed May 30, 2006).

Cochrane, Kira, "The Cult of Cheerfulness; When Barbara Ehrenreich Set Out to Investigate Corporate Culture in America, She Found a Sinister, 'Christianized' World Where Anger Is Outlawed," *New Statesman,* March 27, 2006.

Conniff, Ruth, Barbara Ehrenreich interview, *Progressive*, February 1995.

Dembosky, April, "Bait and Switch: An Interview with Barbara Ehrenreich," *Mother Jones,* September 9, 2005. http://www.motherjones.com/news/qa/2005/09/barbara_ehrenreich.html (viewed May 30, 2006).

Forman, Jack, *Bait and Switch* review, *Library Journal,* September 1, 2005.

Forman, Jack, *Nickel and Dimed* review, *Library Journal,* May 1, 2001.

Mudge, Alden, "Help Wanted: Job-Hunting in Corporate America," *BookPage.* http://www.bookpage.com/0510bp/barbara_ehrenreich.html (May 30, 2006).

Newman, Katherine, "Fear of Falling: The Inner Life of the Middle Class," *Psychology Today,* October 1989.

Owens, Jill, "Undercover with Barbara Ehrenreich," Powells.com. http://www.powells.com/authors/ehrenreich.html (viewed May 30, 2006).

Rowe, Jonathan, *Maid to Order* review, *Washington Monthly,* July-August 2003.

Scott, Joni, *Nickel and Dimed* review, *Humanist,* September 2001.

Sherman, Scott, "Class Warrior: Barbara Ehrenreich's Singular Crusade," *Columbia Journalism Review*, November-December 2003.

Smith, Wendy, "Barbara Ehrenreich: The Nonfiction Writer and Social Activist Has Produced Her First Novel," *Publishers Weekly,* July 26, 1993.

Tim F. Flannery

Adventure, Environment, Science

Benchmark Title: *The Weather Makers*

Melbourne, Australia

1956–

Photo by Adam Bruzzone

About the Author and the Author's Writing

If you "throwim way leg"—a pidgin expression that means go a journey—and follow the trail of Tim Flannery's writings, you find a progression that ranges from documenting the more unusual mammal species of his native Australia (*The Kangaroo*) and examining lost cultures (he made fifteen treks into the New Guinea bush) to looking at the agents of major change. In the last of these books, *The Weather Makers,* he asserts that if global decisions aren't made soon and show results by 2050, the planet is going to be a far different one to live on than we have now.

"Climate change is difficult for people to evaluate dispassionately," he writes in *The Weather Makers,* "because it entails deep political and industrial implications and because it arises from the core processes of our civilisation's success."

Only recently has Flannery recognized the impact of the increased presence of greenhouse gases—from our overreliance on fossil fuels—in our atmosphere. In 2005, he said in a *Publishers Weekly* conversation with Jeff Makos, "It was only when I learned of climate change's impact on Australia's mountain rainforests that I realized how all-pervasive and world-altering climate change could be. Those rainforests had survived for tens of millions of years, yet climate change may destroy them this century."

Global warming is a pretty heady subject, and Flannery's skill is in rendering it comfortably to a general audience. "Flannery has a rare gift for bringing the macro down to the micro," in the opinion of *OnEarth* reviewer George Black. "When he describes the cascade of effects that result from marginal changes in temperature or precipitation, he drives your heart into your throat." Added Ron Gaetz in *Nature Conservancy Magazine,* "His suggestions are not just for lawmakers and captains of industry; he also proposes practical and effective things each of us can do today."

Can the issue be resolved, given the world's political, social, and economic climate? Flannery likens the situation to another that existed three hundred years ago, when slavery thrived. Discussing early abolitionists, he said, "It must have seemed hopeless at first, faced by the opposition of corrupt parliaments and wealthy merchants and planters. Yet, these Abolitionists changed the world by the force of their moral arguments and I believe that moral argument will win the day and lead to solutions for global warming," the author said in *California Literary Review.*

Timothy Fridtjof Flannery was born in 1956 in Melbourne. After receiving a bachelor of arts degree in English in 1977 from LaTrobe University, he worked briefly for the Museum of Victoria's Vertebrate Paleontology department. In 1981, he changed direction and secured a master of science degree in earth science from Monash University. He earned a 1985 doctorate from the University of New South Wales in zoology. Principal research scientist with the Australian Museum in Sydney since 1985, his interests range from paleontology and mammalogy to zoogeography, exploration, medieval literature, fishing, and music.

Flannery's scientific credentials speak for themselves. He has identified and named more than thirty new mammal species, among them tree kangaroos. In 1992, he accepted the Edgeworth David Medal for Outstanding Research; in 2002, he was awarded the Centenary of Federation Medal. He was the first environmentalist to deliver his nation's Australia Day address. He has taught at Harvard University and appeared on-air over ABC Radio, NPR, and the BBC. He presented his own series, *The Future Eaters,* on the Documentary Channel.

Flannery is interested in anthropology and history, particularly the history of exploration. *Throwim Way Leg* features fauna found nowhere else and indigenous people who are nothing if not fascinating. He has edited books about the early years of British colonization and the maritime adventures of John Nicol and Joshua Slocum. *A Gap in Nature* surveys the hundred-plus species of mammals, reptiles, and birds that have gone extinct since Columbus reached America's shores. "These accounts are beautifully written, often anecdotal, and almost always poignant," said *Library Journal's* reviewer.

His best-selling *The Future Eaters* garnered him a wide reputation in Australia and New Zealand. In it, "Flannery demonstrates the subtle interaction that makes an ecosystem work," observed *Publishers Weekly,* "from glaciers to fire, from dung beetles to man. In the process he makes a formidable, sometimes frightening argument for careful cooperation with—rather than domination of—the world." There, as noted, are the seeds of *The Weather Makers*—a topic Flannery is keen on pursuing, with a dedicated Web site and a second book in the pipeline.

Works by the Author

The Kangaroo, with Michael Archer and Gordon Grigg (1986)

Australia's Vanishing Mammals, with Paula Kendall (1990)

The Future Eaters; An Ecological History of the Australasian Lands and People (1994)

Possums of the World: A Monograph of the Phalangeroidea (1994)

Mammals of New Guinea (1995)

Mammals of the South-West Pacific and Moluccan Islands (1995)

Throwim Way Leg: Fifteen Years with Trap in Hand in the New Guinea Bush
(1997), published in United States as *Throwim Way Leg: Tree-Kangaroos,
Possums and Penis Gourds* (1998), also titled *Throwim Way Leg: An Adventure* (1998)

*Astonishing Animals: Extraordinary Creatures and the Fantastic Worlds They
Inhabit* (2001)

The Eternal Frontier: Ecological History of North America and Its Peoples
(2001)

*Fossil Mammals of Australia and New Guinea: One Hundred Million Years of
Evolution,* with John A. Long, Michael Archer and Suzanne Hand (2001)

A Gap in Nature: Discovering the World's Extinct Animals, with Peter Schouten
(2001)

Ill-Starred Captains: Flinders and Baudin, with Anthony J. Brown (2001)

Country (2004)

*The Weather Makers: How Man Is Changing the Climate and What It Means for
Life on Earth* (2006)

*Chasing Kangaroos; A Continent, a Scientist, and a Search for the World's Most
Extraordinary Creature* (2007)

We Are the Weather Makers (2007)

Editor

1788, by Watkin Tench (1996)

The Life and Adventures of John Nicol, Mariner, by John Nicol (1999)

The Explorers: Stories of Discovery and Adventure from the Australian Frontier
(2000)

The Birth of Sydney (2000)

The Birth of Melbourne (2002)

Sailing Alone around the World, by Joshua Slocum (2002)

Contributor

The Life and Adventures of William Buckley, by John Morgan (2002)

Sydney Sandstone; A Pictorial Journey (2002)

Lonely Planet Victoria (2005)

For Further Information

Badger, Lynn C., *A Gap in Nature* review, *Library Journal,* October 1, 2001.

Black, George, *The Weather Makers* review, *OnEarth,* Spring 2006.

Flannery, Tim F., "Civilisation's darkest hour," *Sydney Morning Herald,* September 24, 2005.

Future Eaters review, *Publishers Weekly,* August 21, 1995.

Gaetz, Ron, *Weather Makers* review, *Nature Conservancy Magazine,* autumn
2006.

Harris, Roger, *Astonishing Animals* review, *American Scientist,* March-April
2005.

Makos, Jeff, "Talking about the Weather," *Publishers Weekly,* December 5, 2005.

Sapp, Gregg, "Q&A: Tim Flannery," *Library Journal,* December 1, 2005.

Shotwell, Rebecca, *Throwim Way Leg* review, *Sierra,* May 1999.

Throwim Way Leg review, *Publishers Weekly,* November 30, 1998.

Tim Flannery biography. http://www.abc.net.au.science/slab/flannery/biog.htm (viewed August 29, 2006).

Tim Flannery biography, Weather Makers Web site. http://www.theweathermakers.com/weathermakers (viewed September 4, 2006).

Tim Flannery interview, *George Negus Tonight,* October 3, 2003. http://www.abc.net.au/dimensions/dimensions_in_time/Transcripts/s780702.htm (viewed August 29, 2006).

Tim(othy) (Fridtjof) Flannery entry, Contemporary Authors Online. Reproduced in Biography Resource Center. Farmington Hills, MI: Thomson Gale, 2002. http://galenet.galegroup.com/servlet/BioRC.

Voves, Ed, "Tim Flannery Discusses Global Warming," *California Literary Review*, July 10, 2006. http://www.calitreview.com/Interviews/flannery_8030.htm (viewed August 29, 2006).

Thomas Fleming

Biography, History, Memoir

Benchmark Title: *Washington's Secret War*

Jersey City, New Jersey

1927–

Photo courtesy the author

About the Author and the Author's Writing

Historian Thomas Fleming dotes on secrets. Consider the titles of some of his books: *Washington's Secret War* or *The Secret Trial of Robert E. Lee*. And even if he has no great, untold stories to reveal, he spices his writing with original source materials and finds new perspectives that challenge what we thought we understood of American history, whether it's the immigrant experience of the early twentieth century or the country's jostling on the world stage during World War II.

The Revolutionary War period is the author's first love. When the United States adopted a constitution, more than two centuries ago, it was only after a prolonged arm wrestle. Regional differences were almost too much to overcome. "At one point Thomas Jefferson said to Washington, after one of his brawls with Hamilton and other people, 'There's no doubt in my mind, the only way that we're ever going to get out of this peacefully is the South will have to secede from the North,' " Fleming said in an interview on the American Experience Web site.

The author was born in 1927 in Jersey City, New Jersey, the son of Thomas James "Teddy" Fleming and Katherine "Kitty" Dolan Fleming. His father, son of a poor immigrant Irish family, was a laborer and right hand to corrupt political boss Frank Hague in Jersey City's Sixth Ward. His mother, daughter of a successful carpenter, was a teacher. At an early age, Thomas was exposed to urban politics, and particularly the behind-the-scenes rivalry of the Irish Catholics and the Anglo-Saxon Protestants for political power in the city. " 'My mother was the quintessential idealist," Fleming said in an interview with Tom Deignan of *Publishers Weekly*. "She always said to me: 'Aim high.' Meanwhile, my father was getting out the vote.. . . They were from two different worlds."

From 1945 to 1946 Fleming served in the U.S. Navy. He graduated from Fordham University in 1950 and worked for another year toward an advanced degree. In 1951, he married children's writer Alice Mulcahey; they had four children.

Although his father had urged him to become a lawyer, Fleming gravitated to literature. He was a newspaper reporter in Yonkers, New York, in 1951, worked for two years with *Reader's Digest*, then became literary executor of author Fulton Oursler's estate. From 1954 to 1958, he was an associate editor for *Cosmopolitan,* rising to executive editor. In 1961, he became a full-time writer of both nonfiction and fiction and has produced fifty books so far. A fellow of the Society of American Historians, he was a regular contributor to *American Heritage* and other periodicals.

At the start of his writing career, Fleming alternated between nonfiction examinations of the Revolutionary War period and fictional depictions of the gradual melting of the Irish-American political machine during the late 1940s. Both his fiction and nonfiction works were popularly acclaimed. In fact, he is the only author to have main selections for the Book of the Month Club in both categories of writing. His several generational novels, based somewhat on the powerful New Jersey Stockton and Stevens families, feature his made-up Stapleton characters from the colonial period to modern day.

Fleming accepted a commission to write a history of West Point. But as he researched the topic, he saw a political level that went beyond the career soldiers. He crafted a novel, *The Officers' Wives*, to delve into a more personal aspect of the wars in Korea and Vietnam. Over time Fleming "broadened and deepened his exploration of the clash between America's realities and its ideals," noted a writer on a Get New Jersey Web site.

The plain truth was sufficient to propel Fleming's story of the brutal winter that American forces encamped at Valley Forge, a turning point for George Washington, as is depicted in *Washington's Secret War* (2005). The Continental Army emerged as an empowered, disciplined fighting machine. And the experience turned the future president into a far more politically savvy leader. "Fleming has provided an original and provocative reinterpretation of a critical period in the struggle for independence," Jay Freeman wrote in *Booklist*.

Duel, the author's 1999 history of the conflict between Alexander Hamilton and Aaron Burr, is firmly rooted in the economic and political turmoil of 1804 and President Thomas Jefferson's decision to ditch his Vice President Burr in a run for another term. Hamilton makes some uncharitable remarks at a dinner party. Burr gets word. We know the outcome. "A textured telling of a fateful year," commented *Booklist* reviewer Gilbert Taylor.

Moving forward in American history, Fleming's *The Louisiana Purchase* (2003) "reveals a less than glorious Jefferson, sending signals to Napoleon that we wouldn't mind at all if the French overthrew the black hero of Santo Domingo, Toussaint L'Ouverture," according to *Booklist* reviewer Allen Weakland.

The Secret Trial of Robert E. Lee (2006) offers a fascinating account of a failed attempt to thwart Union General Ulysses S. Grant's terms offered to his Confederate counterpart at Appomattox Courthouse. "Fleming's characterizations of everybody, even [rebel spy] Sophie, show skilled writing and sound historiography," Roland Green said in *Booklist*.

In *The Illusion of Victory* (2003), Fleming offers a new take on President Woodrow Wilson's political decisions during World War I. "This warts-and-all reading characterizes Wilson as an unlovable man who often talked one way and acted another and a successful wartime leader only because he was a good speaker who appealed to both the idealists and the realists," noted Grant Frederickson in *Library Journal*. "Fans of Woodrow Wilson should steer well clear of this book," warned Stephen Svonavec in *Canadian Journal of History*.

But Fleming sought to go beyond reinterpreting political figures. "I explore what I call America's 'covenant with power' which developed from our experience in World War I," Fleming said in a *St. Mihiel Trip-Wire* interview. "We discovered that power, not soaring ideals, was the critical factor in history. At the same time, idealism remained important to Americans. How to balance these two factors has been the problem that has troubled the United States ever since."

The New Dealers' War, published in 2001, is, as one might expect, a new take on the behind-the-scenes grappling of World War II that *Washington Post Book World* reviewer Richard Pearson said "paints a devastating portrait of a Roosevelt whose health and powers were in steep and terminal decline after 1940."

In 2005, the author, having long enough wrestled with his Jersey City origins in his fiction, wrote a memoir, *Mysteries of My Father*, which in the view of *Library Journal*'s Ben Bruton "transcends traditional memoir and becomes a moving examination of the unique challenges faced by 20th-century Irish Americans as they struggled to integrate into American society."

The author says he resorted to memoir to resolve issues in his own past, just as he had before in the nation's. "History had liberated me from a past that was no longer relevant," he said in an essay for History News Network. "I was ready to explore the American side of my hyphenated psyche. I'm still doing it."

Works by the Author

Now We Are Enemies: The Battle of Bunker Hill (1960)

Beat the Last Drum: The Siege of Yorktown (1963)

One Small Candle: The Pilgrims' First Year in America (1964)

Battle of Yorktown, with American Heritage editors (1968)

First in Their Hearts: A Biography of George Washington (1968)

The Man from Monticello: An Intimate Life of Thomas Jefferson (1969)

West Point: The Men and Times of the United States Military Academy (1969)

The Man Who Dared Lightning: A New Look at Benjamin Franklin (1971)

The Forgotten Victory: The Battle for New Jersey (1973)

1776: Year of Illusions (1975)

New Jersey: A History (1977), with historical guide (1984)

The First Stroke: Lexington and Concord and the Beginning of the American Revolution (1978)

The Spoils of War (1985)

Cowpens: Downright Fighting (1988)

Harry S. Truman, President (1993)

Liberty!: The American Revolution (1997)

Lights Along the Way: Great Stories of American Faith (1999)
Duel: Alexander Hamilton, Aaron Burr, and the Future of America (2000)
The New Dealers' War: FDR and the War within World War II (2001)
The Illusion of Victory: America in World War I (2003)
The Louisiana Purchase (2003)
Washington's Secret War: The Hidden History of Valley Forge (2005)
Mysteries of My Father (2005)
Everybody's Revolution (2006)
The Secret Trial of Robert E. Lee (2006)

Editor

Affectionately Yours, George Washington: A Self-Portrait in Letters of Friendship (1967)
Benjamin Franklin: A Life in His Own Words (1972)
The Living Land of Lincoln (1980)

Fiction

All Good Men (1961)
The God of Love (1963)
King of the Hill (1966)
A Cry of Whiteness (1967)
Romans, Countrymen, Lovers (1969)
The Sandbox Tree (1970)
The Good Shepherd (1974)
Liberty Tavern (1976)
Rulers of the City (1977)
Promises to Keep (1978)
A Passionate Girl (1979)
The Officers' Wives (1981)
Dreams of Glory (1983)
Time and Tide (1987)
Over There (1992)
Loyalties: A Novel of World War II (1994)
Remember the Morning (1997)
The Wages of Fame (1998)
Hours of Gladness (1999)
When This Cruel War Is Over (2001)
Conquerors of the Sky (2003)
West Point Blue and Grey (2006)

For Further Information

Bruton, Ben, *Mysteries of My Father* review, *Library Journal,* May 1, 2005.

Conaty, Barbara, *Remember the Morning* review, *Library Journal,* August 1997.

Deignan, Tom, "High-flying Tales: Thomas Fleming," *Publishers Weekly,* January 20, 2003.

Fleming, Thomas, "My Life as a Historian," *History News Network,* Oct. 7, 2002. http://www.historynewsnetwork.com/articles/1008/html (viewed June 16, 2006).

Frederickson, Grant, *The Illusion of Victory* review, *Library Journal,* June 15, 2003.

Freeman, Jay, *Washington's Secret War* review, *Booklist,* October 15, 2005.

Green, Roland, *The Secret Trial of Robert E. Lee* review, *Booklist,* January 1, 2006.

Pearson, Richard, *The New Dealer's War* review, *Washington Post Book World,* July 1, 2001.

Svonavec, Stephen, "The Illusion of Victory: America in World War I," *Canadian Journal of History,* December 2005.

Taylor, Gilbert, *Duel* review, *Booklist*, October 15, 1999.

Thomas Fleming interview, *American Experience.* http://www.pbs.org/wgbh/amex/duel/filmmore/reference/interview/fleming06.html (viewed June 16, 2006).

Thomas Fleming interview, St. Mihiel Trip-Wire, Online Newsletter of the Great War Society. http://www.worldwar1.com/tgws/ei_tf.htm (viewed June 16, 2006).

"Thomas Fleming—Jersey City-born Historian and Novelist, http://www.getnj.com/flemingbio.shtml (viewed June 16, 2006).

Thomas Fleming Web site. http://thomasflemingwriter/com/ (viewed May 30, 2006).

Thomas (James) Fleming entry, Contemporary Authors Online. Reproduced in Biography Resource Center. Farmington Hills, MI: Thomson Gale, 2006. http://galenet.galegroup.com/servlet/BioRC.

Weakland, Allen, *The Louisiana Purchase* review, *Booklist,* July 2003.

John Hope Franklin

Biography, History, Investigative Reporting

Benchmark Title: *From Slavery to Freedom*

Rentiesville, Oklahoma

1915–

Duke University Photography

About the Author and the Author's Writing

There are 350 orchids in his collection, each with a distinct hue and scent, none more precious to the owner than the hybrid *Phalaenopsis Aurelia Franklin,* named by a South Carolina greenhouse in his wife's memory, or the hybrid *Phalaenopsis John Hope Franklin,* named for the horticulturist himself in 1976 by University of Chicago President John T. Wilson.

John Hope Franklin, the history professor, fell in love with the exotic flowers during a teaching assignment in Hawaii. He began to propagate orchids, first in Brooklyn, then in Chicago, now in Durham, North Carolina. His specimens include many collected during his travels.

The same holds for Franklin's ever-growing shelf of awards—more than one hundred honorary degrees and the Presidential Medal of Freedom in 1995. In 2005, the National Newspaper Publishers Foundation honored him with a Lifetime Achievement Award for his more than half-century documentation of African American history. "I'm honored that they would honor me," was Franklin's response, reported in *Jet.* "Black publications have been the knitting machine to help keep together the Black community."

The American Academy of Arts and Letters had already presented Franklin with its Gold Medal in History, its selection committee noting "his scholarship is resourceful and scrupulous; and his wisdom, passion and judgment have made him a moral leader of the historical profession," *Black Issues in Higher Education* reported in 2002. That periodical two years later marked its two-decade anniversary by launching the John Hope Franklin Distinguished Contribution in Higher Education Award and holding a national conference in Virginia on diversity.

111

Franklin was born in 1915 in Rentiesville, Oklahoma, the all-black community in which his parents, attorney Buck Colbert Franklin and schoolteacher Mollie Parker Franklin, had sought relief from prejudice. "My mother and father were irrevocably independent and absolutely disdainful of the whole apparatus of segregation," Franklin told *American Heritage* magazine in 2002. "I was not taught to be deferential to whites. Quite the contrary. I was taught to be independent."

Franklin's early influential reading included W.E.B. Du Bois's *The Souls of Black Folk*; and his parents took him to hear the freedom activist speak in Tulsa, where he was awed by Du Bois's formal attire and erudition. He acknowledged the debt in a small way in 2005 when he joined the board of the Du Bois Center for American History in Great Barrington, Massachusetts, Du Bois's hometown.

In 1935, Franklin received a bachelor of arts degree from Fisk University. "When I finished college in 1935 and wanted to go to graduate school, I couldn't go to graduate school in Oklahoma where I was born, despite the fact that my father paid taxes. Any white person could go to graduate school at the University of Oklahoma. But I couldn't even be caught in the town after sundown," Franklin said in an *Illinois Issues* interview. He earned a master's degree from Harvard University the next year and a Ph.D. from the same university in 1941.

Franklin is a career academic. He has taught and lectured at numerous universities in the United States and abroad. In 1990, the book *Race and History* collected fifty years of essays about teaching and writing.

However, Franklin's writing has been both academic—examinations of the Emancipation Proclamation, of post–Civil War reconstruction from a black perspective —and popular—a biography of George Washington Williams, the nineteenth-century black historian. Franklin's *From Slavery to Freedom,* published in 1947, became a staple in African American history classes and has gone through eight editions. In this and other works, Franklin provides a factual, emotional, intense picture of the black experience in America, in the past and today.

"Few readers of *Runaway Slaves,* especially chapters focusing upon the devastating breakup of families and the chilling hunt to retrieve runaways, will come away from the text with the idea that paternalism was alive and well," reviewer Wilma King wrote in *Black Issues in Higher Education.*

In 1954, Franklin provided research for lawyers pressing the *Brown v. Board of Education* U.S. Supreme Court school desegregation case. He dared become a historian not just of the black experience, but of the South. Franklin asserts, according to Alvin P. Sanoff in *U.S. News & World Report,* "that the region's peculiar social and economic institutions, most notably slavery, held the key to the South's distinctive martial spirit."

Franklin and his wife, the late Aurelia E. Whittington, a librarian, had one son, John Whittington Franklin. Father and son collaborated in editing Buck Colbert Franklin's autobiography for publication in 1997.

Improved race relations has been and remains a major goal for the historian, who believes change can only come through teaching tolerance. "You can create a climate of goodwill," he said in *Jet* in 1998. "The task of trying to reshape our society to bring about a climate of racial healing is so enormous, it strains the imagination."

"I look history straight in the eye and call it like it is," *U.S. News & World Report* quoted the historian in 1990.

◆ Works by the Author

The Free Negro in North Carolina (1943/1995)

From Slavery to Freedom: A History of Negro Americans, with Alfred A. Joss Jr. (1947), reprinted as *From Slavery to Freedom: A History of African Americans* (2000)

The Militant South, 1800–1860 (1956), revised (1970)

Reconstruction after the Civil War (1962/1994)

The Emancipation Proclamation (1963)

Land of the Free: A History of the United States, with John W. Caughey and Ernest R. May (1965)

Racial Equality in America (1976)

A Southern Odyssey: Travelers in the Antebellum North (1976)

George Washington Williams: A Biography (1985)

Race & History: Selected Essays, 1938–1988 (1990)

The Color Line; Legacy for the Twenty-first Century (1993)

Black Intellectuals; Race and Responsibility in American Life, with William M. Banks (1996)

Runaway Slaves: Rebels on the Plantation, with Loren Schweninger (1999)

Mirror to America: The Autobiography of John Hope Franklin (2005)

In Search of the Promised Land: A Black Family and the Old South, with Loren Schweninger (2006)

Editor

The Civil War Diary of J. T. Ayers (1947)

A Fool's Errand, by Albion Tourgee (1961)

Army Life in a Black Regiment, by T. W. Higginson (1962)

Three Negro Classics (1965)

The Negro in Twentieth-Century America: A Reader on the Struggle for Civil Rights, with Isadore Starr (1967)

Color and Race (1968)

The Suppression of the African Slave Trade by W.E.B. Du Bois (1969)

Illustrated History of Black Americans, with the editors of Time-Life Books (1970)

Reminiscences of an Active Life: The Autobiography of John R. Lynch (1970)

Black Leaders of the Twentieth Century, with August Meier (1982)

African Americans and the Living Constitution, with Genna Rae McNeil (1995)

My Life and an Era: The Autobiography of Buck Colbert Franklin, with John Whittington Franklin (1997)

Contributor

Problems in American History (1952), edited by Arthur S. Link and Richard Leopold

The Negro Thirty Years Afterward (1955), edited by Rayford W. Logan

The Americans: Ways of Life and Thought (1956)

Issues in University Education (1959), edited by Charles Frankel

Lincoln for the Ages (1960), edited by Ralph Newman

The Southerner as American (1960), edited by Charles G. Sellars Jr.

American History: Recent Interpretations (1962), edited by Abraham Seldin Eisenstadt

Soon One Morning (1963), edited by Herbert Hill

The Atlantic Future (1964), edited by H. V. Hodson

The South in Continuity and Change (1965), edited by John C. McKinney and Edgar T. Thompson

The American Negro Reference Book (1966), edited by John P. Davis

New Frontiers of the American Reconstruction (1966), edited by Harold Hyman

The Negro American (1966), edited by Kenneth Clark and Talcott Parsons

The American Primer (1966), edited by Daniel J. Boorstin

The Comparative Approach to American History (1968), edited by C. Vann Woodward

William Wells Brown: Author and Reformer (1969), edited by William Edward Farrison

Henry Ossawa Tanner, American Artist (1969), edited by Marcia M. Mathews

Crusade for Justice: The Autobiography of Ida B. Wells (1970), edited by Alfreda M. Duster

Chant of Saints (1979), edited by Michael S. Harper

The Voices of Negro Protest in America (1980), edited by William H. Burns

A Melting Pot or a Nation of Minorities (1986), edited by Robert L. Payton

This Road to Freedom (1990), edited by Eric C. Lincoln

American Studies in Black and White: Selected Essays, 1949–1989 (1991), edited by Sidney Kaplan and Allan Austin

To Be Free (1992), edited by Herbert Aptheker

The Inclusive University (1993)

Jubilee: The Emergence of African-American Culture (2002)

Video

Tutu and Franklin: A Journey Towards Peace (2001)

For Further Information

"Black Issues in Higher Education Marks 20th Anniversary with Inauguration of John Hope Franklin Awards and a National Conference on Higher Education Diversity June 17–19, 2004," PR Newswire, May 12, 2004.

Clarke, John Henrik, "John Hope Franklin: Historian of the Century," *Journal of Blacks in Higher Education,* December 31, 1996.

Color Line review, *Publishers Weekly,* January 4, 1993.

In Search of the Promised Land review, *Ebony,* August 2005.

John Hope Franklin entry, Contemporary Authors Online. Reproduced in Biography Resource Center. Farmington Hills, MI: Thomson Gale, 2006. http://galenet.galegroup.com/servlet/BioRC.

"John Hope Franklin has Remained Dedicated to the Truth about Race in America for More than 40 Years," *Jet,* April 13, 1998.

"John Hope Franklin Honored for Lifetime Achievement," *Black Issues in Higher Education,* June 6, 2002.

King, Wilma, *Runaway Slaves* review, *Black Issues in Higher Education,* May 24, 2001.

Litwack, Leon F., "The Road from Rentiesville: The Greatest Historian of the Black Experience in America Speaks of What Has Changed during His Long Life, and What Has Not. An Interview with John Hope Franklin," *American Heritage,* February-March 2002.

Mirror to America review, *Publishers Weekly*, September 5, 2005.

Morgan, Joan, "The Sage in His Own Words," *Black Issues in Education,* January 18, 2001.

"NNPA honorees," *Jet,* April 3, 2006.

"Phalaenopsis John Hope Franklin," *Black Issues in Higher Education,* September 23, 2004.

"Q&A: John Hope Franklin," *Illinois Issues.* http://www.lib.niu.edu/ipo/1997/ii971124.html (viewed July 3, 2006).

Sanoff, Alvin P., "Revising the Old South History: John Hope Franklin Has Psyched Out the Regional Mind," *U.S. News & World Report,* September 17, 1990.

"Three Blacks Awarded Nation's Highest Medal at White House Ceremony," *Jet,* October 16, 1995.

Ian Frazier

Humor, Investigative Reporting, Memoir, Outdoors, Travel

Benchmark Title: *On the Rez*

Cleveland, Ohio

1951–

Photo courtesy of Granta

About the Author and the Author's Writing

Ian Frazier resents the term "wannabe." True, he immersed himself in the Native American lifestyle when he wrote *On the Rez*. He wore his hair in a ponytail and adopted a few articles of a traditional Indian wardrobe. But he had no interest in performing a sun dance or collecting Indian art or being adopted into a tribe. Few quite understand his goal. "When I'm driving across the field near the town of Oglala on the Pine Ridge reservation and I see my friend Floyd John walking across it the other way, I stop, and he comes over to the car and leans in the window and smiles a big-tooth grin and says, 'How ya' doin', wannabe?' "

He isn't a wannabe; he is a fascinating writer with a growing body of writing that reflects a curious literary DNA: It has the bemused humorous take of a veteran *National Lampoon* writer, refined and enriched with two decades of writing for the *New Yorker*. Combine those influences with a passion for exploring the mundane, the underappreciated, and you have Ian Frazier.

Frazier was born in Cleveland in 1951 and grew up in the neighboring community of Hudson, Ohio. His father, David Frazier, was a chemist. His mother, Peggy Frazier, was a teacher. He graduated with a bachelor of arts degree from Harvard University in 1973. He and his wife, writer Jacqueline Carey, have two children.

You can never be sure of what you'll encounter in one of Frazier's *New Yorker* essays. In one piece, collected in *Dating Your Mom*, for example, Frazier speculates on how the playwright Samuel Beckett might have flown from New York to Chicago as a commercial pilot. In another, in *Nobody Better, Better than Nobody*, he profiles the woman who produces Heloise's Hints etiquette and household comfort. In the title chapter in his book *Coyote v. Acme,* he imagines the Warner Brothers cartoon character Wile E. Coyote writing a consumer complaint letter to Acme Products when one of its devices fails to snag Roadrunner.

In 1982, Frazier and his family moved to Missoula, Montana. He planned to write a novel. Instead, he became curious about his neighbors and began to interview them. The result was *Great Plains,* in which the author visited Lawrence Welk's hometown and Sitting Bull's cabin site. He randomly tracked down figures of the past, and neighbors of the present. He toured one of the two thousand missile silos buried on the plains: "To the eye, it is almost nothing, just one or two acres of ground with a concrete slab in the middle and some posts sticking up behind an eight-foot cyclone fence; but to the imagination it is the end of the world."

Frazier disdains present-tense essays. "God, that's why I love history," he said in a conversation with *Interview.* "If you can't write it in the past tense, then don't write it. Now, everybody writes in the present."

Despite his thorough research, the author doesn't consider himself an expert. "I'm opposed to expertise," he told *Believer* magazine. "For some reason, when I feel I am becoming an expert, I sabotage the whole thing. I mean, I've written about the West but I would never want to think of myself as somebody who writes about the West, as an expert on that subject. The problem is, it's as if you're either going to be an expert or a dilettante, and I don't want to be either."

Frazier certainly used expertise when he wrote about his own family in his book, *Family. Booklist* reviewer Brad Hooper found the account "an effective illustration of the richness of history on the level of ordinary people who are neither kings nor presidents."

Frazier does not tape or write notes when he interviews subjects. He writes his notes afterward and has disciplined himself to recall conversations. His skills as a reporter were put to the test with *On the Rez.* He felt he was being held to the highest of standards, he said in *Publishers Weekly,* because of the convoluted, arcane way full-, half-, and other degrees of the Sioux bloodline at South Dakota's Pine Ridge and other reservations establish not only one's earnings from casino profits but one's standing in the community.

Le War Lance and SuAnne Big Crow are major figures in the book. Lance is a larger-than-life, outrageous yarn spinner whose stories are often true. Big Crow, a high school basketball star who died tragically in an auto accident, is a heroine Frazier couldn't resist—a positive coda to a book headed toward a morose ending. The strength of her character became legend.

"*Great Plains* was about landscapes," the author said in a *Publishers Weekly* interview in 1999. "I had a vision of telephone poles becoming mere dots in the distance. I looked at it with a wide-eyed, hopeful view. *On the Rez* is an attempt to show the native people in that vista looking back."

"I wanted to talk about the question of freedom and the question of heroes," Frazier said in a Powells.com interview with Dave Weich. "I try to do things according to the circumstance of my life, the way you cook according to what's in season. I try to use what's there. I saw in our friendship [with Le War Lance] a way of talking about bigger questions."

On the Rez was a challenge to organize, the author confessed. "The plot of a non-fiction piece is the writer's curiosity, how it proceeds," he explained in an interview with Karl Zimmermann of *The Writer.* "I try and find interesting connections from the point of view of the reader—what he or she is ready for next. I do a lot of revision. I read things over and over. The more writing you do, the more you see how mutable it is."

Frazier did admirably, in the view of Paul Gray in *Time* magazine: "[A]s Frazier serendipitously shuttles his narrative between Pine Ridge visits and snippets of Indian history, a fascinating picture emerges of a people struggling with the consequences of old wrongs and human orneriness."

Frazier returned to the short form for two more collections. *The Fish's Eye* (2002) is about angling. "Frazier's sharp eye and self-implicating wit is at work in these charming but unsentimental pieces," many of them with urban settings. *Gone to New York* (2005) keeps the author in the city—visiting a Holland Tunnel engineer and a typewriter repairman.

As Anthony Pucci summed up in *Library Journal,* "Frazier's varied and quirky essays reflect a blend of keen curiosity, careful observation, and historical accuracy."

Works by the Author

Dating Your Mom (1986), essays
Nobody Better, Better than Nobody (1987), essays
Great Plains (1989)
Family (1994)
Coyote v. Acme (1996), essays
On the Rez (2000)
The Fish's Eye: Essays about Angling and the Outdoors (2002)
Gone to New York: Adventures in the City (2005)

Contributor

They Went: The Art and Craft of Travel Writing (1991)
City Fishing (2002), edited by Jerry Dennis

Editor

The Best American Essays 1997, with Geoffrey C. Ward and Robert Atwan (1997)

Translator

It Happened Like This: Stories and Poems, by Daniil Kharms (1998)

For Further Information

Fish's Eye review, *Publishers Weekly,* March 11, 2002.
Gone to New York review, *Library Journal,* November 15, 2005.
Gray, Paul, "Looking for Lost America; In His Entertaining *On the Rez,* Ian Frazier Recounts the Past and Present of the Oglala Sioux," *Time,* January 24, 2000.
Hall, Gus, "What Is Ian Frazier?" *Interview,* May 1996.

Hooper, Brad, *Family* review, *Booklist,* October 1, 1994.

Ian Frazier entry, Contemporary Authors Online. Reproduced in Biography Resource Center. Farmington Hills, MI: Thomson Gale, 2006. http://galenet.galegroup.com/servlet/BioRC.

Mosle, Sara, *Great Plains* review, *New Republic,* August 7, 1989.

"PW Talks with Ian Frazier," *Publishers Weekly,* December 20, 1999.

Roberts, Jason, "Ian Frazier Interview," *Believer,* September 2004.

Weich, Dave, "Ian Frazier's Heroes," Powells.com. http://www.powells.com/authors/frazier.html (viewed May 30, 2006).

Zimmermann, Karl, "Creative Wanderlust: From New York to Montana, Ian Frazier Turns His Journeys into Literary Gems," *The Writer,* July 2002.

Henry Louis Gates Jr.

History, Investigative Reporting, Memoir

Benchmark Title: *Wonders of the African World*

Keyser, West Virginia

1950–

Courtesy Harvard University

About the Author and the Author's Writing

"What was your name?" Malcom X once asked. "What is your history?"

That's the enormous puzzle Americans of African descent face. It's the reason for the enormous popularity of Alex Haley's *Roots* in 1976 and of Henry Louis Gates Jr.'s documentary television series, *African American Lives,* three decades later.

"Before 1865, when the Civil War ended, most of our ancestors had only one name," said Gates, host of the PBS series that aired during Black History Month in 2006. "That's what the slavery system did. It took away our ancestors' names. It took away their identities." Gates and eight celebrity guests on the program, including T. D. Jakes and Oprah Winfrey set out, with the aid of historians, genealogists, and DNA scientists, to challenge the African diaspora head on, and reestablish links broken by the infamous triangular slave trade of the eighteenth and early nineteenth centuries. The four-part series was Gates's most accessible approach to Americans who are both grappling with the sorriest most shameful? segment of their country's history and looking for a perspective and rationale in a new world of global economics and terrorist politics. Gates followed the series with a how-to book based on Oprah Winfrey's search for family connections. Picking up where Haley's momentum left off, Gates has brought the story to the modern age with the inclusion of sophisticated research techniques and DNA testing.

Henry Louis "Skip" Gates Jr. is America's best-known and most influential humanities professor and a busy writer and editor on subjects ranging from *Uncle Tom's Cabin* author Harriet Beecher Stowe to poet Phillis Wheatley. He was born in Keyser, a Piedmont working-class community in West Virginia, in 1950, the son of Henry Louis and Pauline Augusta Coleman Gates. His father worked as a paper mill loader

120

and telephone company custodian. His mother cleaned houses. At age twelve, when his mother suffered severe depression, Gates pursued a fundamental Baptist faith.

"My mother bred a tremendous amount of self-confidence in my brother and me," Gates told *Observer* interviewer Sean O'Hagan. The future author, scholar, and activist was misdiagnosed as having a psychosomatic ailment at age fourteen when, in fact, he had a hairline fracture. The result was permanent hip damage and the need to use a cane. In the 1960s, he gravitated to the Black Power movement. He devoured the writings of James Baldwin, Ralph Ellison, and Eldridge Cleaver.

Gates graduated summa cum laude and as Scholar of the House in History from Yale University in 1973 with a bachelor of arts degree in history, received a fellowship and earned both his master's and his doctorate in English language and literature from Clare College, University of Cambridge, England, in 1979. The same year, he married Sharon Lynn Adams, a fellow Yale student and campaign worker for Jay Rockefeller; they have two daughters.

Gates worked as a political campaigner, research director, and staff correspondent for *Time* magazine's London Bureau before launching his academic career. He was elected chairman of the Pulitzer Board in 2005. His awards, academic honors, honorary degrees, fellowships, and professional affiliations are so lengthy, they are best viewed on his Harvard Web page (cited in "For Further Information" at the end of the chapter).

Gates floats easily between two worlds in his writing. He is "one of the most powerful academic voices in America," according to *Contemporary Black Biography*. The concentrated prose of *The Signifying Money; Towards a Theory of Afro-American Criticism* is solidly academic, for example, while his television programs are written in a conversational tone. "I adjust my voice depending on the audience I'm reaching, but, really, I don't see any contradiction between the registers," Gates told the *Observer*.

In 1981, a $150,000 MacArthur Foundation "genius grant" afforded Gates the opportunity to unearth and republish Harriet E. Wilson's 1859 *Our Nig*. His scholarly investigation proved the work was not only the first American novel by a black woman, it also came out three decades before anyone had suspected blacks were writing prose. This achievement kicked off the long and impressive body of Gates's work that has followed.

Decrying the lack of works by African Americans in traditional anthologies of American writings, Gates collected many forgotten works in *The Norton Anthology of African American Literature*, which he coedited with Nellie Y. McKay for publication in 1998. In 2006, he was appointed editor in chief for Oxford University Press' Oxford African American Studies Center, which aims to bring materials to a new audience online. In anticipation of an *African American National Biography* from Oxford, Gates and Evelyn Brooks Higginbotham in 2004 compiled the six-hundred-entry *African American Lives*, aimed at students in grades six and up.

Literature is only one of Gates's interests. He coedited with Kwame Anthony Appiah *Africana: The Encyclopedia of the African and African American Experience*, a project envisioned decades before by W.E.B. Du Bois. The 1999 work was revised and expanded in 2003 to contain some four thousand entries.

In 2000, Gates and Cornel West assembled *The African-American Century: How Black Americans Have Shaped Our Country*. It contains profiles of black figures from scholar Du Bois and athlete Jackie Robinson to singer Jessye Norman and aviatrix

Bessie Coleman. Gates profiled other African Americans for the *New Yorker* magazine; a collection of these essays titled *Thirteen Ways of Looking at a Black Man,* published in 1997, includes his interviews with Harry Belafonte, Colin Powell, James Baldwin, and others.

"I'm fascinated with this moment in African American cultural and political and intellectual history," Gates said in a *Booklist* interview. "[W]e're the crossover generation; we're the generation that has benefited more from the opening of American society to affirmative action than any previous generation of African Americans ever possibly could have benefited."

Although sometimes considered an elitist, Gates wrote a 1994 memoir, *Colored People,* which looked at his humble origins. According to *Publishers Weekly's* review, it is an "engrossing narrative of Gates's intellectual, political, sexual and emotional awakening." The author stepped beyond the details of his own life, in his recent PBS documentary, to connect his experiences with that of other blacks in the United States.

In 2005, Gates announced that he would step down as director of Harvard University's W.E.B. Du Bois Institute for Afro-American Research. But Gates shows no signs of reducing his productive examination of the African American experience. In 1999, he articulated one of his many goals to *Publishers Weekly* interviewer Richard Newman: "We're helping to create a new cultural consciousness, one that's pluralistic and diverse."

Works by the Author

Figures in Black: Words, Signs, and the Racial Self (1987)
The Signifying Monkey: Towards a Theory of Afro-American Literary Criticism (1988)
Black Literature and Literary Theory, with Catherine R. Stimpson (1990)
Loose Canons: Notes on the Culture Wars (1992)
Colored People: A Memoir (1994)
Truth or Consequences: Putting Limits on Limits (1994)
Speaking of Race, Speaking of Sex: Hate Speech, Civil Rights, and Civil Liberties (1995)
The Future of the Race, with Cornel West (1996)
Thirteen Ways of Looking at a Black Man (1997)
Afro-American Women Writers (1998)
Wonders of the African World (1999)
The African-American Century: How Black Americans Have Shaped Our Country, with Cornel West (2000)
Back to Africa (2002)
Come Sunday: Photographs by Thomas Roma (2002)
The Trials of Phillis Wheatley: America's First Black Poet and Her Encounters with the Founding Fathers (2003)
America behind the Color Line; Dialogues with African Americans (2004)
Finding Oprah's Roots: Finding Your Own (2007)

Editor

Black is the Color of the Cosmos: Charles T. Davis's Essays on Afro-American Literature and Culture, 1942–1981 (1982)

Our Nig; or, Sketches from the Life of a Free Black, by Harriet E. Wilson (1983)

Black Literature and Literary Theory (1984)

Race, Writing, and Difference (1986)

The Slave's Narrative: Texts and Contexts (1986)

Wole Soyinka: A Bibliography of Primary and Secondary Sources, with James Gibbs and Ketu H. Katrak (1986)

The Classic Slave Narratives (1987)

In the House of Oshugbo: A Collection of Essays on Wole Soyinka (1988)

The Oxford-Schomburg Library of Nineteenth-Century Black Women Writers, 30 vols. (1988), series editor

The Autobiography of an Ex-Colored Man, by James Weldon Johnson (1989)

The Souls of Black Folk, by W.E.B. Du Bois (1989)

Jonah's Gourd Vine, by Zora Neale Hurston (1990)

Mules and Men, by Zora Neale Hurston (1990)

Reading Black, Reading Feminist: A Critical Anthology (1990)

Tell My Horse, by Zora Neale Hurston (1990)

Their Eyes Were Watching God, by Zora Neale Hurston (1990)

Three Classic African-American Novels (1990)

Bearing Witness: Selections from African-American Autobiography in the Twentieth Century (1991)

Black Biography, 1790–1950: A Cumulative Index, with Randall K. Burkett and Nancy Hall Burkett (1991)

The Schomburg Library of Nineteenth-Century Black Women Writers, 10 vols. (1991)

Voodoo Gods of Haiti (1991)

Mulebone: A Comedy of Negro Life, by Langston Hughes and Zora Neale Hurston; coedited with George Bass (1991)

Alice Walker: Critical Perspectives Past and Present, with K. A. Appiah (1993)

Gloria Naylor: Critical Perspectives Past and Present, with K. A. Appiah (1993)

Langston Hughes: Critical Perspectives Past and Present, with K. A. Appiah (1993)

Richard Wright: Critical Perspectives Past and Present, with K. A. Appiah (1993)

Toni Morrison: Critical Perspectives Past and Present, with K. A. Appiah (1993)

Zora Neale Hurston: Critical Perspectives Past and Present, with K. A. Appiah (1993)

The Amistad Chronology of African-American History from 1445–1990 (1993)

Frederick Douglass' Autobiographies (1994)

The Complete Stories of Zora Neale Hurston (1995)

The Dictionary of Global Culture, with Anthony Appiah (1995)

Identities with Anthony Appiah, (1996)

The Norton Anthology of African-American Literature (1996) with Nellie Y. McKay

Ann Petry: Critical Perspectives Past and Present (1997)

Chinua Achebe: Critical Perspectives Past and Present (1997)

Frederick Douglass: Critical Perspectives Past and Present (1997)

Harriet A. Jacobs: Critical Perspectives Past and Present (1997)

Ralph Ellison: Critical Perspectives Past and Present (1997)

Wole Soyinka: Critical Perspectives Past and Present (1997)

The Essential Soyinka: A Reader (1998)

Pioneers of the Black Atlantic: Five Slave Narratives from the Enlightenment, 1772–1815, coeditor (1998)

Black Imagination and the Middle Passage, coeditor (1999)

The Civitas Anthology of African-American Slave Narratives, coeditor (1999)

Wonders of the African World (1999)

Slave Narratives (2000)

Harvard Guide to African-American History (2001)

Schomburg Library of Nineteenth-Century Black Women Writers (2002)

The Bondwoman's Narrative, by Hannah Crafts (2002)

African American Studies: An Introduction to the Key Debates, with Jennifer Burton (2002)

Africana; The Encyclopedia of the African and African-American Experience (2003), 5 vols., with Kwame Anthony Appiah

In the House of Oshugbo: Critical Essays on Wole Soyinka (2003)

Transition 96, with Anthony Appiah (2004)

Transition 97/98, with Anthony Appiah (2004)

African-American Lives, with Evelyn Brooks Higginbotham (2004)

The Annotated Uncle Tom's Cabin, by Harriet Beecher Stowe; coedited with Hollis Robbins (2006)

Television Documentaries

The Image of the Black in the Western Imagination (PBS, 1982)

Wonders of the African World with Henry Louis Gates Jr. (PBS, 1999)

America: Beyond the Colour Line (BBC2, 2003)

African American Lives, executive producer with William R. Grant and Peter W. Kunhardt (PBS, 2006)

For Further Information

African-American Century review, *Publishers Weekly,* October 16, 2000.

Africana review, *Publishers Weekly,* November 1, 1999.

Altschiller, Donald, *Africana* review, *Library Journal,* August 1, 2005.

"Booklist Interview; Henry Louis Gates Jr.," *Booklist,* February 15, 1997.

Colored People review, *Publishers Weekly,* April 18, 1994.

"Definitive 21st Century African American Reference Marks the Start of a New Era in African American Studies," PR Newswire, May 17, 2006.

"Gates to Step Down as African-American Studies Chairman at Harvard," *Black Issues in Higher Education,* May 5, 2005.

"Henry Louis Gates Jr. Elected Chair of Pulitzer Board," *Jet,* June 20, 2005.

Henry Louis Gates Jr. entry, AfricanAmericans.com. http://www.africanamericans.com/HenryLouisGates.htm (viewed May 31, 2006).

Henry Louis Gates Jr. entry, Contemporary Authors Online. Reproduced in Biography Resource Center. Farmington Hills, MI: Thomson Gale, 2006. http://galenet.galegroup.com/servlet/BioRC.

Henry Louis Gates Jr. entry, *Contemporary Black Biography,* Vol. 38, Ashyia Henderson, ed. Detroit, MI: Gale Group, 2003.

Henry Louis Gates Jr. Web page, Harvard University. http://aaas.fas.harvard.edu/faculty/henry_louis_gates_jr/index.html (viewed September 13, 2006).

Henry Louis Gates Jr. Web page, National Endowment for the Humanities. http://www.neh.gov/whoweare/gates/bibliography.html (viewed May 31, 2006).

Newman, Richard, "Henry Louis Gates Jr.," *Publishers Weekly,* June 20, 1994.

O'Hagan, Sean, "The Biggest Brother," *Observer,* July 20, 2003.

Peters, John, *African American Lives* review, *School Library Journal,* August 2004.

Rothstein, Edward, "Digging through the Literary Anthropology of Stowe's Uncle Tom," *New York Times,* October 23, 2006.

Jane Goodall

Environment, Science

Benchmark Title: *The Chimpanzees of Gombe*

London, England

1934–

About the Author and the Author's Writing

When Jane Goodall was a child, her favorite toy was prophetically a stuffed chimp, a gift from her father. "My mother's friends were horrified, because it was quite large," she said in a *New Dimensions* interview. "They said I would get nightmares, but in fact it became my constant childhood companion."

The future author was born in 1934 in London, the daughter of businessman Mortimer Herbert Goodall and his wife, Margaret Myfanwe Joseph Goodall (who wrote under the name Vanne Goodall). Jane's early interest in animals extended to watching the doings of neighborhood cats and dogs. During a visit to a farm, she hid in a chicken house so she could see how a hen laid eggs. This was her first behavioral study. An avid reader at age eleven of Edgar Rice Burroughs's adventure novel *Tarzan of the Apes,* she itched to see the wild species that roamed the wilds of Africa.

After completing her high school studies, Jane began saving her money, and at age twenty-three she traveled to Kenya. She met anthropologist Louis Leakey and became his assistant secretary at the Natural History Museum in Nairobi. She accompanied Louis and his wife, the anthropologist Mary Leakey, to remote Olduvai Gorge to search for fossils.

Dr. Louis Leakey saw links between humans and primates, and at his urging, Goodall accepted a six-month assignment to study the primates at the Gombe Stream Chimpanzee Reserve. Goodall lacked academic training for her new assignment, but she had the determination and stamina to put up with malarial threats, wayward snakes, and scuttling spiders on the shore of Lake Tanganyika. At twenty-six years old, she also had the energy and patience to work her way into the confidence of the chimps. Eventually one elder chimp, David Greybeard, accepted the "white ape" and visited her camp. Day after day, Goodall sat, binoculars in hand, to observe firsthand the chimp's crafting of a primitive tool—a grass reed—to capture ants. Realizing how much there was to be learned, Goodall settled into her research for the long term.

Five years at the reserve gained Goodall enough material for a thesis and to earn her a doctoral degree from Cambridge University. When she accepted her degree, she was only the eighth person in the school's history to have done so without having first completed baccalaureate study. "It is hard to overstate the degree to which Dr. Goodall changed and enriched the field of primatology," suggests the Jane Goodall Institute's Web site.

Goodall documented her early findings in *In the Shadow of Man* and *The Chimpanzees of Gombe*. "I feel very strongly that I was so amazingly lucky to have that incredible opportunity," she said in a conversation with salon.com. "My job now is to save what I love. I seem to have a fairly strong voice and an ability to communicate with most people. And we have to get people's hearts involved."

Goodall's early books, some written with her husband, the nature photographer Hugo van Lawick (they had married in 1964 and had one child), were heavy on scientific details, yet accessible to general readers. After she divorced van Lawick and married Derek Bryceson (a member of Parliament and Tanzania National Parks director) in 1973, she continued to write on her own, and directed herself particularly to younger readers with the "Animal Family" series of books. *The Chimpanzees I Love,* from 2005, typically, is an intense yet accessible summary for middle readers of her adventures at Gombe.

Goodall's love for her subjects is obvious. As Don Lessem observed in *Smithsonian,* "This affection never blurs her scientific focus. Her capacity to be at once sensitive and perceptive is key to Goodall's unique talent and task."

The Jane Goodall Institute for Wildlife Research, Education and Conservation, which Goodall and Genevieve, Princess di San Faustino, set up in California in 1977, works to increase primate habitat conservation through education, training, research, and other activities. The author has periodically recapped her career, as in *Jane Goodall: 40 Years at Gombe,* of which *Library Journal*'s reviewer said, "Her status as a patron saint of chimpanzees seems assured." The book includes anecdotes of her work with chimpanzees and her later work with organizations such as ChimpanZoo.

Goodall has received the Medal of Tanzania, the National Geographic Society's Hubbard Medal, the Kyoto Prize from Japan, and numerous other awards and honorary degrees. In 2002, the United Nations designated her a Messenger of Peace.

The author's more recent work, *Africa in My Blood* (2000), collects letters that afford a chattier, but no less revealing, perspective on her early work. The IMAX film "Jane Goodall's Wild Chimpanzees (2002) presents an overview of her four decades of research and activism. It blends contemporary footage with archival scenes of Gombe.

The naturalist eventually abandoned her field work in Africa for London permanence, although a speaking calendar takes her around the world with great regularity. After her initial fieldwork, Goodall told *Time* in 2001, "my focus changed to protecting chimpanzees and making sure the research continued. Then the focus changed to youth. That was because traveling the world for the conservation message, I found so many young people who had no hope. They thought we'd compromised their future. They were right."

To Goodall, it isn't just about chimpanzees and their behavior. It's about the planet and justice. "The value of a species shouldn't only be determined according to its ecological impact and its commercial value," Goodall said in an *Earth & Sky* interview. "The value of a species is part of our spiritual heritage. It's part of our past, which if we lose it now, our children in future generations may be very sad."

Works by the Author

My Friends, the Wild Chimpanzees, written as Jane van Lawick-Goodall (1967)

The Behaviour of Free-Living Chimpanzees in the Gombe Stream Reserve, written as Jane van Lawick-Goodall (1968)

Innocent Killers, written as Jane van Lawick-Goodall, with Hugo van Lawick, (1970)

Grub the Bush Baby, written as Jane van Lawick-Goodall, (1970), (revised 1972)

In the Shadow of Man, written as Jane van Lawick-Goodall (1971) (revised 1972) as by Jane Goodall; shortened as *Selected from in the Shadow of Man* (1992)

The Chimpanzees of Gombe: Patterns of Behavior (1986)

Through a Window: My Thirty Years with the Chimpanzees of Gombe (1990) reprinted as *Through the Window: Thirty Years with the Chimpanzees of Gombe* (1998)

The Chimpanzee: The Living Link between "Man" and "Beast" (1992)

Visions of Caliban: On Chimpanzees and People, with Dale Peterson (1993)

The Great Apes, with others (1994)

Reason for Hope: A Spiritual Journey, with Philip Berman (1999)

Brutal Kinship, with Michael Nichols (1999)

Jane Goodall—Forty Years at Gombe (1999)

Africa in My Blood: An Autobiography in Letters: The Early Years, edited by Dale Peterson (2000)

Beyond Innocence: An Autobiography in Letters: The Later Years, edited by Dale Peterson (2001)

The Ten Trusts: What We Must Do to Care for the Animals We Love with Marc Bekoff (2005)

Return to Gombe: The Homecoming (2005)

Harvest for Hope: A Guide to Mindful Eating, with Gary McAvoy and Gail Hudson (2005)

The Natural World, with Thomas D. Mangelsen (2007)

For Juvenile Readers

Jane Goodall's Animal World: Chimps (1989)

With Love: Ten Heartwarming Stories of Chimpanzees in the Wild (1994)

My Life with the Chimpanzees (1996)

Dr. White (1999)

The Eagle and the Wren (2000)

The Chimpanzees I Love: Saving Their World and Ours (2001)

Animal Family Series

Baboon Family (1990)

Chimpanzee Family (1990)

Elephant Family (1990)

Giraffe Family (1990)

Hyena Family (1990)
Lion Family (1990)
Wildebeest Family (1990)
Zebra Family (1990)

Contributor

Women in the Wild (1998)

Television Adaptations

Miss Goodall and the Wild Chimpanzees (1965)
Among the Wild Chimpanzees (1984)
Chimps Like Us (1990)
The Gomba Chimpanzees (1990)
The Life and Legend of Jane Goodall (1990)
Nature World (1995), "Fifi's Boys" episode
Animal Zone (1997), "Chimpanzee Diary" episode
People of the Forest: The Chimps of Gombe (1997)
Reason for Hope (1999)
Jane Goodall's Wild Chimpanzees (2002)
When Animals Talk (2005)

For Further Information

"Animal Planet Announces Third Special with Jane Goodall; The Pioneering Primatologist Helps Demystify Animal Communication," PR Newswire, January 13, 2005.

"Born To Be Wild: A Conversation with Jane Goodall," *New Dimensions,* World Broadcasting Network. http://www.newdimensions.org/online-journal/articles/born-to-be-wild.html (viewed June 6, 2006).

"Conversation with the 'Chimpanzee Lady': Jane Goodall on Animals, the Environment and Her Life," *Democracy Now.* http://www.democracynow.org/article.pl?sid=05/11/24/0740243 (viewed June 6, 2006).

Crim, Beth Clewis, *Jane Goodall: 40 Years at Gombe* review, *Library Journal,* January 2000.

Cruickshank, Douglas, "A conversation with Jane Goodall," salon.com, October 27, 1999. http://womenshistory.about.com/gi/dynamic/offsite.htm?zi=1/XJ/Ya&sdn=womenshistory&cdn=education&tm=7&f=22&tt=14&bt=1&bts=1&zu=http%3A//www.salon.com/people/feature/1999/10/27/goodallint/ (viewed September 14, 2007).

Estes, Sally, *Africa in My Blood* review, *Booklist,* March 15, 2000.

Imster, Eleanor, "Everything Is Interconnected," *Earth & Sky* interview. http://www2.earthsky.org/category/humanworld/interviews.php?id=44562 (viewed June 6, 2006).

Jane Goodall entry, Contemporary Authors Online. Reproduced in Biography Resource Center. Farmington Hills, MI: Thomson Gale, 2006. http://galenet.galegroup.com/servlet/BioRC.

Jane Goodall Institute Web site. http://www.janegoodall.org/about-jgi/default.asp (viewed June 6, 2006).

Jane Goodall interview, *U.N. Chronicle*, September-November 2002.

" 'Jane Goodall's Wild Chimpanzees' Swings into California Science Center's IMAX Theater Beginning October 25, 2002; Viewers Will Join the World's Most Famous Female Scientist in Her Revolutionary Studies," PR Newswire, October 10, 2002.

Kephart, Beth, *Beyond Innocence* review, *Book,* September 2001.

Lessem, Don, *Through a Window* review, *Smithsonian,* April 1991.

Peterson, Dale, *Jane Goodall: The Woman Who Redefined Man.* Boston: Houghton Mifflin, 2006.

Rauber, Paul, "People Say That Violence and War Are Inevitable. I Say Rubbish," *Sierra.* http://www.sierraclub.org/sierra/200605/interview.asp (viewed June 6, 2006).

Sachs, Andrea, "Out of Africa; Naturalist Jane Goodall Has Given Up the Bush for the Sake of Her Cause," *Time,* November 12, 2001.

Solomon, Deborah, "The Chimp's Champion," *New York Times Magazine,* July 16, 2006.

Doris Kearns Goodwin

Biography, History, Memoir, Sports

Benchmark Title: *No Ordinary Time*

Rockville Center, New York

1943–

Photo courtesy the author

About the Author and the Author's Writing

What's new to investigate in the life of Abraham Lincoln, certainly the most written about American political figure? Best-selling popular historian Doris Kearns Goodwin had no trouble finding an unexplored angle. She was drawn to Honest Abe because of his charisma—and his being an enigma. If she could travel back in time to visit her hero, "I know, like a good historian, I should ask him how Reconstruction would have been different under his administration," the author said in an interview with Steve Bennett of the *San Antonio Express-News*. "But what I'd most like to say to him is, 'Would you tell me some stories?' "

Lacking such fresh anecdotes, Goodwin took a fresh slant in her 754-page *Team of Rivals: The Political Genius of Abraham Lincoln*, examining the chief executive's genius in appointing William H. Seward as secretary of state, Salmon P. Chase as secretary of treasury, and Edward Bates as attorney general. A mix of Republicans and Democrats, all three were his recent opponents in the 1860 presidential race.

Goodwin assessed Lincoln for *Fortune* interviewer Jia Lynn Yang: "Lincoln had such sensitive antennae. He understood how to share credit and how to shoulder blame.. . . When he was angry. . ., he had this tendency of writing what he called a hot letter. Then he would put it aside, waiting for his emotions to cool down, and never send it."

Doris Helen Kearns was born in Rockville Centre, New York, in 1943, the daughter of bank examiner Michael A. Kearns and Helen Witt Miller Kearns. She grew up on Long Island and attended public high school. When Doris was fourteen, her mother died. Her mother's fondness for reading, the author once said, instilled in her a respect for the power of the written word.

After graduating from Colby College, she interned with the Department of State and the House of Representatives in Washington, D.C. After working in several governmental agencies, she became a special consultant to President Lyndon B. Johnson in 1968, his final year in office, then she went on to teach at Harvard (1969–1972) and eventually worked her way into the media as a political analyst.

In 1975 she married Richard Goodwin, a political consultant, and they raised three sons. She has been a trustee of Wesleyan University, Colby College, and the Robert F. Kennedy Foundation. She has received the Charles Frankel Prize from the National Endowment for the Humanities and the Sara Josepha Hale Award. She resigned as a member of the Pulitzer Prize board in 2002.

When Goodwin had worked with President Johnson, she helped him compile his memoirs; their close association assured she had fresh stories for a biography. "He's still the most formidable, fascinating, frustrating, irritating individual I think I've ever known in my entire life," Goodwin said of Johnson for an Academy of Achievement interview. Three years after LBJ's death, the author published *Lyndon Johnson and the American Dream,* which critics found dug deep into the personal side of the Texan to contrast with his public and political sides. The Vietnam War damaged Johnson's presidency, and probably shortened his life.

Goodwin next delved into the story of Johnson's predecessor, John F. Kennedy, and particularly his Irish-American forebears, in *The Fitzgeralds and the Kennedys,* published in 1987. Her fresh stories came from her husband Richard Goodwin's 150 boxes of material relating to experiences working for the Kennedy "New Frontier" administration. The book presented a revealing picture of patriarch Joseph P. Kennedy Sr.'s manipulations.

Shortly after its publication, writer Lynne McTaggart approached Goodwin's publisher with the challenge that a number of its passages were copied from her work, *Kathleen Kennedy* (1983). McTaggart was acknowledged in footnotes but not in the text. Goodwin blamed it on sloppy note keeping. She then and now uses researchers. Her publisher Simon & Schuster reached a financial settlement with McTaggart and the book was revised. But in 2002, when plagiarism charges arose against military historian Stephen Ambrose, the *Weekly Standard* and the *Los Angeles Times* revealed the McTaggart episode, which had never been publicly disclosed. Goodwin felt some of the sting herself when she charged that author Joe McGinnis swiped from her writing for his Edward Kennedy bio, *The Last Brother* (1993), Thomas L. Jeffers pointed out in *Commentary* in 2002.

In 1995, Goodwin's third presidential book, *No Ordinary Time,* an examination of the relationship of Franklin D. and Eleanor Roosevelt, brought her a Pulitzer Prize. "Confined to a chronology of five years, Goodwin gave taut shape to a small ensemble cast, opening with artful alternations between Franklin and Eleanor Roosevelt on May 10, 1940, while the Nazis are overrunning the Low Countries," writes Thomas Mallon in *Atlantic Monthly*. Against a backdrop of World War II, Goodwin provides a fascinating account of FDR's confrontation with his polio, and Eleanor's confrontation with her husband's dalliance with her personal secretary, Lucy Mercer.

In a change from her insightful presidential biographies that covers Goodwin's own story, the 1997 *Wait till Next Year* is the author's reminiscence about growing up in a family that adored the Brooklyn Dodgers. As a girl of six, she learned to keep box scores of Dodger games so that her father, when he returned home from work, could go over the outcome. He commended her for being a historian. The book was a homer for readers. "Goodwin superbly weaves together the universal and the particular experiences she shared with millions of other war babies and boomers," *Booklist* reviewer Mary Caroll remarked. "And what a great start for life as a historian obsessively following da Bums from 1949 to 1958."

After the uproar over *The Fitzgeralds and the Kennedys,* the author began her opus on Lincoln, *Team of Rivals*; the research alone took a decade. The book charts Lincoln's keen sense of timing, his guidance, his insightful manipulation—and his profound personal tragedy. This was the author's first foray into an earlier century, and a subject with no survivors to interview. Her thoroughness came from investigating not only Lincoln material but also from freshly probing the lives of each of the cabinet members. She unearthed a trove of primary materials.

"They wrote so many letters and kept those extraordinary diaries," she told Edward Morris of BookPage. "I could feel them living day by day, even more intimately than I understood Franklin and Eleanor Roosevelt."

 # Works by the Author

Lyndon Johnson and the American Dream, as by Doris Helen Kearns (1976); as by Doris Kearns Goodwin (1991)

The Fitzgeralds and the Kennedys: An American Saga (1987), revised/corrected edition (2002)

No Ordinary Time: Franklin and Eleanor Roosevelt; the Home Front in World War II (1994)

Wait till Next Year: Recollections of a 50's Girlhood (1997)

Kennedy Weddings: A Family Album, coauthor (1999)

Team of Rivals: The Political Genius of Abraham Lincoln (2005)

Contributor

Telling Lives: The Biographer's Art, edited by Marc Pachter (1979)

For Further Information

Beam, Alex, "Doris Kearns Goodwin's Second Act," *Boston Globe,* October 6, 2005.

Bennett, Steve, "Exploring Lincoln's Unusual Cabinet," *San Antonio Express-News,* May 27, 2006.

Carroll, Mary, *Wait till Next Year* review, *Booklist,* August 1997.

Crain, Caleb, "Rail-Splitting," the *New Yorker*, November 7, 2005.

Doris (Helen) Kearns Goodwin entry, Contemporary Authors Online. Reproduced in Biography Resource Center. Farmington Hills, MI: Thomson Gale, 2006. http://galenet.galegroup.com/servlet/BioRC.

Doris Kearns Goodwin interview, Academy of Achievement, June 28, 1996. http://www.achievement.org/autodoc/page/goo0int-1 (viewed June 6, 2006).

Doris Kearns Goodwin Web site. http://www.doriskearnsgoodwin.com/scroll_about-the-author.pho (viewed June 6, 2006).

Gates, David, "No Ordinary Crime," *Newsweek,* March 18, 2002.

Gewen, Barry, *The Fitzgeralds and the Kennedys* review, *New Leader,* June 1, 1987.

Gray, Paul, "Other People's Words," *Smithsonian,* March 2002.

Jeffers, Thomas L., "Plagiarism High and Low," *Commentary,* October 2002.

Mallon, Thomas, "No Ordinary Tome," *Atlantic Monthly,* November 2005.

Minzesheimer, Bob, "Getting Intimate with Lincoln," *USA Today,* October 19, 2005.

Morris, Edward, "The President's Men," *BookPage.* http://www.bookpage.com/0511bp/doris_kearns_goodwin.html (viewed June 6, 2006).

Noah, Timothy, "Doris Kearns Goodwin, Liar," Slate.com. http://www.slate.com/?id=2061056 (viewed June 6, 2006).

Roberts, Chalmers M., *No Ordinary Time* review, *Washington Monthly,* September 1994.

Shaver, Leslie, "No Ordinary Historian: An Interview with Doris Kearns Goodwin," *Information Outlook,* May 1, 2002. http://www.highbeam.com/doc/1G1-85880887.html (viewed June 6, 2006).

Yang, Jia Lynn, "Lincoln's Genius," *Fortune,* June 12, 2006.

Linda Greenlaw

Adventure, Food, Memoir

Benchmark Title: *The Lobster Chronicles*

Connecticut

1962–

Photo by Anthony Loew

About the Author and the Author's Writing

Guess which of the following was the most exciting moment in Linda Greenlaw's life:

(a) hooking a 635-pound swordfish;

(b) seeing herself portrayed on the big screen by actress Mary Elizabeth Mastrantonio; or

(c) banking a $150,000 advance after her agent auctioned her first memoir.

Greenlaw cherishes all these experiences, but it's (c) that has led her into a new career as a writer.

Greenlaw was minding her own business, more or less, when journalist Sebastian Junger mentioned her in his best-selling adventure tale, *The Perfect Storm*. That book (later turned into a successful motion picture) chronicles the fate of the Gloucester fishing boat *Andrea Gail* on October 28, 1991, when it was caught up in what the National Weather Service called "the perfect storm."

Greenlaw, captain of the sister ship *Hannah Boden,* navigated her vessel and crew to safety, and later provided Junger with technical details about fishing boats. He described her in *The Perfect Storm* as "one of the best captains, period, on the East Coast." Not only was she good, she was the only working female swordfish captain in the entire country. A half-dozen-plus publishers sought rights to her story. She hired an agent, who put *Hungry Ocean* to auction. Published by Hyperion in 1999, the book is a wave-by-wave account of a month on the ocean, hooking and storing 50,000 pounds of fish for market.

Greenlaw was born in 1962 in Connecticut, the daughter of James and Martha Greenlaw. Her father became an information systems manager for the Bath Iron Works in Maine. Her stay-at-home mother raised the four children in Topsham, near Portland, Maine. Linda took to the saltwater, playing along the coast and going out on boat rides as often as she could (despite frequent seasickness). "When other kids got their first 10-speed bicycle, I got my first 10-horsepower outboard," she said in an interview with John Boit in *Christian Science Monitor*.

Greenlaw attended Colby College. After her freshman year, she became summer cook and deckhand on the *Walter Leeman* under Captain Alden Leeman, who encouraged her to become a fisherman. After earning her bachelor of arts degree, she went back to work for Leeman and became the captain in 1986 of his new second boat. Thus began seventeen years as a fisherman.

"Fishermen don't dwell on the fact that they're engaging in the most dangerous profession in the country or maybe even the world," the author said in an interview with Dave Weich for Powells.com. "The biggest evidence of the danger is the price of insurance for a boat. But every time you set out, you don't dwell on *what if what if what if* and *remember so and so*. If you did that, you'd never leave the dock."

In *Hungry Ocean,* Greenlaw shows her skill with details, including the electronic "temperature bird" that gauges the likelihood of finding the fish she needs at a given depth. "After all the gut-wrenching work, there is the suspense of not knowing what the market price of the catch will be," notes John Kenny in *Library Journal*.

Her account is part *Tugboat Annie,* part *Caine Mutiny*. She deals with racism, insubordination, injured egos, long hours, sophisticated equipment, and dinnertime hunger. Her account, in the view of Carolyn Fry in *Geographical*, "paints a colourful picture of the characters who have made fishing their trade and gives an honest insight into what a tough, gritty life it is. As the *Hannah Boden* draws back safely into Gloucester, with her hold full of fish, we join in the crew's collective sigh of relief."

In 1997, Greenlaw left the sea and her career as a fisherman to settle in Isle au Haut, a small community off the northern New England coast. She bought a lobster boat, the thirty-five-foot *Mattie Belle*. As she wrote in her next book, *The Lobster Chronicles,* she decided she needed a crew member, a sternman, preferably a steady, sympathetic one. "[T]he ideal person would be someone who knew less than I did, who would not tell me what to do aboard my own boat, and would do as he was told without question, no matter how ridiculous. Someone with discretion. The natural candidate was a retiree with ties to the Island going back four generations. My father."

The author by now had a fine store of sailor stories, and she put them to paper for *All Fishermen Are Liars* in 2004. "These yarns enchant even as they remind us that angling, no matter where experienced, offers the sort of escape into simplicity and adventure that explains why it is both a way of life and one of America's most popular sporting activities," Jim Casada said in *Library Journal*.

In 2005, Greenlaw collaborated with her mother—a cancer survivor—for a food and cookbook, *Recipes from a Very Small Island*. Although she again had a reliable second mate aboard to compile "Salmon Cakes with Peas and Mint Sauce" and "Lemon-Glazed Blueberry Cupcakes," Greenlaw on her Web site said writing remained something of a chore. "I am very disciplined about my writing. I treat it like I do fishing, in that it's a job, it's hard work, and I have to do it every day to do it well."

Greenlaw says she had to learn the craft of writing just as she did swordfishing and lobstering. "I don't outline," she explained in *The Writer*. "I feel that with both my books I had a natural outline.. . . I'm writing for the most part about my own experience, because they're very personal books." Ultimately, "Writing is harder for me than fishing."

 Works by the Author

The Hungry Ocean: A Swordboat Captain's Journey (1999)
The Lobster Chronicles (2002)
All Fishermen Are Liars: True Tales from the Dry Dock Bar (2004)
Recipes from a Very Small Island, with Martha Greenlaw (2005)

Fiction

Slipknot (2007)

For Further Information

Boit, John, "Master of Her Ship and Her Destiny," *Christian Science Monitor,* August 19, 1999.

Casada, Jim, *All Fisherman Are Liars* review, *Library Journal,* August 2004.

Flynn, Louise Jarvis, "Catch and Don't Release," *New York Times,* June 27, 2004.

Forrest, Rachel, "Small Island, Simple Life, Delicious Food," *Portsmouth Herald.* http://www.seacoastonline.com/2005news/08032005/it/55893.htm   (viewed May 31, 2006).

Fry, Carolyn, *The Hungry Ocean* review, *Geographical,* May 2000.

Greenlaw, Linda, "How I Write," *The Writer,* December 2002.

Kenny, John, *The Hungry Ocean* review, *Library Journal,* May 15, 1999.

Linda Greenlaw entry, *Authors and Artists for Young Adults,* Vol. 47. Detroit, MI: Gale Group, 2003.

Linda Greenlaw entry, Contemporary Authors Online. Reproduced in Biography Resource Center. Farmington Hills, MI: Thomson Gale, 2006. http://galenet.galegroup.com/servlet/BioRC.

Linda Greenlaw Web site. http://www.fishingwithlinda.net (viewed May 31, 2006).

Maryles, Daisy, "Gone Fishin'," *Publishers Weekly*, September 6, 1999.

Maryles, Daisy, and Dick Donahu, "Clawing Its Way up the List," *Publishers Weekly,* July 22, 2002.

"Perfect Storm, 'The Story behind the Movie,' " *LawBuzz.* http://www.lawbuzz.com/movies/perfect_storm/perfect_storm.htm (viewed May 31, 2006).

Sutton, Judith, *Recipes from a Very Small Island* review, *Library Journal,* June 15, 2005.

Weich, Dave, "True Tales from Linda Greenlaw," Powells.com. http://www.powells.com/authors/greenlaw.html (viewed May 1, 2006).

Lee Gutkind

Health, Investigative Reporting, Memoir, Science

Benchmark Title: *Many Sleepless Nights*

Pittsburgh, Pennsylvania

1945–

Photo by C. E. Mitchell

About the Author and the Author's Writing

If the genre of creative nonfiction has a guru, a godfather, a drill sergeant, it's Lee Gutkind, frequent workshop leader, founder of the journal *Creative Nonfiction* (1993), and author of many books, including *The Art of Creative Nonfiction* (1997).

The term "creative nonfiction"—which Gutkind does not claim to have coined—generally refers to the use of fiction writing techniques such as perspective or narrative to tell a factual story. The author is sometimes a participant in the story. Truman Capote's *In True Blood* fits the category, as does Annie Dillard's *Tinker at Pilgrim Creek* and George Plimpton's *Paper Lion*.

On his Web site, Gutkind says that in the early 1970s few dared attempt creative, or literary, nonfiction. "By daring, I mean people who would venture into and experience other lifestyles and then write about it in a literary way. And by literary I mean by using scenes, dialogue, description, first person points of view, all the tools that are available to the fiction writers while consistently attempting to be truthful and factual."

Of course, Gutkind was not afraid, and he quickly embraced creative nonfiction in his own writing.

Born in Pittsburgh, Pennsylvania, in 1945, he was the son of merchant Jack R. Gutkind and Mollie Osgood Gutkind. He served in the U.S. Coast Guard from 1962 to 1963, then attended the University of Pittsburgh, where he received a bachelor of arts degree cum laude in1968. He married twice, and divorced twice.

Gutkind worked briefly as a clown with Ringling Brothers Circus before he went to work for Osgood-McCullough as an account executive and copywriter from 1965 to 1967. He spent two more years with another agency before he became an instructor at Community College of Allegheny County (1969–1972). During this period, he also taught at University of Pittsburgh and gradually worked his way up to a professorship in 1990. In fact, he helped establish a creative writing major at the school. He has received the American Heart Association, Blakeslee Award for Outstanding Achievement in Scientific Journalism and a Carnegie Mellon University award for creative writing. Chatham College in 2004 awarded him an honorary doctorate of letters. He launched PodLit, a biweekly podcast, in 2006.

Gutkind's first book, *Bike Fever,* describes a cross-country trek by motorcycle. His second, the beginning of a prolonged period probing medical and health topics, was *One Children's Place.* It is about two years he spent interviewing patients, nurses, parents, and physicians in a pediatric care facility, Children's Hospital in Pittsburgh. *Stuck in Time,* a sequel, looked at children caught up in the mental health system. The author next profiled a Manhattan animal doctor in *The Veterinarian's Touch* before immersing himself in Major League Baseball to learn what it's like to be an umpire for a year for *The Best Seat in Baseball, but You Have to Stand.*

The author has said he was influenced in his writing by Ernest Hemingway, Gay Talese, John McPhee, Janet Malcolm, James Baldwin, and Robert Frost.

His works exhibit what Gutkind calls an inner point of view. "The nonfiction writer spends so much time with the people about whom he or she is writing that they can visualize the world through the eyes of their character, their inner point of view," he said in a *Smart Writers Journal* interview.

"Employing a journalist's 'fly on the wall' strengths of observations . . . Gutkind recounts hospital procedures—from organ transplants to therapy for child abuse cases—and chronicles a procession of tragedies and triumphs," Genevieve Stuttaford said in a *Publishers Weekly* review of *One Children's Place.*

In 1996, Gutkind published *Creative Nonfiction,* a how-to for aspiring journalists, essayists, historians, and biographers that urged putting out information in a dramatic, although always accurate, manner—heavy on detail, employing dialogue as much as possible. He established the Creative Nonfiction Foundation and established and continues to edit its quarterly journal, *Creative Nonfiction.* In 1997, *Vanity Fair* writer James Wolcott labeled Gutkind the "godfather behind creative nonfiction." Gutkind was so incensed by the revelation that James Frey's best-selling *A Million Little Pieces,* about an addict's efforts to rehabilitate himself, included fabrications, he devoted an entire special issue of his journal in 2006 to the subject, including the necessity of truth.

"I relish the memories and experiences of the journeys I have taken, and although I dreamed of being a novelist, I have never looked back or stopped to rethink my decision to write nonfiction. I continue my total involvement in the creative-nonfiction experience—an odyssey that has consumed me and monumentally enriched my life," the author said in *The Writer.*

Commenting on *Stuck in Time,* a *Publishers Weekly*'s reviewer said, "The author of this sympathetic, eye-opening study, urges a radical change from permanent institution-based care to a flexible system of highly individualized child and family therapy."

"Readers benefit from the realization that the process of learning is both humorous and traumatic. Gutkind recounts his past experiences with clarity and wisdom," Morris Hounion said of *Forever Fat* in a *Library Journal* review.

In an Inkwell Newswatch interview, Gutkind said that anyone looking for a career as a writer should be prepared to work hard. "By this I mean: Plenty of research, plenty of thought and analysis, and an ongoing onslaught of revision. There is tremendous pain and essential honesty involved in recognizing that the first 26 drafts aren't quite there and to keep improving the content."

 Works by the Author

Bike Fever (1973)

The Best Seat in Baseball, but You Have to Stand: The Game as Umpires See It (1975)

The People of Penn's Woods West (1984)

Many Sleepless Nights; The World of Organ Transplantation (1988)

One Children's Place: A Profile of Pediatric Medicine (1990)

Stuck in Time: The Tragedy of Childhood Mental Illness (1993)

Creative Nonfiction: How to Live It and Write It (1996)

The Art of Creative Nonfiction: Writing and Selling the Literature of Reality (1997)

An Unspoken Art: Profiles of Veterinary Life (1998)

The Veterinarian's Touch: Profiles of Life among the Animals (1998)

Forever Fat: Essays by the Godfather (2003)

Almost Human: Making Robots Think (2007)

Editor

Our Roots Grow Deeper than We Know (1985)

Surviving Crisis: Twenty Prominent Authors Write about Events That Shaped Their Lives (1997)

Connecting: Twenty Prominent Authors Write about the Relationships That Shape Our Lives (1998)

The Essayist at Work: Profiles of Creative Nonfiction Writers (1998)

A View from the Divide: Creative Nonfiction on Health and Science (1998)

Lessons in Persuasion: Creative Nonfiction/Pittsburgh Connections (2000)

Healing: Twenty Prominent Authors Write about Inspirational Moments of Achieving Health and Gaining Insight (2001)

On Nature: Great Writers on the Great Outdoors (2002)

In Fact: The Best of Creative Nonfiction, and contributor (2004)

Rage and Reconciliation: Inspiring a Health Care Revolution, and contributor (2005)

Our Roots Are Deep with Passion: Creative Nonfiction by Italian American Writers, with Joanna Clapps Herman (2006)

Unofficial Mexico: Essays from Both Sides of the Divide (2007)

The Best Creative Nonfiction vol. 1 (2007)

Film Adaptation

A Place Just Right (1980)

Fiction

God's Helicopter (1983)

For Further Information

Gutkind, Lee, "Creative Nonfiction: Immersion in Real Life Creates Some of Our Most Memorable Writing," *The Writer,* May 2004.

Halls, Kelly Milner, "Lee Gutkind, a Man of 'Real' Experience," *Smart Writers Journal,* January 2003. http://www.smartwriters.com/index.2ts?page=swjjanuary2003 (viewed June 6, 2006).

Hounion, Morris, *Forever Fat* review, *Library Journal,* December 2003.

Jesus, Diego X., and Mark London, "New New Journalism: Lee Gutkind Gets Royally Real," *Inkwell Newswatch.* http://www.fwointl.com/artman/publish/article_695.shtml (viewed June 6, 2006).

Lee Gutkind entry, Contemporary Authors Online. Reproduced in Biography Resource Center. Farmington Hills, MI: Thomson Gale, 2006. http://galenet.galegroup.com/servlet/BioRC.

Lee Gutkind Web page. http://www.leegutkind.com (viewed June 24, 2006).

PodLit Web page. http://www.creativenonfiction.org/thejournal/podlit.htm (viewed September 12, 2007).

Rogers, Michael, *The Best Seat in Baseball* review, *Library Journal,* June 1, 1999.

Stankovics, Denise J., *Connecting* review, *Library Journal,* April 15, 1998.

Stuck in Time review, *Publishers Weekly*, May 24, 1993.

Stuttaford, Genevieve, *One Children's Place* review, *Publishers Weekly,* May 18, 1990.

Unspoken Art review, *Publishers Weekly,* June 12, 1997.

Wagner, Kathryn, "An Interview with the Godfather: A Conversation with Lee Gutkind," *Adirondack Review.* http://adirondackreview.homestead.com/interviewgutkind.html (viewed June 6, 2006).

David Halberstam

Biography, History, Investigative Reporting, Sports

Benchmark Title: *The Powers That Be*

New York City, New York

1934–2007

Photo by Porter Gifford, Scribner, 2001

About the Author and the Author's Writing

David Halberstam was interested in power. The power of national leaders to conduct war. The power of basketball players to win games. The power of political aspirants to secure office. The power of baseball pitchers to strike out batters.

David Halberstam himself had the power of the printed word and had enjoyed popularity with readers for four decades. The theme of power can be seen in his work.

The author was born in New York City in 1934, not far from Yankee Stadium. He was the son of surgeon Charles A. Halberstam and Blanche Levy Halberstam, a teacher. In 1955, David received a bachelor of arts degree from Harvard University. He has been twice married and has a daughter by his second wife, Jean Sandness Butler.

Halberstam began his journalism career as a cub reporter with the *Daily Times Leader* in West Point, Missouri, working there from 1955 to 1956. "What I learned there (and this is applicable to you as you start your careers)," he told students at the Columbia University Graduate School of Journalism in 2005, when accepting the Columbia Journalism Award, "was this: I learned how to learn. I learned how to talk to people, how to track the politics of the town, and how to find someone on each story who could teach me things."

Halberstam joined the *Nashville Tennessean* for four years and covered sit-ins to protest the growing Vietnam War. In 1960, he became a staff writer for the *New York Times*, which gave him the opportunity to experience Vietnam firsthand. He was a correspondent in the Congo, Poland, and France as well. From 1967 to 1971, he worked as a contributing editor with *Harper's*. After that time, he wrote more than twenty books and uncounted freelance articles.

Halberstam's reports from Vietnam frequently veered radically from official government news releases on particular battles or events, and they earned him a Pulitzer Prize for international reporting. In his 1972 book, *The Best and the Brightest,* which was critical of the Kennedy and Johnson administrations, he compiled the history of American involvement in that Southeast Asian country. His next book, *The Powers That Be,* examined CBS television, *Time* magazine, and the *Washington Post* and *Los Angeles Times;* it offered a critical and scathing assessment of media involvement in national policy.

In *The Breaks of the Game* (1981), Halberstam began his sports odyssey with an investigative-style report on basketball. *The Amateurs* (1985) was about a men's scull team. In 1988, the author returned to the world of politics and wrapped up what many see as a trilogy about strength in America, this time looking at industrial giants Ford and Nissan. The first of these books, *The Reckoning,* reveals "the apparent inability of the richest nation the world has ever seen to maintain the ethic and attitudes that created its strength," Robert Cumberford wrote in *Washington Monthly.*

With *The Summer of '49* Halberstam was back into professional sports, looking at the 1949 American League baseball pennant race between the Red Sox and the Yankees. He spotlighted Ted Williams of Boston and Joe DiMaggio of New York. Although critics praised that book, some took issue with the author's later release, *October 1964,* a book about the 1964 battle between the Yankees and Cardinals. In particular, sport news reviewer Steve Gietschier took issue with Halberstam's suggestion that "the Yankees lost the 1964 World Series because parsimony and racism did them in and that the Cardinals emerged triumphant because they were a racially harmonious team with wise veteran leaders." But then, who ever wins a sports argument?

Moving indoors, Halberstam's *Playing for Keeps* profiles Michael Jordan, the Chicago Bull dynamo who retired in 1998. His assignment was made all the more difficult by Jordan's refusal to grant an interview. That was no problem in *The Teammates,* in which Halberstam followed Boston Red Sox veterans Dom DiMaggio and Johnny Pesky on a motor trip to Florida—this was just after September 11, 2001, and air travel was a major problem—to visit Ted Williams, who was in his eighties and suffering heart disease.

"It's a baseball book, but it's not a baseball book. It's a book about aging and friendship. Ultimately it's a book about love," the author said in an interview with Dave Weich of Powells.com. The sports enthusiast switched playing fields to profile New England Patriots coach Bill Belichick in *The Education of a Coach.*

Ever lured to the White House, Halberstam examined American foreign policy as shaped in the post–Cold War era by the Bush and Clinton administrations in *War in a Time of Peace*—his insights so perceptive, that his book, which was on press when the attacks of 2001 set America back on its heels, mentions in passing the specter of worldwide terrorism. America's relationship with other nations comes as much from within as without, he said. "Foreign policy is not a pure, abstract science," he said in an interview with *Christian Science Monitor.* "It is something that is first and foremost derivative of domestic political equations."

Tackling the national tragedy of September 11, Halberstam wrote more narrowly and personally in *Firehouse*—about members of Engine 40, Ladder 35, which lost a dozen firefighters in the World Trade Center. He reconstructs the day's events and, from interviews with friends and families, profiles the lost men, ably conveying "the sheer chaos at the site and, above all, the immensity of the loss for fellow firefighters," according to a *Publishers Weekly* reviewer.

In his writing career, Halberstam enjoyed a comfortable rhythm. "It's a wonderful privileged life, you know, being a book writer," he said in Brian Lamb's *Booknotes* interview in 1993. "I go out and I write books. I live a good life, and I can have both my private life and my professional life in a way that an anchorman on television or a superstar television reporter can't. There's a wonderful level of privacy and a wonderful level of engagement in the society. I have the best of both worlds."

Halberstam died in a car accident outside San Francisco in April 2007. He was seventy-three years old.

 # Works by the Author

The Making of a Quagmire: America and Vietnam During the Kennedy Era (1965)
The Unfinished Odyssey of Robert Kennedy (1969)
Ho (1971)
The Best and the Brightest (1972)
The Powers That Be (1979)
The Breaks of the Game (1981)
On a Very Hot Day (1984)
The Amateurs: The Story of Four Young Men and Their Quest for an Olympic Gold Medal (1985)
The Reckoning (1986)
The Summer of '49 (1989)
The Next Century (1991)
The Fifties (1993)
October 1964 (1994)
The Children (1998)
Playing for Keeps: Michael Jordan and the World He Made (1999)
New York September 11: As Seen by Magnum Photographers (2001)
War in a Time of Peace: Bush, Clinton, and the Generals (2001)
Firehouse (2002)
Teammates (2003)
The Education of a Coach (2005)
Breaking News: How the Associated Press Has Covered War, Peace, and Everything Else, with Associated Press (2007)
The Coldest Winter: America and the Korean War (2007)

Editor

Great Stories of Heroism and Adventure, by Stephen Crane (1967)
The Best American Sports Writing: 1991 (1991)
The Kansas Century: One Hundred Years of Championship Jayhawk Basketball (1997)
The Best American Sports Writing of the Century (1999)
Defining a Nation: Our America and the Sources of Its Strength (2003)

Contributor

West Point: Two Centuries of Honor and Tradition, with Stephen Ambrose, William F. Buckley, Arthur Miller, George Plimpton, and others (2002)

Fiction

The Noblest Roman (1961)
One Very Hot Day (1968)

For Further Information

Campbell, Kim, "The American Habit of Napping Just before a War Starts," *Christian Science Monitor,* November 8, 2001.

Cumberford, Robert, *The Reckoning* review, *Washington Monthly,* January 1987.

"David Halberstam—Columbia Journalism Award—May 18, 2005," Columbia University Graduate School of Journalism. http://www.journalism.columbia.edu/cs/ContentServer?childpagename=Journalism%2FJRN_News_C%2FJRNNewsDetail&c=JRN_News_C&p=null&pagename=JRN%2FWrapper&cid=1175295298410 (viewed September 14, 2007).

David Halberstam entry, Contemporary Authors Online. Reproduced in Biography Resource Center. Farmington Hills, MI: Thomson Gale, 2006. http://galenet.galegroup.com/servlet/BioRC.

David Halberstam interview, salon.com. http://www.salon.com/books/int/1999/02/18int.html (viewed June 7, 2006).

Fifties review, *Library Journal,* May 15, 1998.

Firehouse review, *Publishers Weekly,* May 27, 2002.

Gietschier, Steve, *October 1964* review, *Sporting News,* September 12, 1994.

Grossman, Lev, "Homers of the Homer: America's Three Savviest Baseball Scholars Weigh in on Our National Pastime. And It's Still Only a Game," *Time,* May 19, 2003.

Hirshberg, Charles, "Fenway Friends: The Lives of Four Old Red Sox, and a Tribute to the Dying Ted Williams, Produce a Literary Home Run," *Sports Illustrated,* August 11, 2003.

Lamb, Brian, "The Fifties by David Halberstam," *Booknotes,* July 11, 1993. http://www.booknotes.org/Transcript/?ProgramID=1157 (viewed June 7, 2006).

Maxymuk, John, *The Education of a Coach* review, *Library Journal,* Oct. 15, 2005.

Teachout, Terry, *War in a Time of Peace* review," *Book,* November-December 2001.

Weich, Dave, "David Halberstam's Hit Streak Continues," Powells.com. http://www.powells.com/authors/halberstam.html (viewed June 7, 2006).

Zibart, Eve, "Halberstam Rediscovers Our Nation's Peaceful Warriors," *BookPage,* March 1998. http://.www.bookpage.com/9803bp/davidhalberstam.html (viewed June 7, 2006).

Pete Hamill

Investigative Reporting, Memoir

Benchmark Title: *Downtown: My Manhattan*

Brooklyn, New York

1935–

About the Author and the Author's Writing

Master of the snappy lead and the succinct quote, champion of the sympathetic victim and challenger of the deceitful crook—Pete Hamill is the consummate tabloid newspaper columnist. And he's a renowned editor and novelist as well.

Hamill was born in Brooklyn, New York, in 1935, the first of seven offspring of Irish immigrants William and Anne Devlin Hamill. When he was sixteen, he left Catholic school to work as a laborer at the Brooklyn Navy Yard. Later, while he served with the U.S. Navy, he completed requirements for a high school diploma. After completing his service, he attended Mexico City College under the G.I. Bill to study painting and writing. He later took courses at Pratt Institute.

Hamill's writing career is varied. He worked as a graphic designer until the *New York Post* hired him as a reporter in 1960. As a correspondent, he covered Vietnam, Nicaragua, Lebanon, and Northern Ireland, and he reported on everything from brutal killings to ravaging fires to World Series baseball games. In addition, he became a columnist for that daily as well as the *New York Daily News, New York Newsday, Village Voice, New York* magazine, and *Esquire.* He is a Distinguished Writer in Residence at New York University.

Hamill's writing career has concentrated mostly on editorial work and reportage for the news media. At different times in his life, he has served as editor-in-chief of the *Post* and the *Daily News,* in both cases leaving under volatile circumstances (in 1991 and 1998, respectively). "They just don't get it," he said of the *Daily News. Editor & Publisher,* in relating the former-editor's speech at an Investigative Reporters & Editors meeting in New Orleans, quoted Hamill further as saying, "what readers want . . . is not entertainment but solid reporting that gives them an understanding of their communities and the world." He was particularly critical of the emphasis on celebrity gossip and the myopic business reporting before that year's savings and loan scandal. Hamill later returned to the paper as a columnist, and he provided text for the 2001 book *New York Exposed: Photographs from the Daily News.*

The author loves New York and has explored its every angle and curve in his newspaper columns—some of which are reprinted in two collections—and in several of his books. *Downtown: My Manhattan* (2004) received wide praise. In a PBS interview, Hamill said he often visited Manhattan when growing up in Brooklyn. "There was a message that the city whispered to its people and to people from all over the United States. 'Come here, everything is possible.' Now, that's a seductive sound. It's a seductive whisper."

On the brighter side, Hamill's twin interests of art and Mexico merged in the illustrated book *Diego Rivera* (2002), about Mexico's well-known muralist. On the darker side, Hamill wrote about the September 11, 2001, terrorist attack on the World Trade Center. (He was on his way to a meeting at the Museum of the City of New York at 8:50 A.M. when the first airplane struck.) Yet he saw the city's strength that day and after. "The city's character was what I had thought it always was," he said in a *New York Voices* interview. "A fairly tough, sometimes rude, city of people who have come from all kids of backgrounds, and all parts of the world, and created this alloy, out of all these mixtures. And that's a pretty tough alloy.. . . I was thrilled by the way New Yorkers reacted to the worst single calamity in their history."

Keenly sensitive to ethnicity—perhaps because of his parents' blue-collar immigrant status—Hamill in his biography of singer Frank Sinatra keyed in on the performer's creation of the "first urban sound," giving voice to, in his case, Italian immigrants, but singing for all, as the author told *East Hampton Star*'s Julia C. Mead.

Hamill has married twice. His union with Ramona Negron ended in divorce. They had two daughters. He married journalist Fukiko Aoki in 1987. They live in Manhattan and Cuernavaca, Mexico.

The author's memoir *A Drinking Life*, which remained on the *New York Times* bestseller list for a third of a year, recounts his Brooklyn childhood years with a hard-drinking father in a hot, oppressive tenement apartment and living with taunts about his tattered clothing when he attended elite Regis High School. In the book, "We feel the powerful pull of the neighborhood, the need to fit in and be one of the guys. We watch stickball games that never end, argue the merits of a black man playing for the Dodgers, listen to great music and spend glorious summer days at Coney Island," *American Journalism Review*'s Robert Borsellino noted in a review.

Hamill's second career has been writing novels, including *Snow in August* (published in 1997) and more recently *Loving Women* (2003), as well as scripts for motion pictures and television programs. In all, he has authored more than twenty book-length works, along with editing and contributing to others.

Works by the Author

Irrational Ravings (1971)

Fighters (1978)

A Drinking Life: A Memoir (1994)

Tools as Art: The Hechinger Collection (1995)

Piecework: Writings on Men and Women, Fools and Heroes, Lost Cities, Vanished Friends, Small Pleasures, Large Calamities, and How the Weather Was (1996)

Times Square Gym (1996)

News Is a Verb: Journalism at the End of the Twentieth Century (1998)

Why Sinatra Matters (1998)

Diego Rivera (1999)
Downtown: My Manhattan (2004)
New York: City of Islands (2007)

Editor

Subway Series Reader (2000)
New York Exposed: Photographs from the Daily News (2001)

Contributor

New York: City of Islands (1998)
American Perspectives: The Bill of Rights (2000)
Brooklyn Noir, edited by Tim McLoughlin (2004)

Fiction

A Killing for Christ (1968)
The Gift (1973)
Flesh and Blood (1977)
Dirty Laundry (1978)
The Deadly Piece (1979)
The Invisible City: A New York Sketchbook (1980)
The Guns of Heaven (1983)
Loving Women: A Novel of the Fifties (1990)
Tokyo Sketches (1993)
Snow in August (1997)
Forever (2002)
Loving Women (2003)
The Gift (2005)
The Guns of Heaven (2006)
North River (2007)

For Further Information

Blackwell, Gordon, *Why Sinatra Matters* review, *Library Journal,* March 15, 2000.

Borsellino, Robert, *A Drinking Life* review, *American Journalism Review,* April 1994.

Downtown review, *Publishers Weekly,* January 3, 2005.

Hoffman, Bill, "We Win! N.Y. Post Scribe's Inside Look at How Tab Staff Drove off Hated Owner," *American Journalism Review,* May 1993.

Hooper, Brad, *New York: City of Islands* review, *Booklist,* December 1, 1998.

"Interview with Pete Hamill," *New York Voices.* http://www.thirteen.org/nyvoices/transcripts/hamill.html (viewed June 7, 2006).

McEvoy, Dermot Kavanagh, "Pete Hamill: The Journalist and Novelist Has Written a Memoir of His Drinking Life," *Publishers Weekly,* January 10, 1994.

Mead, Julia C., "Pete Hamill: A Tough Guy Considers Celebrity," *East Hampton Star,* November 26, 1998.

Patterson, Troy, "He Loves N.Y.: Veteran Journalist-Cum-Novelist Pete Hamill Composes a Fantastical Ode to the City That Never Sleeps," *Entertainment Weekly,* January 10, 2003.

Pete Hamill entry, Contemporary Authors Online. Reproduced in Biography Resource Center. Farmington Hills, MI: Thomson Gale, 2006. http://galenet.galegroup.com/servlet/BioRC.

Pete Hamill interview, WNET. http://www.pbs.org/wnet/newyork/series/interview/hamill.html (viewed June 7, 2006).

Pete Hamill Web site. http://www.petehamill.com/bio.html (viewed June 7, 2006).

Porter, Bruce, "Pete Hamill: Wakes Up the *Daily News,*" *Columbia Journalism Review,* May-June 1997.

Robins, Wayne, " 'Daily News' Tabs Pete Hamill for Return," *Editor & Publisher,* March 12, 2001.

Rogers, Michael, "New York Exposed: Photographs from the *Daily News,*" *Library Journal,* December 2001.

Stein, M. I., "Pete Hamill Raises Hell about Newspaper Publishers," *Editor & Publisher,* June 20, 1998.

Stephen W. Hawking

History, Science

Benchmark Title: *A Brief History of Time*

Oxford, England

1942–

About the Author and the Author's Writing

A wheelchair-bound scientist with severe limitations on mobility wouldn't seem the best prospect as a future best-selling author. But Hawking's *A Brief Theory of Time,* a history of the exploration of physics, published in 1988, was on the *New York Times* best-seller list for more than a year and sold 10 million copies. But that was just the beginning for this astonishing individual. He went on to write a dozen books and edit a dozen others.

Stephen William Hawking was born in 1942 in Oxford, England, where his parents had sought temporary safety during the German bombing of North London. He was born, propitiously, on the 300th anniversary of Galileo's death. By 1950, the Hawking family had settled in St. Albans. Stephen attended St. Albans School, then pursued the study of physics at University College, Oxford. His postgraduate studies were in cosmology at Cambridge University, Cambridge, where he obtained his Ph.D. and was a research fellow. He also worked as a professorial fellow at the Gonville and Caius College.

In 1973, he left the Institute of Astronomy to join the Department of Applied Mathematics and Theoretical Physics at University College, Oxford. Six years later, he accepted the Lucasian Professorship of Mathematics at the University of Cambridge, a position held by Isaac Newton, in the 1660s. Hawking has since received a dozen honorary degrees, the designation Commander of the British Empire in 1982 and a Companion of Honor designation in 1989. He is a Fellow of the Royal Society and a member of the United States National Academy of Sciences. Among his scientific accomplishments are theories regarding general relativity and the emission of radiation from black holes.

The day he decided to pursue cosmology, Hawking solidified his fascination with things gigantic and puny. The General Theory of Relativity, as set forth by Albert Einstein, dealt with large matters, and Hawking himself would eventually unite that work with his own theory of small matters—black holes, or singularities, points of mass in space so dense, even light cannot escape—to establish a continuum in explaining the universe.

Hawking told interviewer David Cherniack of the Canadian Broadcasting Corporation that theoretical physicists "construct mathematical models which represent the universe. And which describe the results of observations. And we can say a model is a good model if it has few arbitrary elements, and if it describes all the observations so far made. And if it predicts the result of new observations correctly."

When he was beginning his doctoral studies in 1962, and soon after Hawking met Jane Wilde, a language teacher, the scientist was diagnosed with amyotrophic lateral sclerosis (ALS), or Lou Gehrig's disease. Before the ALS had set in severely, Hawking proposed to Wilde. As he told biographer Kitty Ferguson for *Stephen Hawking: Quest for a Theory of Everything,* "the engagement changed my life. It made me determined to live." They married in 1965 and eventually reared three children. Hawking was not expected to live even three more years, but he became an anomaly. The disease eventually affected all of his body movement except for his heart and lungs. He has survived more than four decades. The couple later divorced, and the physicist married his longtime private nurse, Elaine Mason, in 1995.

Hawking has become a poster child for those with disabilities. He has shown clearly that physical limitations don't necessarily stifle the intellect—or the sense of humor. He admires Marilyn Monroe and told Benford, of *Reason* magazine, "She's wonderful. Cosmological. I wanted to put a picture of her in my latest book, as a celestial object."

Pneumonia and an emergency tracheotomy in 1985 destroyed Hawking's ability to speak naturally. Specialists developed for him a means of communication using slight finger movement and a computer keypad that allows him to produce text or to speak through a synthesizer. ("Please excuse my American accent," he joked to interviewer Gregory Benford.) He glides in an electric wheelchair; his associates find that his maneuvers with the vehicle at times convey his mood.

Hawking's work naturally raises issues of science versus faith. For example, he argues that space-time has no boundary, no beginning, and thus there was no biblical creation. Much of Hawking's work appears in the scientific press, but the author also strives to explain the complicated in his popular science books. *A Brief History of Time* was not an easy one for the lay reader to digest, and he followed it with others that delved deeper into space and time, such as *The Universe in a Nutshell* (2001) or, less deeply, in the case of *A Briefer Theory of Time* (2005). In *God Created the Integers* (2005), Hawking returned to an early interest in mathematics, and he gave a nod to classic scientists when he edited a series of books by Copernicus, Kepler, and others. (Hawking appeared with actors portraying two of his favorite scientists, Einstein and Newton, in a 1993 episode of the syndicated television series *Star Trek: The Next Generation.*)

Even scientific theories evolve. Hawking in 2004 at the International Conference of General Relativity and Gravitation in Dublin said that he had been wrong about black holes. He said he had determined that black holes "do not forever annihilate all traces of what falls into them," according to a report in *Time.*

Outfitted with a speech synthesizer that is linked to a computer, Hawking is able to speak fifteen words a minute and save material to computer disc. "Using this system," he said on his Web site, "I have written a book and dozens of scientific papers. I have also given many scientific and popular talks." Using another computer program called Equalizer, which is sophisticated enough to produce scientific formulas, he is able to manipulate a screen cursor and select and print words to a body of text.

The physicist's work requires utmost patience, and in Hawking's case, sheer bravado against his affliction. As he related to interviewer Alok Jha for the *Guardian,* "It is no good getting furious if you get stuck. What I do is keep thinking about the problem but work on something else. Sometimes it is years before I see the way forward. In the case of information loss and black holes, it was 29 years."

 # Works by the Author

A Brief History of Time: From the Big Bang to Black Holes (1988), revised and expanded (1998), expanded as *The Illustrated A Brief History of Time* (1996)

Black Holes and Baby Universes and Other Essays (1993)

Life Works (1994)

The Cambridge Lectures (1996)

The Nature of Space and Time, with Roger Penrose (1996)

The Universe in a Nutshell (2001)

The Future of Spacetime, with Kip S. Thorne, Igor Novkiov, Timothy Ferris, and Alan Lightman (2002)

On the Shoulders of Giants: The Great Works of Physics and Astronomy (2002)

The Theory of Everything: The Origin and Fate of the Universe (2002), expanded as *The Illustrated Theory of Everything* (2003)

Three Hundred Years of Gravitation, edited by Werner Israel (2003)

A Briefer History of Time, with Leonard Mlodinow (2005)

God Created the Integers: *The Mathematical Breakthroughs That Changed History* (2005)

Editor

The Large Scale Structure of Space-Time, as S. W. Hawking with G. F. R. Ellis (1973)

General Relativity: An Einstein Centenary Survey, as S. W. Hawking with Werner Israel (1979)

Superspace and Supergravity: Proceedings of the Nuffield Workshop, Cambridge, June 16–July 12, 1980, as S. W. Hawking with M. Rocek (1981)

The Very Early Universe: Proceedings of the Nuffield Workshop, Cambridge, 21 June to 8 July 1982, as S. W. Hawking with G. W. Gibbons and S. T. C. Siklos (1983)

Supersymmetry and Its Applications: Superstrings, Anomalies, and Supergravity: Proceedings of a Workshop Supported by the Ralph Smith and Nuffield Foundations, Cambridge, 23 June to 14 July 1985, as S. W. Hawking with G. W. Gibbons and P. K. Townsend (1986)

Three Hundred Years of Gravitation, as S. W. Hawking with Werner Israel (1987)

The Formation and Evolution of Cosmic Strings; Proceedings of a Workshop supported by the SERC and held in Cambridge 3–7 July 1989, as S. W. Hawking with G. W. Gibbons and T. Vachaspati (1990)

On the Revolutions of Heavenly Spheres, by Nicolaus Copernicus (2004)
Selections from the Principle of Relativity, by Albert Einstein (2004)
Dialogues Concerning Two New Sciences, by Galileo Galilei (2005)
Harmonies of the World, by Johannes Kepler (2005)
Principia, by Isaac Newton (2005)

Contributor

The Large, the Small and the Human Mind, edited by Roger Penrose (2000)

For Young Adults

George's Secret Key to the Universe, with Lucy Hawking (2007)

Television Adaptations

A Brief History of Time (1992, documentary)
Stephen Hawking's Universe (PBS, 1997)

For Further Information

Appignanesi, Richard, editor *Introducing Stephen Hawking.* Cambridge, England: Icon Books, 1995.

Benford, Gregory, "Leaping the Abyss: Stephen Hawking on Black Holes, Unified Field Theory, and Marilyn Monroe," *Reason,* April 2002.

"Descent I," *Star Trek: The Episode Guide.* http://sttng.epiguides.info/?ID=326 (viewed May 11, 2006).

Ferguson, Kitty, *Stephen Hawking: Quest for a Theory of Everything.* New York: Bantam, 1992.

Filkin, David, *Stephen Hawking's Universe: The Cosmos Explained.* New York: Bantam, 1998.

Jerome, Richard, "Of a Mind to Marry: Physicist Stephen Hawking Pops the Most Cosmic Question of All to His Nurse," *People Weekly,* August 7, 1995.

Jha, Alok, "Return of the Time Lord," *The Guardian,* September 27, 2005. http://www.guardian.co.uk/g2/story/0,3604,1578947,00.html (viewed September 16, 2007).

Lemonick, Michael D., "Hawking Cries Uncle: The Famous Physicist Admits He Was Wrong about Black Holes — and Pays Off a Long-Standing Wager," *Time,* August 2, 2004.

Stephen Hawking biography, "About Stephen—A Brief History of Mine," Stephen Hawking Web page. http://www.hawking.org.uk/about/aindex.html (viewed September 16, 2007).

Stephen Hawking entry, Contemporary Authors Online, Gale, 2006. Reproduced in Biography Resource Center. Farmington Hills, MI: Thomson Gale, 2006. http://galenet.galegroup.com/servlet/BioRC.

Stephen Hawking entry, *Scientists: Their Lives and Works,* 7 vols. Online Edition. U*X*L, 2004. Reproduced in Biography Resource Center. Farmington Hills, MI: Thomson Gale, 2006. http://galenet.galegroup.com/servlet/BioRC.

Stephen Hawking interview, David Cherniack Films Interview transcript, Canadian Broadcasting Corp., 1985. http://www.psyclops.com/hawking/resources/cherniack.html (viewed May 7, 2005).

"Stephen Hawking: Star turn," BBC News. http://news.bbc.co.uk/1/hi/in_depth/uk/2000/newsmakers/1609172.stm (viewed September 16, 2007).

Stephen Hawking Web site. http://www.hawking.org.uk (viewed March 19, 2007).

Stone, Gene, *A Brief History of Time Reader's Companion.* New York: Bantam, 1992.

William Least Heat-Moon

Memoir, Outdoors, Travel

Benchmark Title: *Blue Highways*

Kansas City, Missouri

1939–

About the Author and the Author's Writing

William Least Heat-Moon could be described as a literary ferret. He travels routes direct and meandering. He sniffs out places fascinating and mundane. He encounters people, simple and complex. And he writes passionately about them all.

The author was born William Trogdon, the son of Ralph G. Trogdon and Maurine Davis Trogdon, in Kansas City, Missouri, in 1939. His father, a lawyer, was part Osage and he adopted the name Heat Moon from Sioux tradition. Trogdon called his oldest son, William's older brother, Little Heat Moon. And William became Least Heat Moon. The names were for private use, but at the completion of his first book the author decided to use his Native American name so readers would immediately know this work was not coming strictly from a white viewpoint. (The hyphen came later, after some called him Mr. Moon.)

William earned four degrees from the University of Missouri at Columbia: a bachelor of arts degree in literature in 1961, a master's degree in arts in 1962, a doctorate in 1973 and a bachelor of arts degree in photojournalism in 1978. He served in the U.S. Navy from 1964 to 1965. From 1965 to 1968, he taught English at Stephens College in Missouri, then again in 1972 and 1978. He lectured at the University of Missouri School of Journalism from 1984 to 1987. The author's first marriage ended in divorce. His second wife, Linda Keown, is a teacher.

Heat-Moon was on a fairly comfortable academic path in 1978 when his ten-year marriage fell apart; then enrollment was so low that his spring teaching position was eliminated. With John Steinbeck's book *Travels with Charley* fresh in his mind, he assembled necessary goods in his Ford Econoline (which he called "Ghost Dancing") and set out on a meander toward the East Coast, seeking to relieve what he described in *Blue Highways* as "a nearly desperate sense of isolation and a growing suspicion that I lived in an alien land."

That book, named for the narrower highways shown on maps—the blue highways—depicted a range of individuals, from a cop-turned-monk to reservation-bound Native Americans, who have maintained a level of independence in an increasingly homogenized culture. Four years in the writing, it came out in 1982 and was on the best seller list for nearly a year.

155

"I like the digressive kind of traveling, where there's not a particular, set goal," he told Jonathan Miles of salon.com. "Sometimes I may set a goal for a trip, not really caring if I get there or not but knowing, as I try, that a lot of good things will happen —interesting things."

Heat-Moon has admitted to a fondness for unusually named places such as Liberty Bond (in Washington State), or Dime Box (in Texas). "Some of it is just the sheer love of eccentricism. But some names seem to be capsule histories of what's happened in a place, once you know why the name is there," the author told Powells.com interviewer Dave Weich.

The fascination with place names continues in the author's third book, *River-Horse*, in which he abandons roads for waterways but accomplishes much the same. On this journey, he has at different times seven companions—six males, one female—whom he renders into a composite character Pilotus. Heat-Moon told Weich he did this to provide these friends a degree of anonymity and also an emotional link for the reader. Asserting that his mission was different in *River-Horse*, he said he felt himself more akin to nineteenth-century river travelers. He was strongly interested in the relationship of the river to people and communities alongside them, and therefore the profiles of individuals he encountered were briefer.

Between these books, Heat-Moon dug deeply into the men and women and past and present of Chase County, Kansas, an acknowledgment of the spirit of Henry David Thoreau who in *Walden* said, "I have traveled widely in Concord." It took him six years to research and two years to write *PrairyErth*, carefully assembling his portrait of the explorations of Zebulon Pike and the land losses of the Kansas (Kaw) Indians. "Heat-Moon writes of a feminist rancher who hires women primarily, of a farm couple swept aloft by a tornado, of abolitionists who wanted slaves free but not equal," *Publishers Weekly* noted in 1991. "He talks to conservationists and coyote hunters, excerpts pioneer diaries and recreates the 1931 airplane crash that killed football hero Knute Rockne."

"Writing about travel is for me a natural form in that one of the passions I've known in my life is travel," the author said in an *Artful Dodge* interview. "For me to attach writing to this passion, and to draw off of it and use it as a form, as a motif, seems not only perfectly natural for me, but something I think is particularly significant for others. After all, everybody here—red, black, white, yellow—all of us came from the other side, from the other hemisphere. We're all the sons and daughters of travelers."

Works by the Author

Blue Highways: A Journey into America (1982)
PrairyErth (1991)
This Land Is Your Land: Across America by Air (1997)
River-Horse: The Logbook of a Boat across America (1999)
Columbus in the Americas (2002)

Contributor

The Red Couch: A Portrait of America, with Kevin Clarke and Horst Wackerbarth (1984)
Three Essays (1993)
Lewis & Clark: An Illustrated History (1997)

For Further Information

Alexander, Carolyn, *River Horse* review, *Library Journal,* September 1, 2000.

"Conversation with William Least Heat-Moon," *Artful Dodge.* http://www. wooster.edu/ArtfulDodge/interviews/heat-moon.htm (viewed June 13, 2006).

Jones, Malcolm, *River Horse* review, *Newsweek,* November 15, 1999.

Miles, Jonathan, "Road scholar," salon.com. http://www.salon.com/books/int/1999/12/09/moon (viewed June 13, 2006).

PrairyErth review, *Publishers Weekly,* August 16, 1991.

Weich, Dave, "William Least Heat-Moon: Participatory Armchair Rivering," Powells.com. http://www.powells.com/authors/leastheatmoon.html (viewed June 13, 2006).

William Least Heat-Moon entry, *Authors and Artists for Young Adults*, Vol. 66. Farmington Hills, Mich.: Thomson Gale, 2005.

Williamson, Norma B., *Blue Highways* review, *National Review,* May 14, 1983.

James Herriot

History, Memoir, Travel

Benchmark Title: *All Creatures Great and Small*

Sunderland, County Tyne and Wear, England

1916–1995

About the Author and the Author's Writing

James Herriot's first book opens with the unexpected scene of a young veterinarian flat on a cobbled barn floor, his arm extended into a cow's uterus. Creeping numbness threatened his grip as he helped birth a stubborn calf. "With every straining effort from the cow the pressure became almost unbearable, then she would relax and I would push the rope another inch. I wondered how long I would be able to keep this up," we read in *If Only They Could Talk.* "If I didn't snare that jaw soon I would never get the calf away. I groaned, set my teeth and reached forward again."

Herriot's book was nearly as reluctant to find an audience as that newborn bovine. It was several years in creation; dissatisfied with early efforts, the author forced himself to learn the craft of writing. It was not until an American publisher, St. Martin's, packaged his first and second books and retitled them *All Creatures Great and Small* (taken from a line of a hymn), that they gained attention—a lot of attention.

James Herriot was actually James Alfred "Alf" Wight, born in 1916 in the Roker area of Sunderland, a small town in County Tyne and Wear, England. His father, James Henry Wight, was an orchestra leader who often provided accompaniment to silent movies; his mother, Hannah Bell Wight, was a singer. He grew up in Glasgow, Scotland, and was often taken for Scot because of his accent. He attended Glasgow Veterinary College, received his degree in 1938, and qualified as a veterinary surgeon in 1939.

The next year, Wight interviewed with Donald Sinclair, a vet in Thirsk, a village in North Yorkshire, and joined the practice. Except for service with the Royal Air Force during World War II, Wight remained in the Yorkshires for the rest of his life. He married a local woman, Joan Catherine Danbury, in 1941; they had two children.

In the 1960s, his wife encouraged him to compose his memoirs; and he did. *If Only They Could Talk* came out in 1970. It had only modest sales, but he continued with a sequel, *It Shouldn't Happen to a Vet.* Publication of the two books in the United States under the title *All Creatures Great and Small,* as mentioned, found an enormous readership. Wight ultimately went on to write six sequels and several other story or travel books, all populated with richly depicted characters, details of a calmly timeless countryside. At the same time, Herriot included his own wartime experiences with the Royal Air Force and ultimately began to chronicle a declining agrarian economy.

Herriot's partner Sinclair was Siegfried Farnon in the books. His personality and Herriot's were exact opposites—creating both tension and humor. Sinclair's younger brother Brian was the spirited-if-hapless Tristan. The village Thirsk became Darrowby. And his office and home, No. 23 Kirkgate, he called Skeldale House. The author said it was considered unethical for a professional veterinary to advertise. Thus he changed these names and his own. The name James Herriot was based on that of a Birmingham soccer player he saw on television.

The author was surprised by the eventual success of his books. "I was dumb-founded by the reaction to that first book, absolutely dumbfounded," he is quoted on the jamesherriot.org Web site, from a 1981 *Daily Mail* interview. "The most I had hoped for was that someone would publish it and a few people quite enjoy reading it."

On the other hand, he wasn't surprised that his characters and their adventures developed a following. "My stories are not just funny animal tales," he explained to journalist Arturo E. Gonzalez Jr. for *Saturday Review*. "They're about tough pioneering days and hard-bitten old farmers. Because they come from pioneering stock themselves, the Americans saw that at once."

Columnist Mary Ann Grossmann in the *Chicago Tribune* found in Herriot's books "a glow of decency that makes people want to be better humans. I guess we'd call it spirituality these days, this profound belief of Herriot's that humans are linked to all animals, whether they be the calves he helped birth or pampered pets like Tricki Woo, Mrs. Pumphrey's lovable but overfed Pekinese."

Herriot squeezed writing into available hours. It reached a point, after one motion picture and one television series, that he spent more time responding to requests for autographs than tending to patients. In 1979, the author received the Order of the British Empire. In turn, the Humane Society of America established its James Herriot Award in his honor.

His creative name-changing and his richly detailed stories had many readers wondering if Herriot's writings were truth or imagination. His son Jim Wight set the record straight: "The vast majority of these stories were based upon real characters and real incidents," he told interviewer N. Glenn Perett. "I should know—I knew the people and I remember many of the incidents." Herriot was more creative, his son said, with children's books about cats and a dog that only barked once.

Successful though he was with the books, Wight remained Wight, not Herriot, professionally, meeting his obligations to animals. "If a farmer has a sick cow, they don't want Charles Dickens turning up; they want a good vet. And that's what I've tried to be," the author told *People Weekly* in 1995.

More than a decade separated the initial memoirs and the last, *Every Living Thing,* which recounts all of Herriot's latest activities plus those of Calum Buchanan, who by then had joined the practice. Although veterinary medicine had made considerable progress during this time, Herriot's telling of an ill-fated attempt to secure semen from a reluctant bull (to be used in artificial insemination) proved an apt bookend to his earlier experience with the cow.

Wight left his veterinary practice in 1988. In 1995, he died of prostate cancer at his home in Thirlby, near Thirsk. Skeldale House is today the World of James Herriot, a small museum that opened in 1999 (two years after the still-active practice had moved to other premises) and is devoted to the veterinary sciences and the Dales of the 1940s. It greets thousands of tourists annually.

 ## Works by the Author

If Only They Could Talk (Great Britain, 1970)

All Creatures Great and Small (United States, 1972), includes *If Only They Could Talk* and *It Shouldn't Happen to a Vet*

It Shouldn't Happen to a Vet (Great Britain, 1972)

Let Sleeping Vets Lie (Great Britain 1973)

All Things Bright and Beautiful (United States, 1974), includes *Let Sleeping Vets Lie* and *Vet in Harness*

Vet in Harness (Great Britain, 1974)

Vets Might Fly (Great Britain, 1976)

All Things Wise and Wonderful (United States, 1977), includes *Vets Might Fly* and *Vet in a Spin*

Vet in a Spin (Great Britain, 1977)

Animals Tame and Wild, with others (1979), reprinted as *Animal Stories: Tame and Wild* (1985)

James Herriot's Yorkshire: A Guided Tour with the Beloved Veterinarian through the Land of "All Creatures Great" and "Each and Every Living Thing" (1979)

The Lord God Made Them All (1981)

Selected Works (1982)

The Best of James Herriot (1983), expanded as *The Best of James Herriot: Favorite Memories of a Country Vet,* with additional materials from *Reader's Digest* editors (1998)

James Herriot's Dog Stories (1986)

Collected James Herriot, Vol. 1 (1989)

Every Living Thing (1992)

The James Herriot Collection (1992)

The James Herriot Story Book (1992)

James Herriot's Cat Stories (1994)

Seven Yorkshire Tales (1995)

James Herriot's Favorite Dog Stories (1996)

James Herriot's Animal Stories (1997)

James Herriot's Yorkshire Stories (1997)

James Herriot's Yorkshire Revisited (1999)

For Younger Readers

Moses the Kitten (1984)

Only One Woof (1985)

The Christmas Day Kitten (1986)

Bonny's Big Day (1987)

Blossom Comes Home (1988)

The Market Square Dog (1990)
Oscar, Cat-about-Town (1990)
Smudge, the Little Lost Lamb (1991)
Smudge's Day Out (1991)
James Herriot's Treasury for Children (1992)
James Herriot's Yorkshire Village: A Pop-up Book (1995)

Film and Television Adaptations

All Creatures Great and Small (EMI, 1974)
It Shouldn't Happen to a Vet (1975)
All Creatures Great and Small (BBC television, series 1978–1980; Christmas specials, 1983, 1985, 1990; series 1988–1990)

For Further Information

Gonzalez, Arturo F. Jr., "James Herriot," *Saturday Review*, May/June 1986.

Grossman, Mary Ann, "Writer Warmly Detailed Bond between People, Animals," *Chicago Tribune,* March 8, 1995.

"James Alfred Wight OBE," obituary, Thirsk and Sowerby, North Yorkshire Web site. http://www.thirsk.org/uk/herriot1.html (viewed June 13, 2006).

James Herriot entry, Contemporary Authors Online. Reproduced in Biography Resource Center. Farmington Hills, MI: Thomson Gale, 2006. http://galenet.galegroup.com/servlet/BioRC.

James Herriot obituary, James Herriot Web site. http://www.jamesherriot.org/ob.php (viewed September 16, 2007).

Perrett, N. Glenn, "An Interview with Jim Wight." Amorak and Friends Web site. http://www.amorak.net/ArticlesAnInterviewWithJimWight.html   (viewed June 13, 2006).

"Small Wonders: James Herriot Wrote Rural England Alive," *People Weekly,* March 13, 1995.

Wight, Jim, *The Real James Herriot: A Memoir of My Father.* New York: Ballantine, 2001.

World of James Herriot Web site. http://www.worldofjamesherriot.org/ (viewed September 16, 2007).

John Hersey

Adventure, Biography, History, Investigative Reporting

Benchmark Title: *Hiroshima*

Tientsin, China

1914–1994

About the Author and the Author's Writing

It was a story so powerful, the *New Yorker* devoted an unprecedented entire issue —August 31, 1946—to printing it. Copies immediately sold out, and it was then issued as a book. It was a story so compelling, it became a staple on high school and college reading lists. It was a story so important, it has never been out of print.

Titled simply "Hiroshima," journalist John Hersey began his report: "At exactly fifteen minutes past eight in the morning, on August 6, 1945, Japanese time, at the moment when the atomic bomb flashed above Hiroshima, Miss Toshiko Sasaki, a clerk in the personnel department of the East Asia Tin Works, had just sat down at her place in the plant office and was turning her head to speak to the girl at the next desk." Dr. Masakazu Fujii was reading the newspaper. Mrs. Hatsuyo Nakamura was watching construction work outside her window. Hersey relates the experiences of these and three other individuals who survived the bombing that brought an abrupt end to World War II. Without political, tactical, or moral interpretation, Hersey simply and boldly put out the facts.

Hersey was born in China in 1914, the son of Young Men's Christian Association–sponsored missionaries Roscoe M. Hersey and Grace Baird Hersey. He attended English-language schools in China and had the opportunity to see a lot of the native population and countryside while making sojourns with his parents. When Hersey was seven, his father became ill, and the family returned to New York. While he quickly assimilated, his childhood experience would give him an outsider's edge in future years as a war correspondent. He entered Yale in 1932 and wrote for the *Yale Daily News*. He completed degree requirements in 1936 and spent a year at Clare College at Cambridge University in England.

Hersey was twice married. His marriage to Frances Ann Cannon ended in divorce in 1950. He married Barbara Day Addams Kaufman in 1958. He had four children by the first marriage, one by the second.

After working as an assistant to Nobel Prize–winning novelist Sinclair Lewis, he joined *Time* magazine, where he was assigned to Chungking, China, to report on the stirrings of war in the Pacific. In 1942, Hersey returned to New York to write *Men on Bataan,* a report based on interviews, archival research, and his own experience of

General Douglas MacArthur and the American troops in Asia. The book was praised for its even-handedness—it included a little negative along with the positive—and was in what would become a familiar blend of characterization and personal experience highlighting an historical event. *Into the Valley: A Skirmish of the Marines* (1943), Hersey's portrayal of U.S. forces' assault on an airbase at Guadalcanal Island, was in large part reported from his own experiences with the soldiers.

Feeling somewhat confined by reportage and the nonfiction genre, Hersey turned to fiction. For his first novel, *A Bell for Adano,* he made up a town in Sicily after the departure of the Fascists. The book, about a civil servant's efforts to install a new bell in a small town's tower, raised questions about the meaning of democracy, stability, and heroism. It inspired a stage play and a motion picture and won Hersey the Pulitzer Prize in 1945.

Hiroshima, Hersey's next work and his most acclaimed, "struck a chord with a huge number of Americans," observed literary critic Patrick B. Sharp, "providing us with a unique and powerful example of how narrative structures arise to make sense out of new technologies. Using the 'wasteland' imagery of literary modernism, Hersey encapsulated for his American audience the horror of the atomic bomb with a familiar framework."

Bruce Bliven in *New Republic* called the book "one of the great classics of the war." Four decades later (1985), Hersey wrote "Hiroshima: The Aftermath" for the *New Yorker* to relate what had become of the survivors depicted in his book. The material became a new chapter in subsequent printings of *Hiroshima.*

Hersey returned to fiction for *The Wall* (published in 1950), a story of the Holocaust as revealed in goings on in the Warsaw ghetto. The setting is vividly portrayed because Hersey was there during the war. This work, too, inspired a stage play and a motion picture. In 1985, Hersey revisited his childhood world in the novel, *The Call: An American Missionary in China.*

The author continued to write for the *New Yorker*, as well as other periodicals, alternating nonfiction and fiction the rest of his life. He taught writing at Yale University and the American Academy in Rome. He belonged to the Authors League of America and the American Academy of Arts and Letters.

Hersey died in Key West, Florida, in 1993. "The passions he described as the essence of the arts burned in him," *New York Times* columnist Anthony Lewis eulogized, "but he contained them with a restraint that was almost unearthly. To be in his presence was to be in an oasis of gentleness, good humor, kindness, quiet pleasure in others. And yet one sensed underneath, in John, a pain suffered: perhaps personal, or perhaps the pain of knowing so much about man's inhumanity to man."

Works by the Author

Men on Bataan (1942)
Into the Valley: A Skirmish of the Marines (1943)
Hiroshima (1946), reissued as *Hiroshima: A New Edition with a Final Chapter Written Forty Years after the Explosion* (1985)
Here to Stay: Studies on Human Tenacity (1965)
The Algiers Motel Incident (1968)
A Letter to the Alumni (1970)

The President (1975)
Aspects of the Presidency: Truman and Ford in Office (1980)
Blues (1987)
Life Sketches (1989)

Contributor

Robert Capa (1969)

Editor

Ralph Ellison: A Collection of Critical Essays (1973)
The Writer's Craft (1974)

Fiction

A Bell for Adano (1946)
The Wall (1950)
The Marmot Drive (1953)
A Single Pebble (1956)
The War Lover (1959)
The Child Buyer (1960)
White Lotus (1965)
Too Far to Walk (1966)
Under the Eye of the Storm (1967)
The Conspiracy (1972)
My Petition for More Space (1974)
The Walnut Door (1977)
The Call: An American Missionary in China (1985)
Fling and Other Stories (1990)
Antonietta (1991)
Key West Tales (1994), stories

Film, Stage, and Television Adaptations

A Bell for Adano (1944), stage adaptation by Paul Osborn
A Bell for Adano (1945), motion picture
The Wall (1960), stage adaptation by Millard Lampell
The War Lover (1962), motion picture
The Child Buyer (1964), stage adaptation by Paul Shyre
The Wall (1982), CBS television

For Further Information

Bliven, Bruce, *Hiroshima* review, *New Republic,* September 9, 1946.
" 'Hiroshima' by John Hersey" in the *New Yorker* Web page. http://www. herseyhiroshima.com/ (viewed June 13, 2006).

John Hersey biography. http://jhhs.d2314.org/AboutJH/biography.html (viewed June 13, 2006).

John Hersey entry, *Authors and Artists for Young Adults*, Vol. 29. Detroit: Gale Group, 1999.

Lewis, Anthony, "As Others Saw Him," in "A Life in Writing: John Hersey, 1914–1993" by Felicia Kaplan, *Yale Alumni Magazine*, October 1993.

Sharp, Patrick B., "From Yellow Peril to Japanese Wasteland: John Hersey's 'Hiroshima'," *Twentieth Century Literature*, Winter 2000.

Vidal, Gore, "Here to Stay: Studies in Human Tenacity Review," *New York Review of Books,* February 1963.

Widmer, Kingsley, "American Apocalypse: Notes on the Bomb and the Failure of Imagination," in *The Forties: Fiction, Poetry, Drama*. Everett/Edwards, 1969.

Seymour M. Hersh

Adventure, Biography, Investigative Reporting

Benchmark Title: *My Lai Four*

Chicago, Illinois

1937–

About the Author and the Author's Writing

Journalist Seymour M. Hersh is the undisputed pit bull of American journalism. No feints will distract him from the scent. No shaking will loosen his jaws once clamped onto a target. He is fearless, tenacious, and persistent—exactly what an investigative reporter needs to be.

Hersh and his twin brother, Alan, who became a physicist, were born in Chicago in 1937. Their parents, immigrants from Poland and Lithuania, lived in Hyde Park and spoke Yiddish to dry-cleaning customers at their South Side business. Seymour idled his way through the University of Chicago as a history major. After working briefly for Walgreens, he enrolled in the University of Chicago Law School. Poor grades sent him back to the drugstore counter, then to City News Bureau, where he visited his share of crime scenes and learned the rudiments of reporting. He worked for a suburban newspaper; then in 1962, he joined United Press International. He was assigned to South Dakota. It was so quiet in the town of Pierre that Hersh, who was already a fan of the writing of Carl Sandburg and Arthur Schlesinger Jr., began to scan the war reporting of David Halberstam in the *New York Times* and the investigative pieces in *Harper's, Atlantic Monthly*, and the *New Republic*.

After a year, Hersh moved to the Associated Press (AP), which in 1965 sent him to cover the Pentagon in Washington, D.C. There he encountered another influence on his writing: muckraker I. F. Stone. AP placed Hersh in its special investigative section. But when an editor softened a story he wrote about biological and chemical weapons, Hersh quit AP, took the story to *New Republic,* and became press secretary for Eugene McCarthy's presidential campaign. Still itching to do more investigative work, Hersh returned to writing. In the autumn of 1969, he followed up a tip from a fellow reporter, and discovered that the U.S. Army had brought a young lieutenant, William L. Calley Jr., to court martial for killing civilians.

Hersh had the story of the year—but no major newspaper wanted it. He turned to an old friend, David Obst, who accepted it for his left-leaning *Dispatch News Service.* Thirty-six papers ran the article. "The one thing I had going for me was that I had actually interviewed Lieutenant William Calley . . . —he didn't confess, but he told me he thought he had higher authority for what he did. I realized that this was going to be a big story and a long story," Hersh told Amy Tübke-Davidson in a *New Yorker* interview.

The My Lai story brought Hersh a Pulitzer Prize; he wrote books both about the massacre and about the military's attempts to cover it up. In 1972, the *New York Times* hired Hersh as an investigative reporter at a time when the *Washington Post*'s Bob Woodward and Carl Bernstein were scooping everyone else, including the *Times,* on Watergate. Although he didn't quite catch up with Woodward and Bernstein, Hersh shined at the *Times,* covering clandestine CIA activities, among other things.

In 1975, Hersh and his wife, Elizabeth Sarah Klein, relocated to New York. While she attended medical school, he turned his investigative skills onto the corporate world, producing with Jeff Gerth a three-part probe of Gulf + Western Industries. G+W executives—as did others before and since—complained of Hersh's ruthless, often threatening, interview techniques.

Hersh left the *Times* in 1978 and spent four years researching and writing *The Price of Power,* an indictment of Henry Kissinger, secretary of state for President Richard Nixon during the Vietnam years. Many consider it the writer's best book.

Two decades later, he published his take on the John F. Kennedy presidency, and particularly his relationship with actress Marilyn Monroe. *The Dark Side of Camelot* (published in 1997), was controversial from the start. Challengers asserted that material in papers to which Hersh had access—and which quickly proved to be fabrications —nevertheless made their way into the book. Some suggested his zeal in pursuit of an angle overrode his usual penchant for corroboration and accuracy.

"Hersh, of course, is no ordinary reporter," in the view of John J. Miller in *National Review.* "Over the past 30 years, he has won just about every journalism award there is.. . . His articles and books are full of revelations. In the first *New Yorker* piece he wrote after September 11, for instance, he reported that an unmanned aircraft had a clear shot to kill Mullah Omar on the first night of the bombing [of Iraq]—but that a military lawyer forbade the attack."

Hersh has continued to report on national affairs during the second Iraq war. Foreign Affairs reviewer Lawrence D. Freedman praised the writer's *Chain of Command: The Road from 9/11 to Abu Ghraib* (2004) for exposing the scandal at the prisoner camp: "His brilliance lies in his tenacity and readiness to expose the failings of government." That critic couldn't help but add, "His flaw lies in his suspension of critical judgment when hearing a semi-plausible tale that fits with his own prejudices."

Hersh shrugs off criticism. It goes with the job, which he loves. "People talk about the demise of investigative reporting," he told David Barsamian in the *Progressive.* "Newspapers play an amazing role in our society, and I still think they are important. I'm sorry newspaper circulation is down. Ultimately, the importance of newspapers can't be replaced."

Works by the Author

Chemical and Biological Warfare: America's Hidden Arsenal (1968)
My Lai Four: A Report on the Massacre and Its Aftermath (1970)
Cover-Up: The Army's Secret Investigation at the Massacre of My Lai Four (1972)
The Price of Power: Kissinger in the Nixon White House (1983)

"The Target Is Destroyed": What Really Happened to Flight 007 and What America Knew about It (1986)

The Samson Option: Israel's Nuclear Arsenal and American Foreign Policy (1991)

The Dark Side of Camelot (1997)

Against All Enemies (1998)

Chain of Command: The Road from 9/11 to Abu Ghraib (2004)

Television Adaptation

Buying the Bomb (PBS, 1985)

For Further Information

Barsamian, David, "Seymour Hersh Interview," *Progressive*, May 2005.

Brinkley, Alan, "The Dark Side of Camelot," *Time,* November 17, 1997.

Chaudhry, Lakshmi, "Seymour Hersh: Man on Fire," AlterNet, October 27, 2004. http://www.alternet.org/mediaculture/20309/ (viewed September 17, 2007).

Freedman, Lawrence D., *Chain of Command* review, *Foreign Affairs*, January-February 2005.

Hendrickson, David C., "The Dark Side of Camelot," *Foreign Affairs,* May-June 1998.

Miller, John J., "At War—Sly Sy: A Journalist's Latest Tricks," *National Review,* December 3, 2001.

Peretz, Martin, "Unreliable Sources: The Harsh Truth Is Not the Same as the Hersh Truth," *New Republic,* September 12, 1983.

Seymour M. Hersh entry, Contemporary Authors Online. Reproduced in Biography Resource Center. Farmington Hills, MI: Thomson Gale, 2005. http://galenet.galegroup.com/servlet/BioRC.

Sherman, Scott, "The Avenger: Sy Hersh, Then and Now," *Columbia Journalism Review,* July-August 2003.

Tübke-Davidson, Amy, "Q&A: A Reporter's Life," the *New Yorker*, December 23 and 30, 2002.

Laura Hillenbrand

Adventure, Sports

Benchmark Title: *Seabiscuit*

Fairfax, Virginia

1967–

Photo by Lauren Chelec

About the Author and the Author's Writing

If ever there's a formula for a perfect book of sport, of adventure, of human and animal character and endeavor, it is Laura Hillenbrand's *Seabiscuit: An American Legend.* Her proposal was so compelling, she had both a book contract and a motion picture commitment before she began writing.

If ever there's a wrenching story of affliction, of perseverance, of guts, it is Laura Hillenbrand's, for she fought against constant exhaustion to complete that book. Once *Seabiscuit* came out, her stamina was severely tested as she participated in some 250 promotional interviews.

Hillenbrand was born in Fairfax, Virginia, in 1967; and she grew up in Bethesda, Maryland. Her father was a Washington, D.C., lobbyist. She began writing at an early age and recalls, "All through my childhood I wrote short stories and stuffed them in drawers," she told interviewer Anne A. Simkinson for Beliefnet. "I wrote on everything. I didn't do my homework so I could write." She studied history and English at Kenyon College in Ohio, but her plans to become a history professor were cut short when, in 1987, a case of food poisoning sparked onset of an unidentified affliction that kept her in bed for nearly a year with fevers and chills, with no energy whatsoever.

Hillenbrand sufficiently overcame her illness and began to write. She had been an avid horse rider from a young age—she told *Newsweek* her first ride was on a pony named Marylegs—and she pursued that interest with freelance articles for horse racing and trade periodicals such as *Thoroughbred Times, Turf,* and *Sports Digest.* She became a contributing editor and writer for *Equus Magazine* in 1989.

In 1993, Hillenbrand's illness intensified with vertigo, which made it difficult for her to read or write. She was finally diagnosed with chronic fatigue syndrome. "This illness is to fatigue what a nuclear bomb is to a match," she told Jennifer Frey of the

Washington Post in 2001, in a quote that has become a widely used, unofficial motto for CFS charitable organizations. However, knowing what her affliction was brought no assurance of relief.

Hillenbrand recovered somewhat by 1995 and moved to Washington the next year. Always sniffing for a good story, she discovered the jockey Red Pollard while sorting through a collection of documents about Depression-era horse racing. "I saw him first in a photograph, curled over Seabiscuit's neck. Looking out at me from the summer of 1938, he had wistful eyes and a face as rough as walnut bark," she recalled of the jockey in an essay she wrote for the Chronic Fatigue and Immune Dysfunction Syndrome Association of America.

"What really sold me was the epic reach of the tale," Hillenbrand told journalist William Nack. "You had a sweeping view of the breadth of American life in that era."

The too-tall jockey with the shock of red hair emerged into a full-blown and compelling character, as did the dun-colored claimer with the skewed gait, when she wrote a feature article about them for *American Heritage*. The 1998 piece earned her the Eclipse Award for Magazine Writing from the Thoroughbred Racing Association. Her agent secured a book contract with Random House. Two days later, Universal optioned film rights.

Hillenbrand spent two years in further, intense research and another two years in writing, all the while battling CFS. Her longtime companion Borden Flanagan, now a political-science instructor at American University, devised a clipboard device to hold documents vertically for her—so she could read without her head spinning. She worked on a laptop computer from her bed. She conducted 100+ interviews by telephone, several of them eyewitnesses. "Most of them are in their 80s and 90s," she told *Publishers Weekly* in 2001, "but I got a lot of first-hand accounts and I found a lot of film and photographs that could settle disputes."

It was a mixed blessing, certainly, that her CFS afforded Hillenbrand considerable empathy as she wrote about the half-blind, bone-battered, accident-prone jockey. "I think one of the reasons I chose to write about this particular story is that, as a person whose life is very much constricted by physical hardship, the individuals in it were particularly compelling to me. Especially Red Pollard, who battled his body throughout this story," she said in a *USA Today Talk Today* online chat in 2002.

Pollard was only one of the interesting characters in the book. The quiet spoken, down-on-his-luck Wyoming horse trainer Tom Smith was another. Hillenbrand described for the PBS *American Experience* documentary "Seabiscuit" how Smith took the horse to the track one day just to see what it could do. The horse flew down the track. "Horses rarely run as fast in workouts as they do in real races, and Smith knew what he had on his hands, and he was scared to death," she said.

Another fascinating character, Charles Howard, San Francisco car salesman-turned-horse owner, had the sense to give Smith and Seabiscuit their heads. And George "Iceman" Woolf, who visualized every race in his head before leaving the jock's room, was perhaps the only other rider who could steer Seabiscuit to victory when Pollard was injured in a near-deadly accident shortly before the big showdown between Seabiscuit and the East Coast champion War Admiral in 1938. Even Whiskers the goat and Pumpkin the retired Montana cow pony assume depth in the book, so rich is the author's depiction.

"Here was a story I could get lost in, with fascinating subjects whose lives were complicated and vigorous—everything my life wasn't," Hillenbrand told Larry

Katzenstein for ImmuneSupport.com. "Writing it helped me redefine myself, to become Laura the author instead of Laura the sick person."

While the author's illness kept her from attending the Hollywood premiere of the movie *Seabiscuit,* based on her book, Hillenbrand was sufficiently rested by 2003 to describe CFS in "A Sudden Illness" for the *New Yorker*—an article that earned her the 2003 National Magazine Award.

The next big project slated for Hillenbrand after *Seabiscuit*, as her health allows, is a biography of Olympic mile-runner and World War II prisoner-of-war Louis Zamperini.

Works by the Author

Seabiscuit: An American Legend (2001)

Film and Television Adaptations

American Experience: Seabiscuit (PBS, 2003)
Seabiscuit (Universal/Spyglass Entertainment, 2003)

For Further Information

Adriani, Lynn, "PW Talks with Laura Hillenbrand," *Publishers Weekly,* January 1, 2001.

Baker, John F., "Hillenbrand to Tell Hero's Tale," *Publishers Weekly,* August 16, 2004.

Fimrite, Ron, "If Looks Were Everything, This Great Champion Would Have Been Pulling a Cart," *Sports Illustrated,* March 5, 2001.

Frey, Jennifer, "Against the Odds: Laura Hillenbrand Surmounted Illness to Cross the Finish Line with 'Seabiscuit,' " *Washington Post,* March 9, 2001.

Frey, Jennifer, " 'Seabiscuit': Triumph of the Underhorse," *Washington Post,* April 21, 2003.

Hillenbrand, Laura, "A Sudden Illness—How My Life Changed," *New Yorker*, July 7, 2003.

Kantrowitz, Barbara, "A Writer Who Beat the Odds: Hillenbrand Battled Chronic Fatigue to Pen a Best Seller," *Newsweek,* July 28, 2003.

Katzenstein, Larry, "Betting on Seabiscuit: How Laura Hillenbrand Beat the Odds with Chronic Fatigue Syndrome and Wrote a Bestseller," ImmuneSupport.com. www.immunesupport.com/library/showarticle.cfm/ID/4188 (viewed August 21, 2006).

Laura Hillenbrand biography, Seabiscuit Web page. http://www.seabiscuitonline.com/author.asp (viewed August 17, 2006).

Laura Hillenbrand entry, Biography Resource Center Online. Farmington Hills, MI: Thomson Gale, 2003. http://galenet.galegroup.com/servlet/BioRC.

Laura Hillenbrand entry, Contemporary Authors Online. Reproduced in Biography Resource Center. Farmington Hills, MI: Thomson Gale, 2004. http://galenet.galegroup.com/servlet/BioRC.

"Laura Hillenbrand Honored," CFIDS Association of America. http://www.cfids.org/about/hillenbrand.asp (viewed August 17, 2006).

Laura Hillenbrand interview, *American Experience* Web site. http://www.pbs.org/wgbh/amex/seabiscuit/sfeature/sf_hillenbrand_05.html   (viewed August17, 2006).

Nack, William, "A Conversation with Laura Hillenbrand," *Reader's Guide, Seabiscuit: An American Legend,* trade paperback edition. New York: Ballantine, 2002.

Neff, Michael, "An Interview with Laura Hillenbrand," *SolPix.* http://www.webdelsol.com/SolPix/sp-laurainterview.htm (viewed August 17, 2006).

"Seabiscuit: Laura Hillenbrand," online discussion, *USA Today Talk Today*, May 23, 2002. cgi1.usatoday.com/mchat/20020530001/tscript.htm (viewed August 17, 2006).

Simpkinson, Anne A., "What Price Glory?" Beliefnet, May 21, 2001. http://www.beliefnet.com/story/80/story_8043_1.html (viewed August 17, 2006).

bell hooks

Memoir

Benchmark Title: *Ain't I a Woman*

Hopkinsville, Kentucky

1952–

About the Author and the Author's Writing

Educator and social critic bell hooks is a pioneer black feminist who has written critical works about race, gender, politics, class, and power, as well as engaging works of poetry and children's literature.

She was born Gloria Jean Watkins in Hopkinsville, Kentucky, in 1952, one of seven children of custodian Veodis Watkins and his wife, Rosa Bell Watkins, a homemaker and domestic worker. Growing up in a poor Southern community in an abusive household, she took refuge in reading and writing—in fact, her mother once confided that she, too, had written verses as a child. Gloria Jean attended both segregated and integrated schools. She appreciated the first for their sense of community and came to abhor the second for their white teachers, white curriculum, and institutional racism.

Through scholarships, Watkins attended Stanford University, graduating with a bachelor of arts degree in English in 1973. After obtaining her master's degree—also in English—three years later from the University of Wisconsin, she collected poems for a chapbook, *And There We Wept,* in 1978. In 1983, she completed her requirements for a doctorate from the University of California, Santa Cruz, writing her dissertation on author Toni Morrison.

The author has taught English, ethnic studies, and writing at several schools, beginning with her Santa Cruz alma mater. While teaching at San Francisco State University in 1981, she completed her first nonfiction book, *Ain't I a Woman.* The title is inspired by a phrase used by Sojourner Truth in a speech at an Ohio women's rights convention in 1851. Considered one of the seminal works in feminist literature, hooks's work assaulted the advances of white feminists at the expense of black women. In this and later books, she looked at America's media, its school systems, its political institutions, and what she labels in an interview with Rosette Royale an "imperialist white supremacist capitalist patriarchy," all of which hold back blacks—men but, particularly, women.

The author used the penname bell hooks—her great-grandmother's name, which she believed honored her forebears—beginning with her first chapbook of poetry in 1978. The name is rendered in lower-case letters as a statement of anti-ego. Her early works were forceful, adding a feminist perspective to the black experience and limited

173

in their audience. It was several years, and several books, before she came to recognize she had an audience and to think of herself as a writer. Among her works, *Black Looks* (1992) examines depictions of race and ethnicity in a white culture and *Breaking Bread* (1991) looks at the contradictions of black intellectual growth in America. *Teaching Community* (2003), through memoir and storytelling, she continues her theme of a "white supremacist capitalist patriarchy" in a post–September 11 nation.

Strong ideas gave her an advantage, she suggested to Calvin Reid of *Publishers Weekly*: "Writing without money has allowed me to find my voice and not have it shaped by some editor for the marketplace. Obviously, when publishers pay you big sums, they expect to have some control. I have existed on the integrity of my work rather than the machinations of the market."

In 1999, hooks explained to Gary A. Olson for Illinois State University's JAC journal that she has "handwritten all my books. I like to handwrite because I find that I think differently when I do so. Computers are seductive in that you feel that you don't have to edit and rework as much because the printed text can look so good.... I work something through my head, and then I start writing it." She disdains traditional academic style. Her works often float from first to third person.

hooks preaches radical change via "visionary feminism." "Reformist feminism, which is what most people think of as feminism," she told Royale for Real Change News.Org, "isn't concerned with changing society. It's concerned with changing certain aspects of it, like equal pay for equal work, whereas visionary feminism says we've got to change the whole foundation."

While discounting the success of contemporary African American women authors such as Terry McMillan or Alice Walker, suggesting they further stereotypes, hooks embraces Marxist concepts. "I think Marxist thought—the work of people like [Antonio] Gramsci—is very crucial to educating ourselves for political consciousness," she said in an interview in *Z Magazine*. Acknowledging imperfections in much of Marxist writing, she said it is necessary to "extract the resources from their thought that can be useful to us in struggle."

hooks has taught at Oberlin College, Yale University, City College of New York, and, since 2004, at Berea College in Kentucky, where she is a distinguished professor and writer-in-residence.

In reference to one of the three memoirs she has written, *Remembered Rapture,* she explains, "Writing has been for me one of the ways to encounter the divine." She writes painfully of her oppressive childhood, her bisexuality, her encounters with white lovers.

In more recent works, hooks has written about love and about community as means of overcoming race and gender issues. Her children's books such as *Be Boy Buzz* are intended to encourage literacy, particularly among young black males.

The author appreciates that it may take considerable effort for others to adopt her way of thinking. "The practice of mindfulness, the practice of being aware, takes me closer to awakeness," she said in *Shambhala Sun*. "I feel like there is always something trying to pull us back into sleep, that there is this sort of seductive quality in all the hedonistic pleasures that pull on us."

Works by the Author

Ain't I a Woman: Black Women and Feminism (1981)
Feminist Theory: From Margin to Center (1984)
Talking Back: Thinking Feminist, Thinking Black (1989), essays
Yearning: Race, Gender, and Cultural Politics (1990)
Breaking Bread: Insurgent Black Intellectual Life, with Cornel West (1991)
Black Looks; Race and Repression (1992)
Sisters of the Yam: Black Women and Self Recovery (1993)
Emma Amos: Changing the Subject: Paintings and Prints (1994), essay for catalog
Outlaw Culture; Resisting Representations (1994), essays
Teaching to Transgress: Education as the Practice of Freedom (1994)
Art on My Mind: Visual Politics (1995), essays
Killing Rage; Ending Racism (1995)
Black Is a Woman's Color (1996)
Bone Black: Memories of Girlhood (1996)
Reel to Real: Race, Sex, and Class at the Movies (1996)
Cat Island Woman (1996)
Wounds of Passion: A Writing Life (1997)
Remembered Rapture: The Writer at Work (1998)
All About Love: New Visions (2000)
Feminism Is for Everybody: Passionate Politics (2000)
Marcia Lippman Sacred Encounters; East and West, with Barbara Grizzuti Harrison and Marcia Lippman (2000)
Where We Stand: Class Matters (2000)
Salvation: Black People and Love (2001)
Young Wives' Tales: New Adventures in Love and Partnership, with Jill Corral and Lisa Miya-Jervis (2001)
Communion: Female Search for Love (2002)
Rock My Soul: Black People and Self-Esteem (2003)
We Real Cool: Black Men and Masculinity (2003)
Teaching Community: A Pedagogy of Hope (2003)
Space (2004)
The Will to Change: Men, Masculinity, and Love (2004)
Homegrown: Engaged Cultural Criticism, with Amalia Mesa-Bains (2005)
Witness (2006)
A Woman's Mourning Song (2006)
Plantation Culture (2007)
Soul Sister: Women, Friendship, and Fulfillment (2007)
What Lies Beneath: Katrina, Race, and the State of the Nation (2007)

Editor

Gumbo Ya Ya: Anthology of Contemporary African-American Women Artists (1995)

Contributor

Double Stitch: Black Women Write about Mothers and Daughters, edited by Patricia Bell-Scott (1992)

Poetry

And There We Wept (1978)
A Woman's Mourning Song (1992)

Juvenile

Happy to Be Nappy (1996)
Homemade Love (2001)
Be Boy Buzz (2002)
Skin Again (2004)

For Further Information

bell hooks entry, *Notable Black American Women*, book 2. Detroit, MI: Gale Research, 1996.

"Challenging Capitalism & Patriarchy: Third World Viewpoint Interviews bell hooks," *Z Magazine,* December 1995. http://www.zmag.org/ZMag/articles/dec95hooks.htm (viewed August 24, 2005).

Engberg, Giollian, *Homemade Love* review, *Booklist,* February 1, 2003.

Fleming, Robert, "Feminist Revolutionary Comes down to Earth," *Publishers Weekly,* November 25, 2002.

Gloria Watkins entry, Contemporary Authors Online. Reproduced in Biography Resource Center. Farmington Hills, MI: Thomson Gale, 2004. http://galenet.galegroup.com/servlet/BioRC.

hooks, bell, "bell hooks Talks to John Perry Barlow," *Shambhala Sun,* September 1995.

Olson, Gary A., "bell hooks and the Politics of Literacy: A Conversation," Illinois State University's JAC 14.1, 1994. http://jac.gsu.edu/jac/14.1/Articles/1.htm (viewed August 24, 2006).

Reid, Calvin, "Books—and More Books—from bell hooks," *Publishers Weekly,* March 27, 1995.

Royale, Rosette, "Beyond the Binary: bell hooks on Visionary Feminism and the Interdependence of Us All," Real Change News.Org, March 9, 2005. http://www.realchangenews.org/archive3/2005_03_09/current/interview.html (viewed August 24, 2006).

Tony Horwitz

Adventure, History, Travel

Benchmark Title: *Confederates in the Attic*

Washington, D.C.

1958–

Photo by Gerrit Fokkema

About the Author and the Author's Writing

" 'We try to be authentic,' O'Neill said. 'But no one wants to eat rancid bacon and be in the mud all night. This is a hobby, not a religion.' "

That's a Civil War reenactor speaking in Tony Horwitz's fascinating *Confederates in the Attic*. The weekend warriors make a few compromises in their depictions of soldiers North and South. But not many.

"Musty as its title sounds—and fetid as its author got—marching with purist re-enactors in homespun, unwashed woolens just like Johnny Reb and Billy Yank wore" reviewer Roy Blount Jr. wrote in the *New York Times Book Review*, "[this] is the freshest book about divisiveness in America that I have read in some time."

A former staff writer for the *Wall Street Journal* and the *New Yorker,* Horwitz, suggests reviewer Max Boot in *National Review,* has become "a fearless practitioner of 'participatory journalism.' " Much like journalists during the latest Iraqi conflict, he embeds himself in his story; he witnesses it firsthand. In *Confederates,* he found an unexpected—and reader-accessible—focus for his examination of human spirit, quirkiness, stubbornness, and, it would seem, idealism misplaced.

To tell the story of what Southerners think today of the War between the States, he sided with a motley gathering of campaign performers, sought out the widow of the last Confederate soldier, and interviewed a gruff historian, Shelby Foote. He also played soldier along the likes of Robert Lee Hodge, the reenactor of all reenactors, known for his bulge-eyed, pseudo-bloated depictions of a battlefield corpse. ("Hodge clutched his stomach and crumpled to the ground. His belly swelled grotesquely, his hands curled, his cheeks puffed out, his mouth contorted in a rictus of pain and astonishment. It was a flawless counterfeit of the bloated corpses photographed at Antietam and Gettysburg that I'd so often stared at as a child. Hodge leapt to his feet and smiled. 'It's an ice-breaker at parties,' he said.")

177

Horwitz was born in Washington, D.C., in 1958. His journalism career began with the *News-Sentinel* in Fort Wayne, Indiana, where he had moved with his girl-friend (and now wife of some twenty years), Geraldine Brooks. Both had graduated from Columbia University's school of journalism. After they married in 1984, the couple moved to Australia. Horwitz joined the staff of the Sydney *Morning Herald.* Jottings from his cross-continent hitchhiking yielded his first book in 1987, *One for the Road.* He followed that in 1990 with *Baghdad without a Map,* when his wife was covering the Middle East for the *Wall Street Journal.* During that time, he had the op-portunity—sometimes with his wife, sometimes alone—to visit several Muslim coun-tries and give his not-always-reverent opinions. Fortuitously, the book came out just before Operation Desert Storm.

Tired of travel, the couple returned to the United States. Horwitz continued his freelance writing and his regular assignments for the *Wall Street Journal,* where a se-ries of articles about minimum-wage laborers in chicken slaughter houses in Arkansas earned him a Pulitzer Prize. He put in a stint at the *New Yorker,* but since the success of *Confederates,* he has devoted his energies strictly to books.

Newspaper journalism and book writing are not the same, the author told Edward Nawotka of *Publishers Weekly,* and said he went through a slow transition. "I think a lot of people imagine writing is a mystical exercise, and you need to get your aura in just the right place and then somehow, it all magically spills out. The reality is that what it's really about is getting your bum in the seat, day after day, in a very disciplined way and simply cranking it out." A reporter's need to write quickly and succinctly served him well, he added.

In a 2002 conversation with Dave Weich of Powells.com, he challenged the time-honored dictum to reporters: don't place yourself in the story. "I think particu-larly in a place like Baghdad, where it's difficult to get hard information, there is some value in bringing in your own perspective. I think any person who did that would have responded the way I did to Baghdad, which is just the most horrible place in the world."

Horwitz has said he is always curious about places he's never been. And to get a true feel of those places, he seeks out less likely sources. Intrigued with the voyages of Captain James Cook, he set about to visit some of the places Cook visited for his next book, *Blue Latitudes.* He spent a year and half in the Pacific, traveling from Tahiti to New Zealand to Hawaii and beyond. He sailed for a week on a replica ship, the *En-deavor.* He went to Yorkshire, where Cook had grown up in poverty, to see what peo-ple today thought of the man of more than two centuries ago.

"I turned to the journals and art of Cook and his men," he said in a *BookBrowse* interview, "and supplemented this with the work of historians, anthropologists, and in-digenous writers. I discovered that most of those who have written about Cook are old-school British or colonial scholars of nautical bent. They tend to avoid or gloss over the racy and controversial aspects of the story, such as sex, cannibalism, and Cook's eventual breakdown." These ingredients were just what Horwitz needed to en-rich what otherwise might have been a stuffy academic history. *Library Journal* re-viewer Carolyn Alexander had some reservations about too many "searches for and visits with the odds and ends of people (from bartenders to a king) who claim to have some affiliation with Cook." Horwitz in a *BookPage* interview, however, said this de-tail was necessary to crafting a more complete picture of the voyager. "For too long Cook was viewed in the West only in heroic terms, as this great navigator who set off to discover the world. We know what's happened since—in terms of exploitation and the devastation of native cultures."

Horwitz collected fifty adventurous Americans to profile in *The Devil May Care* (2003). *Booklist* reviewer David Pitt found the profiles of, among others, Niagara Falls jumper Samuel Patch and deadbeat philanthropist John Sutter written "with style and readability"—the marks of Horwitz's writing.

 ## Works by the Author

One for the Road: Hitchhiking through the Australian Outback (1987; revised 1999)

Baghdad without a Map, and Other Misadventures in Arabia (1991)

Confederates in the Attic: Dispatches from the Unfinished Civil War (1998)

Blue Latitudes; Boldly Going Where Captain Cook Has Gone Before (2002), published in England as *Into the Blue: Boldly Going Where Captain Cook Has Gone Before* (2002)

The Devil May Care: Fifty Intrepid Americans and Their Quest for the Unknown (2003)

Introduction

South Sea Tales by Jack London (2002)

For Further Information

Alexander, Carolyn, *Blue Latitudes* review, *Library Journal,* March 15, 2003.

Baghdad without a Map review, *Publishers Weekly,* December 21, 1990.

Blount, Roy, "Trekkies of the Confederacy," *New York Times,* April 5, 1998.

Boot, Max, "Cook's Tours," *National Review*, November 25, 2002.

Clemens, Jack, "A Traveler's Tale," *Writer's Digest,* May 2005.

Confederates in the Attic review, *Publishers Weekly,* January 5, 1998.

Devil May Care review, *Publishers Weekly,* August 25, 2003.

Kreyling, Michael, *Confederates in the Attic* review, *Mississippi Quarterly*, fall 1998.

Morris, Edward, "Fantastic Voyages: Tony Horwitz Sails in Search of Captain Cook," *BookPage.* http://www.bookpage.com/0210bp/tony_horwitz.html (viewed August 25, 2006).

Nawotka, Edward, "Tony Horwitz: From Sea to Shining Sea," *Publishers Weekly,* October 14, 2002.

Pitt, David, *The Devil May Care* review, *Booklist,* October15, 2003.

Rider, Shawn, "Coping through History: Tony Horwitz's *Confederates in the Attic,* History, and Reconciliation," wdog.com. http://www.wdog.com/rider/writings/horwitz.htm (viewed August 25, 2006).

Tony Horwitz entry, Contemporary Authors Online. Reproduced in Biography Resource Center. Farmington Hills, MI: Thomson Gale, 2003. http://galenet.galegroup.com/servlet/BioRC.

Tony Horwitz interview, *BookBrowse.* http://www.bookbrowse.com/author_interviews/full/index.cfm?author_number=827 (viewed August 25, 2006).

Vollers, MaryAnne, *Confederates in the Attic* review, salon.com, March 10, 1998. http://www.salon.com/books/sneaks/1998/03/10review.html (viewed August 25, 2006).

Weich, Dave, "Tony Horwitz Boldly Follows," Powells.com. http://www.powells.com/authors/horwitz.html (viewed August 25, 2006).

Pico Iyer

Adventure, Travel

Benchmark Title: *Video Night in Kathmandu*

Oxford, England
1957–

About the Author and the Author's Writing

Want to travel? Want to write about it? Do it because you love it, veteran sojourner Pico Iyer cautions in an interview with Rolf Potts. Don't expect to make a lot of money. And don't think you can just drop into a remote place, chum with a few locals, scratch out a report, and be a success. Travel writing—good travel writing—is hard work.

Iyer's rule one: write down everything, and get it right, "since one seldom has the luxury of being able to return to a place to double-check the names and details and colors... [And] try to catch the feelings—the sound, the smell, the tang, of a place— immediately, before it goes."

Of course, Iyer ends up with too much material. He admitted to Potts that he hated not using every bit of his research, even at the risk of overloading his readers.

Before he uses those building materials—those detailed notes—Iyer fabricates a frame. In a conversation with Dave Weich of Powells.com, the author explained how he built momentum in his book *The Global Soul* to reach a desired peak in the final pages. "I begin deliberately with those dizzying surfaces and passageways—movement, an inundation of data, which I think reflects how the world is today—and you have to fight your way through it to get to the stillness and the space that begins to open up in those last two chapters."

Iyer was born in Oxford, England, in 1957. His Indian parents Raghavan Narasimhan Iyer and Nandini Mehta Iyer were university professors. As a child, a venture on his own to a store in his largely white neighborhood for candy was an excursion into an exotic, frightening, fascinating world. After his parents moved to the United States, Pico remained in England to attend college. In 1978, he obtained his bachelor of arts degree in English from Oxford University. He earned a master of arts from Harvard University in English and American language and literature. For two years, while he worked toward a Ph.D., he taught at Harvard, although he never completed a thesis.

During this time, Iyer contributed essays to St. Martin's Press's Let's Go travel book series. The experience proved invaluable. In 1982, he said in a *Lonely Planet Traveler at Large* interview, "I did France, Italy and Greece and was responsible for covering 27 towns in 29 days. So I got very quickly into a routine of waking up at

181

dawn, getting on a train, going to the next town, and walking and walking and walking around it, transcribing its sites, adding my impressions." He wrote his material at night, got up the next morning, and did it all over again.

Iyer wrote for the *Nation, Saturday Review, Village Voice,* and other periodicals, then became a staff writer with *Time* magazine from 1982 to 1985. He then took a break to travel and gauge Western influences in present-day India, Burma, Nepal, the Philippines, Hong Kong, and China. The result, *Video Night in Kathmandu,* was a popular success and prompted him to further roam Japan for a year and write about it in *The Lady and the Monk.* Iyer returned to *Time* as a contributing editor in 1986, with the freedom to continue his travel writing.

Living mostly in Japan, Iyer is often in California, where his parents now reside. He has said he finds the United States the perfect place for immigrants of means such as himself with multicultural backgrounds to thrive. He thinks of himself as a man of the entire world, rather than any one country.

"I am sitting on a great opportunity because like many people I have grown up with little bits of me in different cultures . . . and so my loyalty is not narrowly limited," he said in an interview for Phayul.com.

Iyer doesn't want to live comfortably at home; he wants new adventures—physical, emotional, and intellectual. His sharp descriptions and flowing prose earmark him as a leading speaker on a burgeoning global culture.

"I am writing about the future, in a sense, because these are the new forms that the world is going to take," he said in an interview with Scott London. "Things we take for granted here acquire a different meaning and value abroad. McDonald's is a status symbol in Thailand, for example . . . so to some extent I am a global village on two legs."

Iyer shares that global village with his readers. "A trip has only really been successful if I come back sounding strange even to myself," he wrote in *Sun after Dark* (2004), a book that roams from the island of Bali to the country of Oman, birthplace of Osama bin Laden.

Fellow travel writer Don George believes Iyer has accomplished much: "Iyer's portraits of these places offer much to admire and emulate," he said on salon.com. "He approaches the world with a fresh heart and wide open eyes. He looks closely and doesn't simply describe what he sees, but constantly analyzes it, trying to understand what things mean and where they fit in the puzzle of the whole."

Why is travel, and travel writing, so popular? The author suggested in a piece he wrote for the Goliards Web site, "We travel to bring what little we can, in our ignorance and knowledge, to those parts of the globe whose riches are differently dispersed. And we travel, in essence, to become young fools again—to slow time down and get taken in, and fall in love once more."

Works by the Author

The Recovery of Innocence (1984)
Video Night in Kathmandu: And Other Reports from the Not-So-Far East (1988)
The Lady and the Monk: Four Seasons in Kyoto (1991)
Falling Off the Map: Some Lonely Places of the World (1993)
The Sudden Disappearance of Japan, with J. D. Brown (1994)

Cuba and the Night (1995)
Tropical Classical: Essays from Several Directions (1997)
Buddha, the Living Way (1998)
The Global Soul: Jet Lag, Shopping Malls, & the Search for Home (2000)
Salon.Com's Wanderlust: Real-Life Tales of Adventure and Romance (2000)
Imagining Canada; An Outsider's Hope for a Global Future (2001)
Himalayan Odyssey: A Visual Journey across the Great Range, with David Samuel Robbins (2002)
The Inland Sea, with Donald Richie (2002)
Sun after Dark: Flights into the Foreign (2004)
A Place I've Never Been (2005)

Contributor

Living in a Dream: Great Residences of the World (1993), with John Julius Norwich, Hakan Groth, Peregrine Hodson, and Raghavan N. Iyer
Traveling Souls: Contemporary Pilgrimage Stories, edited by Brian Bouldrey (1999)
A House Somewhere: Tales of Life Abroad, edited by Don George and Anthony Sattin (2002)
My California: Journeys by Great Writers, edited by Donna Wares (2004)
By the Seat of My Pants, edited by Don George (2005)
Tales from Nowhere: Unexpected Stories from Unexpected Places, edited by Don George (2006)

Editor

The Best American Travel Writing (2004)

Fiction

Cuba and the Night (1995)
Abandon: A Romance (2003)
The Asiatics (2005)

Contributor

Nixon under the Bodhi Tree and Other Works of Buddhist Fiction, edited by Kate Wheeler (2004)

For Further Information

Austa, Sanjay, "Pico Ayer: Chronicler of Modern Times," The South-Asian.com, May-June 2003. http://www.the-south-asian.com/May-June2003/pico_iyer.htm (viewed August 25 2006).

George, Don, "Writers We Love: Pico Iyer," salon.com, September 15, 1999. http://www.salon.com/travel/bag/1999/09/15/iyer/ (viewed May 2, 2006).

"Interview with Pico Iyer," Phayul.com. http://www.phayul.com/news/article.aspx?id=9619&article=Interview+with+Pico+Iyer&t=1&c-5 (viewed May 2, 2006).

Iyer, Pico, "Why We Travel," Goliards.net. http://www.goliards.net/Why%20We%20Travel.htm (viewed September 25, 2006).

London, Scott, "Postmodern Tourism: An Interview with Pico Iyer." http://www.scottlondon.com/interviews/iyer.html (viewed May 2, 2006).

"Lonely Planet Conversations with Pico Iyer." http://www.lonelyplanet.com/columns/traveller_archive/2003may21/index.htm (viewed May 2, 2006).

Pico Iyer entry, Contemporary Authors Online. Reproduced in Biography Resource Center. Farmington Hills, MI: Thomson Gale, 2003. http://galenet.galegroup.com/servlet/BioRC.

Pico Iyer entry, *Notable Asian Americans*. Detroit, MI: Gale Research, 1995.

"Pico Iyer, Novelist, Essayist and Journalist," University of British Columbia. http://www.communityaffairs.ubc.ca/talkofthetown/2003/spring/iyer.html (viewed September 16, 2007).

Potts, Rolf, Pico Iyer interview, *Rolf Potts' Vagabonding.* http://www.rolfpotts.com/writers/iyer/html (viewed May 2, 2006).

Weich, Dave, "Pico Iyer's Mongrel Soul," Powells.com. http://www.powells.com/authors/iyer/html (viewed August 25, 2006).

Sebastian Junger

Adventure, True Crime

Benchmark Title: *The Perfect Storm*

Boston, Massachusetts

1962–

About the Author and the Author's Writing

Sebastian Junger was twenty-nine years old in 1991, a climber for an arborist in coastal Massachusetts. He had cut his leg with a chainsaw, and so was idle for a while. Fresh out of college, he had tried writing stories on speculation. Publishers were seldom interested. Laid up at home, he ruminated on dangerous work. Maybe, he related to NationalGeographic.com, he could write about loggers, firefighters, oil riggers—people who lived at the edge. It was Halloween 1991. Weather turned violent. A storm wiped out a Gloucester fishing boat, the *Andrea Gail*. Maybe he could write about commercial fishermen. That would make a good book, he thought. Maybe it would sell ten thousand copies.

In 1997, W.W. Norton published that book, *The Perfect Storm*. It sold far more than ten thousand copies. It dominated hardcover and then paperback book sales lists for three years and caught another gust of wind when a motion picture version came out in 2000.

"I think my book captured people's imaginations because I didn't resort to fiction to tell a story that, ultimately, could never be fully known," the author said in a *Page One* interview. "Instead, I resorted to a kind of journalism-by-analogy to tell what probably happened on the *Andrea Gail*."

The swordfishing boat sank largely because she was a seventy-two-foot craft in a storm with seventy-foot waves. She never had a chance. Although the implication is there, Junger in the book never quite calls the *Andrea Gail* unsafe—but "it wasn't seaworthy. Its reputation was that it was an unsafe boat and had no business being out there," he said in an interview with Ellen Barry of the *Boston Phoenix*. However, lots of fishing boats would have failed safety inspections. That's the nature of an industry both competitive and failing. "These guys are choosing to go out there," he said. "It's not quite like Russian roulette, but it's a little like that."

Sebastian Junger was born in Boston in 1962. His German-born father Miguel Junger, of Italian, Spanish, and Austrian extraction, was a physicist. His mother, Ellen Sinclair Junger, was an artist. Junger graduated from Concord Academy in 1980 and, four years later, from Wesleyan University. While there, he wrote a thesis on Navajo long-distance runners. "I ran a lot in college," he said in an interview in the *U.S. Naval*

Institute's Proceedings, "and I decided to go to Arizona and train with those talented runners. That turned out to be the most stimulating thing I did in college." He worked for the *City Paper* in Washington, D.C., then for the *Phoenix,* often nudging interesting stories from the waterfront. He was always drawn to adventure.

After *The Perfect Storm* was published, Junger took some heat from his community —and from media critics such as the *New York Observer*, which among other things challenged Junger's assertion that the *Andrea Gail* was less stable because of alterations.

He also took some heat for his technique of making it a mystery to be solved. After all, the six people who disappeared with the boat in that storm were unavailable to give their accounts, so he conjectured. Scholars often do that, and Junger no doubt encountered the device while he studied anthropology at university. Build a body of evidence based on other cases, then surmise how the *Andrea Gail* seamen might have responded.

But in spite of these criticisms, readers loved the book. Junger "weaves a tapestry of fact and detail, history and science, commerce and politics, navigation and meteorology that engages the mind as the saga of the *Andrea Gail* going down fixes the heart," in the view of *Smithsonian* reviewer Paul Trachtman.

Junger expressed great empathy for his subjects. "People who are exhilarated by risk—and I'm one of them, I admit—are almost invariably college-educated. They choose their risks: a Wall Street lawyer who goes rock climbing on the weekend. Those who have to take risks for a living tend not to have gone to college. They take risks in order to eat. The fishermen I wrote about—they dread the risk part of their jobs. It's not an adventure," the author told NationalGeographic.com.

After *The Perfect Storm,* the writer found new adventure in Afghanistan where he interviewed a Taliban leader and in the American West where he worked with a crew of firefighters. *Fire,* published in 2002, collects several of his journalistic pieces, all about people under fire of one sort or another. He looks at wildfire fighters in the western United States and soldiers in Afghanistan. He describes the fur trader and explorer John Colter and diamond traders in Sierra Leone.

For his third book, *A Death in Belmont,* he dug into family lore. He came up with a compelling story that takes place in 1963 in Belmont, the Boston suburb where the Jungers lived. Roy Smith, a black housecleaner, was arrested in the sex-murder of a sixty-three-year-old neighbor, Bessie Goldberg. Coincidentally, Junger said, his mother employed a handyman named Albert DeSalvo. One day Ellen Junger shut and locked the basement door to avoid a strange invitation from DeSalvo, who was working downstairs. DeSalvo was later charged and convicted as the notorious Boston Strangler. Police made no connection between the Goldberg case and the Strangler. Today, some criminologists aren't even certain DeSalvo *was* the Strangler.

Junger again had a story without clear resolution. That is, he can't prove it. But he speculates that Smith was innocent and DeSalvo the real killer of Goldberg. "He's navigating a maze of shadows, and you can see all the more clearly what an enormously skillful prose artist he is," praised Time's Lev Grossman. Again, there were some who found fault with Junger's book, notably victim Goldberg's daughter Lea Scheuerman, who had met with the author for interviews, but adamantly disagreed with his conclusion. "The book is inaccurate," she told the *Boston Globe*. "There is overwhelming circumstantial evidence that proves beyond a reasonable doubt that Roy Smith killed my mother."

New York Times reviewer and law professor Alan M. Dershowitz, writing in the *New York Times Book Review,* also questioned Junger's approach. "Although he acknowledges that 'often the truth simply isn't knowable'—and that this story is 'far messier' than the perfect one he has grown up with—he still tries too hard to fit the messy facts into his payoff narrative."

"As a journalist," Junger responded in a Powells.com interview, "if you have access to the absolute truth, you have to deliver it. But lacking that possibility, pursuing all the possibilities ends up being an interesting inquiry into the world, into the story."

 # Works by the Author

The Perfect Storm: A True Story of Men against the Sea (1997)
Fire (2001)
A Death in Belmont (2006)

Film Adaptations and Documentaries

The Perfect Storm (2000)
Frontline Diaries: Into the Forbidden Zone (2001)

For Further Information

Alvin, Rebecca M., "Probing the 'Idea of Doubt': Sebastian Junger to Speak in Truro Wednesday," *Cape Experience/The Cape Codder,* August 25, 2006.

Barry, Ellen, "Eye of the Storm," *Boston Phoenix,* August 21, 1997.

Dershowitz, Alan M., "The Belmont Strangler," *New York Times Book Review*, April 16, 2006.

Flamm, Matthew, " 'The Perfect Storm' Hits a Summer Squall," *Entertainment Weekly*, September 5, 1997.

Gates, David, "The Perfect Storm," *Newsweek,* June 16, 1997.

Grossman, Lev, "A Murderer in the Home," *Time,* April 10, 2006.

Junger, Sebastian, "Welcome Stranger," *National Geographic Adventure,* May 2006.

Kennedy, Mark, "Another Strangler Case," Waterbury (CT) *Sunday Republican*, May 7, 2006.

Mehegan, David, "The Perfect Story," *Boston Globe,* April 5, 2006.

Nashawaty, Chris, " 'Belmont' Stakes,' " *Entertainment Weekly,* April 21, 2006.

Pumphrey, Mark, *Fire* review, *Library Journal,* April 1, 2002.

Sebastian Junger entry, Contemporary Authors Online. Reproduced in Biography Resource Center. Farmington Hills, MI: Thomson Gale, 2006. http://galenet.galegroup.com/servlet/BioRC.

Sebastian Junger interview, *Page One Lit,* October 2000. http://www.pageonelit.com/interviews/Junger.html (viewed June 20, 2006).

Sebastian Junger interview, Powells.com. http://www.powells.com/authors/junger.html (viewed June 20, 2006).

Sebastian Junger interview, *U.S. Naval Institute Proceedings Magazine,* July 2000. http://www.usni.org/proceedings/Articles00/projunger.htm (viewed June 20, 2006).

Shnayersion, Michael, "Sebastian Junger After the Storm," National Geographic.com. http://www.nationalgeographic.com/afterthestorm/ (viewed June 20, 2006).

Trachtman, Paul, *The Perfect Storm* review, *Smithsonian,* October 1997.

Wetzel, Eric, "Sebastian Junger: The War Reporter, Author and New York Barkeep Shows Us His Souvenir-Strewn Lower East Side Office—But First He's Gotta Take This Call," *Book,* May-June 2003.

Michio Kaku

Environment, Science

Benchmark Title: *Hyperspace*

San Jose, California
1947–

Photo courtesy the author

About the Author and the Author's Writing

To understand Michio Kaku and his meteoric rise to science superstardom, one needs to understand string theory, or at least know what it is. To define string theory, or even to understand it, almost obliges one to hold a university postgraduate degree in physics or mathematics. Even the shortest of definitions goes on for paragraphs and introduces myriad related definitions, from D-branes to quantum gravity to M-theory. Suffice it to say that string theory is an attempt to solve Albert Einstein's quest for a single formula, "a theory of everything," to explain the universe. String theorists are convinced that the universe is made up, not of particles but of one-dimensional threads that are taut and vibrate something like a cello string.

Kaku, the Henry Semat Professor of Theoretical Physics at the City College and the Graduate Center of the City University of New York, although he was not the only scientist to work on string theory, has been instrumental in popularizing it through his writings and television appearances. He explains in an interview with Stephen Marshall of Guerilla News Network: "When these little strings vibrate, they create notes and we believe these notes are in fact the subatomic particles that we see around us. The melodies that these notes can play out is called 'matter' and when these melodies create symphonies, that's called the 'universe.' " To comprehend string theory, he went on, is "to read the mind of God."

Few people fully comprehend the theory. Kaku commented in an interview with Elizabeth Finkel of *Cosmos* magazine, "Engineers want to build bridges; physicists want to understand fundamental laws. Engineers disdained Einstein's theories, but those equations ultimately resulted in the atom bomb."

Michio Kaku was born in San Jose, California, in 1947. His parents Toshio Kaki and Kideko Maruyama Kaku, were interred in camps during World War II. After the war, his father worked as a gardener and his mother as a maid. Young Michio was a precocious youth; he became intrigued, at age eight, with Einstein's unsolved dilemma. Family visits to Golden Gate Park in San Francisco opened his eyes; he saw a carp swimming in the pond, and his mind went into a spin. The fish lived in a two-dimensional world, unaware that there was an unseen world in the third dimension. Likewise, perhaps we live in a three-dimensional world, he thought, unaware that there are unseen, invisible, higher-dimensional universes all around us. Kaku, and his colleague Keiji Kikkawa of Osaka University, later cofounded string field theory, which allows one to summarize all of string theory in an equation barely one inch long. But these are not ordinary strings; they vibrate in ten dimensions, perhaps more. These strings existed at the beginning of time and may explain how the universe was created, and even what happened before creation.

When he was in high school, Kaku, with the help of his parents, constructed an electron volt atom smasher using some twenty-two miles of copper wire, placed in a high school football stadium during the Christmas holiday. The experiment blew out all the electrical fuses in his house but impressed an atomic scientist, Edward Teller, who saw to it Kaku received a scholarship to Harvard University. The young man graduated first in his class in 1968 (summa cum laude) and, after a stint in the U.S. Army, went on to earn his Ph.D. from the University of California, Berkeley, in 1972. His dissertation was about string loops in space. In 1973, he held a lectureship at Princeton University, where he retains a visiting professorship, then moved to City University in New York in 1974.

How does Kaku come up with his theories? He says he is always thinking, as he explained in *New Scientist,* "I find myself spending most of my time staring out the window. I see blocks of equations dancing in my head, and I spend hours trying to fit them together."

In that same article, Kaku noted that Einstein believed that for a theory to be worthwhile, one had to be able to explain it to a child. Or at least to a reasonable adult. Kaku has made it a goal to make physics understandable to the general public; in many respects, he has succeeded. *Hyperspace*, his 1994 stab at explaining quantum physics —including parallel universes and time travel—"will thrill lay readers, SF fans and the physics-literate," in the view of a *Publishers Weekly* reviewer. It grabbed worldwide attention.

The same periodical found the author's next book, *Visions* (1997) exhibited "a rare clarity of scientific thought and exposition" that "convincingly predicts where the next hundred years of technological advancement will take us." Kaku hosts a weekly syndicated science radio program, *Science Fantastic,* and has appeared on a range of television programs, from the *Larry King Show* to *Nightline* to *Nova*. He hosted a four-part TV documentary for BBC-TV in 2006, *Making Time.*

His *Parallel Worlds* (2004) looks at the unreachable "branes," dimensions of hyperspace that may afford a future for civilization should our world on Earth be destroyed. Does the future have time travel in store? The necessary energy would come from stars, Kaku told ScientificAmerican.com. "It would take a civilization far more advanced than ours, unbelievably advanced, to begin to manipulate negative energy to create gateways to the past. But if you could obtain large quantities of negative energy—and that's a big 'if'—then you could create a time machine that apparently obeys Einstein's equation and perhaps the laws of quantum theory."

Works by the Author

Beyond Einstein: The Cosmic Quest for the Theory of the Universe, with Jennifer Trainer Thompson (1987), revised 1995

To Win a Nuclear War: The Pentagon's Secret War Plans, with Daniel Axelrod (1987)

Introduction to Superstrings and M-Theory (1988)

Strings, Conformal Fields, and M-Theory (1991)

Quantum Field Theory: A Modern Introduction (1993)

Hyperspace: A Scientific Odyssey through Parallel Universe, Time Warps, and the Tenth Dimension (1994)

Visions: How Science Will Revolutionize the Twenty-first Century (1997)

Einstein's Cosmos: How Albert Einstein's Vision Transformed Our Understanding of Space and Time (2004)

Parallel Worlds: Creation, Superstrings, and a Journey through Higher Dimensions (2004)

Physics of the Impossible: A Scientific Exploration of the World of Phasers, Force Fields, Teleportation, and Time Travel (2008)

Editor

Beyond Einstein: The Cosmic Quest for the Theory of the Universe, with Jennifer Trainer Thompson (1995)

Nuclear Power, Both Sides: The Best Arguments for and against the Most Controversial Technology, with Jennifer Trainer Thompson (1982)

Beyond Einstein: The Cosmic Quest for the Theory of the Universe, with Jennifer Trainer Thompson (1995)

For Further Information

Finkel, Elizabeth, "Fish out of Water," *Cosmos* magazine, August 2005. http://www.cosmosmagazine.com/node/99 (viewed August 27, 2006).

Hyperspace review, *Publishers Weekly,* March 7, 1994.

Kaku, Michio, "Unifying the Universe," *New Scientist,* April 16, 2005.

Marshall, Stephen, "An Interview with Michio Kaku," Guerilla News Network, reproduced on Water Consciousness Web site, May 2001. http://www. water-consciousness.com/must/must_article25.htm (viewed August 27, 2006).

Michio Kaku entry, Contemporary Authors Online. Reproduced in Biography Resource Center. Farmington Hills, MI: Thomson Gale, 2005. http:// galenet.galegroup.com/servlet/BioRC.

Michio Kaku Web site. http://www.mkaku.org (viewed June 21, 2006).

Minkel, J. R., "Borrowed Time: Interview with Michio Kaku," Scientific American.com, November 24, 2003. http://www.sciam.com/article.cfm?articleID =0000AB94-4016-1FBE-801683414B7F0000 (viewed June 21, 2006).

Parallel Worlds review, *Booklist,* December 1, 2004.

Visions review, *Publishers Weekly,* September 1, 1997.

Weigel, Jack W., *Einstein's Cosmos* review, *Library Journal,* April 15, 2004.

Tracy Kidder

Adventure, Investigative Reporting

Benchmark Title: *House*

New York, New York

1945–

About the Author and the Author's Writing

Tracy Kidder has been a vicarious computer programmer, a carpenter, an elementary teacher, a nursing home aide, and rural town policeman. He has also been a for-real soldier in Vietnam, but we'll get to that later.

Kidder was born in New York City in 1945 and grew up on Long Island. His father, Henry M. Kidder, was a lawyer. His mother, Reine Tracy Kidder, was a high school teacher. He received his bachelor's degree from Harvard University in 1967 and his master of fine arts from the University of Iowa in 1974.

After finishing his studies, Kidder gravitated immediately to journalism. He became a staff reporter for *The Atlantic Monthly,* and one of his first assignments evolved into his first book, *The Road to Yuba City: A Journey into the Juan Corona Murders* (1974). It is the story of a farm labor contractor accused of brutally murdering workers and burying them in an orchard. While the book bore hallmarks of his later works—conversations with the families of victims, notes from the trial, detailed profiles of participants—he was not pleased with its subject and *Road* has since gone out of print.

The Soul of a New Machine, his next book, published in 1981, couldn't have been more pleasing to the author. It gained him both the Pulitzer Prize and the National Book Award in 1982. *Soul* entered the then-fledgling world of microcomputers while a team at Data General works feverishly for a year and a half to perfect the prototype Eagle.

"Kidder reveals a truth of management that all who have worked on a great team know," wrote Jim Collins in *Inc.,* "but that most businesspeople and economists seem to forget: the strongest motivation and the best work do not come primarily from the lure of money, stock options, formal recognition, or advancement."

In 1981, Kidder married Frances T. Toland. They have two children and live near Northampton, Massachusetts. His next four books found subjects close to home, beginning with *House,* the story of a couple who commission an architect to design a home for them in Holyoke, Massachusetts, and engage a quartet of carpenters to build it. It's something of Eric Hodgins's *Mr. Blandings Builds His Dream House* with less humor, more detail, more angst, more emphasis on relationships.

192

"His impartial, probing, thoughtful narrative follows the house from its inception in the mind's eye of the owners, Judith and Jonathan Souweine, to its formal definition on the drafting table of their friend and architect, Bill Rawn, to the saws and hammers of the four partners who together make up Apple Corps construction company," said Sal Alfano in *Psychology Today*.

Critics noted, as they had with his previous book, Kidder's ability to deftly depict personalities, isolate relationships, to identify motivations. Despite frequent disagreements, everyone worked together to get the job done.

The author went back to school for a year to prepare his next book, *Among Schoolchildren* (1989). He sat at a desk at the front of elementary teacher Chris Zajac's Holyoke classroom to record her trials and rewards in nurturing a class of twenty through the three Rs. Even though she has two children of her own, Zajac spends more than classroom time with her young scholars. "Nearly all of her daylight hours are devoted to her students, as well as a good portion of her night hours," *New Republic* reviewer Anne Tyler observes. "After supper she grades papers, stopping now and then to care for her own two children. When she goes to bed, she often lies awake mulling over various students' problems."

Moving to the other end of the age spectrum, Kidder in *Old Friends* focuses on two roommates at Linda Manor, a 121-bed nursing home near Northampton—gruff seventy-two-year-old Joe and gentle ninety-year-old Lou, as well as assorted of their fellow residents to create a picture of a growing segment of our population in which the spark still burns. In this and his next book, *Hometown*, in which he rides in Northampton police offer Tommy O'Connor's cruiser to see what makes the bustling college town of thirty thousand tick, the author shows great maturity of approach. The books are rich in detail, comfortable in language, poignant in anecdote, and informative about the taken-for-granted.

In an essay for *The Writer* magazine, Kidder said he collects a mound of research for each book then wrestles the material into a first draft. That draft may go through ten rewrites before he's through. He often searches for the single representative story that carries the load. His notes, he said, must be "extremely concrete. I try not to write down what I'm thinking or feeling at the moment; I want to get down what people say, how things look and how people look, gestures, all the stuff you can see and hear and smell." Solid notes rekindle his memories during the writing.

A chance meeting in Haiti with Dr. Paul Farmer, founding director of Partners in Health and a specialist in infectious diseases, led to *Mountains beyond Mountains*, published in 2004. "A challenging person," Kidder said of Farmer in a *BookBrowse* interview, "the kind of person whose example can irritate you by making you feel you've never done anything as important, and yet, in his presence, those kinds of feelings tended to vanish."

The writer's more recent *My Detachment*, published in 2005, is something of a departure from his usual type of subject matter and style. This is a memoir of his noncombat experiences in Vietnam in 1968–1969. Although factual, it is looser in style than his other prose. "It's a book, I think, about various lunacies of youth, or at least of my youth, especially the romanticism that accompanies wars, that seems indeed to help make wars possible," he said on "Ink Q&A."

Publishers Weekly found the book "an introspective, demythologizing dose of reality seen through the eyes of a perceptive, though immature, army intelligence lieutenant at a rear-area base camp. War isn't hell here; it's 'an abstraction, dots on a map.' "

Works by the Author

The Road to Yuba City: A Journey into the Juan Corona Murders (1974)
The Soul of a New Machine (1981)
House (1985)
Among Schoolchildren (1989)
Old Friends (1993)
Home Town (1999)
Mountains beyond Mountains: The Quest of Dr. Paul Farmer, a Man Who Would Cure the World (2003)
My Detachment: A Memoir (2005)

Editor

The Best American Essays: 1994 (1994)

For Further Information

Alfano, Sal, *House* review, *Psychology Today,* December 1985.

Collins, Jim, "The Soul of a New Machine," *Inc.,* December 1996.

Kanner, Ellen, "Our Town: Both Sides of Main Street," *BookPage,* May 1999. http://www.bookpage.com/9905bp/tracy_kidder.html (viewed August 28, 2006).

Kidder, Tracy, "How I Write: Tracy Kidder," *The Writer,* April 2004.

My Detachment review, *Publishers Weekly,* June 13, 2005.

Old Friends review, *Publishers Weekly,* July 26, 1993.

Selwyn, Laurie, *Mountains beyond Mountains* review, *Library Journal,* July 2004.

Skow, John, *The Soul of a Small Town* review, *Time Canada,* May 3, 1999.

Tracy Kidder entry, Contemporary Authors Online. Reproduced in Biography Resource Center. Farmington Hills, MI: Thomson Gale, 2004. http://galenet.galegroup.com/servlet/BioRC.

Tracy Kidder interview, *Bookbrowse.* http://www.bookbrowse.com/author_interviews/full/index.cfm?author_number=940 (viewed June 21, 2006).

Tracy Kidder interview, "Ink Q&A," Powells.com. http://www.powells.com/ink/kidder/html (viewed August 28, 2006).

Tyler, Anne, *Among Schoolchildren* review, *New Republic,* November 13, 1989.

Jonathan Kozol

Investigative Reporting

Benchmark Title: *Death at an Early Age*

Boston, Massachusetts

1936–

About the Author and the Author's Writing

"Jonathan Kozol has been writing variations of the same righteously indignant book ever since his National Book Award–winning *Death at an Early Age* in 1967," David Gates wrote in *O, The Oprah Magazine.* Gates marveled at the author's longevity. Kozol's first book came out a decade after the landmark court decision in the case of *Brown v. Board of Education* in Topeka, Kansas, supposedly ended segregated schools. As Kozol expounds in his 2005 *The Shame of the Nation,* urban black and Hispanic students are still largely taught apart from their white peers. "This book will make your blood boil," reviewer Gates asserted.

Kozol was born in Boston in 1936. His father Harry was a psychiatrist and his mother Ruth (Massell) a psychiatric social worker. He grew up in the well-to-do Boston suburb of Newton, leading a comfortable and privileged childhood. Kozol graduated from Harvard University, summa cum laude, in 1958 and did graduate studies at Magdalen College, Oxford University, in 1958 and 1959.

In 1964 and 1965, he taught elementary school in Boston's Dorchester section and in Newton the following year. The 1964 Mississippi murders of three young freedom workers energized his political beliefs. He developed Storefront Learning Center, an alternative school in Boston, from 1968 to 1971. A marriage in the 1970s ended in divorce. Over the next decade, he served as an administrator or a teacher at a variety of schools ranging from the Intercultural Documental Institute in Cuernavaca, Mexico, to South Boston High School to the National Literacy Coalition to Yale University and the University of Massachusetts to Trinity College.

Since then, he has lectured at dozens of universities, libraries, and public schools; worked as a reporter-at-large for the *New Yorker* (1988); and was a regular contributor to *The Nation* (1990–2001). Additionally, his essays have appeared in the *New York Times Book Review,* the *Los Angeles Times, Saturday Review of Literature, Psychology Today, Newsweek, Harper's,* and the *Washington Post.*

Kozol's early experience teaching children in Boston's Roxbury section opened his eyes wide to the inequities of, particularly, inner-city education for blacks. That was decades before Boston was forced by the court to integrate its public schools. In his first book, *Death at an Early Age* (1967), Kozol described his colleagues' repressive methods in the classrooms, the inadequate textbooks, the discouraging environment. Although some critics suggested the author was intentionally tunnel-visioned in his approach—and never said a harsh word about a black child—Elizabeth M. Eddy in *Harvard Educational Review* found he "eloquently describes the consequences of this system for both child and teacher, and Kozol himself is a dramatic example of the way in which the teacher is often discouraged from initiating creative learning activities in the classroom."

There is good public education, Kozol believes. It just isn't universal, he asserts —with statistical grounding. Kozol's goals for education include smaller class sizes and higher salaries for teachers. He told *Christian Century* that he has had conversations with conservative friends "who send their children to private schools in New England at a cost of $25,000 to $30,000 a year. They ask me, 'Can you really solve these education problems by spending more money?' I generally respond by saying, 'It seems to do the trick for your children, doesn't it?' "

In *Savage Inequalities,* an examination of schools in Camden, New Jersey; Washington, D.C.; South Bronx, New York; Chicago; and San Antonio, Texas, in the late 1980s, the writer charged that minority children were forced into slots. "He lets the pupils and teachers speak for themselves," said *Publishers Weekly*'s reviewer, "uncovering 'little islands of … energy and hope.' This important, eye-opening report is a ringing indictment of the shameful neglect that has fostered a ghetto school system in America."

"There's the greatest irony of all: If you want to see the most segregated school in America today, ask to see the school named after Martin Luther King. Or Rosa Parks, or Thurgood Marshall," he told Elana Berkowitz for *Campus Progress.* A school named for Jackie Robinson in New York City, he said, is 96 percent black and Hispanic. One named for Langston Hughes is 99 percent nonwhite.

Throughout his career, Kozol has vigorously advocated for educational—and social—reform. *Rachel and Her Children* (1988) is a powerful portrayal of a family living in a Manhattan welfare hotel. *Amazing Grace,* published in 1995, relates his findings in a South Bronx community called Mott Haven. "Perhaps nothing can halt the juggernaut of resurgent social Darwinism, but, if anything can," *Booklist*'s Mary Carroll wrote, "it may be Kozol's prophetic vision and the openness and humanity of the remarkable people whose amazing grace he so eloquently describes."

After Kozol returned to Public School 30 in Mott Haven to chronicle its committed teachers and the innovative St. Ann's Episcopal Church after-school program, he was enraged. "I hear public policy debates today about how we have to drill inner-city kids for the next exam, and if their grades aren't good enough, put them in summer school and don't worry about whether it's going to make much difference," he said in *U.S. Catholic.* "The collective body of discussion about urban children now has a vaguely punitive, almost adversarial tone—as though our young people, especially young people of color, are the enemy." Why, he asks, can't the dollars the public appears willing to spend on juvenile detention centers be spent instead on the education system?

Kozol in *The Shame of the Nation* (2005), based on visits to sixty schools in eleven states and using extensive quotes from children and teachers, describes what he asserts is America's resegregation. He advocates for a new civil rights movement to achieve educational justice.

Kozol won't be swayed by arguments that it is class, not race, that defines educational differences. "It's a distinction without a difference because the most deeply hypersegregated schools in America are far, far more likely to be schools of concentrated poverty than are racially integrated schools. So I still believe race is at the heart of it," he said in a salon.com interview.

And he continues with the struggle.

Works by the Author

Death at an Early Age: The Destruction of the Hearts and Minds of Negro Children in the Boston Public Schools (1967)

Free Schools (1972), revised as *Alternative Schools: A Guide for Educators and Parents* (1982)

The Night Is Dark and I Am Far from Home (1975)

Children of the Revolution (1978)

Prisoners of Silence: Breaking the Bonds of Adult Illiteracy in the United States (1979)

On Being a Teacher (1981)

Illiterate America (1985)

Rachel and Her Children: Homeless Families in America (1988)

Savage Inequalities: Children in America's Schools (1991)

Amazing Grace: The Lives of Children and the Conscience of a Nation (1995)

Ordinary Resurrections: Children in the Years of Hope (2000)

Will Standards Save Public Education?, with Deborah Heler (2000)

The Shame of the Nation: The Restoration of Apartheid Schooling in America (2005)

Letters to a Young Teacher (2007)

For Further Information

Berkowitz, Elana, "Five Minutes With: Jonathan Kozol," CampusProgress.org, September 19, 2005. http://www.campusprogress.org/features/552/five-minutes-with-jonathan-kozol (viewed August 28, 2006).

Brock, Ted and Winnie Brock, "Falling Behind: An Interview with Jonathan Kozol," *The Christian Century*, May 10, 2000.

Carroll, Mary, *Amazing Grace* review, *Booklist,* September 15, 1995.

Eddy, Elizabeth M., *Death at an Early Age* review, *Harvard Educational Review,* spring 1968.

Gates, David, "Every Child Left Behind: Jonathan Kozol Takes Furious Aim at Our Schools," *O, The Oprah Magazine*, October 2005.

Jonathan Kozol entry, *Authors and Artists for Young Adults,* Vol. 46. Detroit, MI: Gale Research, 2002.

Jonathan Kozol entry, Contemporary Authors Online. Reproduced in Biography Resource Center. Farmington Hills, MI: Thomson Gale, 2004. http://galenet.galegroup.com/servlet/BioRC.

Karnasiewicz, Sarah, "Apartheid America," salon.com, September 19, 2005. http://dir.salon.com/story/mwt/feature/2005/09/22/kozol/index.html (viewed August 28, 2006).

Lodge, Sally, "Jonathan Kozol—Quiet Time for a Crusader," *Publishers Weekly,* May 15, 2000.

Savage Inequalities review, *Publishers Weekly,* August 16, 1991.

"Still Separate and Unequal," *U.S. Catholic,* October 2000.

Jon Krakauer

Adventure, Environment, History

Benchmark Title: *Into Thin Air*

Brookline, Massachusetts

1954–

Photo by Linda Moore

About the Author and the Author's Writing

The mountain is on the border between Nepal and the Tibet Autonomous Region of China, part of the frigid Himalayan chain. Its temperature never rises above freezing. The Nepali call it *Sagarmatha,* or "Forehead in the Sky." To the Tibetans, it is *Chomolunga,* "Goddess Mother of the World." The British named it Mount Everest in 1856, after Surveyor General of India Sir George Everest. At 29,035 feet, it was and continues to be an open invitation to adventurers. In 1924, mountain climber George Mallory, who wanted to scale its ice walls simply "Because it is there" perished in his attempt. It was still there when Edmund Hillary declared, "Well, we knocked the bastard off." Hillary and Tenzing Norgay, a Sherpa mountain guide, were the first to plant a flag at the acme in 1953. "No one remembers who climbed Mount Everest the second time," declared Na Nook, a Sherpa.

Or the third or fourth. Nor does anyone know what number Jon Krakauer held when he reached the top in 1996. "But now that I was finally here," he's widely quoted, "standing on the summit of Mount Everest, I just couldn't summon the energy to care." However, Krakauer made sure no one forgot others who attempted to breast the peak that season. Several of them died in the trying. He wrote their epitaph.

Jon Krakauer was born in 1954 in Brookline, a suburb of Boston, Massachusetts. His father Lewis, a physician, moved the family to Corvallis, Oregon, when Jon was two. Following his father's interest, Jon began to climb mountains at the age of eight; he never lost interest. He idolized leading mountaineers of the day, such as Willi Unsoeld, and aspired to reach Everest's peak some day. Jon attended Hampshire College in the 1970s. In 1980, he married fellow climber Linda Moore. He labored as a carpenter and a commercial fisherman, all the while climbing mountains in his spare time. After the American Alpine Club asked him to write an account of his ascent of

199

the Alaskan Arrigetch Peaks, he found a new career. He wrote articles about climbing for *Outside* and *Smithsonian* magazines. His first book, *Eiger Dreams* (1990), was a collection of those articles.

Krakauer mostly wrote about his own experiences, but in 1992 at the request of his *Outside* editors, he wrote a profile of Christopher McCandless, who never came back from an attempt to live off the land in the Alaskan wild. The article later grew into the book, *Into the Wild* (1996). "Krakauer probes the mystery of McCandless's death, which he attributes to logistical blunders and to accidental poisoning from eating toxic seed pods," said *Publishers Weekly*. Sean Penn turned the book into a movie in 2007.

The author found the transition from periodicals to books to be an easy one. "I research enough to write a book. Almost every magazine piece I've ever written, I felt like I haven't done it justice, like it was just a gloss," he said in an interview on the Random House Web site. "So to write a book, and to spend a year or two and tell a story right is really satisfying."

In 1990 Krakauer produced a travel/photo book, *Iceland: Land of the Sagas* with David Roberts.

Krakauer's 1996 ascent of Mount Everest was another *Outside* assignment. Originally he intended to document the increasing commercialism of Everest climbing. He joined a team organized by seven-time veteran Rob Hall. From base camp at 17,600 feet, Krakauer noticed what he felt was rampant inexperience among other climbers. When he reached the top, the adrenalin faded. He felt little exuberance.

Krakauer had no anticipation of writing another postmortem on an adventure gone wrong. But a savage storm struck the mountain during his descent. He reached a camp unaware there were twenty-eight hikers behind him, some already dead. He interviewed survivors, studied evidence, and wrote his article—later expanded into the best-selling *Into Thin Air* (1998). "The intensity of the tragedy is haunting," said a *Publishers Weekly* reviewer, "and Krakauer's graphic writing drives it home."

Other climbers and family members and friends of those lost on the mountain that day complained bitterly about Krakauer's book. But he defended his writing, noting that the mountain was swarming with amateurs and half-planners. He got details wrong, others countered. He admitted to some factual mistakes when his article was reprinted in *The Best of Outside: The First 20 Years*. Although Krakauer portrayed head guide Anatoli Boukreev as something of a villain, the American Alpine Club honored Boukreev as a hero and noted that none in his party died. Later a more serious accusation was made by fellow mountaineer and writer Galen Rowell in *American Alpine Journal* in 1998—that the presence of a celebrity journalist on the mountain that day precipitated bad decisions—that expedition leaders Scott Fischer and Rob Hall (both of whom died) wanted to make a good impression so as to "lure more $65,000 clients."

When Krakauer turned to history in his next book, *Under the Banner of Heaven,* published in 2003, he met controversy again. Krakauer tells the story of a fundamentalist Mormon family and a double murder—of polygamist Allen Lafferty's wife and daughter by Lafferty's brothers Ron and Dan, following, to their minds, divine directive. The Church of Jesus Christ of Latter-Day Saints, upon the book's publication, issued a strongly worded negative review, charging the author maligned the congregation. The book sold very well.

Krakauer's heart remains in the wild. "I think we Americans have a special affinity for the back of beyond because of the exalted place it holds in our national mythology, the author told an interviewer for Trust for Public Land. "We grew up learning in school about Lewis and Clark, Sieur de La Salle, Father Escalante, and the Donner Party.... Even at this late date, some of us like to imagine that there is still a frontier out there somewhere, an expanse of untamed country."

Works by the Author

Eiger Dreams: Ventures among Men and Mountains (1990), essays
Iceland: Land of the Sagas, with David Roberts (1990)
Into the Wild (1996)
Into Thin Air: A Personal Account of the Mount Everest Disaster (1998)
High Exposure: An Enduring Passion for Everest and Unforgiving Places, with David F. Breashears (2000)
Under the Banner of Heaven: A Story of Violent Faith (2003)

Modern Library Explorations Series (Editor)

The Last Place on Earth: Scott and Amundsen's Race to the South Pole, by Roland Huntford (1999)
Starlight and Storm: The Conquest for the Great North Faces of the Alps, by Gaston Rebuffat (1999)
La Salle and the Discovery of the Great West, by Francis Parkman (1999)
Farthest North, by Fridtjof Nansen (1999)
The Brendan Voyage, Vol. 1, by Tim Severin (2000)
Weird and Tragic Shores, Vol. 1, by Chauncey Loomis (2000)
The Land of White Death, by Valerian Albanov (2000)
The Shameless Diary of an Explorer, by Robert Dunn (2001)
Great Exploration Hoaxes, by David Roberts (2001)
The Mountains of My Life, by Walter Bonatti (2001)
Notes from the Century Before, by Edward Hoagland (2002)

Contributor

Out of the Nanosphere: Adventure, Sports, Travel, and the Environment: The Best of Outside Magazine (1992)
The Best of Outside: The First 20 Years (1997)

Contributor of Forewords or Prefaces

The Mountain of My Fear, by David Roberts (1991)
Escape Routes: Further Adventure Writings of David Roberts, by David Roberts (1997)
Touching My Father's Soul: A Sherpa's Journey to the Top of Everest, by Jamling Tenzing Norgay with Broughton Coburn (2001)
Into the Land of White Death: An Epic Story of Survival in the Siberian Arctic, by Valerian Albanov (2001)

Television or Film Adaptations

Into Thin Air (ABC-TV 1997)
Into the Wild (2007)

For Further Information

Boynton, Robert S., *The New New Journalism: Conversations with America's Best Nonfiction Writers on Their Craft.* New York: Vintage Books, 2005.

DeWalt, Weston, "Everest Debate, Round Two," "Wanderlust," salon.com, August 14, 1998. http://www.salon.com/wlust/feature/1998/08/14featureb.html (viewed September 20, 2007).

"Frontier Daydreams: A Conversation with Jon Krakauer," Trust for Public Land Web site, December 1, 2001. http://www.tpl.org/tier3_cd.cfm?content_item_id=660&folder_id=266 (viewed June 27, 2006).

Into the Wild review, *Publishers Weekly,* November 6, 1995, and March 17, 1997.

Jon Krakauer, Contemporary Authors Online. Reproduced in Biography Resource Center. Farmington Hills, MI: Thomson Gale, 2004. http://galenet.galegroup.com/servlet/BioRC.

Kreyche, Gerald F., *Under the Banner of Heaven* review, *USA Today* magazine, March 2004.

Maryles, Daisy, "Into the Mormon Wild," *Publishers Weekly*, July 28, 2003.

Miles, Jonathan, "Left for Dead," salon.com, April 25, 2000. http://archive.salon.com/books/review/2000/04/25/weathers/index.html (viewed August, 28, 2006).

Plummer, William, "Everest's Shadow: Still Haunted by the Deaths of Fellow Climbers, Writer Jon Krakauer Knows Even a Bestseller Can't Kill the Pain," *People Weekly,* June 2, 1997.

Rowel, Galen, review of *The Climb* by Anatoli Bourkreev and G. Weston DeWalt, *American Alpine Club Journal,* reprinted on Mountain Light Photography Web site. http://www.mountainlight.com/reading.html (viewed August 31, 2006).

Stuttaford, Genevieve, *Eiger Dreams* review, *Publishers Weekly,* February 2, 1990.

Stuttaford, Genevieve, *Iceland* review, *Publishers Weekly,* October 19, 1990.

Weissman, Larry, "An Interview with Jon Krakauer" Random House Web site. http://www.randomhouse.com/boldtype/0697/krakauer/interview.html (viewed June 27, 2006).

Jane Kramer

Investigative Reporting, Travel

Benchmark Title: *The Politics of Memory*

Providence, Rhode Island

1938–

Photo by Sigrid Estrada

About the Author and the Author's Writing

Journalist Jane Kramer divides her time between Europe and the United States. Each time she makes the switch, going back to a place she hasn't been for a while, she has to reacquaint herself with her surroundings. That's one thing that helps keep her writing fresh and exciting.

"The best reporting works the way she does it," *New York Times* Paris Bureau chief James M. Markham wrote in his review of Kramer's *Europeans* in 1988, "notebooks packed with names, telltale quotations, colors and marginal details that together achieve a critical mass and become a compelling tale. Solid reporting sustains generalizations. Ms. Kramer's leaps to the macrolevel are sometimes so elegant and so satisfying that one is tempted to make one's own private album."

Markham wasn't the only one keen on Kramer's prose. With the book, she was both the first woman and the first American to win the Prix Européen de l'Essai, Europe's prestigious nonfiction award. It's on her desk along with an American Book Award for *Unsettling Europe* and a National Book Award for *The Last Cowboy*.

Jane Kramer was born in Providence, Rhode Island, in 1938, the daughter of physician Louis Kramer and his wife, Jessica Shore Kramer. She received her bachelor of arts degree in English from Vassar College in 1959 and her master's two years later from Columbia University. She wrote for a free weekly newspaper, the *Morningsider,* in New York City in 1961 and 1962, then joined the *Village Voice* staff. Several of her feature stories for that paper were collected in her first book, *Off Washington Square,* published in 1963.

In 1964, Kramer began to write for William Shawn's *New Yorker*. She married anthropologist Vincent Crapanzano, now a distinguished professor at the City University of New York's Graduate Center, in 1967. They have one child. She honed her interview technique while she helped her husband interview women in Morocco as part of his field work in 1969. Kramer and Crapanzano wrote up their results for the *New York Times Magazine,* and Kramer eventually reshaped the material for another book, *Honor to the Bride Like the Pigeon That Guards Its Grain under the Clove Tree* (1970).

Eight years later, Kramer found one of a vanishing breed, cowboy Henry Blanton, and profiled him, covering America's Western myth in *The Last Cowboy* (1978). The book is a compelling account of a range rider who resists agri-industrialization. Kramer spent a year with her subject, whom she calls Hank Blanton, a ranch foreman in the Texas Panhandle. Blanton hates unions, hates nonwhites, hates gun control, hates government meddling. "Yet there is a certain charm in Henry Blanton's bluster and his stubborn belief in old values. You admire it, the way you might admire a small boy who refuses to eat his oatmeal on the grounds that he don't want no damned oatmeal," reviewer Larry L. King wrote in *New York Times Book Review.*

In 1980, she submitted regular "Letters from Europe" to the *New Yorker.* Her book published that year, *Unsettling Europe,* painted a fascinating, grittier, more political picture of the continent than that found in tourism brochures and most guidebooks. *Europeans* in 1988 collected later columns. *The Politics of Memory* focused closely on one country, Germany, on East Germans and West Germans, on secret police and skinheads, as the "two Germanies" attempted to reconcile their shared past.

Kramer credentials reach beyond her writing. She has been writer-in-resident or visiting lecturer at several schools including Bernard M. Baruch College, University of California at Berkeley, and Princeton University. She is a founding board member of the Journalists Human Rights Committee and is an associate of the Environmental Defense. She edited a series of travel books for Public Planet Books, beginning with her own *Whose Art Is It?,* a look at tensions between modern artists and their patrons.

In a more recent work, Kramer returned to the American West for *Lone Patriot* (2002), a not particularly sympathetic examination of a right-wing John Pitner, of Whatcom County, Washington, leader of the Washington State Militia. "Kramer's strengths are her inquisitiveness, insight and graceful prose," *Publishers Weekly* said, "but one ends up wondering whether the FBI—and Kramer—might have better spent time pursuing real militiamen rather than this sad band of malcontents."

Yet the book fits the Kramer pattern of looking at individuals of little political sway. Robert S. Boynton, in his book *The New New Journalism,* praised Kramer for writing about both the haves and the have-nots, about the power brokers and political leaders and about the seldom-named people who live at the fringe. He found her particularly adept at bringing telling detail to what otherwise is widely abstract. Kramer told Boynton, "I like looking at a larger story through a particular personal lens so that I'm not simply analyzing or asking 'Whither the world?' I try to find the people within the larger story. I look for marginal figures who by definition look at the world with the skepticism of a journalist."

Works by the Author

Off Washington Square: A Reporter Looks at Greenwich Village (1963)
Allen Ginsberg in America (1969), published in England as *Paterfamilias* (1970)
Honor to the Bride Like the Pigeon That Guards Its Grain under the Clove Tree (1970)

The Last Cowboy (1978)
Unsettling Europe (1980)
The Europeans (1988)
Eine Amerikanerin in Berlin (1993)
Sondebare Europäen (1993)
Whose Art Is It? (1994)
The Politics of Memory: Looking for Germany in the New Germany (1996)
Unter Deutschen (1996)
Lone Patriot: The Short Career of an American Militiaman (2002)

Television Documentary

This Is Edward Steichen (1966)

For Further Information

Boynton, Robert S., *The New New Journalism: Conversations with America's Best Nonfiction Writers on Their Craft*. New York: Vintage Books, 2005.

Collins, James, *Politics of Memory* review, *Time*, October 28, 1996.

Jane Kramer entry, Contemporary Authors Online. Reproduced in Biography Resource Center. Farmington Hills, MI: Thomson Gale, 2006. http://galenet.galegroup.com/servlet/BioRC.

"Jane Kramer, Sidney Harman Writer-in-Residence, Fall 1999," Baruch College. http://www.baruch.cuny.edu/wsas/harman/kramer.html (viewed September 1, 2006).

King, Larry L., *The Last Cowboy* review, *New York Times Book Review*, January 22, 1978.

Kramer, Jane, "Letter from Europe: Blood Sport," *New Yorker*, January 24, 2005.

Lone Patriot review, Powells.com. http://www.powells.com/cgi-bin/biblio?isbn=067944873x (viewed September 1, 2006).

Lone Patriot review, *Publishers Weekly*, May 27, 2002.

Markham, James M., "Cities, Like Old Friends," *New York Times*, December 25, 1988.

Politics of Memory review, *Publishers Weekly*, August 26, 1996.

"Q&A: Beneath the Veil," *New Yorker*, November 15, 2004. http://www.newyorker.com/archive/2004/11/22/041122on_onlineonly01 (viewed September 20, 2007).

Whose Art Is It? review, *Publishers Weekly*, October 10, 1994.

Mark Kurlansky

Food, Investigative Reporting, Travel

Benchmark Title: *Cod*

Hartford, Connecticut

1948–

Photo courtesy Penguin Group

About the Author and the Author's Writing

Mark Kurlansky looks at things differently than most of us. His recent overview of New York City, for example, is told from the perspective of oysters. From the author of books about codfish and sea salt, it makes sense that the metropolis, which is situated on the Hudson River estuary rife with natural oyster beds, can be viewed from a food perspective.

The Big Oyster is one of Kurlansky's trademark microhistories. "By framing larger social history through one tiny item—caffeine, flattery, the pencil, the number zero—an author risks either drowning in a tar pit of obscurity or losing the narrative thread that holds the tale together," commented Ted Anthony in a review in the *Seattle Times*. Kurlansky, he attested, got it all right and is "a towering accomplishment that offers genuine insight into the world through an accessible doorway."

From that single hinge, the oyster, Kurlansky delves into everything from waste treatment plants to Lanape Indians, lower Manhattan slums, New Jersey moonshiners, and Delmonico's restaurant. "*The Big Oyster* is a cautionary tale of man's nature," *Publishers Weekly* noted, "which lays waste to any exploitable resource, with conservation always a tardy afterthought."

Kurlansky was born in Hartford in 1948. After receiving a bachelor of arts degree from Butler University in 1970, he worked as a chef and pastry maker in New York and elsewhere in the Northeast. Food is a major point of interest for the author. He writes a food history column for *Food & Wine* magazine. He developed his journalism skills in the foreign bureaus of the *Chicago Tribune, Miami Herald, Philadelphia Inquirer,* and the *International Herald Tribune* (Paris). He and his wife and daughter live in New York City.

"I have always written, long before I had any readers, starting at about the age of ten," the author said in a Powells.com interview. "As best I can understand it, I am enjoying a conversation that I have with myself. It is clear to me that writing is about being alone, about wanting to be alone, about craving your own company. Strange, isn't it?"

Along with food, a Kurlansky interest is cultures on the wane. He immersed himself in the Basque country for his *The Basque History of the World,* published in 1999. With their distinct language and culture, the Basque "have historically coexisted with powerful neighbors by insisting primarily upon keeping their own laws and customs, which during most of the twentieth century have been denied to them, leading to the creation of self-conscious, militant nationalism and the label Basque separatist," *Booklist* reviewer Ray Olsen notes.

In his earlier book, *Cod* (1997), which earned the Glenfiddich Food and Drink Award for Best Book and the James Beard Award for Excellence in Food Writing, Kurlansky revealed that Basque fishermen in quest of new trolling grounds "discovered" America before Columbus. Over the years, the quest for this fish has become unrelenting. The species may disappear.

"By the end of Mark Kurlansky's *Cod,* we know nobody is to blame, except the entire human race, and only because we are such phenomenally proficient predators," said *Smithsonian* reviewer Richard Wolkomir. Kurlansky provides six hundred historic cod recipes, which readers can purportedly use as long as cod is still available at fish markets. Many of those recipes call for salt. That is the subject of another Kurlansky book, *Salt: A World History* (2002). The book is not a science text, as one might assume from the title. Instead, "Kurlansky is primarily a social historian," Raymond Sokolov wrote in *Natural History.* "Or perhaps he should be called an economic mineralogist, since his focus is on the intersection of salt with civilization." Kurlansky looks at how salt as a vital preservative triggered taxes, trade wars, and remarkable technical innovation.

Kurlansky in another microhistory looks, not at a single topic but at an array of subjects in a single year. He was in college during the vibrant 1960s, and he felt strongly enough that 1968 was a seminal year that he wrote a book about it—*1968: The Year That Rocked the World,* published in 2003. The Soviet Union began to crumble in 1968. America underwent an enormous political shift. Vietnam saw its worst death toll. "It's a very different experience to write about history that you've lived through," the author told *Publishers Weekly*'s Martin Schneider. "On the one hand, you're constantly informed and enriched by your personal knowledge.... On the other hand, it's much easier to deal with history when it's not your experience. You have a built-in distance."

Kurlansky also writes short fiction and novels. He finds differences between writing fiction and nonfiction. "How you solve your problems are quite different," he said in an interview in the *New Zealand Herald.* "In non-fiction you can always go back to the research, whereas in fiction you have to go back to yourself—which is a little bit scary."

Works by the Author

A Continent of Islands: Searching for the Caribbean Destiny (1992)
A Chosen Few: The Resurrection of European Jewry (1994)
Cod; A Biography of the Fish That Changed the World (1997)
The Basque History of the World (1999)
Salt: A World History (2002)
Choice Cuts: A Savory Selection of Food Writing from around the World and throughout History (2002)
1968: The Year That Rocked the World (2003)
The Big Oyster: History on the Half Shell (2006)
Nonviolence: 25 Lessons from the History of a Dangerous Idea (2006)

Juvenile

The Cod's Story (2001)
The Girl Who Swam to Euskadi: Euskadiraino Igerian Joan Zen Neska (2006)

Contributor

The Junky's Christmas, edited by Elise Seagrave (1994)

Fiction

The White Man in the Tree: And Other Stories (2000)
Boogaloo on 2nd Avenue: A Novel of Pastry, Guilt, and Music (2005)

For Further Information

Anthony, Ted, "Prying Open the History of New York," *Seattle Times*, March 26, 2006.

Big Oyster review, *Publishers Weekly,* April 3, 2006.

Mark Kurlansky entry, Contemporary Authors Online. Reproduced in Biography Resource Center. Farmington Hills, MI: Thomson Gale, 2002. http://galenet.galegroup.com/servlet/BioRC.

Mark Kurlansky interview, "Ink Q&A," Powells.com. http://www.powells.com/ink/kurlansky.html (viewed September 2, 2006).

Olson, Raty, *Basque History of the World* review, *Booklist,* October 15, 1999.

Reid, Graham, Mark Kurlansky interview, *New Zealand Herald,* March 24, 2005.

Schneider, Martin, "From Cod to Salt to … 1968," *Publishers Weekly,* December 8, 2003.

Sokolov, Raymond, *Salt* review, *Natural History,* March 2002.

Williams, Wilda, *Choice Cuts* review, *Library Journal,* December 2002.

Wolkomir, Richard, *Cod* review, *Smithsonian,* May 1998.

Anne LaBastille

Adventure, Environment, Memoir, Science

Benchmark Title: *Woodswoman*

New York, New York

1938–

About the Author and the Author's Writing

Anne LaBastille was born in the twentieth century, obtained a modern education and sensibility, then crawled back into the nineteenth century to embrace a lifestyle of wilderness isolation.

She works with yellow pad and pen, or a portable typewriter—no electronics. The author said in *Woodswoman II* she finds mornings best suited for writing, her equivalent to a corporate executive's power period for drafting memos, writing letters, and clearing the desk. "However, instead of coffee breaks and committee meetings, my work is broken by such distractions as meeting the mail boat, tramping to the outhouse, putting fresh wood in the stove, or admiring the hummingbirds. I am alone with time yet never really alone. On sunny, calm days I may even work in the bottom of my canoe, floating on the lake."

LaBastille was born in 1938 in New York City, the daughter of Ferdinand Meyer LaBastille, a college professor, and Irma Goebel LaBastille, a musician and writer. While other girls her age were thinking about clothes or boys, Anne was reading naturalist and Sierra Club founder John Muir and fingering catalogs of camping equipment. She decided she would one day be a naturalist.

"When I started out, women just did not go into the woods the way they do now," she told Cynthia Potts in an interview on the EclecticEveryday Blog. "I was only the second woman to enroll at the Cornell School of Natural Resources. The first was from way out in Alaska. Now the program is something like sixty percent women."

She received a bachelor of science degree from Cornell University in 1955. After securing her master's in science degree from Colorado State University, she obtained her doctorate from Cornell in 1969. She then worked in various locations, leading wildlife tours, working as a ranger, a naturalist, a biologist, and a field director. She conducted surveys for World Wildlife Fund, Defenders of Wildlife, and the U.S. Environmental Protection Agency.

From 1969 to 1971, LaBastille was an assistant professor in Cornell University's Natural Resources and Science and Environmental Education Departments. She has been a research associate, consultant, freelance wildlife ecologist, photographer, and writer since 1971. She has lectured widely—from Harvard University and Cornell to

East Tennessee State University. She has given writing workshops and served on the boards of several environmental organizations. For her contributions, she has been acknowledged with the World Wildlife Fund Gold Medal for conservation (1974) and the Explorer's Club's Citation of Merit, which she was the first woman to receive.

Between sojourns into the academic world, LaBastille took refuge in the Adirondack wilds, in a cabin she built on twenty-two acres she purchased following her divorce. In 1976, she began to write about her remote life (shared with her beloved German shepherds), and the books proved popular and inspirational, particularly to women who embrace the outdoors. In fact, others have found LaBastille exemplar. Madelyn Holmes in *American Women Conservationists* and Kate Winter in *Woman in the Mountain* include her among their dynamic outdoorswomen. LaBastille has run workshops to introduce and train women for wilderness experiences and environmental initiatives. She has also written about other outdoors women in *Women and Wilderness.* "With a great deal of insight," wrote a Powells.com reviewer, "the author provides a background of the historical role of women in America's frontier wilderness and contrasts that role with the drastically different and ever-changing involvement of women in the outdoors today."

The *Woodswoman* book became a quartet as LaBastille revealed more of her forest adventures. In the first book, she built her retreat. In the second, she wrote of the next decade and threats of acid rain and trespassers, of old Adirondack guides and the prospect of romance. The two later sequels she published under her own imprint, West of the Wind Publishing, a further statement of her independence.

LaBastille acknowledged Henry David Thoreau in an essay "Fishing for the Sky" for *New Essays on Walden,* a collection published in 1992. LaBastille said that although she struggled in her college years to read *Walden*, after hearing it on tape when she was in her forties, she came not only to enjoy the work but to feel a sense of kinship with the sage of Concord.

LaBastille has written several other books that have looked at aspects of ecology and conservation. *Mama Poc* (1993), for example, describes her encounter, as a Caribbean naturalist, with the giant pied-billed grebe, or poc. "Mama Poc" is what natives came to call her, as she conducted a grebe census at Lake Atitlán in the Guatemalan Highlands. They also called her "crazy bird lady," as she sought grants to protect the endangered, flightless birds. Her effort proved futile in a country unaware of the need to save a species.

"Anne's books convey her strong belief that wild lands and wildlife everywhere need constant care and attention, wrote James Lassoie, chairman of Cornell's Department of Natural Resources, in a foreword to LaBastille's *Jaguar Totem,* her recent chronology of various of the projects for which she served as ecological consultant over the years.

Although she has slowed her pace some, and maintains a regular house, she still is most comfortable in the woods at her cabin. "This is my home," she told *Mother Earth News,* "the place I can always come back to. Here I can be perfectly alone and undisturbed to focus on my thoughts, and here I can be at peace."

Works by the Author

Birds of the Mayas, as by Anne La Bastille Bowes (1964)
Bird Kingdom of the Mayas, as by Anne La Bastille Bowes (1967)
Ecology and Management of the Atitlan Grebe, Guatemala (1974)
Woodswoman: Young Ecologist Meets Challenge Living alone in the Adirondack Wilderness (1976)
Assignment: Wildlife (1980)
Women and Wilderness (1980)
The Wilderness World of Anne LaBastille (1992)
Mama Poc: An Ecologist's Account of the Extinction of a Species (1993)
Woodswoman II: Beyond Black Bear Lake (2000)
Woodswoman III: Book Three of the Woodswoman's Adventures (1996)
Jaguar Totem: The Woodswoman Explores New Wildlands & Wildlife (1998)
The Extraordinary Adirondack Journey of Clarence Petty; Wilderness Guide, Pilot, and Conservationist, with Christopher Angus (2002)
Woodswoman IIII: Book Four of the Woodswoman's Adventures (2004)

Contributor

Wildlife Country (1977)
Wildlife '78 (1978)
Orbits and Opportunities (1980)
New Essays on Walden, edited by Robert F. Sayre (1992)

Juvenile

Ranger Rick's Best Friends Series
   White-Tailed Deer (1973)
   The Oppossums (1974)
   The Seal Family (1974)
   Wild Bobcats (1974)

For Further Information

Anne LaBastille entry, Contemporary Authors Online. Reproduced in Biography Resource Center. Farmington Hills, MI: Thomson Gale, 2001. http://galenet.galegroup.com/servlet/BioRC.

Anne LaBatsille profile, *Mother Earth News,* March/April 1978.

"Ecologist, Author, Alumna Anne LaBastille Is on Campus for Reading April 29," *Cornell Chronicle,* April 22, 1999.

Holmes, Madelyn, *American Women Conservationists: Twelve Profiles.* Jefferson, NC: McFarland, 2004.

Potts, Cynthia, Anne LaBastille interview, Eclectic Everyday Blog, August 2004. http://eclecticeveryday.blogspot.com/2004/08/woodswoman.html (viewed September 2, 2006).

Tregaskise, Sharon, "A Walk in the Woods: Anne Labastille's Adirondack Life," *Cornell Currents*, July/August 2004.

Winter, Kate H., *Woman in the Mountain: The Reconstruction of Self and Land by Adirondack Women Writers*. Albany: State University of New York Press, 1989.

Women and Wilderness review, Powells.com. http://www.powells.com/biblio?isbn=0871568284 (viewed September 2, 2006).

Anne Lamott

Biography, Memoir, Spirituality

Benchmark Title: *Bird by Bird*

San Francisco, California

1954–

About the Author and the Author's Writing

Anne Lamott isn't out to proselytize or to win converts to Christianity. She's out to reassure, to give testimony that God will accept anyone—since God has accepted her. In a loose, conversational, comfortable style, she tackles many of the world's problems. Or at least, she looks at solutions that may or may not work.

Someone once observed to the author that she typically endured trials and came to a moment of grace. "I just felt my skin crawl," she said on the Bookreporter.com Web page. "I thought, 'Well, I hope not. I hope I'm not suggesting that.' And at the same time I do experience a lot of grace and I think that most people, paying attention and looking for it, will find it. And notice it."

Anne Lamott was born in San Francisco in 1954, the daughter of Kenneth and Pamela Lamott. She grew up in Marin County, California, where she still lives. Her father, raised in Japan by his Presbyterian missionary parents, was a writer. Her mother went to law school after her children were grown and began the first all-female law firm in Honolulu. "I didn't grow up in a close family," she explained to Pamela Feinsilver for *Publishers Weekly.* "I grew up in a traditional American family where no one talked about their emotions." Her parents' marriage was not a happy one, and it ended in divorce.

Anne attended Goucher College on a tennis scholarship from 1971 to 1973 to study English, philosophy, and religion. After dropping out, she became a staff writer for *WomenSports* from 1974 to 1975. She has been a professional writer since 1980. In addition to books, she has written a food review column for *California* magazine, book reviews for *Mademoiselle,* and a "Word by Word" column for salon.com. She has a son, whose father maintains a relationship with the two. She has an ongoing relationship with painter and advertising copywriter Rory Phoenix.

Lamott's first published books were critically popular novels in which she created characters and situations, often comically portrayed, not too far from those from her own life. In particular, *Crooked Little Heart* (published in 1997) found a wide readership. However, when she moved to nonfiction, beginning with *Operating Instructions* (1993), she became increasingly popular with readers. Lamott addressed issues directly and bluntly in the book, which might be described as a how-not-to for contending with a firstborn. She found she was far from alone in her tribulations and fears of motherhood.

Her success only grew with *Bird by Bird,* an inspirational guide to writing. "She has learned that writing is more rewarding than publication, but that even writing's rewards may not lead to contentment," observed *Publishers Weekly.* Start small, her father once told her brother as he struggled with a school report about avifauna: "Just take it bird by bird."

When she published *Traveling Mercies,* the story of her conversion to Christianity, in 1999, her readership exploded. "In four sparkling, idiosyncratic books of nonfiction, novelist Anne Lamott has married a razor-sharp wit to a disarming spiritual sincerity. *Operating Instructions,* Lamott's beautiful and brutally honest 1993 account of her first years as a single parent, should be required reading for high-strung new mothers, married or not," proclaimed Jennifer Reese in *Entertainment Weekly.*

Lamott says she strives to communicate to others in a way she yearned for herself. "I was so starved for people who could speak the same language," she said in a *People Weekly* article by Galina Espinoza. She sampled several religions before settling on Presbyterianism. "I talked to God and asked for help," she said. When God answered, in the mid-1980s, it was through Jesus, whom she first encountered, she said in a ChristianityToday.com interview, in a lavatory while on an airplane. Through His intervention, she says, she became sober. "I think Jesus is divine love manifest on earth," she said, "as it comes through the community of Christians." She likens Him to a kindly Jewish uncle who gently shows the way. His guidance was greatly appreciated when she lost her father to brain cancer, her mother to Alzheimer's.

Discussing her conversion in an interview for *The Writer* in 2003, she commented "For the last twenty-some years I have tried everything in sometimes suicidally vast quantities—alcohol, drugs, work, food, excitement, good deeds, popularity, men, exercise, and just rampant compulsion and obsession—to avoid having to be in the same room with that sense of total aloneness."

Lamott writes essays on spiritual themes for salon.com that have emerged into two books about faith. "That's where I try out most of my material," the author said in a conversation with Powells.com's Dave Weich. "The pieces tend to be about faith. They tend to be spiritual, but they're really about very, very ordinary life."

Lamott's viewpoint has shifted from book to book. Writing at the launch of the Iraq war, she felt Jesus had been betrayed. *Grace (Eventually),* essays collected mostly from the online magazine salon.com, "is a less angry book. I like how I'm aging, except that my back hurts more often," she said in a conversation on Amazon.com, adding on a more serious note, "During every single terrible problem and tragedy, I have been given enough guidance and stamina and even humor to bear up, and be transformed, for the good."

The author's unconventional, liberal, loose approach to Christianity at times draws fire: "Some 'right-wingers,' often with Southern accents, occasionally call her to tell her that she will rot in hell (she received thirty such calls after writing a negative review of a 'God-awful' thriller by Pat Robertson)," she said on ChristianityToday.com.

Lamott says she lives to express herself. "I write because writing is the gift God has given me to help people in the world," she said on an "Ink Q&A" Web site. "I came with curly hair, green eyes, and the ability to shape and tell stories in a way that a certain kind of person finds helpful, and funny."

"If Jesus does not have a sense of humor," she summed up on the Religion & Ethics Web site, "I am so doomed that none of this matters anyway."

 Works by the Author

Operating Instructions: A Journal of My Son's First Year (1993)
Home and Other Stories (1993)
Bird by Bird: Some Instructions on Writing and Life (1994)
Traveling Mercies: Some Thoughts on Faith (1999)
Plan B: Further Thoughts on Faith (2005)
Grace (Eventually): Thoughts on Faith (2007)

Editor

Imagine: What America Could Be in the 21st Century, with Marianne Williamson, Joseph Sohm, and Thom Hartmann (2000)

Contributor

Between Mothers and Sons: Women Writers Talk about Having Sons and Raising Men, edited by Patricia Stevens (1999)
Not So Funny When It Happened: The Best of Travel Humor and Misadventure, edited by Tim Cahill (2000)

Forewords

When You Eat at the Refrigerator, Pull Up a Chair, by Geneen Roth (1999)
Mothers Who Think: Tales of Real-Life Parenthood, by Camille Peri and Kate Moses (1999)
Finding God When You Don't Believe in God: Searching for a Power Greater Than Yourself, by Jack Erdmann and Larry Kearney (2003)
What Would You Do If You Had No Fear? Living Your Dreams While Quakin' in Your Boots, by Diane Conway (2004)
Truth Is Beauty That Hurts: The Collected Poems of Elizabeth M. Come (2004)

Fiction

Hard Laughter (1980)
Rosie (1983)
Joe Jones (1985)
All New People (1989)
Crooked Little Heart (1997)
Blue Shoe (2002)

For Further Information

Anne Lamott entry, Contemporary Authors Online. Reproduced in Biography Resource Center. Farmington Hills, MI: Thomson Gale, 2005. http://galenet.galegroup.com/servlet/BioRC.

Anne Lamott interview, *BookBrowse.* http://www.bookbrowse.com/author_interviews/full/index.cfm?author_number=125 (viewed June 28, 2006).

Anne Lamott profile, Bookreporter.com. http://www.bookreporter.com/authors/au-lamott-anne.asp (viewed June 28, 2006).

Anne Lamott profile, "Ink Q&A," Powells.com. http://www.powells.com/inmk/lamott/html (viewed June 28, 2006).

Bird by Bird review, *Publishers Weekly,* July 18, 1994.

Espinoza, Galina, "Open Book: Drawing on Her Trials—from Alcoholism to Her Mom's Alzheimer's—Writer Anne Lamott Bares All in Her Work," *People Weekly,* November 25, 2002.

Feinsilver, Pamela, "Anne Lamont: The California Writer Talks about the Birth of Her Son and the Rebirth of Her Career," *Publishers Weekly,* May 31, 1993.

Freeman, Franklin, "Still Struggling," *America,* August 29, 2005.

Jones, Malcom Jr., "Lowercase, High Class: Profile: Anne Lamott," *Newsweek,* April 28, 1997.

Kovach, Ronald, "Straight Shooter; Anne Lamott Succeeds with Honest Writing," *The Writer,* April 2003.

Medwick, Cathleen, "Present Imperfect; Anne Lamott Takes on the Hip-Hugging Chaos of Kids, Exes, Aging Parents, and Complex Memories in Her Dead-on, Charming New Book," *O, The Oprah Magazine,* October 2002.

"Profile: Anne Lamott," *Religion & Ethics* Web site, February 17, 2006. http://www.pbs.org/wnet/religionandethics/week925/profile.html (viewed June 28, 2006).

"Questions for Anne Lamott," Amazon.com, http://www.amazon.com/Grace-Eventually-Thoughts-Anne-Lamott/dp/1594489424/ref=pd_bbs_1/102-6264343-5849734?ie=UTF8&s=books&qid=1174675811&sr=8-1 (viewed March 23, 2007).

Reese, Jennifer, "Twist of Faith," *Entertainment Weekly,* March 4, 2005.

Tennant, Agnieszka, " 'Jesusy' Anne Lamott: Chatting with a Born-Again Paradox," *Christianity Today,* January 2003.

Traveling Mercies review, *Publishers Weekly*, December 7, 1998.

Weich, Dave, "Word by Word with Anne Lamott," Powells.com, September 26, 2003. http://www.powells.com/authors/lamott.html (viewed June 28, 2006).

William Langewiesche

Investigative Reporting, Travel

Benchmark Title: *American Ground*

Unknown

1955–

About the Author and the Author's Writing

September 11, 2001, was a day of both tragedy and heroism in America. As its implications spiraled onto the world stage, many sought, in the smallest of details, to understand what had happened, to find comfort in the nation's response. William Langewiesche, veteran journalist with the *Atlantic Monthly,* took to heart the assignment of following the massive cleanup of the World Trade Center collapse in New York City. He spent six months with Kenneth Holden and Michael Burton, officials with New York City's Department of Design and Construction, and with the several thousand policemen and firefighters and engineers and professional laborers who wrestled an unmanageable situation into a system to clean up the site, methodically and conscientiously. In these individuals he found new courage, resolve, and hope.

Langewiesche's descriptions, such as this one below-ground, are vivid: "The ruins … were closing in oppressively, with crazily angled slabs tilting down into the waters ahead amid a confusion of rubble slopes that obscured the blackness beyond, where an access route might possibly be found. The place looked like a trap, and dangerous as hell." His three-part report in the *Atlantic* became the book *American Ground,* which *Library Journal*'s Nathan Ward said "is a marvelous work of committed reporting, following every detail of the Ground Zero effort down to the Turkish freighter that hauled the Tower's last steel out to sea."

Ward had reservations about the author's depiction of firemen, a criticism that mushroomed into a vocal assault by firefighters and widows, who took particular issue with his descriptions of widespread looting and the discovery, in the rubble, of a fire truck with a cab full of blue jeans apparently taken from a Trade Center store. Protests caused cancellation of author book-signing appearances, in both New York and Boston. The *Atlantic* stood by its writer.

A thorough examination of the book by *Slate* columnist Timothy Noah found only six "extremely minor" errors, according to Steve Ritea, who recapped the controversy for *American Journalism Review.* Protest by the New York Uniformed Fire Officers Association reached as far as the National Book Critics Circle, which had nominated *American Ground* for an award. The book publisher, North Point Press, stood by its writer.

William Langewiesche graduated from Stanford University in 1977, at age twenty-two, with a degree in anthropology and a yen, thanks to his father, to fly. His father, Wolfgang Langewiesche, was a pilot and author of *Stick and Rudder,* a classic how-to about flying, in 1944.

After working as a pilot for a dozen years, William followed his father's literary bent. He joined *Atlantic Monthly* in 1991; his first article was "The World in Its Extreme," about the Sahara desert. His topics have ranged from pieces on American environmentalist Douglas Tompkins in Chile, wine connoisseur Robert Parker, and the 1990 crash of EgyptAir 990. His essay on the U.S.-Mexico border and Anglo-Mexican relations became the book *Cutting for Sign* (1993), in which he combined "trenchant observations with an understated style," *Publishers Weekly* suggested in its review.

Langewiesche's second book, *Sahara Unveiled,* published three years later, showed he is "a man who knows how to travel lightly, observe intently, and transform his complex experiences into prose as polished as glass," *Booklist*'s Donna Seaman said. The book expands on his early *Atlantic* piece. Following that, he published *Inside the Sky* (1998), which is a collection of essays on aspects of flying. "Writing with poetic authority," *Publishers Weekly* said, "he uses this 'meditation' to unfold, partially, the mysteries of flight, and to recommend flight as a metaphor for understanding elements of the human condition."

The author in an interview with Robert S. Boynton, author of *The New New Journalism,* outlined what he believes his role is as a journalist: "I am my readers' eyes and ears. If I have one job, it's to tell my cherished readers to look beyond the façade, to have the courage to embrace the ugly and the real, and to avoid romanticizing the world. I am their agent on the ground."

After his book on September 11, Langewiesche went out into the ocean to tackle his next subject, the relatively unregulated business of commercial shipping, in *The Outlaw Sea* (2004). "If there's one place where the rule of law breaks down it's out on the open ocean," said Chris Edwards in *Geographical.* "As described by William Langewiesche, the law of the sea barely exists, making it possible for ships to sail when they are barely able to float and for pirates to operate with impunity." Among the anecdotes the author recounts in his book is the nighttime 1994 capsizing of the *Estonia,* a Baltic Sea ferryboat, which killed 852 of the people aboard. Based on records and interviews with some of the 137 survivors, Langewiesche relates how the ship's owners, with cooperation of Swedish maritime officials, had operated an ill-maintained, unsafe craft.

Langewiesche thrives on writing, which he sees as an inviting door into myriad interesting subjects. "It's not at all like being a tourist—a writing profession allows a deep relationship with the world," he explained in *The Writer.* "And then the actual process of writing allows you to think about it. You often don't know what you really have until you sit down to write it, and the reason is not that you don't know what's in your notes. But you haven't been forced to put it into a form that communicates, and that process is a very severe, intellectually rigorous discipline, which is, I suppose … satisfying."

Works by the Author

Cutting for Sign: The 1,951-Mile Mexican Border, It Can Be Crossed but Never Ignored (1993)
Sahara Unveiled: A Journey across the Desert (1996)
Inside the Sky: A Meditation on Flight (1998)
American Ground: Unbuilding the World Trade Center (2002)
The Outlaw Sea: A World of Freedom, Chaos and Crime (2004)
The Atomic Sky (2007)

For Further Information

Boynton, Robert S., *The New New Journalism: Conversations with America's Best Nonfiction Writers on Their Craft.* New York: Vintage Books, 2005.

Cutting for Sign review, *Publishers Weekly*, November 15, 1993.

Edwards, Chris, *Outlaw Sea* review, *Geographical,* March 2005.

Inside the Sky review, *Publishers Weekly,* May 18, 1998.

Langewiesche, William, "How I Write," *The Writer,* August 2004.

Ritea, Steve, "Ground for Contention," *American Journalism Review,* January-February, 2003.

Seaman, Donna, *Sahara Unveiled* review, *Booklist,* August 1996.

Ward, Nathan, *American Ground* review, *Library Journal,* November 1, 2002.

William Langewiesche entry, Contemporary Authors Online. Reproduced in Biography Resource Center. Farmington Hills, MI: Thomson Gale, 2004. http://galenet.galegroup.com/servlet/BioRC.

William Langewiesche profile, Lettre Ulysses Award Web page. http://www.lettre-ulysses-award.org/authors04/langewiesche.html (viewed June 28, 2006).

Zeitchik, Steven, "Author in NBCC Flap," *Publishers Weekly,* February 24, 2003.

Erik Larson

History, Investigative Reporting, True Crime

Benchmark Title: *The Devil in the White City*

Unknown

1954–

Photo by Mary Cairns

About the Author and the Author's Writing

Erik Larson does all his own research. "No researchers, no assistants. I need first-hand contact with my sources," he said on a Random House Web page for *The Devil in the White City*. "I love a good archive. Call me boring, but to me every book is a detective story, every archive a misty alley full of intrigue and desire." His account of the 1893 World's Fair in Chicago, interwoven with the drama of a serial murderer, won the author the 2004 Edgar Award for best fact crime book.

Besides the tangible details that he secures through research—from holding in his hands the postcards bearing the heavy pencil script by the delusional Patrick Prendergast, for example—Larson also comes by unexpected ideas. "I had begun looking into a turn-of-the-century murder," he said on the Random House Web page, "when I turned the page of an old newspaper and saw banner headlines about the storm and some amazingly clear black-and-white photographs showing devastation that evoke photographs of post bomb Hiroshima. I was instantly captivated." His book, *Isaac's Storm,* published in 1999, is an account of the storm that demolished Galvaston, Texas, in 1900. "The sheer magnitude of the disaster practically guarantees that any book about it will be fascinating," R. Kent Rasmussen wrote in *Library Journal,* "but Larson goes further, weaving in the story of government meteorologist Isaac Cline, who lost his wife and home in the storm and barely survived himself."

Larson knows bad weather. Although he and his wife, Dr. Christine Gleason, and their daughters now live in Seattle, where the climate is relatively mild, Larson spent most of his childhood in Freeport, Long Island, where he experienced weather extremes. Born in 1954, he grew up in Freeport, Long Island, in what he has described as a major period of East Coast hurricanes. He swam at Jones Beach before and after each storm.

After graduating summa cum laude from the University of Pennsylvania in 1976, where he studied Russian history, he saw the film *All the President's Men*. The film inspired him to become a reporter. He attended the Columbia University Graduate School of Journalism, graduating in 1978. After securing his degree, Larson wrote investigative pieces for the *Bucks County Courier Times* in Levittown, Pennsylvania. Later, he became features writer for the *Wall Street Journal* and *Time* magazine. Since then, he has written for the *New Yorker, Atlantic Monthly, Harper's,* and other periodicals. He regularly makes public presentations and has taught nonfiction writing at San Francisco State University and the University of Oregon and for the Johns Hopkins Writing Seminar.

While working for the *Wall Street Journal*, Larson was given a full month to craft one of its trademark front-page simple, funny, oblique stories. "And that's where I honed a lot of things that actually went into [*Isaac's Storm*]. First of all, the idea of a nut graph—the idea of getting readers into the story and then stepping back and explaining why you should read this. And also the attention to little nuggets of detail," Larson explained in a profile in *The Writer*.

But Larson is not a formulaic writer and his subjects are wide-ranging. *The Naked Consumer* (1992) looks at how vulnerable consumers are to sales pitches. "Instead of concentrating on offering better goods and services, he charges, companies develop invasive marketing and motivation research to 'manipulate our needs, values and shopping habits,' " noted *Publishers Weekly*. With *Lethal Passage,* Larson examined the case of Nicholas Elliot, a sixteen year old who went on a rampage and killed a teacher at his Virginia high school in 1988. From this, the author broadened his book's scope to examine the gun culture in the United States and the "paranoid, Constitution-thumping" National Rifle Association.

In *Isaac's Storm,* Larson stepped further back in time but again focused on one interesting individual—Isaac Cline—to give human dimension to his story. For his next book, *The Devil in the White City,* Larson put two men in the spotlight: Architect Daniel H. Burnham, who orchestrated the World's Fair in Chicago in 1894; and Herman Webster Mudgett (better known as Dr. H. H. Holmes), the killer of as many as two hundred people. "Larson's breathtaking new history is a novelistic yet wholly factual account of the fair and the mass murderer who lurked within it," *Publishers Weekly* said, adding that it was an apt companion to Caleb Carr's gaslight thriller *The Alienist*. This was no accident; Larson devoured Carr's novel and was keen to evoke the same sense of period in his own work. He didn't want to write a straight history of the exposition. He didn't want to concentrate on Holmes's crimes. But merging the two achieved what he wanted.

How did he get into writing novels? "When I was a mainstream journalist I always wanted to do a novel," Larson told interviewer Robert Birnbaum. "To do something creative that was just me. But what I found with *Isaac's Storm,* initially and with this book also, is that for now at least, maybe I don't have a novelist's sensibility, but what I do have is a terrific ear and eye for the little stories that bring an era alive."

Larson retold another true story of passion, murder, and invention in *Thunderstruck* (2006), set in Edwardian England. In this book, as in *Devil in the White City,* he uses two characters to tell the story. He meshes the stories of Hawley Crippen, who murders his wife and hides her body in the basement of their London home and flees with his mistress on a ship bound for Canada, and Guglielmo Marconi, who is anxious to perfect his invention, the radio.

"Larson is, at the end of the day, an admirably thorough historian whose grasp of his chosen era and personalities really shouldn't be caged," concludes *Chicago Tribune* reviewer Beth Kephart. "So we're treated to mini-histories of the first battery and sidebar biographies of social reformers in the course of this story. So Beatrix Potter makes an appearance, and also Virginia Woolf. What the heck. This is a Larson book. Why not take the ride?"

Novelistic in approach, Larson's books are rich with detail. In an interview with Dave Weich of Powells.com, Larson said he tells his writing students "the most important thing in narrative nonfiction is that you not only have to have all the research; you have to have about 100% more than you need. That's sort of my rule of thumb: If you have twice as much stuff, you can feel comfortable that in the end you will have enough."

 ## Works by the Author

> *The Naked Consumer: How Our Private Lives Become Public Commodities* (1992)
>
> *Lethal Passage; How the Travels of a Single Handgun Expose the Roots of America's Gun Crisis* (1994), reprinted as *Lethal Passage: The Story of a Gun* (1995)
>
> *Isaac's Storm: A Man, a Time, and the Deadliest Hurricane in History* (1999)
>
> *The Devil in the White City: Murder, Magic, and the Madness at the Fair That Changed America* (2003)
>
> *Thunderstruck* (2006)

For Further Information

> Birnbaum, Robert, Erik Larson profile, identitytheory.com. http://www.identitytheory.com/interviews/birnbaum95.html (viewed July 2, 2006).
>
> *Devil in the White City* review, *Publishers Weekly*, December 16, 2002.
>
> Erik Larson entry, Contemporary Authors Online. Reproduced in Biography Resource Center. Farmington Hills, MI: Thomson Gale, 2005. http://galenet.galegroup.com/servlet/BioRC.
>
> Erik Larson interview, Random House Web site. http://www.randomhouse.com/crown/devilinthewhitecity/interview.html (viewed July 2, 2006).
>
> Erik Larson profile, Random House Web site. http://www.randomhouse.com/features/isaacsstorm/book/author.html (viewed September 10, 2006).
>
> Huntley, Kristine, *Devil in the White City* review, *Booklist,* February 15, 2003.
>
> Kephart, Beth, "Erik Larson Again Finds Intrigue in Coincidence," *Chicago Tribune,* October 22, 2006.
>
> Kovach, Ronald, "A Devil of a Good Writer: Erik Larson on Choosing the Right Topic, and Making It Compelling," *The Writer,* September 2003.
>
> *Lethal Passage* review, *Publishers Weekly,* January 31, 1994.

Mudge, Alden, "The Devil Is in the Details: Fortune and Fate at the Chicago World's Fair," *BookPage.* http://www.bookpage.com/0302bp/erik_larson.html (viewed July 2, 2006).

Naked Consumer review, *Publishers Weekly,* August 17, 1992.

Rasmussen, R. Kent, *Isaac's Storm* review, *Library Journal,* May 1, 2000.

Reese, Jennifer, "Aside Tracked," *Entertainment Weekly,* October 27, 2006.

Weich, Dave, "Eric Larson in the City of Books," Powells.com. http://www.powells.com/authors/larson.html (viewed July 2, 2006).

Michael Lewis

Investigative Reporting, Sports

Benchmark Title: *Moneyball*

New Orleans, Louisiana

1960–

Photo by Tabitha Soren

About the Author and the Author's Writing

Michael Lewis's first career, as a bond salesman for a Wall Street firm, gave him solid grounding for his second career as a journalist with a knack for finding interesting people and stories with a financial hook.

Lewis was born in New Orleans in 1960. His father, J. Thomas Lewis, was a corporate lawyer. His mother, Diana Monroe Lewis, was a community activist. After receiving his bachelor of arts from Princeton University in 1982, he went on for a master's from the London School of Economics and Political Science in 1985. He and his wife, photographer and television journalist Tabitha Soren, and their daughters and son live in Berkeley, California.

After three years in Manhattan's financial district, Lewis left to write about his experiences. *Liar's Poker,* published in 1989, details how internal bickering, short-sighted planning, and greed undermined famed investment firm Solomon Brothers and led to its giant losses in October 1987. A *Forbes* reviewer remarked on the author's "wit and keen insights into the rise and fall of this investment giant."

The author next looked at Japanese capitalism as it evolved from pre–World War II family monopolies. Although General Douglas MacArthur tried to eliminate the *zaibatzu,* as these monopolies are called, as a step in introducing American-style democracy; they survived and today dominate the nation's business culture. Lewis concludes, "every important American-style change in Japan has been made while staring into the barrel of a gun or under the threat of American trade sanctions. Take away the gun and the threats and Japan reverts to its former self."

The author found the minor candidates in the 1996 elections more interesting than the frontrunners, in his next book, *Trail Fever.* (It came out in paperback as *Losers.*) Few today even remember the businessman Morry Taylor, who mounted an (obviously) unsuccessful bid for the presidency, as did Alan Keyes and Pat Buchanan. "Covering the campaign for the *New Republic,* journalist Michael Lewis was smart enough to leave the pack and take that yellow brick road, turning in dispatches that were fresh, hilarious must-reads," Tamala Edwards wrote in *Time.* The articles emerged as *Trail Fever.*

Lewis eavesdropped on Senator Alphonse D'Amato in the toilet and pawed through Bill Clinton's trash for *Trail Fever.* He had it a lot easier for *Next New Thing,* an examination of Silicon Valley and particularly businessman Jim Clark, who by 1999 had shaped three billion-dollar firms, Silicon Graphics, Netscape, and Healtheon. "Lewis was apparently given unlimited access to Clark," *Publishers Weekly* observed, "a man motivated in equal parts by a love of the technology he helps to create and a desire to prove something to a long list of people whom he believes have done him wrong throughout his life."

For *Next New Thing,* Lewis analyzed the impact of the Internet revolution. "The Internet creates chaos in any relationship that's premised on an imbalance of access to information," the author wrote. "The legal profession, the medical profession and parents in relation to their children have enjoyed superior status because they have had better access to information. I found myself looking for the effects in the world of eliminating those imbalances." The Internet, he said, was a great democratizer, and in fact, favors the fringe.

Moneyball, published in 2003 and Lewis's best-known work, is an examination of a revolution in Major League Baseball. It looks specifically at how Oakland Athletics General Manager Billy Beane looked at different statistics when he hired players others perceived as slow or overweight. Beane's scouts looked for on-base percentages, for example, instead of batting averages. The Oakland A's valued outs over base advances and shunned base-stealing or bunts while waiting for three-run homers. They didn't win the pennant, but they made a fantastic stab.

In an interview in *Mudville* magazine, Lewis said he didn't immediately see a book on the subject. Not until he looked at numbers and saw that a team with a $40 million budget was winning against foes that spent three times that on their players. "When I got in, what really hooked me were two things: one was Billy Beane as a character.... [The second was] that for a guy to become an Oakland A he had to be defective in some way."

The author found it difficult to explain this playing philosophy to old-time sports journalists. "I'm telling you people who think they know what they are talking about when they talk about baseball, including the announcers and all of the sports press—no matter how much evidence you present them to the contrary they will continue to think that what they think is right."

Heart, more than finances, energized Lewis's 2005 publication, *Coach,* a look at gruff Coach Fitz from his private school in New Orleans, who taught his charges to fight "the natural instinct to run away from adversity." Parents years after Lewis played under Fitz's direction thought the coach an old-school anachronism—thus Lewis's "Lessons on the Game of Life," as the book is subtitled, in support of naming the school gym for his old mentor.

Bringing his *Moneyball* sensitivity and descriptive writing style to football, Lewis looks at high-paid talent in the National Football League in his more recent book, *The Blind Side* (2006).

In a conversation with ESPN.com's Rob Neyer, the author acknowledged he usually developed an affinity for his subjects. "I can't imaging writing a book about people for whom I feel no sympathy," he said. "I was very fond of my main subjects, and I assumed my affection would bleed through into the prose."

Works by the Author

Liar's Poker: Rising through the Wreckage on Wall Street (1989)
The Money Culture (1991)
Pacific Rift: Adventures in the Fault Zone Between the U.S. and Japan (1991)
Trail Fever: Spin Doctors, Rented Strangers, Thumb Wrestlers, Toe Suckers, Grizzly Bears, and Other Creatures on the Road to the White House (1997), reprinted as *Losers: The Road to Everyplace but the White House* (1998)
Altering Fate: Why the Past Does Not Predict the Future (1998)
The Next New Thing: A Silicon Valley Story (1999)
Next: The Future Just Happened (2001)
Moneyball: The Art of Winning an Unfair Game (2003)
Coach: Lessons on the Game of Life (2005)
The Blind Side: Evolution of a Game (2006)

Editor

The Best American Sports Writing 2006 (2006)

For Further Information

Birnbaum, Robert, Michael Lewis interview, identitytheory.com. http://www.identitytheory.com/interviews/birnbaum110.php (viewed September 20, 2007).

Cheuse, Alan, *Liar's Poker* review, *Forbes,* March 18, 1991.

Coach review, *Publishers Weekly,* April 4, 2005.

Edwards, Tamala, *Trail Fever* review, *Time,* July 7, 1997.

Gordon, Devin, "How to Build a Ballclub: A Best-Selling Journalist on the Secrets of Oakland," *Newsweek,* May 12, 2003.

Michael Lewis interview, *Mudville* magazine. http://www.mudvillemagazine.com/archives/05_2003/index.html (viewed August 15, 2006).

Mudge, Alden, "Michael Lewis Monitors Social Shuffling and Feather Ruffling," *BookPage.* http://www.bookpage.com/0108bp/michael_lewis.html (viewed August 15, 2006).

Next New Thing review, *Publishers Weekly,* September 27, 1999.

Neyer, Rob, "Examining the Art of Evaluating," ESPN.com. http://espn.go.com/mlb/columns/neyer_rob/1553233.html (viewed September 20, 2007).

Pacific Rift review, *Publishers Weekly,* March 9, 1992.

Zimbalist, Andrew, "The American Game," *American Prospect,* October 2003.

Robert Lindsey

Adventure, Biography, True Crime

Benchmark Title: *The Falcon and the Snowman*

Glendale, California

1935–

About the Author and the Author's Writing

It's a story of buddies; a story of joyous youth. And it's the story of the sale of some of America's most closely held secrets to the Soviet Union. Richard Lindsey's first true-crime book, *The Falcon and the Snowman*—made into a motion picture with Sean Penn and Timothy Hutton—captivated its readers from the day it was published in 1979. *Newsweek*'s Walter Clemons said it was "a book quite unlike any other spy story you have ever read."

Lindsey covered the story of Christopher "The Falcon" Boyce and Daulton "The Snowman" Lee as a journalist. The two men, who grew up together and later sold CIA satellite intelligence to the Soviets, were arrested in 1977, tried, and imprisoned. As Aaron Latham described in a *New York Times* story in 1983, "Managing to develop a rapport with Mr. Boyce, the reporter soon learned some of the spy's dark secrets, mining his motivations and methods just the way the spy had opened up the Black Vault."

Interestingly, that wasn't the end of the story. Boyce broke out of federal prison in Lompoc, California, in 1980, and, using his wilderness skills, successfully eluded recapture for months. He adopted a new identity in Idaho and openly worked for a nursery. He took flying lessons in Washington State. But he also began to rob banks. An informant finally turned him in after he bragged too openly about his accomplishments.

Lindsey's sequel, *The Flight of the Falcon,* told the story. Evan "Ed McBain" Hunter, Grand Master of crime fiction, certainly knew a good story when he saw it. He had only high praise for the book: "Lindsey, the Los Angeles bureau chief of *The New York Times,* details the 19-month manhunt that resulted in Mr. Boyce's eventual capture, and he does so at a headlong pace that makes the book read like a suspense thriller. Indeed, as the story hurtles toward its breathless climax, it is virtually impossible to turn the pages fast enough."

In a structural variation from his first book, as the story unfolded in *Flight*, Lindsey began to alternate viewpoints between Boyce and his pursuers, between prey and hunters. *Washington Post Book World* reviewer Michael Collins found Lindsey presented the espionage story "with clarity and sensitivity."

Born in Glendale, California, in 1935, the son of Robert Hughes and Claire Elizabeth Schulz Lindsey, Lindsey received a bachelor of arts degree from San Jose State University in 1956. He was a reporter for the *San Jose Mercury News* from 1956 to 1968 and then joined the *New York Times* as a reporter. In 1975, he became that newspaper's Los Angeles bureau chief. He and his wife, Sandra Jean Wurts, have two children.

In addition to the true-espionage books, Lindsay has written two true-crime novels and two celebrity biographies. The biographies were *Brando,* published in 1994, about the famous actor, and *Reagan*, which he wrote with several other *New York Times* reporters and published in 1981.

One of Lindsey's crime novels, *A Gathering of Saints,* tells the story of Mark Hofmann, a dealer in Church of Latter Day Saints (LDS) documents, who "discovered" a (forged) nineteenth-century letter written by Martin Harris. Harris, one of the three Witnesses to the Book of Mormon, purportedly described to his correspondent, W. W. Phelps, the story of Joseph Smith and his unearthing of the gold plates thanks to the appearance of a spirit. The occult nature of the letter disturbed LDS hierarchy. Hofmann let out word of the letter, hoping to sell it and other sensitive items to the church. Negotiations ended when a pipe bomb exploded in his car, nearly killing him. Lindsey, in the view of the Mormons in Transition Web site, wrote up the crime with balance and without the sensationalism of some other books on the subject. "His sharp investigative journalism and insightful analysis united and organized a potentially fragmented tale," the reviewer wrote.

Although he has yet to find another subject as engaging to readers as the Falcon or the Snowman, his position since 1986 as the *New York Times'* chief West Coast correspondent affords him considerable versatility in his search.

Works by the Author

The Falcon and the Snowman: A True Story of Friendship and Espionage (1979)
Reagan: The Man, the President, with Hendrick Smith, Adam Clymer, Leonard
    Silk, and Richard Burt (1981)
The Flight of the Falcon (1983)
A Gathering of Saints: A True Story of Money, Murder, and Deceit (1988)
Irresistible Impulse: A True Story of Blood and Money (1992)
Brando: Songs My Mother Taught Me, with Marlon Brando (1994)

Films Adaptations

The Falcon and the Snowman (1985)

For Further Information

Clemons, Walter, *The Falcon and the Snowman* review, *Newsweek*, November
    26, 1979.
Collins, Michael, *The Falcon and the Snowman* review, *Washington Post Book
    World,* December 16, 1979.

Gathering of Saints review, Mormons in Transition Web site. http://www.irr. org/mit/gathering.html (viewed September 11, 2006).

Hunter, Evan, *The Flight of the Falcon* review, *New York Times Book Review,* November 23, 1983.

Irresistible Impulse review, *Publishers Weekly,* June 29, 1992.

Latham, Aaron, "Caught Twice," *New York Times*, November 27, 1983.

Robert (Hughes) Lindsey entry, Contemporary Authors Online. Reproduced in Biography Resource Center. Farmington Hills, MI: Thomson Gale, 2006. http://galenet.galegroup.com/servlet/BioRC.

Smothers, Bonnie, *Brando* review, *Booklist,* October 1, 1994.

Barry Lopez

Environment, Investigative Reporting

Benchmark Title: *Arctic Dreams*

Port Chester, New York

1945–

Photo courtesy Knopf

About the Author and the Author's Writing

"I grew up in a rural landscape in Southern California," Barry Lopez said in an interview on the Calypso Consulting Web site. "I spent a lot of time in the Mojave Desert as a child, so in those early years I came to look at the world in terms of those images. I raised pigeons. The release of pigeons, the way they flew, and the way they described the air above me were the first ways I came to understand the complexity of life."

In the three decades of his writing, Lopez has looked at the natural world—within and beyond—to better understand how humans relate to it. And he has done remarkably well, garnering a National Book Award in 1986 for *Arctic Dreams*.

How did Lopez, a native of Port Chester, New York, end up in Southern California? His family, including one brother, moved west when he was three; within two years, his parents, divorced. The boys made the best of their big, rugged backyard. "Lopez turned to the natural world for solace," according to Nicholas O'Connell in a profile of the author for *Commonweal*. "By foot and bike, he explored the local farms, rivers, and mountains. His mother encouraged this appreciation of landscape, taking him and his younger brother Dennis to the Mojave Desert, the Santa Monica Mountains, Zuma Beach, Big Bear Lake, Hoover Dam, and the Grand Canyon."

His mother, Mary Holstun, remarried in 1956. Their new father, Adrian Bernard Lopez, adopted the boys and moved the family to Manhattan, where Barry attended a Catholic school. He traveled in Europe the summer before he entered Notre Dame University, where he took courses in aeronautical engineering, but he ended up an English major. Inspired by the weekend excursions of his youth, Lopez traveled whenever he could during these years, and by the time he graduated in 1966, he had visited all of the continental United States except Oklahoma.

Lopez briefly considered joining a monastery. In 1967, he met and married Sandra Landers (they divorced in 1999), settled in the Cascade Mountains, and entered the University of Oregon's fine arts program. He took a course with folklorist Barre Toelken, who had an enormous influence on Lopez's future career. Lopez became entranced by the possibilities of anthropology and researching other cultures, particularly as they related to their land. He abruptly changed his major to anthropology. He earned a master's in 1968.

Lopez collected and edited for publication Native American oral folk tales in books such as *Giving Birth to Thunder, Sleeping with His Daughter.* He also wrote short stories, including those gathered in the trilogy of *Desert Notes, River Notes,* and *Field Notes.* In the last, *Backpacker* reviewer Jeff Rennicke noted the author has demonstrated a progression. "Gone is much of the youthful, clear cut world view of the earlier works. Yet Lopez is still pursuing many of the same themes—a sense of place, the human responsibility for the planet, how we come to know our surroundings and ourselves."

The author enjoys working in both fiction and nonfiction. Nonfiction, obviously, is bound by factual truth. "The basis for fiction is emotional truth," he said in a *January Magazine* interview. "It's got to be the case that the reader reading the work of fiction says: This is plausible, this could happen. I know this. And one of the reasons I would say that is in non-fiction you're often reading something that maybe you didn't know."

Lopez has written extensively and on a wide range of topics for *Harper's, North American Review, GEO, Outside,* the *New York Times Book Review,* and other periodicals. "My ideal is that the writer is a servant in some way of the society in which he resides," Lopez mused in a Capitola Book Cafe interview in 1998. "That society can be defined in a variety of ways; geographic communities, intellectual communities, or even political communities."

As he has explored nature themes, Lopez has increasingly added metaphorical and spiritual elements, in the spirit of Thoreau. His message is that the modern generation of humans lives without an engagement to the environment that was evident in earlier, "primitive" cultures. An experience, described in *Arctic Dreams,* published in 1986, brought this home to him. He and a trio of scientists working off the North Slope of Alaska, nearly became icebound when the weather suddenly and drastically changed for the worse. They worked furiously to break the ice and navigate their craft into open water. Lopez suffered severe chill when rain penetrated his parka, and hovered near unconsciousness. "Arctic history became for me, then, a legacy of desire —the desire of individual men to achieve their goals," he wrote. "But it was also the legacy of a kind of desire that transcends heroics and which was privately known to many—the desire for a safe and honorable passage through the world."

Lopez yearns to answer the big questions: "What is the relationship of the individual to the state, what is the relationship of the individual to society, what is the relationship of human culture to place? All of those questions now, at least in the United States, are being most rigorously addressed in this genre called 'nature writing,' " he said in a conversation with Mark Mordue.

The author says he frequently puts in ten- or twelve-hours days at his desk. "I'm always writing," Lopez told journalist Douglas Marx. "There's no difference for me between my life and my work: they're completely of a part, totally related. I'm reading when I get up in the morning and I'm reading when I go to bed at night. I'm walking out and traveling and doing all that feeds my work during all my waking hours, and I'm certain that during my sleeping hours stories gestate."

 Works by the Author

Of Wolves and Men (1978)
Arctic Dreams: Imagination and Desire in a Northern Landscape (1986)
Crossing Open Ground (1988)
The Rediscovery of North America (1990)
About This Life: Journeys on the Threshold of Memory (1998)
Apologia (1998)

Anthologies

On Nature: Nature, Landscape, and Natural History, edited by Daniel Halpern (1987)
Modern American Memoirs, edited by Annie Dillard and Cort Conley (1995)
Writers Harvest 3, edited by Tobias Wolff and William Spruill (2000)

Editor

Home Ground: Language for an American Landscape, with Debra Gwartney (2006)

Fiction

Desert Notes: Reflections in the Eye of a Raven (1976)
Giving Birth to Thunder, Sleeping with His Daughter, Coyote Builds North America (1977)
River Notes; The Dance of Herons (1979)
Desert Reservation (1980), chapbook
Winter County (1981)
Coyote Love (1989), chapbook
Crow and Weasel (1990)
Desert Notes: Reflections in the Eye of a Raven/River Notes: The Dance of Herons (1990)
Field Notes; The Grace Note of the Canyon Wren (1994)
Lessons from the Wolverine (1997)
Light Action in the Caribbean (2000)
Resistance (2004)
Vintage Lopez (2004), includes fiction and nonfiction selections

Stage Adaptation

Crow and Weasel, with Jim Leonard Jr. (1993)

For Further Information

Barry Lopez entry, *Authors and Artists for Young Adults*, Vol. 63. Detroit, MI: Thomson Gale, 2005.

Barry Lopez interview, Calypso Consulting Web site. http://www.calypsoconsulting.com/lopez.html (viewed August 23, 2006).

Barry Lopez interview, Capitola Book Cafe, June 28, 1998. http://www.capitolabookcafe.com/andrea/lopez.html (viewed September 20, 2007).

Marx, Douglas, "Barry Lopez: 'I Am a Writer Who Travels,' " *Publishers Weekly,* September 26, 1994.

Mordue, Mark, "A Conversation with Barry Lopez." 12gauge.com. http://www.12gauge.com/issue9/r_barry_lopez.html (viewed August 23, 2006).

O'Connell, Nicholas, "At One with the Natural World—Barry Lopez's Adventure with the World & the Wild," *Commonweal,* March 24, 2000.

Rennicke, Jeff, *Field Notes* review, *Backpacker,* August 1995.

Richards, Linda L., Barry Lopez interview, *January Magazine,* January 2001.

Seaman, Donna, *About This Life* review, *Booklist,* April 1998.

Tredinnick, Mark, *The Land's Wild Music: Encounters with Barry Lopez, Peter Matthiessen, Terry Tempest William, and James Galvin*. San Antonio, TX: Trinity University Press, 2005.

Peter Maas

Adventure, Biography, True Crime

Benchmark Title: *Serpico*

New York, New York

1929–2001

About the Author and the Author's Writing

"It's amazing to me how the details of first events get etched in your mind," said the subject of Peter Maas's 1997 biography, *Underboss*. "We kidded and joked as we slowly drove down the street. Tommy turned up the radio. A Beatles song was on. The seating arrangement wasn't exactly what I wanted. I reached under my jacket for my gun, which was a .38."

The speaker is Salvatore Gravano, known to his peers as "Sammy the Bull," the Brooklyn construction contractor/Mafioso underboss who broke the "Omerta" and testified in 1992 against John the "Dapper Don" Gotti. Gravano's testimony tore up the Gambino Family's organized crime operations; after that, "The Bull" was more often called "The Rat." Gravano spent five years in prison then was a free man again—forgiven for an alleged nineteen gangland slayings. But he couldn't stay out of trouble. He eventually pleaded guilty to drug trafficking charges in 2002 and began a twenty-year sentence. Then New York City police unearthed sufficient evidence to charge him in the killing of a corrupt New York policeman.

That's the character who, so conversationally, in Maas's *The Underboss,* relates a gangland slaying.

"Sammy Gravano is the defector from the Mafia who brought John Gotti down. And 'defector,' as Peter Maas points out in this brilliantly constructed and grimly fascinating history-cum-memoir, is the right word, not 'fink' or 'rat'," wrote mystery novelist Donald E. Westlake in reviewing the book. "He switched sides only after his own team proved disloyal to him."

Criminals and cops were Maas's strong suit, in a half-century writing career that stretched from his days as a reporter with the *New York Herald Tribune* in Paris in 1955 and 1956 to stints in New York with *Collier's* the next year, a run as senior editor for *Look* from 1959 to 1962, and an assignment as the *Saturday Evening Post*'s senior writer from 1963 to 1966. Standouts of his work from this time are an investigative piece for *Look* in 1960 about a man held longer than anyone else on death row in Louisiana and an expose for the *Post* of a syndicated columnist, Cholly Knickerbocker, who was really a spy for the Dominican Republic. From then, he concentrated on columns for *New York* and the *New York Times* and on books.

Of Dutch and Irish ancestry, Maas was born in New York City in 1929. He studied history and political science and earned a bachelor of arts from Duke University in 1949. While a reporter for the student newspaper, he landed a scoop when he eluded security and interviewed Walter Reuther, the labor leader who was then recovering in a hospital from an attempted assassination. He served in the U.S. Navy during the Korean War. Maas married producer Audrey Gellen in 1962. Following her 1975 death, he married real estate broker Laura Parkins in 1976. He had one child in each marriage.

Maas wrote *Underboss* with the help of his subject, Gravano. The New York State Crime Victims Board didn't appreciate the fact that Gravano may have profited from the book; it sued Maas and his publisher, HarperCollins. The New York State Appellate Division in 2000 upheld Maas and said the New York State "Son of Sam" law, enacted to recover any profits a criminal might look to profit from the notoriety of his crime, belonged to the victims, didn't apply in this case because Gravano had pled guilty to charges against him.

Underboss wasn't Maas's first crime book with an insider angle. That was *The Valachi Papers,* about another high-profile mob informant, hit man Joe Valachi. The 1969 book was rejected by twenty-four publishers before making its way into print—over governmental objections, according to *Guardian* reporter Tony Thompson. "Finally published, the first print run sold out in three days. The book went on to sell 2.5 million copies, [and] was translated into 14 languages." Maas inadvertently pioneered a new genre in fiction; Mario Puzo's novel *The Godfather* came out the next year.

In between was a variation, *Serpico,* in which the supposed good guys were, in fact, the criminals, and a man who had ached to be a cop from his boyhood couldn't stomach the corruption. No one would listen—until he went to the *New York Times* and blew off the lid. The hastily formed Knapp Commission made a very public investigation. Serpico, still on the force, was shot in the face during a drug raid. His fellow officers, to his mind, were too slow in coming to his assistance. He eventually quit the force and moved to Europe.

"In *Serpico* and in the unjustly little known *Marie,* Maas has given compelling portraits of honest, decent people who refused to participate in criminal activities and then had the remarkable courage to reveal the existence of the conspiracies that almost all of those around them were involved in," noted a reviewer on the Bruthersjudd.com Web site.

Maas was fascinated by character. "When I write nonfiction, it's like fiction," he is quoted in a *New York Times* obituary. "All the research, and the writing too, is a continual process of discovery for me. I never have an outline."

The author's last book was *The Terrible Hours,* published in 1999, an account of U.S. Navy officer Charles "Swede" Momsen and his valiant effort, in the face of bureaucracy and uncooperative seas, to save sailors trapped aboard the submarine *Squalus* when the craft sank in 250 feet of water off the New England coast in 1939.

It was his last book. Maas died in 2001 of complications following surgery for an ulcer.

Works by the Author

The Rescuer (1968)
The Valachi Papers (1969)
Serpico (1973)
King of the Gypsies (1975)
Marie: A True Story (1983)
Manhunt: The Incredible Pursuit of a CIA Agent Turned Terrorist (1986)
In a Child's Name: The Legacy of a Mother's Murder (1990)
Killer Spy: The Inside Story of the FBI's Pursuit and Capture of Aldrich Ames, America's Deadliest Spy (1995)
Underboss: Sammy the Bull Gravano's Story of Life in the Mafia (1997)
The Terrible Hours: The Man behind the Greatest Submarine Rescue in History (1999)

Fiction

Made in America (1979)
Father and Son (1989)
China White: The Ultimate International Conspiracy (1994)

Film Adaptations

The Valachi Papers (1972)
Serpico (1973)
Serpico: The Deadly Game (1976)
The King of the Gypsies (1978)
Marie: A True Story (1985)
In a Child's Name (1991)
Submerged (2001), based on *The Terrible Hours*

For Further Information

Barron, James, "Peter Maas, Writer Who Chronicled the Mafia, Dies at 72," *New York Times,* August 24, 2001.

"New York State Appellate Division Affirms Dismissal of Crime Victims Board Case against Peter Maas and HarperCollins Publishers," Business Wire, March 7, 2000.

Peter Maas entry, Contemporary Authors Online. Reproduced in Biography Resource Center. Farmington Hills, MI: Thomson Gale, 2004. http://galenet.galegroup.com/servlet/BioRC.

Serpico review, Brothersjudd.com. http://www.brothersjudd.com/index.cfm/fuseaction/reviews.detail/book_id/524 (viewed September 24, 2006).

Thompson, Tony, "Peter Maas: Mixing Fact and Fiction to Tell the Stories of Joe Valachi and Serpico," the *Guardian,* August 25, 2001.

Westlake, Donald E., "A Good Family Man," *New York Times Book Review,* May 18, 1997.

Dave Marsh

Biography, Investigative Reporting

Benchmark Title: *Glory Days*

Pontiac, Michigan
1950–

About the Author and the Author's Writing

"Music can't change the world," Dave Marsh wrote on RockRap.com of Bruce Springsteen's *We Shall Overcome* CD in 2006. "But sometimes, it delivers some pretty great marching orders."

Marsh, so long a voice on the popular music scene some have called him "the Methuselah of rock criticism," seemed destined for a career on the auto assembly line in Pontiac, Michigan, where he was born in 1950, the son of railroad worker O. K. Marsh and his wife, Mary Evon Marsh. It was a city of laborers. Music was an aural relief, but no one was expected to write about it. Marsh wanted to write about it.

His first words on paper brought him favorable feedback. "When I wrote, people displayed their emotions," he told Paula Span in a *Washington Post* story. "Sometimes they even laughed when I wanted them to. Just as important, my own confused thoughts and feelings seemed clear. Writing for me has always been a way of disentangling the conflicting impressions of events and people and experiences, the basic circumstances of living in the world."

At Wayne State University in Detroit, Marsh met another student, Barry Kramer, who published a magazine about rock music, *Creem*. Marsh dropped out, took command of the tabloid for four years, learned the craft as he went, and fully launched himself into the world of popular music literature. Setting the tone for the rising genre, Marsh moved on to *Newsday* and the *Real Paper* in Boston and finally to *Rolling Stone,* where he wrote a record review column from 1975 to 1978. Still a contributor to that periodical, Marsh has written for a nonadvertising newsletter, Rock and Roll Confidential (later Rock and Rap Confidential). He has also been music critic for *Playboy* and for Web sites StarPolish and ParadigmTSA. The writer and his wife, Barbara Carr, a recording executive and one of Springsteen's managers, have one daughter. Marsh serves on the board of the National Writers Union and of the Kristen Ann Carr Fund for Sarcoma Research, named in honor of a second daughter, who died of cancer.

Marsh described to interviewer Scott Woods how he perceives his role as "trying to look at this thing, the music thing, and how it expresses things for people who don't have any other means of public expression.… I'm trying to write from the point of view of an informed and intelligent and at this stage I would guess it's fair to say 'expert' audience member. I'm not trying to write from the point of view of the musician."

Born to Run, Marsh's first book, and his first of several about Bruce Springsteen, was one of the earliest popular rock 'n' roll biographies. The author looks beyond the music to its social context. In a discussion of Springsteen's *We Shall Overcome* CD with journalist Alan Maas, for example, Marsh recalls a remark in musicologist Christopher Small's book, *Music of the Common Tongue,* "He begins by saying that English is a deficient language for explaining music because it thinks that music is a noun, and music is really a verb. We need the verb 'musicking.' Musicking is what this album is about. Bruce talks about this in the liner notes—that this album is about the making of the music."

Marsh elaborates on music's larger social context: every song that has endured and been recorded or performed by other than the originator, he told *Socialist Worker Online,* "has its individual, specific history. But the history of all of them… is that somebody picks them up and puts themselves into them. It's always particular to the people who are singing them, and it's always a link back to the origins—you're looking backward while you look forward."

Marsh's writing goes beyond listening and reacting; it involves at times lengthy research, as when he examined diaries, read stories and verses, reviewed letters and song lyrics, and pored over newspaper articles for *Pastures of Plenty,* a collection of material that offers a different view of iconic folk singer Woody Guthrie.

Marsh is also no stranger to the stage: he has played with Rock Bottom Remainders, the rock band made up of Stephen King, Amy Tan, Dave Barry, and other authors that mostly plays at bookseller conventions.

Marsh has a take on all popular music's leading lights. Neil Young, he wrote in *Illustrated History of Rock* (in a chapter deleted from later editions), "is Dylan's greatest disciple, not only because of a shared sound—a wracked voice, an inability to stay in one stylistic space for long—but also because of a shared cunning: Young has mastered Dylan's greatest trick, the art of self-mythology."

Marsh has been criticized for at times becoming too close to his subjects, specifically to Bruce Springsteen. Journalist Jacob Weisberg accused him in *Washington Monthly* of promoting a "vapid, pretentious tone that has infected rock reviewers at alternative papers and music magazines around the country." Marsh countered, in an interview with Susan Whitall for the *Detroit News,* that he writes subjectively and honestly. "Objective criticism is an oxymoron to me."

One of his more interesting books is the biography not of an individual, but of a song: Richard Berry's 1956 "Louie Louie," an anthem for teenage garage bands and dance clubs for decades. Marsh describes how the Kingsmen issued a version in 1963 which, with slurred (and to some adult ears suggestive) lyrics intoned by a singer who wore braces, has since been recorded by performers from Frank Zappa to Nirvana. "Crammed with trivia and wit, this text convincingly argues in mock-profound terms its thesis that "Louie" is a melodic phenomenon far bigger than the mere mortals who perform it," a *Publishers Weekly* reviewer wrote.

Works by the Author

Born to Run: The Bruce Springsteen Story (1979)

The Book of Rock Lists (1980)

Elvis (1981)

Before I Get Old: The Story of the Who (1982)

Rocktopicon, with Sandra Charon and Deborah Geller (1984)

Fortunate Son: The Best of Dave Marsh (1985)

The First Rock & Roll Confidential Report inside the World of Rock & Roll (1985)

Sun City by Artists United against Apartheid: The Struggle for Freedom in South Africa (1985)

Trapped: Michael Jackson and the Crossover Dream (1986)

Glory Days: Bruce Springsteen in the 1980s (1987)

The Heart of Rock and Soul: The 1001 Greatest Singles Ever Made (1989)

50 Ways to Fight Censorship (1991)

Louie, Louie: The History and Mythology of the World's Most Famous Rock 'n' Roll Song (1993)

Merry Christmas, Baby: Holiday Music from Bing to Sting (1993)

The New Book of Rock Lists (1994)

Born to Run (1996)

George Straight (1996)

Neil Young (1996)

Soul Asylum, with Danny Alexander (1996)

Sam and Dave: An Oral History with Sam Moore (1998)

Bruce Springsteen (2003)

Forever Young: Photographs of Bob Dylan, with Douglas R. Gilbert (2005)

The Trouble with Music, with Mat Callahan and Ian Mackaye (2005)

Bruce Springsteen on Tour 1968–2005 (2006)

The Beatles' Second Album (Rock of Ages) (2007)

Contributor

Illustrated History of Rock (1976)

The Great Rock 'n' Roll Joke Book (1997)

Editor

Rolling Stone Record Guide: Reviews and Ratings of Almost Ten Thousand Currently Available Pop, Rock, Soul, Country, Blues, Jazz, and Gospel Albums, with John Swenson (1980), revised as *The New Rolling Stone Record Guide,* with Kevin Stein (1984)

Pastures of Plenty: A Self-Portrait, by Woody Guthrie, with Harold Leventhal (1990)

Heaven Is under Our Feet: A Book for Walden Woods, with Don Henley (1991)

Mid-life Confidential: The Rock Bottom Remainders Tour America with Three Chords and an Attitude (1994)

Black Sabbath: An Oral History, with Mike Stark (1998)

George Clinton and P-Funk: An Oral History (1998)

Sly and the Family Stone: An Oral History, with Joel Selvin (1998)

Up Around the Bend: The Oral History of Creedence Clearwater Revival, with Craig Werner (1998)

For Further Information

Dave Marsh entry, *Authors and Artists for Young Adults*, Vol. 52. Detroit, MI: Gale Group, 2003.

Dave Marsh entry, Contemporary Authors Online. Reproduced in Biography Resource Center. Farmington Hills, MI: Thomson Gale, 2001. http://galenet.galegroup.com/servlet/BioRC.

Louie, Louie review, *Publishers Weekly,* June 28, 1993.

Maas, Alan, "An Interview with Dave Marsh," *CounterPunch.* http://www.counterpunch.org/maass05222006.html (viewed September 17, 2007).

Marsh, Dave, "Boy from the North Country," *American Grandstand,* July 2, 2001. http://www.starpolish.com/news/article.asp=id114 (viewed May 24, 2006).

Marsh, Dave, "Bruce Springsteen in New Orleans," RockRap.com, June 15, 2006. Reproduced at http://scottpeterson.typepad.com/leftofthedial/2006/06/index.html (viewed September 20, 2007).

Marsh, Dave, "Marsh on Music," *American Grandstand,* April 16, 2001. http://www.starpolish.com/news/article.asp?id=77 (viewed May 24, 2006).

Marsh, Dave, *We Shall Overcome* review, May 19, 2006. http://www.socialistworker.org/2006-1/589/589_11_DaveMarsh.shtml (viewed September 20, 2007).

Pfeiffer, Scott, Dave Marsh interview, *People's Tribune,* January 1998.

Span, Paula, "Dave Marsh, Boswell to 'The Boss,' " *Washington Post*, April 26, 1978.

Weisberg, Jacob, "The Heart of Rock and Soul: The 1001 Greatest Singles Ever Made," *Washington Monthly,* December 1989.

Whiteall, Susan, Dave Marsh profile, *Detroit News*, May 17, 1987.

Woods, Scott, "A Meaty, Beaty, Big, and Bouncy Interview with Dave Marsh," Rockcritics.com. http://www.rockcritics.com/interview/davemarsh.html (May 24, 2006).

Peter Matthiessen

Adventure, Environment, Spirituality

Benchmark Title: *The Snow Leopard*

New York, New York

1927–

Photo by Alix Smith

About the Author and the Author's Writing

"The langur is sacred to all Hindus as the manifestation of the monkey god Hanuman," Peter Matthiessen writes in *The Snow Leopard,* his highly respected description of a 1973 journey into Nepal's rugged Dolpo region in the company of zoologist George Schaller, "and is also the beast most commonly brought forth to account for footprints of the 'abominable snowman' although bears, snow leopards, great-footed birds, and melting snow have their supporters."

The scientist and the journalist were in search of the elusive Himalayan blue sheep—but yeti, snow leopards, and spiritual manifestation were also on the agenda. Matthiesen's *The Snow Leopard* was a result of the trek. The travel Web site World Hum identified *The Snow Leopard* as one of the all-time best travel books. "As he takes the reader deep into the mountains," it states, "we realize that Matthiessen is using this scientific journey as a metaphor to reflect on much broader matters of life, death and existence itself."

Matthiessen and Shaller never found the snow leopard. But that only reinforced the positive that came from the excursion, which points out the obvious: We need to live in the moment.

"I was always writing something down," the author told interviewer Michael Sims for *BookPage.* "I don't know if that was the beginning or not. But even when I was a little boy, I would make strange lists—even of my phonograph records. I don't know why."

Matthiessen was born in 1927 in New York City, the son of Erard A. and Elizabeth Carey Matthiesen. His father, a well-established architect, served on the board of the National Audubon Society. Peter attended The Hotchkiss School in Lakeville, Connecticut. From 1945 to 1947, he served in the U.S. Navy. In 1948 and 1949, he attended La Sorbonne, the University of Paris, after which he completed his studies at Yale, receiving a bachelor of arts in 1950.

The author has said his eyes were first opened to his life's direction when he was a counselor at a charity camp and witnessed boys wolf their food. "And I realized these kids had never been able to relax and eat their fill in their whole life," he said in an interview with Hillel Italie. "And I thought, 'What kind of country is this were we have all this money and people are as poor as that?' "

The writer's interest in the downtrodden and abused first emerged in his fiction, although Matthiesen has also written broadly of his travels to sparsely populated lands, of unusual wildlife, unknown landscapes, forgotten and oppressed people, and struggling cultures.

One of his early short stories garnered the 1951 Atlantic Prize. He taught at Yale for a year, then returned to Paris and there cofounded the *Paris Review* with Harold L. Humes, where he served as its first fiction editor. Once he was back on American shores, Matthiesen continued to write but also worked as a commercial fisherman on Long Island—something he has described as a necessary physical counterpoint to his intellectual bent.

In 1956, the author set off on an automobile tour of the country; the end result, his *Wildlife in America,* signaled a change in his writing direction to nonfiction. He traveled to the Canadian northwest, to Asia and Australia and beyond for his next several books, including *The Cloud Forest* and *Under the Mountain Wall.* In the early 1960s, he completed two more novels. One, *At Play in the Fields of the Lords* (1965), was nominated for a National Book Award. Showing considerable research, it is about a remote group of South American Indians and the man sent to "pacify" them. *New York Times* reviewer Emile Capouya noted the author's "detailed picture of Indian customs, his insight into character, and his physical descriptions are almost always convincing and absorbing."

The author's nonfiction *The Tree Where Man Was Born* (1972) also earned the author a National Book Award nomination. *New York Times* reviewer Eric Pace noted Matthiessen's journalistic integrity and attention to detail in sounding an environmental alarm and called it "the first nonfiction book on Africa with a surprise ending." The book is about the loss of animal species and habitat. Matthiessen in the book quotes Tanzania game department agent Peter Enderlein, who nicely sums up the theme: "This valley, this people—it is a tragedy we are watching. And it is a sign of what is happening everywhere in this country, in the whole world." (Matthiessen kept his eye on the continent; his *African Silences* [1991] two decades later merged his hallmark environmental reportage with a travelogue and nature study.)

In 1974, he was elected to the National Institute of Arts and Letters. Four years later, *The Snow Leopard* won a National Book Award. A blend of natural history with a Zen undercurrent, Matthiessen wrote the book following the 1972 death of his second wife, Deborah Love, with whom he had two children. There were also two children from his first marriage, to Patricia Southgate in 1951 (it ended in divorce in 1958). In 1980, he married a third time, to Maria Eckert. They live on Long Island.

Matthiessen says he is equally comfortable writing fiction or nonfiction. In nonfiction, one is bound by the truth, and likely has an idea of the direction in which he is headed, he has explained. Fiction, on the other hand, is made up, and while he may have a hint of where his characters may take him, for the most part, he has to let them lead the way.

The author returned to the jungle for *Tigers in the Snow,* published in 2000. The book relates trips he made to Russia in 1992 and 1996 in pursuit of the Siberian tiger.

While there, he met the biologist Maurice Hornocker, codirector of the Siberian Tiger Project.

Matthiessen is not without hope, though he may sometimes sound as if he is. He told interviewer Kay Bonetti, "We must all make an effort for the betterment of mankind, even though we know it won't do any good."

Matthiessen visited South Georgia and Antarctica for his recent *End of the Earth.* In reviewing the book for *Booklist,* Donna Seaman described the author as "The grand master of the purposeful and philosophical nature-oriented travelogue."

Works by the Author

Wildlife in America (1959), revised (1987)

The Cloud Forest: A Chronicle of the South American Wilderness (1961)

Under the Mountain Wall: A Chronicle of Two Seasons in the Stone Age (1962)

Comingmak: The Expedition to the Musk Ox Island in the Bering Sea (1967)

The Shorebirds of North America (1967), reprinted as *The Wind Birds* (1973)

Sal Si Puedes: Cesar Chavez and the New American Revolution (1970) reprinted as *Sal Si Puedes (Escape If You Can)* (2000)

Blue Meridian: The Search for the Great White Shark (1971)

Everglades: With Selections from the Writings of Peter Matthiessen, edited by Paul Brooks (1971)

The Tree Where Man Was Born (1972/revised 1995)

The Snow Leopard (1978)

Sand Rivers (1981)

In the Spirit of Crazy Horse (1983)

Indian Country (1984)

Men's Lives: The Surfmen and Baymen of the South Fork (1986)

Nine-Headed Dragon River: Zen Journals 1969–1982 (1986)

African Silences (1991)

Shadows of Africa (1992)

East of Lo Mothang (1995)

Tigers in the Snow (2000)

The Peter Matthiessen Reader (2000)

The Birds of Heaven: Travels with Cranes, with Robert Bateman (2002)

End of the Earth: Voyages to the White Continent, with Kenneth Garrett (2003)

Arctic National Wildlife Refuge: Seasons of Life and Land: A Photographic Journey, with Subhankar Banerje (2003)

Editor

North American Indians (2004)

For Juvenile Readers

Seal Pool (1972), reprinted as *The Great Auk Escape* (1974)

Fiction

Race Rock (1954)
Partisans (1955)
Raditzer (1961)
At Play in the Fields of the Lord (1965)
Far Tortuga (1975)
On the River Styx, and Other Stories (1989)

Watson Trilogy

Killing Mister Watson (1990)
Lost Man's River (1997)
Bone by Bone (1999)

Film, Television, and Stage Adaptations

Adventure: Lost Man's River—An Everglades Journey with Peter Matthiessen (1991)
At Play in the Fields of the Lord (1992)
Men's Lives (1992), stage production

For Further Information

Bonetti, Kay, *Peter Matthiessen Interview with Kay Bonetti*. Columbia, MO: American Audio Prose Library, 1987.

Capouya, Emile, "The Bible and Bombs," *New York Times,* November 7, 1965.

Italie, Hillel, "Zen Buddhist Writer Enjoys Easygoing Life," *Nashville Telegram,* November 14, 2004.

Page, Eric, "The Dark Fate of Africa's Elephants," *New York Times,* August 22, 1991.

Peter Matthiessen entry, Contemporary Authors Online. Reproduced in Biography Resource Center. Farmington Hills, MI: Thomson Gale, 2005. http://galenet.galegroup.com/servlet/BioRC.

"Peter Matthiessen State Author, 1995–1997," New York State Writers Institute, State University of New York. http://www.albany.edu/writers-inst/matsnsa.html (viewed September 20, 2007).

Seaman, Donna, *End of the Earth* review, *Booklist,* September 15, 2003.

Shepard, Paul, *The Tree Where Man Was Born* review, *New York Times, Book Review*, November 26, 1972.

Sims, Michael, "A Series of Tiny Astonishments: An Interview with Peter Matthiessen," *BookPage,* 2000. http://www.bookpage.com/0002bp/peter_matthiessen.html (viewed August 28, 2006).

Skow, John, "Lost Man's Tale: Peter Matthiessen Caps a Dense, Fascinating Trilogy about a Brawling Florida Planter," *Time,* May 17, 1999.

Tigers in the Snow review, *Publishers Weekly,* January 10, 2000.

Top 30 Travel Books, World Hum Web site. http://www.worldhum.com/weblog/item/no_11_the_snow_leopard_by_peter_matthiessen_20060521/ (viewed August 28, 2006)

Tredinnick, Mark, *The Land's Wild Music: Encounters with Barry Lopez, Peter Matthiessen, Terry Tempest William, and James Galvin.* San Antonio, TX: Trinity University Press, 2005.

Frances Mayes

Memoir, Travel

Benchmark Title: *Under the Tuscan Sun*

Fitzgerald, Georgia

Unknown

Photo by John Gillooly

About the Author and the Author's Writing

It's enough of a challenge to purchase and renovate an old home in the United States. But in Italy? "I was afraid I might be crazy," Frances Mayes said in an interview for *San Francisco State University Magazine*. "I knew it was a risk. It was the sense of risk that was appealing. I wanted to do something I didn't know how to do."

Mays not only bought and fixed up the house, she wrote about the experience in *Under the Tuscan Sun*. "It takes a determined effort to read this account of restoring and enjoying a Tuscan farmhouse without experiencing a violent attack of adolescent jealously," suggested Bill Ott in *Booklist*. "Why her and not me, you'll be screaming as writer and professor Mayes describes languorous lunches on the patio, local wine flowing freely and olive pits casually pitched toward the nearby stone wall."

Mayes's adventure in Italy is shelved in the travel sections of the library and bookstore. But its widest appeal was to other women who, as William R. Smith wrote in his *Library Journal* review, were thrilled to read "an unusual memoir of one woman's challenge to herself and its successful transformation into a satisfying opportunity to improve the quality of her life."

Echoing that sentiment, Mayes told salon.com, "From my mail I've ... learned that many, many people identify with me taking a huge risk in mid-career. You know, at a time when most people are thinking of settling down, [my husband] Ed and I decided to take this huge risk and buy a house in a foreign country and fix it up."

Frances Mayes hasn't revealed the year of her birth. The daughter of cotton mill manager Garbert Mayes and his wife, Frankye Davis Mayes, she grew up in Fitzgerald, Georgia. She attended Randolph-Macon Woman's College, the University of Florida, and San Francisco State University, where she received her master of arts in 1975. She has one daughter from her marriage to William Frank King. They were divorced, and in 1998, she married poet Edward Kleinschmidt. He took her last name. The couple has homes in Cortona, Italy, and in North Carolina.

Prior to writing books, Mayes compiled copy for cookbook publishers and crafted stories for newspapers. Her poetry appeared in *Atlantic Monthly* and in *Iowa Review,* as well as other literary journals. She wrote several volumes of poetry and put together a college textbook for Harcourt Brace. In 1988, the National Endowment for the Arts awarded her a fellowship. She joined the English Department at San Francisco State University and while there directed the Poetry Center and chaired its creative writing department until taking a sabbatical to devote her time to her writing. In addition, she led writing workshops at Foothill College and Cañada College.

Then her *Under the Tuscan Sun* (1996) caught fire. The author said she began visiting that region of Italy right after college. "I studied Renaissance art and architecture —medieval art and architecture—so the minute I got there, *there* it all was right before me. And I just loved Italy from the outset," she told Linda Richards for *January Magazine.* She rented a farmhouse in 1985 and eventually purchased a fixer-upper, "Bramasole," high on a hill in Cortona. She felt right at home there—despite language differences—and found the Tuscans shared her enjoyment of leisurely pace, good company, and good food—a lifestyle honed in her Southern childhood.

"So many of us are work-obsessed," Mayes said on her Random House Web page. "I've loved experiencing how Italian friends take the time to enjoy family and friends, how they pursue their interests with so much pleasure, how they enter the community life of the piazza. I'm fascinated by the importance of the table, the central role it plays."

Mayes wrote a sequel, *Bella Tuscany,* a continuation of her house story. *In Tuscany,* with her husband as coauthor, and *Bringing Tuscany Home,* solidifying her brand. And speaking of brands, Drexel Heritage furniture company brought out Mayes's "At Home in Tuscany" collection of furnishings. "It's their most successful line in twenty years," she said in an interview with the travel newsletter *Dreams of Italy.* "Much of it is based on my own antiques.... The line is personal for me and translates well to my desire to 'bring Tuscany home.' "

That sense of place, of belonging, of home permeates Mayes's writing. Her first novel, *Swan,* is set in a small Georgia town reminiscent of her childhood. And her recent *A Year in the World* takes the author and her husband beyond their beloved Bramasole to Portugal and Greece and Scotland. "I went to places that I had always dreamed of as places to live," she said in an interview with Michelle Jones. "For me, it was an exploration of the idea of home. I decided to go to these places and see what it would take to be at home there."

Diane Lane played Mayes in the 2003 motion picture version of *Under the Tuscan Sun.* The film departs from the book in plot, particularly in that Mayes's character is divorced and pursuing the renovation alone and the film's inclusion of a brief romantic affair. The affair never happened, although the author laughed as she told *SFSU Magazine,* "I'd love for my relatives back in Fitzgerald to think I had an affair with a hot Italian guy."

 **Works by the Author**

The Discovery of Poetry (1987)
Under the Tuscan Sun: At Home in Italy (1996)

Bella Tuscany: The Sweet Life in Italy (1999)
In Tuscany, with Edward Mayes (2000)
Bringing Tuscany Home: Sensuous Style from the Heart of Italy (2004)
A Year in the World: Journeys of a Passionate Traveller (2006)

Editor

The Best American Travel Writing 2002 (2002)

Fiction

Swan (2002)

Poetry

Sunday in Another Country (1977)
Climbing Aconcagua (1977)
After Such Pleasures (1979)
The Arts of Fire (1982)
Hours (1984)
Ex Voto (1995)

Film Adaptations

Under the Tuscan Sun (2003)

For Further Information

Bee, Adrianne, "It Takes a Villa," *SFSU Magazine* Online, fall/winter 2003. http://www.sfsu.edu/~sfsumag/archive/fall_winter_03/mayes.html (viewed August 29, 2006).

Bringing Tuscany Home review, *Publishers Weekly,* July 19, 2004.

Frances Mayes interview, Dream of Italy Web site, February 2005. http://www.dreamofitaly.com/public/112.cfm (viewed September 18, 2006).

Frances Mayes interview, Frances Mayes Web page. http://www.randomhouse.com/features/mayes/interview.html (viewed August 29, 2006).

George, Don, Frances Mayes interview, salon.com, April 14, 1999. http://www.salon.com/travel/bag/1999/04/14/mayes/ (viewed September 18, 2006).

Jones, Michelle, "Out of Tuscany," BookPage. http://www.bookpage.com/0603bp/frances_mayes.html (viewed September 18, 2006).

Ott, Bill, *Under the Tuscan Sun* review, *Booklist*, September 15, 1996.

Richards, Linda, Frances Mayes interview, *January Magazine*. http://www.janmag.com/profiles/mayes.html (viewed August 29, 2006).

Smith, William R., *Under the Tuscan Sun* review, *Library Journal,* September 1, 1996.

Wise, Olga B., *In Tuscany* review, *Library Journal,* February 1, 2001.

Peter Mayle

Food, Travel

Benchmark Title: *A Year in Provence*

Brighton, East Sussex, England
1939–

Photo by Jennie Mayle

About the Author and the Author's Writing

Talk about a dream life: Peter Mayle is an expatriate who periodically rolls out a literary tribute to the good life in southern France and sells millions of copies, which pays for his lifestyle for a few more years. Many travel writers wish they could live this way. But not every writer can convey the rich detail, with the contained humor and in the lively prose that Mayle specializes in. Lonely Planet's travel editor Don George began reading Mayle's *French Lessons,* determined to resist its allures. "But by page six, I was immersed in his first unforgettable feast.. . . We were in a Parisian restaurant discovering the joys of chewy French bread and slabs of pale butter, fish fragrant with fennel, crisp, pencil-thin pommes frites, textured cheeses, and a topless, glistening tarte aux pommes. I had been happily seduced once again."

It took Mayle a while to find his literary niche. He spent fifteen years writing advertising copy. "I always wanted to write ever since I was 19," he said in a Washingtonpost.com interview. "I eventually started writing in the advertising business, writing commercials and ads." He began to write lighthearted parenting and children's books—the simplicity of the language wasn't much different. Then he longed to write something more ambitions. He moved to Europe. "France provided me with a huge amount of inspiration, which led to my first grown-up book, which was *A Year in Provence*."

Mayle was born in England in 1939. He has been a writer since 1975 and is a columnist for *Gentleman's Quarterly*. He has three sons from his first marriage, two daughters from his second. He and his third wife, Jennie, decided on a radical career change and left the United States to acquire an eighteenth-century farmhouse in the Luberon Mountains in Provence. Their experiences trying to fit in with the rural lifestyle provided meat for the 1990 *Year in Provence*, which *Publishers Weekly*'s Genevieve Stuttaford said, "In nimble prose ... captures the humorous aspects of visits to markets, vineyards and goat races, hunting for mushrooms. Even donating blood is an occasion for fun. The Provencal cuisine is Mayle's leitmotif, however."

The theme of food comes to the fore in Mayle's later books, such as *French Lessons,* which describes visits to regional French festivals. "Mayle is always a pleasant enough companion: the charming outsider who makes up for his lack of expertise and savoir faire with good-natured humility and curiosity," James Schiff commented in *Book.* The author narrowed his focus in *Confessions of a French Baker* (2005) to one kitchen master, Gerard Auzet, and his art of baking French bread. It comes with recipes. "Mere words may not begin to encompass the technique and art involved in producing a perfect loaf of French bread," Mark Knoblauch said in *Booklist,* "but Mayle and Auzet present an entrée for the home breadsmith."

French food isn't always a great experience for Mayle. He recalled in a Lonely Planet interview a particularly displeasing *andouillette* (that is, a sausage) that he couldn't finish eating, but insisted it was the only bad dining experience he's had in France.

The good food he easily defines: "The basis of it all is olive oil, wonderful vegetables in their various seasons like peppers, tomatoes, beans. Goat's cheese is terrific down there. There is something like thirty-eight different kinds of goat's cheese," he said in an interview with *Restaurant Report*'s Philip Silverstone.

Beyond food, Mayle fell in love with the people of southern France and captures them well in his writing. "I think it was the sight of a man power-washing his underpants [using a hose] that really brought home the difference, cultural and otherwise, between the old world and the new," he wrote in *Encore Provence.*

Mayle alternates his nonfiction with fiction, which he has said offers enormously greater freedom of character and flexibility of plot.

While readers may assume otherwise, Mayle doesn't dine out expensively every night. "One of the great thrills of it all is its rarity," he said in a conversation with *BookPage*'s Henry Alford. "I think if you drank Chateau Lafitte twice a day with your ham sandwich, there would be a danger of ennui. That's why we normally live a very simple sort of life, and occasionally we go off on one of these wonderful benders."

Works by the Author

How To Be a Pregnant Father: An Illustrated Survival Guide for the First-time Father (1977)

Baby Taming (1978)

Great Moments in Baby History (1980)

Anything but Rover—The Art and Science of Naming Your Dog: A Breed by Breed Guide, Including Mongrels (1985)

A Year in Provence (1989)

Dangerous Candy: A True Drug Story by Someone Who Did Them and Kicked Them, with Raffaella Fletcher (1990), reprinted as *Dangerous Candy: A True Story about Drug Addiction* (1991)

Toujours Provence (1991)

Acquired Tastes: A Beginner's Guide to Serious Pleasures (1992)

Up the Agency: The Funny Business of Advertising (1993)

Provence (1995)

Provence from the Air, with Jason Hawkes (1996)

Encore Provence: New Adventures in the South of France (1999)

French Lessons: Adventures with Knife, Fork, and Corkscrew (2001)

An Englishman in Paris, with Michael Sadler (2002)

A Chef in Provence, with Edouard Loubet (2004)

Confessions of a French Baker; Breadmaking Secrets, Tips, and Recipes, with Gerard Auxet (2005)

Provence A–Z (2006)

For Juvenile Readers

Where Did I Come From? The Facts of Life without Any Nonsense and with Illustrations (1973)

What's Happening to Me? The Answers to Some of the World's Most Embarrassing Questions (1975)

Will I Go to Heaven? (1976)

Will I Like It? Your First Sexual Experience, What to Expect, What to Avoid and How Both of You Can Get the Most Out of It (1977)

Divorce Can Happen to the Nicest People (1979), revised as *Why Are We Getting a Divorce?* (1988)

As Dead as a Dodo, with Paul Rice (1981)

Congratulations! You're Not Pregnant: An Illustrated Guide to Birth Control, with Arthur Robbins (1981)

Grown-ups and Other Problems: Help for Small People in a Big World (1982)

The Honeymoon Book (1983)

Chilly Billy (1983)

Man's Best Friend: Introducing Wicked Willie in the Title Role (1984)

Sweet Dreams and Monsters: A Beginner's Guide to Dreams and Nightmares and Things That Go Bump under the Bed (1986)

Wicked Willie's Guide to Women: A Worm's Eye View of the Fair Sex (1987)

Wicked Willie's Guide to Women: The Further Adventures of Man's Best Friend (1988)

Contributor

Adventures in Wine, edited by Thom Elkjer (2002)

Fiction

Hotel Pastis: A Novel of Provence (1993)

A Dog's Life (1995)

Anything Considered (1996)

Chasing Cézanne (1997)

A Good Year (2004)

Film and Television Adaptations

A Year in Provence (BBC, 1992), television series

A Good Year (20th Century Fox, 2006), film

For Further Information

Alford, Henry, "How Exactly Does One Find the Best $1,300 Shoes? Peter Mayle Can Help," *BookPage,* July 1992. http://www.bookpage.com/BPinterviews/mayle792.html (viewed August 29, 2006).

Bly, Laura, "Toujours Peter Mayle," *USA Today,* November 3, 2006.

Encore Provence review, *Publishers Weekly*, May 10, 1999.

George, Don, Peter Mayle interview, "Traveller at Large," Lonely Planet Web site, June 13, 2001. http://www.lonelyplanet.com/columns/traveller_archive/13june01/traveller_index.htm (viewed September 18, 2006).

Guttman, Robert J., *Encore Provence* review, *Europe*, March 2000.

Knoblauch, Mark, *Confessions of a French Baker* review, *Booklist*, October 1, 2005.

"Off the Page: Peter Mayle," Washingtonpost.com., June 10, 2004. http://www.washingtonpost.com/wp-dyn/articles/A4225-2004May31.html (viewed September 18, 2006).

Peter Mayle entry, Contemporary Authors Online. Reproduced in Biography Resource Center. Farmington Hills, MI: Thomson Gale, 2004. http://galenet.galegroup.com/servlet/BioRC.

Schiff, James, *French Lessons* review, *Book*, July 2001.

Silverstone, Philip, "An Interview with Peter Mayle," *Restaurant Report.* http://www.restaurantreport.com/Departments/w_petermayle.html (viewed August 29, 2006).

Stuttaford, Genevieve, *A Year in Provence* review, *Publishers Weekly,* March 23, 1990.

Toujours Provence review, *Publishers Weekly,* May 10, 1991.

Frank McCourt

Autobiography, Memoir

Benchmark Title: *Angela's Ashes*

Brooklyn, New York

1930–

Photo by Gasper Tringale

About the Author and the Author's Writing

For years—even decades—Frank McCourt was ashamed of his Irish background, of his unshakable brogue, of his father who drank up the weekly paycheck, of his mother who contended with no food on the table, and of serious illness in the home (three of McCourt's siblings died in childhood). "And concurrent with shame is anger," the author said in an Academy of Achievement interview. "When we joked around about this in New York, my brothers and I, my mother would say, 'Will you stop talking about that? That's the past.' " He may have stopped talking about it, but he wrote, instead, first in notebooks, then in his best-selling memoir, *Angela's Ashes*.

Angela's Ashes was the memoir of the 1990s. It sold four million copies, was translated into twenty-two languages, and earned its author a National Book Critics Circle Award and a Pulitzer Prize.

Frank McCourt was born in Brooklyn, New York, in 1930, the son of Irish immigrants Malachy and Angela Sheehan McCourt. The family returned to Ireland when Frank was four and settled in Limerick, in hopes of improved job prospects. Their small cottage saw spurts of happiness, but no prosperity. The children all slept in a flea-plagued bed. McCourt's father drank away his meager earnings while the family eked by on public welfare and occasional family assistance. In Frank's view, his schoolteachers were conceited and uncaring. He quit school when he was fourteen, and five years later, he returned to the United States. He worked at the Biltmore Hotel until, fired from his job, he joined the U.S. Army's K-9 unit and served in Germany during the Korean War. In 1954, he enrolled at New York University on the G.I. Bill, attending class during the day and working the docks at night.

With both bachelor's and master's degrees from New York University, McCourt taught at a Staten Island vocational school before being hired on at Manhattan's Peter Stuyvesant High School, where he taught English and creative writing for nineteen years. He has one daughter from a first marriage. A second marriage ended in divorce. His third wife, Ellen Frey, is a television publicist. After retiring in 1987, he dug out the fragments of a memoir he'd put together over the years. Through writer friends, his manuscript made its way to an agent who showed it to a Scribner editor, who published it. The title refers to the fireplace ashes, at which his mother often stared at despairingly.

"When I look back at my childhood," the author states in the book, "I wonder how I survived at all. It was, of course, a miserable childhood: the happy childhood is hardly worth your while. Worse than the ordinary miserable childhood is the miserable Irish childhood, and worse yet is the miserable Irish Catholic childhood."

Miserable, perhaps. But in the telling, the story is compelling. "McCourt's magical memoir, his first book, evokes so persuasively the voices and images of a ragged and hungry Irish childhood that we suspend disbelief in his total recall," a *Publishers Weekly* reviewer said of *Angela's Ashes*. "The sights, the stinks, the savage comedy of survival in the slums of 1930s and 1940s Limerick are mesmerizing."

As to the accuracy of the book's detail, McCourt related to *Newsweek* writer Malcolm Jones Jr. that he was approached at a book signing in Limerick by an aged-looking man who turned out to be Willie Harrell, one of the neighborhood boys he'd grown up with. "He leaned across the table and said, 'In your book you give me a sister, and Frankie, I had no sister.' ... This was true. Somehow or other, I invented a sister for him who had none." They spoke further, then Harrell, as he was leaving, asked for a copy of McCourt's book—a pensioner, he couldn't afford to buy one—but figured it would be fair trade for forgetting about the invented sister.

McCourt's memoir ended with his return to New York as a young man. In response to public demand, McCourt extended the volume with *'Tis* (about his early working life) and *Teacher Man* (about his experiences in the classroom). As much as an autobiography, *Teacher Man* is a tribute to educators. "You rarely read anything about teachers," McCourt said in an interview with Dermot McEvoy. "Movie stars, judges, cops, doctors, but not teachers. I ... just wanted to tell the story of what it was like with my own particular experience, which was unusual—I had no high school diploma, very little formal education, and I had to make my own way."

Along with his actor-author-brother Malachy, McCourt wrote and appeared in a 1980s musical review, *A Couple of Blaguards,* which has been staged several times with other performers since.

McCourt took the backdoor to a writing career; he taught others how to do it before he did it himself. It finally dawned on him, as he discussed poetry with students, that literature was also meant to be practiced. "Nobody ever told me in college. 'This stuff is all about you. This guy Iago's about you, about aspects of all of us,' " he said in *Instructor,* "When I learned that I felt lifted. I was so enthusiastic I wanted to share it."

Works by the Author

Angela's Ashes: A Memoir (1996)
'Tis: A Memoir (1999)
Ireland Ever, with Malachy McCourt (2003)
Teacher Man (2005)

Drama and Musical Reviews

> *A Couple of Blaguards,* with Malachy McCourt (1980s)
> *The Irish ... and How They Got That Way* (1997)

Fiction

> *Yeats Is Dead: A Mystery by Fifteen Irish Writers,* contributor (2001)
> *Angela and the Baby Jesus* (2007)

Film Adaptation

> *The McCourts of Limerick* (1998)
> *Angela's Ashes* (1999)
> *The McCourts of New York* (1999)

For Further Information

Angela's Ashes review, *Publishers Weekly*, July 1, 1996.

Frank McCourt entry, *Authors and Artists for Young Adults*, Vol. 61. Detroit, MI: Thomson Gale, 2005.

Frank McCourt interview, Academy of Achievement. http://www.achievement. org/autodoc/page/mcc1int-3 (viewed August 28, 2006).

Frank McCourt interview, Online NewsHour, March 17, 1999. http:// www.pbs.org/newshour/bb/entertainment/jan-june99/mccourt_3-17.html (viewed August 28, 2006).

Frank McCourt Web page, Soldier Creek Associates. http://www. soldiercreek.com/mccourt.cfm (viewed May 4, 2006).

Jones, Malcolm Jr., "From 'Ashes' to Stardom: Frank McCourt's Tragicomic Tale of Growing Up Poor in Ireland Is the Woebegone Publishing Industry's Cinderella Story of the Decade," *Newsweek,* August 25, 1997.

Maxwell, Gloria, *'Tis* review, *Library Journal,* May 1, 2000.

McEvoy, Dermot, "Angry Teacher Man: PW Talks with Frank McCourt," *Publishers Weekly,* October 17, 2005.

Truby, Dane, "Frank McCourt: The Author of *Angela's Ashes* Looks Back on 30 Years of Teaching in New York City Classrooms," *Instructor,* January-February 2006.

David McCullough

Biography, History

Benchmark Title: *John Adams*

Pittsburgh, Pennsylvania

1933–

Photo by William B. McCullough

About the Author and the Author's Writing

With his honed sense of time and place, with his rich baritone voice, with his shock of white hair and squint-eyed look of curiosity, David McCullough is one of America's preeminent historical writers. Twice winner of the National Book Award, twice recipient of the Pulitzer Prize, McCullough compiles massive examinations of national events and presidential accomplishments in a small writing camp behind his Martha's Vineyard home.

"If you look around here, you see no sign of the 21st century—or the 20th," the writer told *Boston Globe* reporter Mark Feeney. "This could be a view, could it not, from the 18th century? That's the way I like it."

In 1965, with the modest advance for his first book, McCullough found a manual Royal typewriter in a secondhand shop in White Plains, New York and began his project. He's written all of his books since on that typewriter, and just as with the first effort, the pages that rolled from the platen have been scrutinized by the author's in-house editor. "After finishing a chapter, he gives it to Rosalee, his wife, companion, and editor in chief of 47 years, who reads it aloud to him. Adverbs, complicated sentences, convoluted thoughts—out they go," David R. Gergen reported in *U.S. News & World Report* in 2001. "This is a writer who wants to make sure each paragraph rings truly in the ear."

David McCullough was born in Pittsburgh, Pennsylvania, in 1933, the son of Christian Hax McCullough (who ran an electrical company) and Ruth Rankin McCullough. He married Rosalee Ingram Barnes in 1954; they have five children. In 1955, he earned his bachelor of arts in English from Yale University and went to work for Time Inc. in New York City as a writer and editor. He left in 1961 to work for three years with the U.S. Information Agency in Washington, D.C. From 1964 to 1970, he was with American Heritage Publishing in New York, after which he became a freelance writer. He has provided voice narration for a number of television documentaries and series—for *Smithsonian World* for four years and *American Experience* for a decade-plus.

His early books were about big events—coping with the Johnstown flood, digging the Panama Canal, or erecting the Brooklyn Bridge—and myriad historical characters, some heroes, some thugs, some innocent bystanders. He became adept at biography—much of *The Great Bridge* is about John Roebling and his son Washington, for example—and with *Mornings on Horseback*—which is about Theodore Roosevelt—he began to write mostly biography.

While he works best in an anachronistic setting at his home in Massachusetts, McCullough writes very much for a contemporary audience of thoughtful readers. He stresses the importance of environment and context in writing history, to get across "What was it like when smallpox or yellow fever swept through a city? What was it like to go from Boston, Mass., to Philadelphia on horseback in the dead of winter…?" the author told Edward Newotka for *Publishers Weekly* in a 2001 interview.

Too much material can sometimes overwhelm a historian. Gerald Carson, who reviewed *The Great Bridge* for the *New York Times,* said McCullough is "a writer with a sound intuitive sense of what to put in and what to leave out of his narrative."

There's no question that McCullough has succeeded in his quest. *Publishers Weekly*'s review of *Truman,* for example, noted the author "has written a surefooted, highly satisfying biography of the 33rd president, one that not only conveys in rich detail Truman's accomplishments as a politician and statesman, but also reveals the character and personality of this constantly surprising man—as schoolboy, farmer, soldier, merchant, county judge, senator, vice president and chief executive."

That book earned McCullough critical acclaim and enormous public attention. But it took him ten years to complete. He has said he would never again take on a subject for which there is almost too much material available—as was the case of the Truman papers housed in Missouri. McCullough has occasionally written short pieces; for example, *Brave Companions* collects his shorter profiles of the likes of Harriet Beecher Stowe and Louis Agassiz. However, most of his works run over five hundred pages in length.

The writer's more recent *1776* (2005) is something of a companion to *John Adams* (2001), which related the political side of the war for independence. *1776* covers the military operation, an aspect of the war that McCullough felt was underplayed. "I want people to see that all-important time in a different way—in the way it was. For a number of reasons, including the absence of photographs, we tend to see the men and women of the Revolution as not quite real. And we have far too little sense of what they suffered," he said in a conversation with Bookreporter.com.

Because he immerses himself in his subjects, McCullough said in *The Writer,* he is loathe to take on a subject with whom he doesn't empathize. He once dropped a Pablo Picasso project, for instance, and has no interest in world figures such as Adolf Hitler. "We're fascinated by monsters. And some people like to write about monsters. I don't. I like to tell a good story," he told *The Writer*'s Ronald Kovach. However, that doesn't mean he omits the dirty laundry. "You need the unpleasant; you can't see the light if you don't have the shadow."

In a 2005 *Newsweek* feature story, Jon Meacham said of McCullough: "Some professional historians find McCullough's work too safe and too smooth. A careful reading of his books, however, does not really support that academic critique. McCullough is the least cynical of writers, but he is also among the most clear-eyed."

"History teaches, reinforces what we believe in, what we stand for, and what we ought to be willing to stand up for," McCullough summed up for Powells.com's Dave

Weich. "History is—or should be—the bedrock of patriotism, not the chest-pounding kind of patriotism but the real thing, love of country."

 Works by the Author

The Johnstown Flood (1968), revised (2004)

The Great Bridge: The Epic Story of the Building of the Brooklyn Bridge (1972), revised (2001)

The Path between the Seas; The Creation of the Panama Canal, 1870–1914 (1977), revised (1999)

Mornings on Horseback: The Story of an Extraordinary Family, a Vanished Way of Life, and the Unique Child Who Became Theodore Roosevelt (1981), revised (2001)

Brave Companions: Portraits in History (1992)

Truman (1992)

Why History? (1996)

John Adams (2001)

1776 (2005)

Contributor

A Sense of History: The Best Writing from the Pages of American Heritage (1985)

Extraordinary Lives: The Art and Craft of American Biography, edited by William Zinsser (1986)

A Bully Father: Theodore Roosevelt's Letters to His Children, edited by Joan Patterson Kerr (1995)

Letters of Great Americans to Their Children, edited by Dorie McCullough Lawson (2004)

Editor

The American Heritage Picture History of World War II, by C. L. Sulzberger (1967), revised as *World War II* (1970)

Smithsonian Library (1968–1970), six volumes

Remington: The Masterworks, with Michael E. Shapiro and Peter H. Frederick (1988)

Television Host or Narrator

Brooklyn Bridge (1981)

Smithsonian World (1984–1988)

Huey Long (1985)

The Statue of Liberty (1985)

The Shakers (1985)

"A Man, a Plan, a Canal—Panama" episode, *Nova* (1987)

American Experience (PBS, 1988–2000)

The Civil War (1990)
Abraham and Mary Lincoln: A House Divided (2001)

For Further Information

Brave Companions review, *Publishers Weekly,* September 27, 1991.

Carson, Gerald, *The Great Bridge* review, *New York Times,* October 15, 1972.

David (Gaub) McCullough entry, Contemporary Authors Online. Reproduced in Biography Resource Center. Farmington Hills, MI: Thomson Gale, 2005. http://galenet.galegroup.com/servlet/BioRC.

David McCullough biography, Bookreporter.com. http://www.bookreporter. com/authors/au-mccullough-david.asp (viewed August 28, 2006).

David McCullough biography, Electriceggplant.com. http://www. electriceggplant.com/davidmccullough/author.htm (viewed August 28, 2006).

David McCullough biography, Soldier Creek Associates Web site. http:// www.soldiercreek.com/mccullough.cfm (viewed May 4, 2006).

Feeney, Mark, "Tracing the Steps of American Icons, McCullough Becomes One Himself," *Boston Globe,* May 30, 2005.

Gergen, David R., "A Blast from the Past," *U.S. News & World Report*, August 6, 2001.

Kovach, Ronald, "David McCullough on the Art of Biography," *The Writer,* October 2001.

"McCullough to Step Down as Host of the *American Experience,*" PR Newswire, December 7, 1999.

Meacham, Jon, "Rethinking Washington," *Newsweek,* May 23, 2005.

Nawotka, Edward, "PW Talks with David McCullough," *Publishers Weekly,* April 2, 2001.

Truman review, *Publishers Weekly*, May 4, 1992.

Weich, Dave, "Connecting with David McCullough," Powells.com. http://www. powells.com/authors/mccullough.html (viewed August 28, 2006).

Joe McGinniss

Investigative Reporting,
Sports, True Crime

Benchmark Title: *Fatal Vision*

New York, New York

1942–

About the Author and the Author's Writing

True crime writer Joe McGinniss has been in and out of court nearly as often as his subjects, sometimes as an observer, sometimes as a defendant. It began with *Fatal Vision,* his 1983 examination of Dr. Jeffrey MacDonald, a veteran of the Green Berets prosecuted and convicted for the murder of his wife and two children. To this day proclaiming his innocence, MacDonald was delighted at the prospect of having veteran author McGinniss tell his story. But in the course of his research, McGinniss became convinced of MacDonald's guilt. And he said so in *Fatal Vision,* in which he depicted MacDonald as a maniacal drug addict.

MacDonald was convicted in 1979, then released a year later on appeal. A higher-court justice said MacDonald had been denied a speedy trial. MacDonald brought civil suit against McGinniss and received $325,000 from the author in an out-of-court settlement. MacDonald's in-laws, the Kassabs, however, received $80,000 of that amount in their own unlawful death suit against MacDonald; his mother received $93,000; and his lawyers $104,000. The Supreme Court later reversed that decision, and MacDonald, who had returned to his medical practice, went back to prison. He refused to apply for parole in 1991 because it would require an admission of guilt. At this writing, on the thirty-seventh anniversary of the crime, Mac-Donald awaits District Court consideration of new evidence including DNA test results, according to Themacdonaldcase.org Web site.

MacDonald's remarkably convoluted case inspired another book about the case, written from the perspective that the physician is innocent and McGinniss's drug-use allegations were bogus (Jerry Potter and Fred Bost's *Fatal Justice: Reinvestigating the MacDonald Murders,* 1994), as well as a book about the relationship between McGinniss and MacDonald (Janet Malcolm's *The Journalist and the Murderer,* 1990) in which the writer is charged with being deceitful and unethical.

It's highly unusual that a writer become so wrapped up in his story. All that would have discouraged a fledgling writer. But McGinniss wrote two more true crime books before moving (equally controversial) to political biography and then sports subjects.

The author was born in New York City in 1942, the son of Joseph and Mary Leonard McGinniss. He grew up in Rye, New York, and received a bachelor of science degree from Holy Cross College in 1964. He has two daughters from his first marriage, to Christine Cooke, and two sons from his second marriage, to Nancy Doherty.

Fresh out of college, McGinniss joined the newsroom of the *Portchester* (New York) *Daily Item,* soon moving to the *Worcester* (Massachusetts) *Telegram.* He became a sports writer with the *Philadelphia Bulletin* in 1966 and, two years later, a general columnist for the rival *Philadelphia Inquirer.* His topics included the assassination of Dr. Martin Luther King Jr. and the 1968 presidential primaries. He left that newspaper to travel with the Richard Nixon political team for five months and was afforded unusual access to that campaign's marketing strategies. *The Selling of the President, 1968* caused a sensation when it came out, not the least to those of the Nixon camp who had been so open with their information.

"My great advantage was that I wasn't considered press," McGinniss told *Life* magazine. "I was the guy writing a book."

McGinniss wrote a novel, *The Dream Team* (1972), about a novelist who is obsessed with women, and two nonfiction books, a collection of interviews that explore the theme of fame (*Heroes,* 1976) and an examination of Alaska's experiences with big oil (*Going to Extremes,* 1980). He spent four years putting together *Fatal Vision,* published in 1983. His next book, *Blind Faith,* was about a New Jersey man, Rob Marshall, convicted of killing his wife for the life insurance payment. McGinniss employed novelistic techniques in the book, recreating conversations.

A 1991 release, *Cruel Doubt,* chronicled another family crime, the 1990 stabbings of Leith and Bonnie Von Stein. He died, and she lived; her son Chris (Leith's stepson) was charged with arranging the killing and attempted killing with a Dungeons and Dragons–playing friend. "This book goes beyond my last two, because here was a woman who was a victim in a very real way," the author told *Publishers Weekly*'s Robert Dahlin. "She was almost killed, and then the legal system treated her as though she might have been in some way responsible."

McGinniss's *The Last Brother: The Rise and Fall of Teddy Kennedy,* released in 1993, was almost universally disparaged by reviewers for what was viewed as a reliance on hearsay and innuendo.

Although he sat through nine months of proceedings in the 1995 O. J. Simpson trial, McGinniss ultimately abandoned the project, disgusted at the outcome.

McGinniss's 1999 *The Miracle of Castel di Sangro* was based on a year with an Italian soccer team. The author was ultimately disappointed with sales and charged that his publisher, Little, Brown, and Company, failed to promote the book adequately.

The writer took his next sports book, *The Big Horse,* to Simon & Schuster. Published in 2004, it is about Hall of Fame horse trainer P. G. Johnson and the horse Volponi during the 2003 racing season.

As accustomed as McGinniss is to twists and turns in his writing life, he was caught by surprise in spring 2006 when working on a new true crime book about the 2003 death of American financier Robert Kissel (he was drugged with a strawberry milkshake then bludgeoned to death by his wife, Nancy, his body put in a basement storage room). Nancy Kissel was found guilty and appealed her conviction.

McGinniss believed he had a winner in a new book about the high-profile trial, which was held in Hong Kong. When the victim's brother, Andrew M. Kissel, a money manager, was stabbed to death in his Connecticut home, the writer, now living in Amherst, Massachusetts, was dumbfounded.

"This is not a piece of luck for me," McGinniss told the *New York Times'* David Carr of the press's sudden interest in his book. "This is a horrible thing." Nevertheless, he continued the project. *Never Enough* came out in late 2007.

"Once I start on a project, my only goal is to write the most compelling narrative I can," the author told an interviewer for *Holy Cross Magazine.* "I set out to tell the best possible story that I can."

 # Works by the Author

> *The Selling of the President, 1968* (1969), reprinted as *The Selling of the President* (1988)
> *Heroes* (1976)
> *Going to Extremes* (1980)
> *Fatal Vision* (1983)
> *Blind Faith* (1988)
> *Cruel Doubt* (1991)
> *The Last Brother: The Rise and Fall of Teddy Kennedy* (1993)
> *The Miracle of Castel di Sangro* (1999)
> *The Big Horse* (2004)
> *Never Enough* (2007)

Fiction

> *The Dream Team* (1972)

Film and Stage Adaptations of the Author's Work

> *The Selling of the President, 1968* (1969)
> *Fatal Vision* (1984), miniseries
> *Blind Faith* (1990), two-part television movie
> *Cruel Doubt* (1992), two-part television movie

For Further Information

Carr, David, "2nd Case of Murder Adds Twist to a Book," *New York Times,* April 6, 2006.

Cohen, Jacob, *Last Brother* review, *National Review,* September 20, 1993.

Dahlin, Robert, "Joe McGinniss: Fascinated by American Family Traumas, McGinniss Perseveres in a Painful Trade: True Crime," *Publishers Weekly,* October 18, 1991.

Dodge, Dennis, *Big Horse* review, *Booklist,* July 2004.

Ferguson, Andrew, "His Brothers' Last Keeper," *National Review,* September 6, 1993.

Hendin, Josephine, *Fatal Vision* review, *New Republic,* October 24, 1983.

Joe McGinniss entry, Contemporary Authors Online. Reproduced in Biography Resource Center. Farmington Hills, MI: Thomson Gale, 2006. http://galenet.galegroup.com/servlet/BioRC.

Merron, Jeff, Joe McGinniss interview, SportsJones.com. http://www.sportsjones.com/mcginniss.htm (viewed August 29, 2006).

Moore, Steve, "The Rebel," *Holy Cross Magazine*, winter 2000.

Offman, Craig, "McGinniss vs. Little, Brown: Publisher Avoids the 'S' Word," salon.com, June 25, 2999. http://www.salon.com/books/log/1999/06/25/mcginniss/ (viewed August 29, 2006).

Ott, Bill, *Miracle of Castel di Sangro* review, *Booklist,* September 1, 1999.

Selling of the President, 1968 review, *Life,* October 10, 1969.

Themacdonaldcase.org Web site, viewed March 26, 2007.

Ward, Geoffrey C., *Last Brother* review, *American Heritage,* November 1993.

Bill McKibben

Environment, Memoir, Travel

Benchmark Title: *The End of Nature*

Palo Alto, California

1960–

About the Author and the Author's Writing

Yes, Bill McKibben is an alarmist. He yanked the alarm cord in 1989, when with *The End of Nature* he sounded his first warning about unbridled consumerism, rampant use of fossil fuels, waste of natural resources, and rise of global warming. That book, translated into twenty languages and available on six continents, is considered a keystone of environmental crisis literature.

"If the temperature [is] increasing a degree per decade," he wrote in his characteristic reasonable tone in *The End of Nature,* "the forest surrounding my [Adirondack region] home would be due at the Canadian border sometime around 2020."

But besides raising awareness of the environmental problems we face, McKibben is a constructivist. In subsequent books, he posited potential solutions for our seeming worldwide dilemma. *Hope, Human and Wild* offers uplifting stories of wildlife returning to the northeastern United States; of an urban planner's ideas for a human-scale city in Brazil; of progress in the income level of inhabitants of a village in India. In *Maybe One* (1999), he asserts that small families will conserve food, fuel, and environment. *Hundred Dollar Holiday* (1998) makes a case for decommercializing Christmas, improving family ties, and saving vital resources.

"McKibben, indeed, is an interesting mix of hope and despair," Michael Coffey wrote in *Publishers Weekly*. "On the one hand, the political situation is at its worst, he notes, with the gutting of the Clean Water Act and other environmental rollbacks sponsored by the Republican congress; on the other, he senses that these acts will hasten the circumstances that will make reform a necessity."

McKibben was born in Palo Alto, California, the son of Gordon C. and Margaret Hayes McKibben. He and his wife, Sue M. Halpern, have one child. McKibben joined the *New Yorker* as a staff writer fresh out of Harvard University in 1982. He left in 1987 to become a freelance writer and frequent contributor to the *New York Review of Books, Outside,* and the *New York Times.*

McKibben takes heart that there is now wide recognition of the effects of a population boom on the planet. "Over the last 30 years, human beings have realized it's necessary to bring our numbers under control, so educated and empowered women have seen their average fertility drop from 4.5 children to 2.7," he said in an interview with Jennifer Hattam of *Sierra Magazine*. "That's a pretty remarkable accomplishment."

In similar fashion, global warming has become much more accepted in the scientific—and general—populations. "No single hurricane is the result of global warming," he said in a piece he wrote for *Sierra* magazine. "But a month before Katrina hit [in 2005], Massachusetts Institute of Technology hurricane specialist Kerry Emmanuel published a landmark paper in the British science magazine *Nature* showing that in the past half century tropical storms have been lasting 60 percent longer and spinning winds 50 percent more powerful."

Many of McKibben's ideas are controversial. In *Enough* (2003), he questions technologies that allow the "design" of human babies. He rejects human cloning but values other aspects of the science: "The insights that genetics have provided already have yielded all sorts of useful treatments for real people with real illnesses," he said in an interview for Center for Genetics and Society. "So-called 'somatic' gene therapy, involving the insertion of better-functioning genes into living individuals to, say, keep their lungs from malfunctioning due to cystic fibrosis, does not raise the kind of existential problems that come from designing people before they're born."

Political in more subtle ways, McKibben's contributions to John Elder's *The Return of the Wolf* (2000) reflect on the success of the Wolf Restoration Project in the Northeast; *Wandering Home,* published in 2005, documents the author's meander from Vermont into New York's Adirondack wilds. "McKibben, charmingly self-deprecating and funny, isn't only communing with nature," notes reviewer Donna Seaman, "but also visiting individuals committed to living 'green,' including organic farmers, a vintner, a beekeeper, environmental studies students, wildlands philanthropy promoter John Davis, and writer Don Mitchell. Thanks to their efforts, this once hard-used land is now restored and rebounding."

The author's recent *Deep Economy,* in his lively, philosophic, and journalistic tone, charges that the relentless quest for corporate profit does nothing for our future. "With the threat of energy crises and global warming, McKibben's vision of nurturing communities rooted in traditional values and driven by 'green' technologies, however utopian, may provide ideas for constructive change," said *Booklist* reviewer Donna Seaman.

McKibben has a long wish list of environmental and social concerns. Given one shot at bringing down global warming, he told *Meteor Blades,* he would go for "the rapid phase-in of a 40 mpg average for new cars. Because the technology is there to do it easily, because it would demonstrate to us that the change in our sacred lifestyles will be very small at first—and because it will give everyone the added benefit of saving some money on gas."

Works by the Author

The End of Nature (1989)

The Age of Missing Information (1992)

Look at the Land: Aerial Reflections of America (1993)

Three Essays, with Terry Tempest Williams and William Least Heat-Moon (1993)

The Comforting Whirlwind: God, Job, and the Scale of Creation (1995)

Hope, Human and Wild: True Stories of Living Lightly on the Earth (1995), reprinted 2007

Twenty-Five Bicycle Tours in the Adirondacks: Road Adventures in the East's Largest Wilderness (1995)

Hundred Dollar Holiday: The Case for a More Joyful Christmas (1998)

Maybe One: A Case for Smaller Families (1998)

Long Distance: Testing the Limits of Body and Spirit in a Year of Living Strenuously (2000)

The Adirondacks: Wild Island of Hope, with Gary Randorf (2002)

Profits Pending, with Matthew Albright (2002)

Enough: Staying Human in an Engineering Age (2003)

Wandering Home: A Long Walk across America's Most Hopeful Landscape: Vermont's Champlain Valley and New York's Adirondacks (2005)

Welcome to Doomsday (New York Review of Books Collection), with Bill Moyers (2006)

Deep Economy: The Wealth of Communities and the Durable Future (2007)

Editor

Birch Browsings: A John Burroughs Reader (1992)

Contributor

Radiant Days: Writings by Enos Mills, edited by John Dotson (1994)

Walden: Lessons for the New Millennium, by Henry David Thoreau (1997)

Adirondacks: Views of an American Wilderness, by Carl E. Heilman (1999)

The Return of the Wolf: Reflections on the Future of Wolves in the Northeast, edited by John Elder (2000)

The Mountains of California, by John Muir (2001)

Wild Earth: Wild Ideas for a World Out of Balance, edited by Tom Butler (2001)

Wilderness Comes Home: Rewilding the Northeast, edited by Christopher McGrory Klyza (2001)

Hamish Fulton: Walking Journey (2002)

Life's Philosophy: Reason and Feeling in a Deeper World, by Arne Naess and Per Invgar Haukeland, translated by Roland Huntford (2002)

Backwoods Ethics: A Guide to Low-Impact Camping and Hiking, by Laura Waterman and Guy Waterman (2003)

For Further Information

Bill McKibben entry, Contemporary Authors Online. Reproduced in Biography Resource Center. Farmington Hills, MI: Thomson Gale, 2006. http://galenet.galegroup.com/servlet/BioRC.

Blades, Meteor, "Global Warming Walk: Five Qs&As with Bill McKibben," *The Next Hurrah.* http://thenexthurrah.typepad.com/the_next_hurrah/2006/08/global_warming_.html (viewed September 24, 2006).

Coffey, Michael, "Bill McKibben: Environmental Hope in Conservative Times," *Publishers Weekly,* November 13, 1995.

Easterbrook, Gregg, *End of Nature* review, *Washington Monthly,* October 1989.

Emerson, Deborah, *Return of the Wolf* review, *Library Journal,* November 1, 2000.

End of Nature review, *American Forests,* January-February 1990.

Enough review, *Booklist,* January 1, 2004.

Hattam, Jennifer, "Bill McKibben on Brash Plans to Tinker with Our Genes," *Sierra.* http://www.sierraclub.org/200311/interview.asp (viewed September 24, 2006).

Little, Larry R., *Long Distance* review, *Library Journal,* February 1, 2001.

McKibben, Bill, "Year One: Climate Chaos Has Arrived," *Sierra.* http://www.scierraclub.org/sierra/200601/year_one.asp (viewed August 30, 2006).

"Q&A: Bill McKibben on Staying Human," Center for Genetics and Society, AlterNet, May 29, 2003. http://www.alternet.org/story/15963 (viewed August 30, 2006).

Seaman, Donna, *Deep Economy* review, *Booklist,* January 1, 2007.

Seaman, Donna, *Wandering Home* review, *Booklist,* March 1, 2005.

Talbot, Margaret, "The Perfectionist: Nature and the Morality of Family Size," *New Republic,* July 20, 1998.

Turney, Jon, "*Genes by Design?* review, *New Scientist,* May 10, 2003.

John McPhee

Environment, Food, History, Science, Sports, Travel

Benchmark Title: *Annals of the Former World*

Princeton, New Jersey

1931–

About the Author and the Author's Writing

John McPhee shouldn't be mistaken for one of the New Journalists, insists William L. Howarth in his introduction to *The John McPhee Reader,* "those celebrities who parade their neuroses or stump for public causes. McPhee never confesses, rarely preaches. He avoids publicity; other writers barter families and agents for good notice." McPhee's image has never appeared on one of his books, Howarth went on, because the author is both shy and private. Instead, McPhee gravitates to garrulous, opinionated individuals, such as the crusty, reclusive New Jerseyite Bill Wasovwich in *The Pine Barrens* (1968) and Vermont craftsman Henri Vaillencourt in *The Survival of the Bark Canoe* (1975) for anecdotes and perspective.

Despite Howarth's suggestion that McPhee never preaches, there is often a message in McPhee's books. *Pine Barrens*, for example, exposed the Garden State's disinterest in conservation. That changed with (now former) Governor Brendan T. Byrne, who told Jonathan Miller of the *New York Times* in 2004, "There's one sentence in John's book in which he says in effect, based on the realities of things, the Pinelands is bound to disappear. And I sort of took that as a challenge." Late 1970s state and federal laws were enacted to help preserve much of the 1.1 acres of south New Jersey land.

McPhee's hallmark is covering subjects otherwise overlooked. His *Coming into the Country* (1977), which appeared first as a long article in the *New Yorker,* focused on a state residents of the Lower Forty-Eight know little about—Alaska: its geology, its oil pipelines, its native inhabitants, its politics.

"When John McPhee writes about something, you don't need any advance knowledge of that subject," wrote blogger Rick Terrien. "You don't have to have any prior interest in it. But rest assured, you'll come away from his writing not just informed but graced, embraced and made better by Mr. McPhee's immense talent."

John McPhee was born in 1931 in Princeton, New Jersey, where he continues to live. His parents were Harry Roemer McPhee and Mary Ziiegler McPhee. His father, team physician for Princeton University and numerous U.S. Olympics athletes, enrolled John in Deerfield Academy for a postgraduate year before he entered Princeton. McPhee received an A.B. degree from Princeton in 1953, and did graduate study at Cambridge University in 1953 and 1954. From 1955 to 1957, he wrote scripts for the

Robert Montgomery Presents television show. In 1957, he married Pryde Brown; they had four children. After his marriage ended in divorce, McPhee married Yolanda Whitman in 1972. She had four children from a previous marriage. Until 1964, McPhee worked as a *Time* magazine associate editor in New York City.

Aspiring to write for the *New Yorker*, McPhee repeatedly submitted ideas. Finally, in 1964, the periodical accepted his 17,000-word profile of basketball star Bill Bradley. Soon after, editor William Shawn offered McPhee a position as staff writer. Since then, his essays for the *New Yorker* have been repackaged as books by his publisher Farrar, Straus and Giroux.

McPhee is drawn to many diverse subjects, with no apparent pattern.

After publishing *Coming into the Country,* he said in a 1978 interview, "The next project I'm thinking about is vague. It may be a short piece about geology, something to do with cretaceous extinction. What caused it when the dinosaurs disappeared? It's not as clear as people think. I might get into that subject."

McPhee researches thoroughly and collects mounds of resource material. For *Looking for a Ship* (1990), in which he examined U.S. Merchant Marines, the author sailed with Captain Andy Chase aboard the *Stella Lykes* for a month-and-a-half trek from Charleston, South Carolina, through the Panama Canal to South America, encountering porpoises and avoiding tropical storms and cocaine smugglers. McPhee's "clean, lean prose displays his sharp eye for telling detail and arresting incident," Genevieve Stuttaford wrote in her *Publishers Weekly* review.

Howarth described McPhee's writing technique, at least in the 1970s, as laborious, involving myriad note cards and a detailed outline. His intense pre-planning he attributed to an early grade-school teacher, Olive McKee, who required his three weekly school essays to have suitable introduction, body, and conclusion.

Geology and technology are among topics addressed in *Irons in the Fire* (1997), which includes his profile of a "forensic geologist" and a blind writer who uses a talking computer. *The Founding Fish,* published in 2002, vents the author's long enjoyment of shad fishing. "McPhee is in great form here, as informative as always but also funny, unusually self-revealing, and quite passionate in his discussions of the dire effects dams have had on shad and rivers alike," Donna Seaman wrote in her review for *Booklist.*

McPhee won the Pulitzer Prize for general nonfiction in 1999 for *Annals of the Former World,* a book which took two decades to write and actually encompasses four works that were first published as separate books: *Basin and Raznge, In Suspect Terrain, Rising from the Plains,* and *Assembling California.* As a whole, *Annals* is a geological history along the 40th parallel. Praising the book, John Skow in *Time* said, "McPhee, who is beguiled by his geologists and can make you see why, has a good feel for when to ease off into anecdotes. He goes after the rock wonks with butterfly net and magnifying glass."

Transportation has long fascinated McPhee; his 2006 title, *Uncommon Carriers,* offers his experiences riding an eighteen-wheel semitrailer truck and sitting in the cab of a Union Pacific coal train. There's a visit to a UPS sorting facility and an excursion along New England rivers to retrace the routes taken by his spiritual mentor, Henry David Thoreau. "McPhee breathes life into these experiences through his legendary eye and ear for detail, his talent for observation and description and his sardonic wit," Robert Braile wrote in the *Boston Globe.* Jesse Leavenworth in the *Hartford Courant* marveled at McPhee's prose—"He is a great describer and will tell you things you didn't know."

New York Times Book Review writer Adam Hochschild concluded that McPhee "has found wonderfully fertile terrain by simply doing things that small boys dream of. For what other thread connects his flying with a bush pilot, hanging out with blimp enthusiasts, or going on maneuvers with the Swiss Army?"

 Works by the Author

A Sense of Where You Are: A Profile of William Warren Bradley (1965)
The Headmaster: Frank L. Boyden of Deerfield (1966)
Oranges (1967)
The Pine Barrens (1968)
The Crofter and the Laird (1969)
A Roomful of Hovings and Other Profiles (1969)
Levels of the Game (1970)
Encounters with the Archdruid (1972)
Wimbledon: A Celebration (1972)
The Deltoid Pumpkin Seed (1973)
The Curve of Binding Energy (1974)
Pieces of the Frame (1975)
The Survival of the Bark Canoe (1975)
The John McPhee Reader, edited by William Howarth (1977), revised as *The Second John McPhee Reader,* edited by David Remnick and Patricia Strachan (1996)
Coming into the Country (1977)
Giving Good Weight (1979)
Alaska: Images of the Country, with Rowell Galen (1981)
Basin and Range (1981), included in *Annals of the Former World*
In Suspect Territory (1983), included in *Annals of the Former World*
Heirs of General Practice (1984)
La Place de la Concorde Suisse (1984)
Table of Contents (1985)
Rising from the Plains (1986), included in *Annals of the Former World*
Outcroppings (1988), includes portions of *Encounters with the Archdruid, Basin and Range* and *Rising from the Plains*
The Control of Nature (1989)
Looking for a Ship (1990)
Assembling California (1993), included in *Annals of the Former World*
The Ransom of Russian Art (1994)
Irons in the Fire (1997)
Annals of the Former World (1984), includes *Basin and Range, In Suspect Terrain, Assembling California,* and *Rising from the Plains*
The Founding Fish (2002)
Uncommon Carriers (2006)

Editor

The Princeton Anthology of Writing: Favorite Pieces by the Ferris/McGraw Writers at Princeton University, with Carol Rigolot (2001)

For Further Information

Berkes, Howard, "John McPhee: A Reporter's Reporter," National Public Radio, September 6, 2006. http://www.npr.org/templates/story/story.php?storyId=55-8203 (viewed September 6, 2006).

Braile, Robert, "McPhee's 'Carriers' Is Transporting," *Boston Globe,* June 26, 2006.

Grossman, Lev, "Hook, Line and Thinker," *Time,* Nov. 25, 2002.

Hoshschild, Adam, "Trains, Planes & Automobiles," *New York Times Book Review*, June 18, 2006.

John (Angus) McPhee entry, Contemporary Authors Online. Reproduced in Biography Resource Center. Farmington Hills, MI: Thomson Gale, 2004. http://galenet.galegroup.com/servlet/BioRC.

Leavenworth, Jesse, " 'Carriers' Makes the Wheels Go Round," *Hartford Courant,* June 25, 2006.

Pearson, Michael, *John McPhee*. New York: Twayne, 1997.

Reid, Calvin, "Libel Suit Against McPhee, FSG, 'New Yorker' Dismissed," *Publishers Weekly,* March 11, 1996.

Seaman, Donna, *Founding Fish* review, *Booklist,* September 1, 2002.

Seaman, Donna, *Irons in the Fire* review, *Booklist,* January 1, 1997.

Skow, John, *Annals of the Former World* review, *Time,* July 6, 1998.

Stuttaford, Genevieve, *Looking for a Ship* review, *Publishers Weekly,* July 20, 1990.

Terrien, Rick, "John McPhee in the Garage," Sustainablework Web site, 2005. http://sustainablework.com/blog/2005/10/john-mcphee-in-garage.html (viewed September 6, 2006).

Ved Mehta

Autobiography, Biography, Memoir, Travel

Benchmark Title: *Continents of Exile*

Lahore, India (Pakistan)

1934–

Photo by Jerry Bauer, 1977

About the Author and the Author's Writing

Ved Parkash Mehta's life has been one of more heartache than joy. He was born in 1934 in relatively promising circumstances to Hindu parents in Lahore, then part of colonial British India (now Pakistan); but Ved's life was fractured from the start.

His father, Amolak Ram Mehta, was an ambitious, English-trained physician involved in India's public health service. Before he turned four, Ved lost his sight to cerebrospinal meningitis. His mother, Shanti Mehra Mehta, believed the affliction was only temporary and resorted to herbal cures and flogging with twigs as ineffectual cures. Eventually, his father sent him to Bombay's Dadar School for the Blind, expressing the hope that the youth could avoid a life of begging or chair caning. The school was pure misery. Family life was further disrupted by religious unrest that led to the partition of India in 1947.

"Deprivation often makes a writer," Mehta wrote in *1985 Medical and Health Annual.* "In India, one of the poorest countries the world has ever known, the lot of the blind was to beg with a walking stick in one hand and an alms bowl in the other.... But my father, a doctor, tried to fight the superstition and give me an education, like his other children, so that I could become, as he used to say, a self-supporting citizen of the world."

With his father's help, Ved wrote letter after letter to schools in the United States and finally was accepted at the Arkansas School for the Blind in Little Rock. He traveled there by himself, at age fifteen, not knowing the racism his dark features would bring. After completing his course work, he went to Pomona College in California. Interested in one of the girls in the class but too shy to ask her for a date, he came up with the scheme of hiring her to help type his autobiography. The romance never happened, but the book did. Little, Brown, and Company brought out *Face to Face* in 1957. The publisher expected it was a one-time effort.

Mehta continued to write as he went off, on a Hazen Foundation scholarship, to study history at Balliol College, Oxford University. In 1959, he received a bachelor of arts degree with honors. He received a master's degree from Harvard University in 1961 and master of arts from Oxford University the next year.

Mehta met legendary *New Yorker* editor William Shawn in 1960. He had pitched an idea for a 14,000-word article about a recent return visit he had made to India. Shawn not only bought the piece, he put Mehta on the staff, where he remained for three decades.

Mehta has not shunned controversy in his writings; in 1993, his *Mahatma Gandhi and His Apostles* was both applauded for its originality—he was the first writer to seek out Gandhi's former disciples to see how they were carrying on the legacy—and its honesty—many of those disciples had warped or strayed from their mentor. Mehta's treatment of Gandhi's unusual approach to celibacy—many young women slept with him even though he was a *brahamachari* (a celibate), a test of his will, he said, as there were no sexual relations—not surprisingly created a stir.

Mehta's life has provided content for more than a dozen autobiographical works and memoirs, including the eleven-volume Continents of Exile series. Noting that the books are unlike anything else in literature, *Smithsonian*'s Suzanne Green said, "It would be too limiting to regard him primarily as a blind writer or an Indian writer, but being both blind and Indian gives him a special perspective on the extraordinary event that shaped his childhood."

Mehta's books deal with various periods and people in his life: his parents, his attendance at a school for the blind, his construction of a new house for his family, his efforts to develop loving relationships with three women (he did marry Linn Fenimore Cooper Cary in 1983, and they have two children). *The Red Letters,* the final volume, published in 2004, explores an unexpected topic, one he had delayed confronting: his father's love affair with a friend of the family. "Mehta's unique outlook as a native-born Indian educated and living in the West since 1949 gives readers a comfortable entrée to a world that he knows but no longer inhabits," Jan Brue Enright wrote in *Library Journal.*

Although some of Mehta's books are written with vivid visual imagery, one that does not is *Vedi*: "We follow the blind child into the orphanage, and, like him we never learn what the place or any of the people in it looked like," Janet Malcom wrote in *New York Review of Books.* "We hear, we feel, but we see nothing." Not the least of *Vedi*'s originality is this very stylistic denial, which amounts to an approximation of the experience of blindness."

Mehta on his Web site said he takes no notes and keeps no journal. He used a tape recorder for interviews only one time, when he wrote the Gandhi biography, because he wanted to be able to verify his quotes from wary disciples of the leader. Otherwise he relies on his keen memory, which he developed after losing his sight.

Mehta has received numerous fellowships including ones from the Guggenheim and the John D. and Catharine T. MacArthur Foundations, and honorary doctoral degrees from Pomona, Bard, Williams, and Vassar Colleges. He has taught at Balliol College, Oxford, Williams, Vassar, and Yale.

Mehta acknowledged loss as a major theme of his writing, he told journalist Anil Padmanabhan, "loss of sight, of home and, with Partition, the loss of all the familiar landmarks of my childhood. The loss of language. I should ordinarily have written in Hindu, Punjabi or Urdu, but I ended up writing in what is really a foreign tongue. In the old days no one became a writer unless they became part of a national tradition. Now writers don't belong to any tradition. That in itself is a kind of a loss."

 # Works by the Author

Face to Face: An Autobiography (1957)
Walking the Indian Streets (1960), revised (1971)
Fly and the Fly-Bottle: Encounters with British Intellectuals (1963)
The New Theologian (1966)
Delinquent Chacha (1967)
Portraits of India (1970)
John Is Easy to Please: Encounters with the Written and Spoken Word (1971)
Mahatma Gandhi and His Apostles (1977)
The New India (1978)
The Photographs of Chachaji: The Making of a Documentary Film (1980)
A Family Affair: India under Three Prime Ministers (1982), sequel to *The New India*
Rajiv Gandhi and Rama's Kingdom (1994), sequel to *A Family Affair*
A Ved Mehta Reader: The Craft of the Essay (1998)

Continents of Exile Series

Daddyji (1972), included in *Daddyji/Mamaji* (1984)
Mamaji (1979), included in *Daddyji/Mamaji* (1984)
Vedi (1982)
The Ledge between the Streams (1984)
Sound-Shadows of the New World (1986)
The Stolen Light (1989)
Up at Oxford (1993)
Remembering Mr. Shawn's New Yorker; *The Invisible Art of Editing* (1998)
Ved Mehta Reader: The Craft of the Essay (1998)
All for Love (2001)
Dark Harbor: Building House and Home on an Enchanted Island (2003)
The Red Letters: My Father's Enchanted Period (2004)

Contributor

Adventures in Living, edited by Henry I. Christs and Herbert Potell (1962)
Perspectives, edited by Leo Kneer (1963)
Interpreting Literature, by K. L. Knickerbocker and H. W. Reninger (1965)
Profiles of Nehru, edited by Norman Cousins (1966)
Readings for Liberal Education, edited by George Arms, William M. Gibson and Louis G. Locke (1967)

Exploring Literature, by Walter Havighurst, Arno Jewett, Josephine Lowery, and Philip McFarland (1968)

Background Readings in Building Library Collections, by Mary V. Gaver (1969)

Profiles of Gandhi, edited by Norman Cousins (1969)

Purpose and Function in Prose, edited by Nicholas P. Barker (1969)

Rajaji-93 Souvenir, edited by T. Sadasivan (1971)

A Reader for Writers: A Critical Anthology of Prose Readings, edited by Jerome W. Archer and Joseph Schwartz (1971)

Voices from India, edited by Margaret Cormack and Kiki Skagen (1971)

Linguistics for Teachers, edited by John F. Savage (1973)

A Primer of Linguistics, edited by Anne Fremantle (1974)

Style and Synthesis, edited by Albert R. Kitzhaber (1974)

Through Indian Eyes, edited by Donald J. Johnson and Jean E. Johnson (1974)

Experiencing Biography, edited by Robert E. Beck (1978)

Houghton Mifflin Literature Series, Grade 8, edited by Havighurst, Jewett, Lowery, and McFarland (1978)

Ordinary Lives: Voices of Disability and Disease, edited by Irving Kenneth Zola (1983)

1985 Medical and Health Annual (1984)

Self-Esteem and Adjusting with Blindness: The Process of Responding to Life's Demands, edited by Dean W. Tuttle (1984)

India: A Teacher's Guide (1985)

Great Writing, edited by Harvey Weiner (1987)

World Geography: The Earth and Its People, edited by Phillip Bacon (1989)

The Oxford Book of Marriage, edited by Helge Rubinstein (1990)

Kaleidoscope, edited by George Perkins and Barbara Perkins (1993)

Transitions; Paragraph to Essay, edited by Linda Bates (1993)

The Foloi Anthology of Autobiography, edited by Angela Thirwell (1994)

Living in America; Poetry and Fiction by South Asian American Writers, edited by Roshni Rustomji-Ierns (1995)

Scott Foresman Literature and Integrated Studies, edited by Alan C. Purves (1996)

Traveller's Literary Companion: The Indian Sub-Continent (1996)

The Human Family, edited by Stevan Harrell (1997)

Mirrorwork: 50 Years of Indian Writing 1947–1997 (1997)

Multitude: Cross-Cultural Readings, edited by Chitra B. Divakaruni (1997)

Staring Back: The Disability Experience from the Inside Out, edited by Kennedy Fries (1997)

Transitions: An Interactive Reading, Writing, and Grammar Text, edited by Linda Bates (1997)

Progress: Topics, edited by Eva Hedencrona and others (1999)

Regions: Adventures in Time and Place, edited by James A. Banks and others (1999)

Asian American Writers (2000)

Texts from Other Cultures (2000)

Along These Lines: Writing Sentences and Paragraphs, edited by John Biyas and Carol Wershoven (2001)

Public Lives, Private Prayers, edited by Mary Reath (2001)

Globe Literature 2001 (2001)

Interactions: A Thematic Reader, edited by Anne Moseley and Jeanette Harris (2003)

Fiction

Three Stories of the Raj (1986)

Documentary Film

Chachaji: My Poor Relation (1978)

For Further Information

Dark Harbor review, *Publishers Weekly,* May 19, 2003.

Dowd, Maureen, "A Writing Odyssey through India Past and Present," *New York Times Magazine,* June 10, 1984.

Enright, Jan Brue, *Red Letters* review, *Library Journal,* September 15, 2004.

Heidmann, Ilse, *All for Love* review, *Library Journal,* August 2001.

Heidmann, Ilse, *Ved Mehta Reader* review, *Library Journal,* November 1, 1998.

Malcolm, Janet, *Vedi* review, *New York Review of Books,* October 7, 1982.

Padmanabhan, Anil, "Talent Knows No Borders," *India Today International,* November 1, 2004.

Staples, Suzanne Green, "The Ledge between the Streams," *Smithsonian,* August 1984.

Tiwana, Jagpal Singh, *Mahatma Gandhi and His Apostles* review, *Canadian India Times,* February 2, 1978.

Ved Mehta Web site. http://www.vedmehta.com (viewed September 5, 2006).

Ved (Parkash) Mehta entry, Contemporary Authors Online. Reproduced in Biography Resource Center. Farmington Hills, MI: Thomson Gale, 2003. http://galenet.galegroup.com/servlet/BioRC.

Farley Mowat

Adventure, Autobiography, Environment, Investigative Reporting, Memoir, Science

Benchmark Title: *Never Cry Wolf*

Belleville, Ontario

1921–

About the Author and the Author's Writing

The forty-two members of the Sea Shepherd Conservation Society's *Farley Mowat* sailed from Auckland harbor in December 2002. Under a pirate flag, Skipper Paul Watson considered himself an international maritime enforcer, his target Japanese Antarctic sailors who killed minke whales for "scientific" purposes. In truth, the whales were sold at market in Japan. By January 2006, Watson stated he was willing to back off on his harassment campaign if the Australian or New Zealand governments would take Japan to international court.

The conservation organization not only named its flagship for Canada's best-known nonfiction author, Farley Mowat, it mirrored Mowat's technique: muster solid data (favorite Mowat topics include aboriginal people, endangered animal species, and grand adventure), broadcast it worldwide, and irritate powers that be into taking action.

Farley McGill Mowat was born in 1921 in Belleville, Ontario, Canada, the son of Angus and Helen Elizabeth Thomson Mowat. A veteran of World War I, Angus Mowat moved the family frequently until he became head librarian in Saskatoon, Saskatchewan. Young Farley immersed himself in books. He also explored the woods with his dog, Mutt, and raised a small zoo of odd animals including Wol the owl. Most important, he absorbed the adventures of his peripatetic uncle Frank Farley, who showed him how to mount wildlife specimens and collect birds' eggs for museums. Uncle Frank on one trip introduced the youth to northern caribou herds—and opened the future writer's eyes to the fragility and enormous wonder of nature.

After Farley graduated from high school, with World War II in full bloom, he enlisted in the Hastings and Prince Edward Regiment (the same as his father had once belonged to) and led a rifle platoon in the invasion of Sicily (1940–1946). This experience, too, shaped his thinking—he would soon yearn for warless solitude and wilderness. Mowat went on to major in biology at the University of Toronto (where he earned his bachelor's degree in 1949). Mowat had two sons with his wife, Frances Thornhill. After that marriage ended, he married Claire A. Wheeler in 1964.

On a scientific trip to the Canadian north, to the land of the Ihalmiut, he discovered the plight of the Inuit—and they became the subject of his first book, *People of the Deer* (1952).

Mowat had always had a natural bent for writing. It became his life's career. As a teenager, he had written a bird column for the Saskatoon *Star Phoenix*. Certainly other occupations seemed unlikely. As he writes with bemusement in *Born Naked*, a biography of his early years, he had little mechanical ability. "One day when I had made a cut half an inch short in a piece of wood for the caravan's frame, he [father Angus]—said to me, quite unkindly, 'Bunje, my lad, you are without doubt the roughest carpenter one man ever told another about. Why don't you take up knitting or finger-painting?'"

Mowat wrote about his military experiences in *The Regiment*, published in 1954. His children's book, *Lost in the Barrens* (1956), brought him wide recognition and a Governor General's Award. It is about children of different backgrounds—one is white, one Native American—who survive winter in the Arctic thanks to an Inuit boy they meet. Mowat wrote two more books for young readers, *The Dog Who Wouldn't Be* (1957) and *Owls in the Family* (1961), both based on family experiences. He wrote of the daring rescues of the oceangoing tug *Foundation Franklin* in his 1958 release, *Grey Seas Under*.

Then, on assignment from the Canadian government, he went back to the Arctic to monitor caribou herds. While ranchers believed wolves were eating the caribou, Mowat observed that the wolves mostly subsisted on mice and ate only the weakest of the deer. It was, he believed, the ranchers themselves who were responsible for the diminished caribou herds. His book *Never Cry Wolf*, published in 1963, not only entertained readers all over the world, it inspired the Soviet Union to ban the wholesale killing of wolves.

Years later, Mowat admitted that some of his "scientific findings" were embellished for that book. "I am an entertainer," he told journalist Joe Shepstone. "I do like to pleasure my audience. If that makes my writing more acceptable then it will be more effective. My writing is a communication between myself and the reader." Mowat's biographer James King defended the author, stating that Mowat felt a universal truth had to be asserted even at the loss of factual accuracy.

Mowat's reputation appears undiminished as he continues to produce a stream of books. Two of the most recent are *No Man's River* (2004), which is about a two-man zoological expedition to an isolated Arctic camp, and *Bay of Spirits* (2006), a tale of a Newfoundland coastal steamer and a love affair with a woman and a place. *Canadian Geographic* reviewer Julie McCann notes a complexity to Mowat's eight-year sojourn in Burgeo, Newfoundland. Mowat is appalled that dragger fishermen throw back small fish caught in their nets—even though their rapid rise to the surface has already spelled their doom. "For a conservationist like Mowat, these practices—conducted by people he otherwise adores—are hard to rationalize."

"He is a national icon," John Goddard wrote in *Saturday Night*. "He is part storyteller, part crusader. He is famous for the fearlessness with which he is ready to confront and ridicule established authority, and for the affinity he often shows in his books for animals, native peoples, and the natural environment."

Mowat's long list of awards began with a President's Medal for best Canadian short story in 1952, from the University of Western Ontario, for "Eskimo Spring." He received a Book of the Year for Children award from the Canadian Association of Children's Librarians for *Lost in the Barrens*, a Stephen Leacock Foundation Medal for *The Boat Who Wouldn't Float* and an Author of the Year designation from the Canadian Booksellers Association in 1988.

Whether he is totally comfortable with it or not, Mowat has accepted his status as an environmental champion. In 2005, the library in Port Hope, Ontario, where he and his second wife live part of the year (the rest in Nova Scotia), held a Farley Mowat Week and screened several films based on his books, including *Lost in the Barrens* and *Never Cry Wolf*.

"It's always a great pleasure to be celebrated before you're dead," he quipped to a reporter for *Sea Shepherd News*.

 ## Works by the Author

People of the Deer (1952), revised (1975)

The Regiment (1954), revised (1973)

Grey Seas Under: The Perilous Rescue Missions of a North Atlantic Salvage Tug (1958)

The Desperate People (1959), revised (1975)

The Serpent's Coil: An Incredible Story of Hurricane-Battered Ships and the Heroic Men Who Fought to Save Them (1961)

Never Cry Wolf (1963/1973)

Westviking: The Ancient Norse in Greenland and North America (1965)

Canada North (1968)

This Rock Within the Sea: A Heritage Lost (1968)

The Boat Who Wouldn't Float (1969)

The Siberians (1970), in Canada as *Sibir: My Discovery of Siberia* (1970/1973)

A Whale for the Killing (1972)

Wake of the Great Sealers (1973)

The Snow Walker (1975)

The Great Betrayal: Arctic Canada Now (1976), sequel to *Canada North*, published in Canada as *Canada North Now: The Great Betrayal* (1976)

Top of the World Trilogy (1976), includes *Ordeal by Ice, Polar Passion*, and *Tundra*

And No Birds Sang (1979)

Sea of Slaughter (1984)

My Discovery of America (1985)

Woman in the Mists: The Story of Dian Fossey and the Mountain Gorillas of Africa (1987), published in Canada as *Virunga: The Passion of Dian Fossey* (1987)

The New Founde Land (1989)

Rescue the Earth: Conversations with the Green Crusaders (1990)

My Father's Son: Memories of War and Peace (1992)

Born Naked: The Early Adventures of the Author of Never Cry Wolf (1993)

Aftermath: Travels in a Post-War World (1995)

A Farley Mowat Reader (1997)

The Farfarers: Before the Norse (1998), published in England as *The Alban Quest: The Search for a Lost Tribe* (1999)
Walking on the Land (2000)
High Latitudes: An Arctic Journey (2002)
No Man's River (2004)
Bay of Spirits: A Love Story (2006)

Editor

Coppermine Journey: An Account of a Great Adventurer (1958)
Ordeal by Ice: The Search for the Northwest Passage (1960), reprinted (1973)
The Polar Passion: The Quest for the North Pole (1967), reprinted (1973)
Tundra: Selections from the Great Accounts of Arctic Land Voyages (1973)

For Juvenile Readers

The Dog Who Wouldn't Be (1957)
Owls in the Family (1961), reprinted (1973)

Fiction

Lost in the Barrens (1956), also issued as *Two against the North* (1977)
The Black Joke (1962) reprinted (1973)
The Curse of the Viking Grave (1966)

Film Adaptations

In Search of Farley Mowat (1981), documentary
Never Cry Wolf (1983)
Lost in the Barrens (1990)
The Curse of the Viking Grave (1991)
The Snow Walker (2003)

For Further Information

Born Naked review, *Publishers Weekly,* February 7, 1994.
Burgess, Steve, "Northern Exposure," "Brilliant Careers," salon.com1995. http://www.salon.com/people/bc/1999/05/11/mowat/ (viewed September 20, 2007).
Farley (McGill) Mowat entry, Contemporary Authors Online. Reproduced in Biography Resource Center. Farmington Hills, MI: Thomson Gale, 2002. http://galenet.galegroup.com/servlet/BioRC.
Farley Mowat profile, Canada Reads. http://www.cbc.ca/canadareads/cr_2002/k_%20mowat.html (viewed September 20, 2007).
"Farley Mowat Week in Port Hope, Ontario," *Sea Shepherd News,* April 21, 2005.
Farley Mowat (ship) Web page. http://www.newzeal.com/theme/Ships/Shepherd/farleymowat.htm (viewed September 12, 2006).

Gardner, James, "Sea Shepherd vs. Japan's Whaling Fleet," Cyber Diver News Network Web site. http://www.cdnn.info/eco/e020826/e020826.html (viewed September 29, 2006).

Goddard, John, "A Real Whopper," *Saturday Night,* May 1996.

High Latitudes review, *Publishers Weekly,* February 24, 2003.

King, James, *Farley: The Life of Farley Mowat.* Hanover, NH: Steerforth Press, 2003.

Lessem, Don, *Woman in the Mists* review, *Smithsonian,* May 1988.

McCann, Julie, *Bay of Spirits* review, *Canadian Geographic,* September/October 2006.

My Father's Son review, *Publishers Weekly,* November 23, 1992.

Rogers, Michael, *Grey Seas Under* review, *Library Journal,* June 1, 2001.

Shepstone, Joe, "Farley Mowat on Writing Fiction, Non-fiction and Autobiography," *CM* magazine. http://www.umanitoba.ca/cm/vol3/no1/farleymowat.html (viewed September 12, 2006).

Smith, Stephen, "Horror on the Barrens," *Canadian Geographic,* November 2000.

Takver, "Sea Shepherd: Prosecute Japan over Whaling and We Will Withdraw," Melbourne.indy.media.org. http://melbourne.indymedia.org/news/2006/01/103737.php (viewed September 20, 2007).

"Uncle Sam Cries Wolf at Border," *U.S. News & World Report*, May 6, 1985.

Susan Orlean

Investigative Reporting, Sports, Travel

Benchmark Title: *The Orchid Thief*

Cleveland, Ohio

1955–

About the Author and the Author's Writing

Travel writer Susan Orlean is anxious to go anywhere. Even to Houston, to the surprise of one friend, who warned her that the city was a bore. Orlean didn't believe him; how could such a sprawling metropolis full of oil and gas facilities be dull? "My friend was disgusted," she related in the introduction to *My Kind of Place* (2004). "I will confess that he was almost right: Of all the places I've been, Houston was one of the hardest to love, but its blankness and shapelessness fascinated me and made a great backdrop to the story I had gone there to see."

Orlean goes places not so much to see the places as to see what interesting people she can find in those places. In *My Kind of Place,* for instance, she explores the African music scene in Paris and chats with taxidermists in Illinois and speaks with Little League ballplayers in Cuba. They're all in a day's work for the veteran *New Yorker* writer and journalist.

The author was born in 1955 in Cleveland, Ohio, the daughter of Arthur and Edith Gross Orlean. Her father was a real estate developer, her mother a bank official. She studied literature and history at the University of Michigan in Ann Arbor. In 2001, she married investment broker John Gillespie; they have one child.

Orlean began her writing career with the *Boston Phoenix,* working there from 1983 to 1986; then became a *Boston Globe* columnist for a year. In 1987, she went to New York City to become a *Rolling Stone* contributing editor and a staff and freelance writer for the *New Yorker.*

On her Web site Orlean says she was largely self-taught: I "always dreamed of being a writer, but had no idea of how you went about being a writer—or at least the kind of writer I wanted to be: someone who wrote long stories about interesting things, rather than news stories about short-lived events."

Orlean's curiosity is enormous. "Everything amazes Orlean; curiosity is her thing," Chris Colin asserted in his salon.com interview with the author. "It got her the *New Yorker* job—she wanted to know more about those great shirt folders at Benetton stores—and it gets her readers through potentially boring articles about how supermarkets work or what some Maui surfer girls are like."

Orlean has collected many of her magazine pieces in four books. She is drawn, not to celebrity, but to anonymity. "I didn't want to write about famous people simply because they were famous," she told Powells.com interviewer Dave Weich in 2001, "and I didn't want to write about charming little things that were self-consciously charming and little.... The subjects I was drawn to were often completely ordinary, but I was confident that I could find something extraordinary in their ordinariness."

Saturday Night (1990) describes Saturday nights spent everywhere from a Park Avenue soiree to a Midwest missile silo. *The Bullfighter Checks Her Makeup* (2000) includes the author's pieces about figure skater Tonya Harding, who was disgraced at the 1994 Olympics, and fashion designer Bill Blass and the leading female matador Cristina Sánchez.

One 1995 *New Yorker* feature article had sufficient promise that she expanded it into a full-length (and best-selling) book, *The Orchard Thief.* The book is about a curiously personable if eccentric poacher of rare orchids, Floridian John Laroche. The investigation into Laroche's story became the focus of a 2002 motion picture, *Adaptation,* which was loosely based on the book. Meryl Streep starred in the film, playing the role of Orlean.

Orlean say she does not rely on outlines before she starts writing. "There are times when I certainly envy people who do that because it seems like a more deliberative and rational process," she told Julie Hale of *BookPage.* "For me, a big part of figuring out a story is actually sitting down to write it."

She said she favors the writing aspect of her craft over the reporting. "I think, all the time, about the art of writing and how I'm going to write the story," she said in an *Identity Theory* interview. "I had an editor who told me there are three parts to what you want to do: reporting, thinking and writing. Of those three, his feeling was that they could not be separated. I get the most pleasure about people remarking on the written part of it rather than the reporting thing or the thought."

Orlean's life of late has gone to the dogs. She ghostwrote a cookbook for her Welsh springer spaniel, Cooper Gillespie, and at this writing is delving into the biography of movie star Rin Tin Tin.

In an article in *The Writer,* she offered this advice: "Report more than you think you have to, and then do a little more reporting—it will always, always pay off in the writing.... Read good writing. And most of all, put your heart in it, in every single word and every single sentence."

 # Works by the Author

Red Sox and Bluefish: Meditations on What Makes New England New England (1987)

Saturday Night (1990)

The Orchid Thief: A True Story of Beauty and Obsession (1998)

The Bullfighter Checks Her Makeup: My Encounters with Extraordinary People (2000)

My Kind of Place: Travel Stories from a Woman Who's Been Everywhere (2004)

Editor

The Best American Essays 2005, with Robert Atwan (2005)

Contributor

Literary Journalism, edited by Norman Sims and Mark Kramer (1995)

Best American Sports Writing 1996, edited by John Feinstein (1996)

Making Contact: Readings from Home and Abroad, edited by Carol J. Verburg (1997)

Telling Stories/Taking Risks: Journalism Writing at the Century's Edge, edited by Alice M. Klement and Carolyn Matalene (1997)

Da Capo Best Music Writing 2000, edited by Peter Guralnick and Douglas Wolk (2000)

Best American Travel Writing 2001, edited by Jason Wilson and Paul Theroux (2001)

Fierce Pajamas: An Anthology of Humor Writing from the New Yorker, edited by David Remnick and Henry Finder (2001)

Life Stories: Profiles from the New Yorker, edited by David Remnick (2001)

The New Gilded Age: The New Yorker Looks at the Culture of Affluence, edited by David Remnick (2001)

Sweet Breathing of Plants: Women Writers on the Green World, edited by Linda Hogan and Brenda Peterson (2002)

Flowers in Shadow: A Photographer Discovers a Victorian Botanical Journal, by Zeva Oelbaum (2002)

The Writers Presence: A Pool of Readings, edited by Donald McQuade and Robert Atwan (2003)

The Good City: Writers Explore 21st Century Boston, edited by Emily Hiestand and Ande Zellman (2004)

This Side of Paradise, by F. Scott Fitzgerald (2005)

Under Name Cooper Gillespie

Throw Me a Bone: Fifty Healthy, Canine Taste-Tested Recipes for Snacks, Meals, and Treats, with Sally Sampson (2003)

Film Adaptations

Adaptation (2002)

For Further Information

Birnbaum, Robert, Susan Orlean interview, *Identity Theory.* http://www.identitytheory.com/people/birnbaum6.html (viewed September 12, 2006).

Colin, Chris, Susan Orlean interview, salon.com, February 2001. http://archive.salon.com/people/conv/2001/02/26/orlean.index.html (viewed September 12, 2006).

Hale, Julie, "Susan Orlean: Unveiling a Cast of 'Extraordinary' Characters," *BookPage,* January 2001. http://www.bookpage.com/0101bp/susan_orlean.html (viewed April 19, 2006).

Hopkins, Alison, *My Kind of Place* review, *Library Journal,* October 1, 2004.

Orchard Thief review, *Publishers Weekly,* November 23, 1998.

Orecklin, Michele, *The Bullfighter Checks Her Makeup* review, *Time,* February 19, 2001.

Orlean, Susan, "How I Write," *The Writer,* March 2002.

Sanoff, Alvin P., "The Culture of Hanging Out," *U.S. News & World Report,* June 4, 1990.

Susan Orlean entry, *Authors and Artists for Young Adults*, Vol. 64. Farmington Hills, MI: Thomson Gale, 2005.

Susan Orlean Web site. http://www.susanorlean.com/about/index.html (viewed September 12, 2006).

Weich, Dave, "Susan Orlean Returns with Stories from the Road," Powells.com, 2001. http://www.powells.com/authors/orlean2001.html (viewed September 12, 2006).

Nathaniel Philbrick

Adventure, History, Sports

Benchmark Title: *In the Heart of the Sea*

Pittsburgh, Pennsylvania

ca. 1957–

Photo courtesy Penguin Group

About the Author and the Author's Writing

Melissa Philbrick stopped in at the Nantucket library just before Christmas in 1998 to pick up an interlibrary loan for her husband. The reference librarian gave her a curious look and inquired after Nat. He's confined to the house but is doing fine, she replied. Only as she was in the parking lot did she look at the article she had retrieved and understand the source of the librarian's concern: "The Nutritional Value of Cannibalism."

Historian Nathaniel Philbrick didn't get *that* deeply into his research, but he did immerse himself in whaling lore and the South Seas as he wrote *In the Heart of the Sea,* the National Book Award–winning account of the crew of the ill-fated *Essex* and their fifteen-month struggle to survive on the open sea. They ate some of their dead mates to survive.

As director of the Egan Institute of Maritime Studies on Nantucket, Philbrick had written earlier local histories and books about sailing. He provided an introduction to a 1995 reprint of Joseph C. Hart's *Miriam Coffin; or, The Whale-Fishermen,* a work that novelist Herman Melville had consulted as he crafted his sea epic *Moby Dick* in 1851. With his account of the *Essex, In the Heart of the Sea,* Philbrick made a second link with Melville, using the sinking of a ship by an angry whale to conclude his adventure.

Philbrick grew up in Pittsburgh—his ocean blood developing in his college years when he was an intercollegiate All-American sailor and North American Sunfish champion. He received a bachelor's degree from Brown University and a master's in American literature from Duke University. Although he had anticipated becoming a teacher, as his parents had been, he began to write for a variety of publications ranging from *Vanity Fair, Sailing World,* and the *New York Times Book Review* to the *Wall Street Journal, Los Angeles Times,* and *Boston Globe.* After writing and editing books about sailing both serious (*Second Wind,* 1998) and not (*Yachting: a Parody,* 1984), he compiled two histories for the Egan Institute, *Away Off Shore* (1994), a history of Europeans on the island, and *Abram's Eyes* (1998), about Native Americans there. In 2002, he was named Nathaniel Bowditch Maritime Scholar of the Year by the American Merchant Marine Museum.

Philbrick and his wife uprooted from Boston when she, an attorney and Cape Cod native, discovered an employment opportunity on Nantucket, south of New Bedford. For a time, Philbrick stayed at home with their two children while his wife worked. His mobility limited, he took an interest in the island's history. Poring over materials about sailing crews, he discovered the story of the *Essex*—and particularly, he learned of the recent discovery of a years-later account by a cabin boy, which, paired with the first mate's diary, gave a firsthand account of the episode. This became his spark for *In the Heart of the Sea.*

"I am trained as a journalist," the author said on the Penguin Web site, "and instead of inventing anything, the way a fiction writer would, I was trying to figure out, as best I could, what really happened. Where information concerning the *Essex* and her crew was lacking, I turned to other whaling voyages for examples of what had occurred under similar circumstances."

The irony of the *Essex* experience, the author explained to *News Hour*'s Ray Suarez, is, "Their fear of cannibalism drove them on this impossible voyage [they rowed their whaleboats toward mainland to avoid the island natives] and ultimately required them to enact their own worst fears."

Philbrick developed a reputation for being able to find the unexpected within the familiar. *Sea of Glory,* his 2003 retelling of the U.S. Exploring Expedition of 1838–1840, brought to life Lieutenant Charles Wilkes, the explorer-scientist who remained mostly overlooked although he was first to plant an American flag on Antarctica.

"When I'm writing I read and write every day—seven days a week," Nathaniel Philbrick said in an interview with Carol Standish of *Maine Harbors*. "*Sea of Glory* took a year and a half of 'solid writing.' "

Mayflower, published in 2006, has given the story of the Pilgrims much-needed perspective. Few outside of southern New England, for example, are aware of the devastating toll the English settlers wrought on the Native Americans and the failed King Philip's War of Wampanoags and their allies in the 1670s to drive the Europeans away.

"Philbrick has a gift for drawing telling details from the primary accounts on which much of his book is based," Jenny Hale Pulsipher said in a *Globe* review. " 'Mayflower' is a surprise-filled account of what are supposed to be some of the best-known events in this country's past but are instead an occasion for collective amnesia," Janet Maslin commented in the *New York Times*.

"I too grew up thinking there was the *Mayflower* and Thanksgiving," the author said in a conversation with Andrew Richards. "What got lost in there was the Indians. The Native American experience then became part of the winning of the west. Learning about King Philip's War was shocking."

It took Philbrick thirteen years to amass sufficient material to write *Mayflower*. Native American accounts passed down through oral tradition were particularly difficult to come by. "I realized that exploring the Native American past requires a whole different side of the brain almost, a whole different discipline. I took a couple of years just coming up to speed in that way," he said in a *BookPage* interview.

Americans need to hear and understand their entire history, the author says. "I think [*Mayflower* is] a story that has real relevance to where we are now," Philbrick told journalist David Mehegan of the *Boston Globe,* "because in many ways the world today is a kind of 17th-century New England, in terms of all the groups that don't understand one another. But we need to do the best we can to live together."

Works by the Author

The Passionate Sailor (1987)

Away Off Shore: Nantucket Island and Its People, 1602–1890 (1994)

Second Wind: A Nantucket Sailor's Odyssey (1998)

Abram's Eyes: The Native American Legacy of Nantucket Island (1992)

In the Heart of the Sea: The Tragedy of the Whaleship "Essex" (2000)

Sea of Glory: America's Voyage of Discovery, The U.S. Exploring Expedition, 1838–1842 (2003)

Mayflower: A Story of Courage, Community, and War (2006)

For Juvenile Readers

Revenge of the Whale: The True Story of the Whaleship "Essex" (2002)

Editor

Yachting: A Parody (1984)

The Loss of the Ship "Essex" Sunk by a Whale, with Thomas Nickerson and others (2000)

American Sea Writing: A Literary Anthology, with Peter Neill (2000)

The Private Journal of William Reynolds: United States Exploring Expedition, 1838–1842, with Thomas Philbrick (2004)

The Mayflower Papers: Selected Writings of Colonial New England, with Thomas Philbrick (2007)

Contributor

Miriam Coffin, or, The Whale-Fisherman, by Joseph C. Hart (1995)

Moby-Dick, or The White Whale, by Herman Melville (2001)

Remarkable Observations of the Whaling Journal of Peleg Folger 1751–54, edited by Thomas Philbrick (2006)

For Further Information

Gates, Davie, "Pilgrims' Bloody Progress: Nathaniel Philbrick Takes on Mayflower Fairy Tales," *Newsweek,* May 1, 2006.

Golden, Frederic, "Cannibals of Nantucket: *In the Heart of the Sea* Recounts the Real Events That Inspired *Moby Dick,*" *Time,* May 1, 2000.

Martin, Chris, *In the Heart of the Sea* review, *Geographical,* June 2000.

Maslin, Janet, "Pilgrims, the Forgotten Years," *New York Times*, May 4, 2006.

Mehegan, David, "Author Seeks Balance in Pilgrims' Story," *Boston Globe,* May 16, 2006.

Mudge, Alden, "New World Order," *BookPage,* May 2006. http://www. bookpage.com/0605bp/nathaniel_philbrick.html (viewed September 23 2007).

Nathaniel Philbrick profile, "Meet the Writers," Barnes&Noble.com. http:// www.barnesandnoble.com/writers/writer.asp?cid=1017017 (viewed September 20, 2007).

Nathaniel Philbrick profile, Penguin. http://us.penguingroup.com/static/ rguides/us/in_the_heart_of_the_sea.html (viewed October 3, 2006).

Nathaniel Philbrick profile, Smithsonian Institution Libraries. http://www. sil.si.edu/Press/backgrounder-nathaniel-philbrick_12_03.htm (viewed May 4, 2006).

Nathaniel Philbrick, Contemporary Authors Online. Reproduced in Biography Resource Center. Farmington Hills, MI: Thomson Gale, 20064. http:// galenet.galegroup.com/servlet/BioRC.

Pulsipher, Jenny Hale, *Mayflower* review, *Boston Sunday Globe,* May 7, 2006.

Richards, Andrew, "Rediscovering America," Library Journal Academic Newswire, April 24, 2006. http://www.publishersweekly.com/article/ CA6327024.html?display=current (viewed May 4, 2006).

Standish, Carol, Nathaniel Philbrick profile, *Maine Harbors,* January 2004.

Suarez, Ray, "Conversation with Nathaniel Philbrick," *NewsHour* Web site. http://www.pbs.org/newshour/conversation/july-dec00/philbrick_9-5.html (viewed May 4, 2006).

Toth, Deborah, "Q&A: Nathaniel Philbrick, '78," *Brown Alumni Magazine,* January/February 2001.

George Plimpton

Biography, Investigative Reporting, Sports

Benchmark Title: *Paper Lion*

New York, New York

1927–2003

About the Author and the Author's Writing

"There are people who would perhaps call me a dilettante, because it looks as though I'm having too much fun," George Plimpton is quoted in the London *Guardian* in 2003. "I have never been convinced there's anything inherently wrong in having fun."

If Plimpton was born with a silver spoon in his mouth, it didn't stop him from taking chances, from working hard, and from making a mark in the crowded field of literary nonfiction authors. He is widely identified as the premiere "participatory journalist," and an undaunted "professional amateur." He ran the football field or golfed or struck hockey pucks with the pros to be able to write about the sports accurately and colorfully.

He was born in New York City in 1927, the son of Francis T. P. and Pauline Ames Plimpton. His father was an attorney, who was appointed a U.S. deputy representative to the United Nations. He also served as president of the Bar Association of the City of New York. George attended private schools, then Harvard (Robert Kennedy was a classmate) for an A.B. in 1948. Drafted into the U.S. Army in 1945, he afterward said his work in Italy defusing land mines spawned his lifelong affection for fireworks. To avoid military assignment to Korea, he entered King's College, Cambridge, where he attained a B.A. in 1952 and an M.A. two years later. He was twice married, to Freddy Medora Espy in 1968 and, after a divorce, to Sarah Whitehead Dudley in 1991. He had two children from each marriage.

Plimpton was a busy writer, a consummate editor, and a keen interviewer. He was also a film celebrity.

His first stint as an editor was for the Harvard *Lampoon,* from 1948 to 1950. He later became an associate or contributing editor for a range of periodicals including *Horizon, Harper's, Food and Wine,* and *Sports Illustrated*. It was with the last periodical that he developed his signature essays as an aspiring professional athlete. He told journalist Andrew Anthony that his first actual experience as a befuddled sportsman was while he was at Oxford. When he was asked to try out for the rowing crew, he showed up on the dock and couldn't figure out how to get into the scull.

Never one to let embarrassment or inexperience get in the way, in 1963 Plimpton found a willing coach and became a "last-string quarterback" for the Detroit Lions, losing thirty-two yards during his minutes on the field during a scrimmage. That experience became *Paper Lion,* published in 1966, which became a bestseller. There followed a series of diverse life experiences, playing golf on the Pro-Am circuit, basketball with the Boston Celtics, baseball in Yankee Stadium, and boxing against a light heavyweight Archie Moore. He played hockey as an Edmonton Oiler so he could write *Open Net* (2003) in his easy, engaging style. When he expended most of his athletic options, he played kettledrums with the New York Philharmonic, photographed for *Playboy* magazine, and even joined a circus as a trapeze artist.

The six-foot four-inch tall, rugged Plimpton claimed that although his experiences on the playing fields were significant, writing was his most important ability. "What seems to often be overlooked is the most important part—you have to be able to write," he said in an interview with Doug Blackburn of the *Albany Times Union.* "The point of doing it is to sit down and write."

One personal episode was almost surreal. He was in the Ambassador Hotel kitchen in Los Angeles in June 1968 when Sirhan Sirhan fired the shots that killed Robert F. Kennedy. Football star Rosie Grier grappled with the assailant, and Plimpton wrested the .22-caliber Iver Johnson revolver from his hands. Plimpton's close ties with RFK resulted in his work on a memoir-collection in 1970. Similarly, his friendship with starlet-celebrity Edie Sedgwick and *In Cold Blood* author Truman Capote precipitated his involvement in biographies of those individuals.

As editor of the *Paris Review* from 1953 until his death in 2003, Plimpton nurtured up-and-coming authors ranging from Jack Kerouac to Philip Roth, and he honed his trademark long interviews with myriad literary personalities—providing material for more than a dozen book collections. One early interview was with Ernest Hemingway, whom he had met in France.

Plimpton enjoyed his conversations with celebrities: "There's always something intriguing about the raw material of a biography," he told interviewer Ron Hogan. While it's easy enough to interview someone and cull the best material for an article, Plimpton considered the interview itself an artifact. "I'm fascinated by the entire transcript, by the depth of material that's available in it."

Plimpton wrote scripts for and appeared in a number of television programs based on his own books. To mention a few they were *Plimpton: The Man on the Flying Trapeze* (1970); *Plimpton! The Great Quarterback Sneak* (1971); and *Plimpton! Adventure in Africa* (1972), all for ABC-TV. Alan Alda played him in the film *Paper Lion* (1968). Although Plimpton's role as an extra in *Lawrence of Arabia* was cut, he had cameo appearances in *Rio Lobo, Beyond the Law, Reds,* and *Good Will Hunting.*

In the *New Yorker,* David Remnick described Plimpton as "a serious man of serious accomplishments who just happened to have more fun than a van full of jugglers and clowns. He was game for anything and made a comic art of his Walter Mitty dreams and inevitable failures." Plimpton died in his New York home in 2003, at age seventy-six.

Works by the Author

Out of My League (1961)

Paper Lion: Confessions of a Last-String Quarterback (1966)

The Bogey Man: A Month on the PGA Tour (1968)

Mad Ducks and Bears: Football Revisited, with Alex Karras and John Gordy (1973)

One for the Record: The Inside Story of Hank Aaron's Chase for the Home Run Record (1974)

One More July: A Football Dialogue, with Bill Curry (1977)

Shadow Box: An Amateur in the Ring (1977)

Sports! with Neil Leifer (1978)

A Sports Bestiary, with Arnold Roth (1982)

Open Net (1985)

The Best of Plimpton (1990)

The X Factor (1990), revised (1995)

The Norton Book of Sports (1992)

The Official Olympics Triplecast Viewer's Guide (1992)

Chronicles of Courage: Very Special Artists, with Jean Kennedy Smith (1993)

Truman Capote: In Which Various Friends, Enemies, Acquaintances, and Detractors Recall His Turbulent Career (1997)

Pet Peeves; or, Whatever Happened to Doctor Rawff? (2000)

A&E Biographies: Ernest Shackleton (2003)

George Plimpton on Sports (2003)

Editor

Writers at Work: The Paris Review Interviews, 9 volumes (1957–1992)

The American Literary Anthology, nos. 1 to 3, with Peter Ardery (1968–1970)

American Journey: The Times of Robert Kennedy, with Jean Stein (1970)

Pierre's Book: The Game of Court Tennis, by Pierre Etchebaster (1971)

Edie: An American Biography, by Jean Stein (1982), reprinted as *Edie: American Girl* (1994)

D.V., by Diana Vreeland, with Christopher Hemphill (1984)

Fireworks: A History and Celebration (1984)

Poets at Work: The Paris Review Interviews (1989)

Women Writers at Work (1989)

The Writer's Chapbook: A Compendium of Fact, Opinion, Wit, and Advice from the Twentieth-Century's Preeminent Writers (1989)

The Best of Bad Hemingway: Choice Entries from the Harry's Bar & American Grill Imitation Hemingway Competition, Vols. 1 and 2 (1989 and 1991)

The Paris Review Anthology (1990)

Playwrights at Work (2000)

Home Run (2001)

As Told at the Explorers Club: More than Fifty Gripping Tales of Adventure (2003)

Latin American Writers at Work: The Paris Review (2003)

The Paris Review Book: of Heartbreak, Madness, Sex, Love, Betrayal, Outsiders, Intoxication, War, Whimsy, Horrors, God, Death, Dinner, Baseball, Travels, the Art of Writing, and Everything Else in the World Since 1953, with Paris Review editors (2003)

The Man in the Flying Lawn Chair and Other Excursions and Observations, with Sarah Dudley Plimpton (2005)

Fiction

The Curious Case of Sidd Finch (1987)

For Juvenile Readers

The Rabbit's Umbrella (1955)

For Further Information

Anthony, Andrew, "Been There, Done That," *Guardian Unlimited,* October 5, 2003. http://observer.guardian.co.uk/review/story/0,6903,1055918,00.html (viewed September 13, 2006).

Bakkum, Beth, "Six Writers Who Made a Difference," *The Writer,* January 2005.

Bing, Jonathan, "George Plimpton: A Most American Boswell," *Publishers Weekly,* November 17, 1997.

Blackburn, Doug, "Literary Lion," *Albany* (N.Y.) *Times Union,* May 6, 1999.

Edwards, Owen, *As Told at the Explorers Club* review, *Smithsonian,* May 2004.

George (Ames) Plimpton entry, Contemporary Authors Online. Reproduced in Biography Resource Center. Farmington Hills, MI: Thomson Gale, 2005. http://galenet.galegroup.com/servlet/BioRC.

Hogan, Ron, George Plimpton interview, "Beatrice Interview," 1997. http://www.beatrice.com/interviews/plimpton (viewed September 13, 2006).

McDonnell, Terry, George Plimpton obituary, *Sports Illustrated,* October 6, 2003.

Remnick, David, George Plimpton obituary, *New Yorker,* October 6, 2003.

Michael Pollan

Food, Investigative Reporting, Science

Benchmark Title: *The Botany of Desire*

Long Island, New York

1955–

Photo courtesy Penguin Group

About the Author and the Author's Writing

The way farmers grow our food would seem a simple enough subject. But writer Michael Pollan has dug deeply into the way large corporations raise beef animals, and he's not pleased with what he's found.

"Is knowledge about our food a burden or a pleasure?" Pollan wondered in an interview with Dave Weich of Powells.com. "A lot of people don't want to know where their 99-cent hamburger comes from, in the same way that people don't want to know how their sausage is made. There are people who are happy to eat in ignorance."

Once people read the author's *The Omnivore's Dilemma,* they may have second thoughts about the way agribusinesses cut corners. As serious as he is, Pollan doesn't preach his message; he simply presents it in detail, examining the industrial, organic and hunter-gatherer approaches. Describing *The Omnivore's Dilemma, New York Times Book Review*'s David Kamp wrote, "The first quarter of the book is devoted to a shocking, page-turning expose of the secret life of that most seemingly innocent and benign of American crops, corn." In an expansion of articles he originally wrote for the *New York Times Magazine,* the author describes how governmental policy during the Clinton and George H. W. Bush administrations have fostered an industrial approach to food production that relies heavily on corn.

Pollan comes by his information not from library research but from firsthand observation, "attempting to get up at 5:30 A.M. to do chores at Polyface Farm in the Shenandoah Valley…, traipsing up and down burned-off California forest hillsides in search of morels…, following food sources Rosie the chicken and a steer known only as 534 to their respective demises … and hunting wild pigs," noted *Globe and Mail* reviewer Gordon Morash.

Pollan was born on Long Island, New York, in 1955, the oldest of four children and the only boy. His father, Stephen Pollan, is also a writer. His mother, Corky

294

Pollan, was the editor of the "Best Bets" column in *New York* magazine. Michael attended Bennington College and earned a bachelor of arts degree in English. In 1981, he received a master's degree in English literature from Oxford. Joining *Harper's* magazine in 1983, he worked as senior editor and was responsible for its "Harper's Index" feature, as well as its "Readings" section. He went on to serve as executive editor for the magazine for another ten years. He has also been a freelance writer for *House & Garden* and other periodicals. Since 2003, he has been professor of journalism at the University of California at Berkeley. He and his wife, painter Judith Belzer, have one son.

Before moving west, Pollan wrote three books from and about his home in Litchfield County, Connecticut. Reviewers frequently describe his work in terms of what it is not. *Second Nature* "isn't so much a how-to on gardening as a how-to on thinking about gardening," a *Publisher's Weekly* article said. *A Place of My Own,* according to *Booklist*, is "not so much a how-to as a how-and-why-it-happened" tale of building a writing cabin behind his place.

A Botany of Desire began what Pollan calls his "food detective stories." One point of focus is a Monsanto genetically modified potato, the New Leaf, which he plants and nurtures in his home garden. The author also describes his visits to the chemical giant's plant in St. Louis and potato farmers in Idaho.

"I very much like to have a personal stake in what I'm writing about," the author told interviewer Russell Schoch. "One of the most influential books I read growing up was George Plimpton's *Paper Lion,* where he described his experience playing football with the Detroit Lions. Most journalists are in the stands, or in the press box. Plimpton inserted himself onto the field of play."

In the same interview, Pollan dismissed the idea that journalists must be objective. That's virtually impossible, he said. But they should be absolutely fair and present all sides.

From writing about vegetables, Pollan went to meat. He purchased a steer (from its photo in the *New York Times Magazine* for March 31, 2002, it is a steer, although in the story he calls it a cow—he's yet to become a real country boy) and followed its life from barn birth to feedlot to slaughterhouse. In the manner of Thoreau, he kept track of expenses. The cost of the animal plus its upkeep came to $917. It sold for $934. He netted $17.

Profit, of course, was not his objective. It was to understand what we eat.

So what does Pollan eat? He won't eat the genetically manipulated potato. He will eat organic vegetables. And he still consumes beef, as long as it is grass-fed. His rule of thumb, he has said, is this: If your great-grandmother wouldn't recognize it as food, don't eat it.

Works by the Author

The Harper's Index Book, with Eric Etheridge (1987)
The Field Guide to Home Buying in America: A Home Buyer's Companion from House Hunting to Moving Day, with Stephen M. Pollan and Mark Levine (1988)
Second Nature: A Gardener's Education (1991)
A Place of My Own: The Education of an Amateur Builder (1997)

The Botany of Desire: A Plant's-Eye View of the World (2001)
The Omnivore's Dilemma; A Natural History of Four Meals (2006)
In Defense of Food: The Myth of Nutrition and the Pleasures of Eating (2008)

Contributor

Best American Essays 1990 (1990)
Norton Book of Nature Writing (1990)
Best American Essays 2003 (2003)
Best American Science Writing (2004)

For Further Information

Genco, Barbara A., *The Botany of Desire* review, *School Library Journal,* December 2001.

Grandfield, Kevin, "A Place of My Own," February 15, 1997.

Morash, Gordon, "The Omnivore's Dilemma," *Globe and Mail,* April 29, 2006.

Pollan, Michael, "A Gardener's Guide to Sex, Politics and Class War," *New York Times Book Review,* July 21, 1991.

Pollan, Michael, "This Steer's Life," *New York Times Magazine,* March 31, 2002.

Roberts, David, "Eat the Press," Michael Pollan interview, *Grist.* http://www.grist.org/news/maindish/2006/05/31/roberts (viewed September 13, 2006).

Schoch, Russell, "Michael Pollan on Food Chains, Dead Zones, and Licensed Journalism," *California Monthly,* December 2004.

Second Nature review, *Publishers Weekly,* April 26, 1991.

Weich, Dave, "Michael Pollan Comes to Dinner," Powells.com. http://www.powells.com/interviews/polan.html (viewed September 13, 2006).

Weintraub, Irwin, *The Omnivore's Dilemma* review, *Library Journal,* April 15, 2006.

Ron Powers

Biography, History, Memoir, Sports

Benchmark Title: *Mark Twain: A Life*

Hannibal, Missouri

1941–

Photo by Dean Powers

About the Author and the Author's Writing

On an autumn day in 2005, Ron Powers talked about his new Mark Twain biography, appropriately, at the Mark Twain House in Hartford, Connecticut. Powers gave an engaging overview of his subject, including Twain's evolution from writer into public speaker. In a conversation during a book signing that followed, Powers mentioned that in 1871, two years after Twain's *The Innocents Abroad* had come out, Twain tried to give a humorous talk in rural Massachusetts. And the audience hated it. The next time Twain appeared there, Powers said, Twain tried to give a serious talk. And the crowd roared with laughter.

Powers has immersed himself in Twain—the subject of four of his books so far. The *New York Times* deigned his *Mark Twain: A Life* a notable nonfiction work of 2005; the *Christian Science Monitor* called it one of the year's best biographies. But Powers's career has hardly focused on a single topic. His criticism earned him a Pulitzer Prize, his spot television news reporting garnered an Emmy Award, and his military history of Iwo Jima earned a Christopher Award.

Powers was born in Hannibal, Missouri, in 1941, the son of Paul S. and Elvadine Toalson Powers. He earned a degree in journalism from the University of Missouri in 1963. In 1978, he married Honore Flemming. From 1963 to 1969, he was a sports and general assignment reporter for the *St. Louis Post-Dispatch.* Subsequently, he worked as a news reporter for the *Chicago Sun Times.* He was a television critic in Chicago and New York, including with CBS News *Sunday Morning,* where he worked from 1983 to 1988. From 1990 to 1996, he taught creative writing at Middlebury College in Vermont; at the same time, he taught nonfiction at the Bread Loaf Writer's Conference from 1980 to 1996.

Powers's early books focused on the medium of television. *The Beast, the Eunuch and the Glass-Eyed Child* (1990), for example, collects the author's *GQ* columns, which he wrote from 1984 to 1990. "The pieces reveal an articulate, civilized reviewer who is profoundly disturbed by certain trends in televisionland," commented a *Publishers Weekly* reviewer. These trends include hyped children's programming and "non-news" news shows.

The author believes the print media is superior to broadcast media, and he says so in *The Cruel Radiance,* which was published in 1994. *Publishers Weekly* noted that the book, "has as its theme the author's faith in the redemptive power of the written word and his parallel belief that exploitative broadcast media are eroding our cultural heritage."

In *Far from Home* (1991), exploring what he sees as the diminishment of small-town America, Powers looks closely at attempts in Cairo, Illinois, to reinvigorate itself, and of Kent, Connecticut (where Powers lived before moving to Middlebury, Vermont, in 1990), to survive an influx of developers and well-to-do urbanites such as Henry Kissinger. The author notes, "If town life in this country [is] over, so [is] an essential culture rooted in obligations and the perception of a common good."

Powers's favorite author—Mark Twain—had close connections with their mutual hometown Hannibal, Missouri. And so does Powers. For *White Down Drowsing* (1986), he revisited Hannibal and wrote of both his own reaction to going home and home's wild attempts to shape itself as a theme town and celebrate the Twain sesquicentennial. Powers revisited Hannibal on Twain's behalf more than a decade later. The result was *Dangerous Water* (1999), a work which a reviewer for *Publishers Weekly* found "illuminating both the sorrow and the exhilaration of a boyhood that provided a lifetime of inspiration."

In a *Vermont Magazine* interview, Powers said he actually intended to write a full Twain biography. "Then one day I picked myself up off the ground, rubbed my forehead, and realized I'd just run into the side of Mount Everest at full tilt. The life he led was just too big. I needed years more study and research."

A decade later, thanks to the ongoing work of the Mark Twain Project at the University of California, Berkeley, which has collected an estimated twelve thousand Twain letters from attic boxes and library drawers, Powers was ready to compile that full biography. He used the new material to give Twain the voice so often missing in other biographies. Powers said he had no interest in psychoanalyzing his subject. He did, however, want to show up the critics who have diminished Twain's literary achievement because of his reliance on vernacular and on satire and humor.

Powers's editor gave him great freedom with the endeavor. Bruce Nichols told *Publishers Weekly*'s Edward Nawotka, "With any other writer, I wouldn't have let through so many puns. But here, it seems appropriate." Twain and Powers, he said, are "an extraordinary match of writer and subject."

Critics agreed. "The author goes the extra mile by including details of what developed the character of the man, the reality versus the myth, and leads the reader through a chronologically segmented and enjoyable look at history," in the view of *Decatur Daily*'s Tracy W. Tubbs.

In 2000, Powers's helped James Bradley write *Flags of Our Fathers,* the story of the six men (only three of whom survived the war) who raised the flag in the famous Joe Rosenthal photo snapped at Iwo Jima on February 23, 1945. The book garnered considerable attention, particularly when producer Steven Spielberg and director Clint Eastwood turned it into a motion picture in 2006.

Powers followed up with an assist to Colonel Robert Morgan to write his memoir of flying a B-17 bomber on twenty-five missions over Europe during World War II and to John Baldwin to chronicle the story of the last Confederate warship.

Works by the Author

The Newscasters: The News Business as Show Business (1977)

Supertube: The Rise of Television Sports (1983)

White Town Drowsing (1986)

The Beast, the Eunuch, and the Glass-Eyed Child: Television in the '80s (1990)

Far from Home: Life and Loss in Two American Towns (1991)

The Cruel Radiance: Notes of a Prosewriter in a Visual Age (1994)

Dangerous Water: A Biography of the Boy Who Became Mark Twain (1999)

Flags of Our Fathers, with James Bradley (2000)

The Man Who Flew Memphis Belle: Memoir of a World War II Bomber Pilot, with Colonel Robert Morgan (2001)

Tom and Huck Don't Live Here Anymore: Childhood and Murder in the Heart of America (2001)

Mark Twain: A Life (2005)

Last Flag Down: The Epic Journey of the Last Confederate Warship, with John Baldwin (2007)

Fiction

Face Value (1979)

Toot-Toot-Tootsie, Good-Bye (1981)

Motion Pictures Based on the Author's Works

Flags of Our Fathers (2006)

For Further Information

Auchincloss, Kenneth, "Six Men and a Flag: How One Episode on Iwo Jima Reshaped Three Lives," *Newsweek,* May 29, 2000.

Carroll, Mary, *Tom and Huck Don't Live Here Anymore* review, *Booklist,* September 15, 2001.

Cruel Radiance review, *Publishers Weekly,* November 21, 1994.

Dangerous Water review, *Publishers Weekly,* May 17, 1999.

Flags of Our Fathers review, *Publishers Weekly,* May 8, 2000.

Flags of Our Fathers Web site. http://www.randomhouse.com/features/jamesbradley/index3.html (viewed October 6, 2006).

Gillespie, Nick, "Mark Twain vs. Tom Sawyer: The Bold Deconstruction of a National Icon," *Reason,* February 2006.

Man Who Flew the Memphis Belle review, *Publishers Weekly,* July 2, 2001.

Nawotka, Edward, "The Destiny of Ron Powers: Making the Case for Mark Twain," *Publishers Weekly,* September 26, 2005.

Ron Powers interview, *Vermont Magazine,* September/October 2006.

Ron(ald) (Dean) Powers entry, Contemporary Authors Online. Reproduced in Biography Resource Center. Farmington Hills, MI: Thomson Gale, 2002. http://galenet.galegroup.com/servlet/BioRC.

Stuttaford, Genevieve, *Far from Home* review, *Publishers Weekly,* April 12, 1991.

Stuttaford, Genevieve, *The Beast, The Eunuch, and the Glass-Eyed Child* review, *Publishers Weekly,* April 6, 1990.

Tubbs, Tracy W., "Mark Twain: The Man behind the Stories," *Decatur Daily,* October 23, 2005.

Beth Powning

Environment, Investigative Reporting, Memoir

Benchmark Title: *Home: Chronicle of a North Country Life*

Putnam, Connecticut

1949–

Photo by Peter Powning

About the Author and the Author's Writing

In the early 1970s, Beth and Peter Powning, newly married and celebrating the first Earth Day, were very concerned about the direction things were going in the United States, so they went in search of a new lifestyle. They drove to the Canadian Province of New Brunswick—her grandfather's family was from St. Stephen—with a dream of homesteading. They would harvest their own crops, raise their own animals, and be self-sufficient. While driving down a country road not far from the coast, they came upon a white, 1870 farmhouse and barn nestled in a valley, two work horses lolling beneath the trees. They fell in love with the place, in Sussex, bought it, and have lived there ever since.

"It's wonderful to be 20 or 21," Beth Powning said in an interview with James O'Hearn for *Engaging the Word*. "You have that ability to truly believe in your dreams. Soon you realize you need to make money." Peter began to make pottery. Beth gravitated to photography and writing how-to books such as *Roses for Canadian Gardens* and *Hardy Trees and Shrubs*. That's how they still make their living these days, though they also have a few chickens and raise a lot of their own food.

The author was born in Putnam, Connecticut, in 1949. "I spent my childhood in a creaky, mouse-ridden farmhouse in northeast Connecticut," she said on a Dropped Threads 3 Web site. In 1972, she received a bachelor's degree in creative writing from Sarah Lawrence College. She and her husband have one son.

The Powning farmstead in maritime Canada has proved a rich backdrop to several of her writings, which, according to Contemporary Authors Online, have been critical hits because of "her ability to evoke a setting and demonstrate how places affect the people who live in them.... Her works often intermingle personal stories with observations of nature." It's for that approach that she's sometimes been called a female Thoreau.

Home: Chronicle of a North Country Life combines the author's photos with words that follow the seasons and the joys of the outdoors. "Powning longs for a blizzard; without storms, winter creeps by duly," noted *Publishers Weekly*. "She writes about fields and forests, vegetable gardens and wild fruits, and finds that her life and where she lives are inextricably entwined. This book imparts a feeling of serenity."

Booklist's Alice Joyce commented, "Powning recounts a vibrant life filled with the awesome recognition of their secluded Canadian environment's raw beauty and uncharged forests.... Powning forms a seamless testament to a fragile yet wondrous wilderness."

With *Shadow Child,* published in 1999, Powning moved deeper into autobiography to discuss her rural childhood, her discovery of her artistic abilities, her career decisions—she gave up thought of studying in Europe and instead married her college boyfriend. "Then," *Library Journal*'s reviewer Annette Haines noted, "the story's central focus becomes the prolonged and suppressed grief and guilt over the loss of her first pregnancy, but, in a broader sense, it also stands as a commentary on modern-day womanhood: the conflict between fulfilling the traditional roles of daughter, wife, and mother at the expense of realizing one's metamorphosis as she learns to accept herself and penetrates the complexities of relationships in family and community."

The author's first novel, *The Hatbox Letters* (2004), works in the same personal territory. It is about a widow who comes to terms with the emotional pain of her husband's sudden death. She finds solace in a hatbox full of family papers. Powning, reviewer Joanne Wilkinson wrote, "has a real affinity for crafting delicate descriptions of the natural world."

Personal experience is critical to composing fiction, the author said in an interview on the Random House Canada Web site. "You have to be living in it; it's almost happening to you as much as you're making it," she said.

The author returned to memoir for her 2005 *Edge Seasons,* which looks at midlife, when dreams have been achieved or not. The book began as a collection of essays without a narrative thread. At her editor's insistence, Powning spread the essays on the floor, stood on her desk, and stared at them until their coherence came to her. They were all, she told interviewer O'Hearn, about reaching that time in life when you're again on the edge of change. There may have been soaring successes or dismal failures, but one still has to move on. Her son has gone off to college. Parents are aging. The three-hundred-acre farm is a handful to maintain.

"Late one August, Powning reflects on the sauna she and Peter had built with great enthusiasm when they first arrived in Sussex," Nancy Schiefer wrote in a *London Free Press* review. "Now abandoned and run down, the once-busy bath seems to her to symbolize the energy and faith in the future that marked its construction. She and Peter decide to repair it and the project becomes a metaphor for the importance of renewal."

They had stopped listening to the sounds of the brook. Now they hear its trickle and burble and are moving on.

Works by the Author

Roses for Canadian Gardens, with Robert Osborne (1991), revised as *Hardy Roses: A Practical Guide to Varieties and Techniques* (2001)

Hardy Trees and Shrubs: A Guide to Disease-Resistant Varieties, with Robert Osborne (1994)

Seeds of Another Summer: Finding the Spirit of Home in Nature (in Canada, 1996), published in the United States as *Home: Chronicle of a North Country Life* (1996)

Shadow Child: A Woman's Journey through Childbirth Loss (1999)

New City Gardener, with Robert A. Osborne (2001)

Edge Seasons: A Mid-life Year (2005)

Contributor

Northern Wild: Best Contemporary Canadian Nature Writing, edited by David R. Boyd (2001)

When the Wild Comes Leaping Up: Personal Encounters with Nature, edited by David Suzuki (2002)

The Sea's Voice: An Anthology of Atlantic Canadian Nature Writing, edited by Harry Thurston (2005)

Dropped Threads 3, edited by Marjorie Anderson (2006)

Fiction

The Hatbox Letters (2004)

For Further Information

Beth Powning entry, Contemporary Authors Online. Reproduced in Biography Resource Center. Farmington Hills, MI: Thomson Gale, 2006. http://galenet.galegroup.com/servlet/BioRC.

Beth Powning profile, *Dropped Threads* contributors, Random House of Canada. http://www.randomhouse.ca/features/droppedthreads/powning.html   (viewed October 6, 2006).

Beth Powning Web page, Random House Canada. http://www.randomhouse. ca/catalog/author.pperl?authorid=54948 (viewed October 6, 2006)

Beth Powning Web site. http://www.powning.com/beth/index.html (viewed September 22, 2007).

Haines, Annette, *Shadow Child* review, *Library Journal,* December 1999.

Home review, *Booklist,* July 1996.

Home review, *Publishers Weekly,* May 13, 1996.

O'Hearn, James, Beth Powning interview, *Engaging the Word.* http://www. engagingtheword.net/archive.html (viewed October 6, 2006).

Schiefer, Nancy, *Edge Seasons* review, *London Free Press,* October 29, 2005.

Wilkinson, Joanne, *The Hatbox Letters* review, *Booklist,* February 15, 2005.

Richard Preston

Investigative Reporting, Science

Benchmark Title: *The Hot Zone*

Cambridge, Massachusetts

1954–

Photo by Richard Lewis

About the Author and the Author's Writing

> *The red spots on the skin grow and spread and merge to become huge,*
> *spontaneous bruises, and the skin goes soft and pulpy, and can tear off if it is*
> *touched with any kind of pressure. Your mouth bleeds, and you bleed around*
> *your teeth, and you may have hemorrhages from the salivary glands—liter-*
> *ally every opening in the body bleeds no matter how small.*
>
> —From The Hot Zone

Richard Preston writes books of biotech horror, of nature gone frightfully awry, but they're not shelved with the works of novelists Charles L. Grant or Michael Crichton.

Because they're true.

"Whatever Preston writes about eerily becomes the news," an AnnOnline profile said. "This became most evident recently when two men were arrested carrying what was thought to be weapons-grade Anthrax. It almost seems that the words bioterrorism and bioweapon were coined by Preston."

Preston was born in Cambridge, Massachusetts, in 1954, the son of lawyer Jerome Preston Jr. and art historian and painter Dorothy McCann Preston. A shy boy and an avid book reader, he grew up in Wellesley. His high school grades were so low that he was rejected by every college where he applied. He managed to enter the second semester at Pomona College and ended up graduating summa cum laude in 1977 with a bachelor of arts degree in English. In 1983, he earned his Ph.D. from Princeton. While at Princeton, he took John McPhee's course, Literature of Fact, and discovered what has become his life's career.

Preston is an avid outdoorsman who frequently whitewater canoes and mountain bikes. He married editor Michelle Parham in 1985; they have three children. In 1983, Preston was a lecturer in English at Princeton before becoming a staff writer for the university. In 1985, he became a freelance writer—selling stories to the *New York Times, Washington Post, New Yorker, National Geographic,* and other publications.

Preston's debut book, *First Light,* published in 1987, profiles astronomers Carolyn and Eugene Shoemaker at CalTech. The book won him an American Institute of Physics Award and led to the scientists naming an asteroid for him. The book offers a fascinating and personal look at today's astronomers and their efforts to understand the universe. Preston was praised for his skill at narrative and his deftness at getting across character.

The author's *American Steel* (1991) follows the construction of a new steel mill in an Indiana cornfield by a brash new company, Nucor, that hoped to challenge existing steel-making giants.

His best-selling *The Hot Zone* was expanded from a *New Yorker* piece and published in 1994. It describes the outbreak of the Ebola virus in Reston, Virginia, and how it came to this country from a cave in Uganda. The book has been translated into thirty languages. Author Stephen King, quoted in *The New New Journalism,* called it "one of the most horrifying things I've ever read in my life." Preston's book inspired the motion picture *Outbreak* with Dustin Hoffman.

Preston followed *Hot Zone* with two more books that he labels his "dark biology" series. One, *The Cobra Event,* is actually fiction, although it took the author three years to research. The novel is about how a doctor, collaborating with the FBI, quashes a potential New York City bioterrorism attack. Movie rights sold to Fox in 2000 for $3 million.

"Like a hybrid of William S. Burroughs and John McPhee, this book combines the unspeakable insect horror of the former with the clarity and humanity of the latter," reviewer Robert Glantz wrote in *Whole Earth Review.*

The third dark biology book, *The Demon in the Freezer,* published in 2002, is about how smallpox, anthrax, and other deadly viruses that we thought were wiped out by strategic inoculations actually survive in very small samples in secure, artificial scientific environments. But just how secure?

"Preston humanizes his science reportage by focusing on individuals—scientists, patients, physicians, government figures," noted a *Publishers Weekly* reviewer. "That, and a flair for teasing out without overstatement the drama in his inherently compelling topics, plus a prose style that's simple and forceful, make this book as exciting as the best thrillers, yet far scarier."

Although most outbreaks have been natural, Preston wants the public to be aware: biological warfare could happen. "We're living now in an age of biological weapons and terrorism," the author told CNN's Paula Zahn in 2002. "Because it is a weapon, it's the kind of thing that public health doctors always have to consider as—you know, we have to think about this as terrorism."

If Preston's subjects seem at times overblown, it's intentional. "I have an apocalyptic streak as a writer," he told interviewer Robert S. Boynton of *The New New Journalism.* "In my books there are always immense forces swirling around the human stories I tell—themes that dwarf the human species."

The author has come back to earth, somewhat, for *The Wild Trees,* the story of a botanist who studies his subjects—giant California redwoods—from a canopy thirty-five stories above the soil. As the author relates, the art of observing these re-markably high treetops and their unusual ecosystems only began in the 1980s. Steve Sillett, a main figure in Preston's book, is a daredevil known to "free climb"—without ropes—more than thirty stories up, in the name of science (and adventure).

On his Web site Preston describes how he writes: "When I'm researching a book, I conduct large numbers of in-depth interviews with people, and I also try to experi-ence their lives and work…. I write many drafts. The first chapter of every book I write typically goes through 20 to 30 drafts. (Having to do all these revisions drives me nuts, but revision is the soul of writing.)"

 # Works by the Author

First Light: The Search for the Edge of the Universe (1987)
American Steel: Hot Metal Men and the Resurrection of the Rust Belt (1991)
The Hot Zone: A Terrifying True Story (1994)
The Demon in the Freezer: A True Story (2002)
Pure Fuel, with Peter Miles and Damon Murray (2007)
The Wild Trees: A Story of Passion and Daring (2007)

Fiction

The Cobra Event (1997)
The Boat of Dreams: A Christmas Story (2003)

For Further Information

Boynton, Robert S., *The New New Journalism: Conversations with America's Best Nonfiction Writers on Their Craft.* New York: Vintage Books, 2005.

Demon in the Freezer review, *Publishers Weekly,* September 23, 2002.

Glantz, Robert, *Hot Zone* review, *Whole Earth Review,* spring 1995.

Jost, Amy, *Hot Zone* review. http://www.haverford.edu/biology/edwards/disease/reviews/jostR.html (viewed October 8, 2006).

Richard (McCann) Preston entry, Contemporary Authors Online. Reproduced in Biography Resource Center. Farmington Hills, MI: Thomson Gale, 2005. http://galenet.galegroup.com/servlet/BioRC.

Richard Preston biography, AnnOnline. http://www.annonline.com/interviews/980924/biography.html (viewed October 7, 2006).

Richard Preston Web site. http://www.richardpreston.net/about.html (viewed October 7, 2006).

Zahn, Paula, "Interview with Richard Preston," CNN.com. http://transcripts.cnn.com/TRANSCRIPTS/0211/07/ltm.07.html (viewed September 19, 2006).

Ruth Reichl

Food, Memoir

Benchmark Title: *Tender at the Bone*

New York, New York

1948–

Photo by Brigitte Lacombe, printed with permission,
The Gourmet Cookbook, Houghton Mifflin, 2004

About the Author and the Author's Writing

"Bread with cold, sweet butter is my favorite food," good food aficionado Ruth Reichl told interviewer Francine Sagan. "Bite into a piece of bread topped with icy butter. Now try the same bread, but with room-temperature butter. Taste the difference?"

At first pause, one wonders how an individual so simply pleased by bread and butter could, in her sharply written newspaper and magazine reviews, have become the nemesis of so many restauranteurs. But then again, notice the detail: only cold, sweet butter will do.

The author was born in 1948 in New York City, the daughter of book designer Ernst Reichl and musicologist Miriam Brudno Reichl. She received a B.A. with honors from the University of Michigan in 1968 and an M.A. in art history from the same school two years later. She married and later divorced Douglas Hollis. In 1983, she and her second husband, Michael Singer, married; they have one son. Reichl's early career passion was art; after college she worked as a book designer for her father's firm, Ernst Reichl Associates. In 1973, she became art director for *Glass Art* magazine in Berkeley, California. At the same time, she opened and worked as chef for her Swallow Restaurant in Berkeley. After a stint as food writer and editor for *New West Magazine,* she began a restaurant column for the *Los Angeles Times,* where she worked as food editor from 1990 to 1993. In 1993, she moved back east to join the *New York Times* as its restaurant critic.

Her reputation at the *Times* was such that one restaurant owner issued a staff memo (reproduced in *Harper's* in 1996) with a bad photocopy picture of Reichl—who sometimes wore disguises when she ate out. "Ruth uses a tape recorder to record her thoughts during dinner," Thomas W. Monetti advised his Tavern on the Green employees. "If you see a woman in the dining room who fits the description speaking into a small tape recorder, most likely it will be Ruth."

Despite dining in restaurants—for work—a dozen times a week, Reichl still weighs the same today as when she graduated from college, attested journalist Daniel Okrent in *People Weekly*.

Reichl was very popular with her *New York Times* readers. "I learned early that the most important thing in life is a good story," she told Okrent.

Beyond a good story, she adopted a discerning attitude. "She has written from an outsider's perspective about the snobbery and pretension of some well-known New York restaurants," Dwight Garner wrote on salon.com, "and she has delved into the sexism that often confronts women while eating out." Accepting no gifts, she made sure her subjects knew she wasn't fooled when, once identified, she was offered a better table or extremely personalized service.

"Reichl doesn't just judge meals, she critiques manners and mores," Anastasia Toufexis wrote in *Psychology Today*. "Do waiters automatically give the bill to the man at the table? Where are women diners seated? How are ordinary folk treated?"

In 1999, Reichl joined the venerable *Gourmet* magazine as its editor-in-chief. She is also editor for Modern Library's culinary books. These assignments came to her because she was remarkably knowledgeable. "You can be a decent critic if you know about food," she said in a Powells.com interview, "but to be a really good one you need to know about life."

Reichl has written three memoirs about food and her own life. *Tender at the Bone*, published in 1998, describes her growing up years and early adulthood. Professional chef Ruth Adams Bronz found that "At every major juncture of Ms. Reichl's life, food and the people who love it are there to mitigate the hard journey." A sequel, *Comfort Me with Apples* (2001) picks up where the previous volume leaves off, while Reichl's most recent memoir, *Garlic and Sapphires* (2005), portrays her experiences dining out with flair.

Reichl has said she finds writing a challenge. She prefers to dig in during early morning hours, before the day's bustle. She writes in large spurts and returns to the material later to shape and edit, she said in *The Writer*. Reviews and recipes and food writing generally are different than memoir. "You have to decide how closely you want to adhere to the truth," she said in *that periodical*. "This can be a problem, especially when dealing with people who are still alive. Then, too, you have to consider other people's feelings. I've never thought that writing should be a way of evening scores or working out problems."

Reichl coedited the landmark, five-and-a-half-pound, 1,283-recipe *Gourmet Magazine Cookbook*. She said in a Seattlepi.com interview she considers the cookbook as "the book you use as your default.... It would sort of grow with you if you were starting to cook, with enough easy recipes with very clear instructions so you could cook from it, but as you grew as a cook the book would continue to work for you."

A few pleasant surprises came to the author as she and the *Gourmet* kitchen staff discovered and tried old recipes from the magazine's files. "The most obvious one was Lobster Thermidor. Just the name of it sounds gooey and old-fashioned. And we made it, and it was wonderful—and not that complicated," she said in an interview with *Publishers Weekly* in 2004.

Reichl's philosophy? She explained to Eve Zibart of *BookPage*, "You can't be a good cook if you don't have a generous soul and the impulse to take care of people."

Works by the Author

Mmmmm: A Feastiary (1972)

The Contest Book, with Ken Dollar and Susan Suble (1979)

Tender at the Bone: Growing up at the Table (1998)

The New York Times Guide to Restaurants in New York City, 2000, with others (2000)

Comfort Me with Apples; More Adventures at the Table (2001)

Garlic and Sapphires: The Secret Life of a Critic in Disguise (2005)

Editor

Endless Feasts: Sixty Years of Writing from Gourmet, with *Gourmet* magazine editors (2002)

The Gourmet Cookbook: More Than 1000 Recipes, with John Willoughby and Zanne Early Stewart (2004)

Remembrance of Things Paris: Sixty Years of Writing from Gourmet, with the editors of Gourmet Magazine (2005)

The Unprejudiced Palate: Classic Thoughts on Food and the Good Life, by Angelo M. Pellegrini (2005)

History in a Glass: Sixty Years of Wine Writing from Gourmet, with the editors of *Gourmet* magazine (2006)

Contributor

Clementine in the Kitchen, by Samuel Chamberlain (2001)

Japanese Cooking; A Simple Art, by Shizuo Tsuji and Yoshiki Tsuji (2007)

For Further Information

Adler, Jerry, "Check, Please," *Newsweek,* February 8, 1999.

Andriani, Lynn, "Bringing the Past into the Future at Gourmet," *Publishers Weekly*, August 2, 2004.

Bronz, Ruth Adams, "Overcoming Obstacles by Learning to Cook Well," *New York Times,* March 11, 1998.

Denn, Rebekah, "A Moment with … Ruth Reichl, *Gourmet* Editor," Seattlepi.com. http://seattlepi.nwsource.com/food/192789_reichl29.html (viewed September 19, 2006).

Garlic and Sapphires review, *Publishers Weekly,* February 14, 2005.

Garner, Dwight, "Palate Revolt," salon.com. http://www.salon.com/nov96/interview96118.html (viewed September 19, 2006).

Jones, Malcolm, "Putting It All on the Table: Career Chowhound Ruth Reichl Has No Reservations," *Newsweek,* April 4, 2005.

Monetti, Thomas W., "Watch Out for Ruth," *Harper's Magazine,* January 1996.

Okrent, Daniel, "Going Public: Food Guru Ruth Reichl Stands Unmasked at Last," *People Weekly,* December 6, 1999.

Reichl, Ruth, "How I Write," *The Writer,* November 2002.

Ruth (Molly) Reichl entry, Contemporary Authors Online. Reproduced in Biography Resource Center. Farmington Hills, MI: Thomson Gale, 2005. http://galenet.galegroup.com/servlet/BioRC.

Sagan, Francine, "Gourmet Girl," *Berkshire Living,* March/April 2006.

Toufexis, Anastasia, "Dishing with Ruth Reichl," *Psychology Today*, November/December 1998.

Weich, Dave, "Ruth Reichl's Home Cooked Comforts," Powells.com, September 2006. http://www.powells.com/authors/reichl.html (viewed September 19, 2006).

Zibart, Eve, "A Second Serving of Sensual Memories from Food Writer Ruth Reichl," *BookPage,* April 2001. http://www.bookpage.com/0104bp/ruth_reichl.html (viewed September 19, 2006).

Mary C. Roach

Investigative Reporting, Science

Benchmark Title: *Stiff*

New Hampshire

1959–

Photo courtesy W.W. Norton

About the Author and the Author's Writing

Morbid isn't the first word that comes to mind when seeing journalist Mary Roach's probing eyes and huge grin. And Mary Roach isn't morbid, really, even if she does have an enormous fascination with morbid topics, such as dead bodies.

Born in New Hampshire in 1959, Roach is the daughter of a college professor, Walter Roach, and his wife, Clare Falkner Roach, a secretary. She received a B.A. in 1981 from Wesleyan University and went on to become a freelance writer for *Outside, GQ, Wired, New York Times Magazine, Vogue, Esquire, Islands, Glamour,* and other periodicals. In addition, she has written a humor column, "My Planet," for *Readers Digest,* has contributed a regular column to salon.com, and is a contributing editor to *Discover* magazine. Married to illustrator Ed Rachles, she lives with her husband in San Francisco.

"When I first started writing, I was doing health, lifestyle and travel pieces," she said in an Identitytheory.com interview. "I find science so much meatier, so much more interesting and surprising."

Roach's first book, *Stiff,* published in 2003, entranced readers with its dark humor, fascinating anecdote, and compelling interviews. The book dares ask—and answer—those questions about death that most of us avoid, such as how rapidly do bodies decay in the ground, how are body organs harvested and how are corpses used to research automobile safety? Of course, with popular television shows such as *Six Feet Under* and *CSI* and *Bones,* people are seeing a lot more of cadavers today—rest assured Roach has done her part.

The author told a Booknoise.net interviewer that she finds laboratory cadavers fascinating. She's also fascinated by human attitudes about them. "I'm intrigued by the decision to will one's body to science," she said. "I admire the blunt practicality of it.

It's a pretty evolved mindset: Go ahead and parcel me out to ten different labs and do what you will, because I won't be around to care."

Roach delights in research, and she fills her books with details, many in free-for-all footnotes. "It's me stumbling onto something that I can't bear to leave out of the book," she explained to Dave Weich of Powells.com. "I get distracted easily, and I come across these things in my research."

Similarly, she told Weich that she allows her sense of humor to go wild as something of a safety valve, with all that deathly discussion going on.

With *Spook,* her 2005 release, the author went to the next step after death, to examine the human spirit that inhabits those bodies. "Bear in mind just because science hasn't delivered proof yet, that doesn't mean an afterlife or a soul doesn't exist," she said in a Scifidimensions.com interview. "It just means science isn't (yet) equipped to provide it."

Roach said people in this day and age want at least a dram of scientific proof of something. That's why biotechnician Duncan MacDougall's efforts to prove a body loses twenty-one grams in weight when a person dies—he set up an experiment using scales and patients dying from tuberculosis in an effort to verify the assertion as to the soul's physical weight—so appealed to the author.

"A creative, if mildly naïve approach to the issue," Roach commented on MacDougall's endeavor in a *California Literary Review* interview. "I do love this can-do spirit. He made a cameo in my first book, *Stiff,* and was sort of the inspiration for *Spook,* which is all about people seeking evidence, or proof, of a soul or an afterlife."

If Roach has found a niche audience, so far it's an avid one. "What she celebrates" summed up reviewer Kate Zernike, in discussing *Spook* in the *New York Times Book Review,* "is the passion that drives the inquiry, that keeps people at their research despite the loneliness—and mockery. She may have a skeptic's mind, but she writes with a believer's heart."

Works by the Author

Stiff: The Curious Lives of Human Cadavers (2003)
Spook: Science Tackles the Afterlife (2005)

For Further Information

Borondy, Matt, Mary Roach interview, identitytheory.com. http://www.identitytheory.com/interviews/roach_interview.html (viewed September 20, 2006).

"Chronicling the Lives of the Non-Living," booknoise.net. http://www.booknoise.net/stiff/interview/index.html (viewed September 20, 2006).

Comstock, Paul, "An Interview with Author Mary Roach," *California Literary Review*, December 2005.

Gallagher, Aileen, "Play It Fast and Loose with Mary roach, Author of *Stiff,*" The Black Table Web site. http://www.blacktable.com/gallagher041027.htm (viewed March 31, 2007).

Mary C. Roach entry, Contemporary Authors Online. Reproduced in Biography Resource Center. Farmington Hills, MI: Thomson Gale, 2004. http://galenet.galegroup.com/servlet/BioRC.

Snider, John C., "Interview: Mary Roach," *SciFi Dimensions* Web site. http://www.scifidimensions.com/Dec05/maryroach.htm (viewed October 9, 2006).

Weich, Dave, "A Second Time, Mary Roach Comes Back from the Dead," Powells.com. http://www.powells.com/authors/roach.html (viewed September 20, 2006).

Zernike, Kate, *Spook* review, *New York Times Book Review,* October 9, 2005.

Ann Rule

True Crime

Benchmark Title: *The Stranger beside Me*

Lowell, Michigan

1953–

About the Author and the Author's Writing

Ann Rule leads a life of crime—crime writing, that is. She has turned out a string of best-selling true crime books, including *The Stranger beside Me.*

Rule was born in Lowell, Michigan, in 1935. Her family moved frequently and also lived in Pennsylvania, California, and Oregon. Her father, Chester R. Stackhouse, was a high school athletics coach, and her mother, Sophie Hansen Stackhouse, was a teacher. Justice was no doubt a frequent topic at family gatherings as her grandfather was sheriff in Stanton, Michigan, a cousin was a prosecuting attorney, and an uncle was medical examiner.

Ann attended Coatesville (Pennsylvania) High School, then went to the University of Washington, where in 1954 she obtained a B.A. in creative writing with psychology, criminology, and penology minors. At the University of Washington, she did further graduate study in police science. Her marriage to Bill Rule ended in divorce in 1972. She raised five children, including one foster child.

Rule became a police officer in Seattle but left the force because she could not pass a vision examination. She was a student intern at Oregon State Training School for Girls and a caseworker with the Washington State Department of Public Assistance before she became a writer.

"I started by writing for *True Confessions* magazine, then became the stringer for *True Detective* and *Master Detective*. That entailed going down to the police department, the sheriff's office, to get the story. I went back to school to get a degree in police science," Rule told *Time* magazine's Andrea Sachs. Since then she has written about a thousand or more crime cases, mostly involving killers, some rapists, and bank robbers, for various periodicals.

Through her research and writing, the author became extremely knowledgeable in criminal behavior and has lectured widely, testified in court cases as an expert witness, and served on a U.S. Justice Department task force that established VI-CAP (Violent Criminal Apprehension Program) used by FBI.

Rule gained a wide audience for her 1980 book *The Stranger beside Me*, which is about serial killer Ted Bundy. She had an unusual inside track on the story; she actually worked beside Bundy for a short time at a suicide hotline at Seattle Crisis Center.

Another book ... *And Never Let Her Ago* (1999) is about killer Thomas Capano; *Bitter Harvest* (1998) follows the case of killer Debora Green; *If You Really Loved Me (1991)* describes a millionaire slayer; and *Everything She Ever Wanted* (1992) portrays a Georgia socialite's fatal attractions.

Rule isn't likely to run out of subjects any time soon. *Green River, Running Red* (2004) tells the story of another serial killer. "Interweaving her individual profiles of the murdered women with the story of [Gary] Ridgway and the officials who caught him (presciently swabbing his mouth years before DNA testing would finally give him away), Rule gives full, heartbreaking emotional weight to what America's most notorious serial killer truly wrought," reviewer Alan Moores said in *Booklist*.

Discussing the perpetrators in her books, Rule told Edward Morris of *BookPage,* "All of them, I would say, have deeply entrenched personality disorders. In their minds, the world revolves around them, and the rest of us are one-dimensional paper-doll figures who are put on earth to make them happy."

Rule has identified a number of writers who have influenced her work: Jerry Bledsoe, James Neff, Kathryn Casey, in the true crime field, and Anne Tyler, Wally Lamb, Garrison Keillor, and Anne Quindlen in general literature. The author has written one novel. She said in an interview with Cheryl Dellasega of *Writers Write* that it "was inspired by the Stockholm syndrome case I later wrote about as nonfiction in *Empty Promises*. I originally fictionalized the story to avoid embarrassment to the young woman involved."

She described her approach to writing in a piece for *The Writer* in 2001: "I pretty much go for [a good first draft], and I will usually write 10 to 30 pages a day. I usually start the next morning by going over what I've done the day before in order to prime the pump." She took on a pseudonym, Andy Stack, for a while because, she has said, some editors didn't believe women authors would appeal to readers.

Many of the author's magazine articles have been collected in a series from Pocket Books, called Ann Rule's Crime Files. "Rule brings the same respect for detail to her short work that is evident in the book-length accounts," asserted David Pitt in *Booklist*.

The author's books frequently appear on the *New York Times* best-seller list and she has won two Anthony Awards from mystery writers at Bouchercon, three nominations for an Edgar from Mystery Writers of America, a Washington State Governor's Award, and a Peabody Award for her *Small Sacrifices* miniseries.

Is it a downer, to spend so much time with criminals? "I get to know the victim so well that I can see and feel the pain that these people go through: the victim, the victim's family and the family of the perpetrator," she said in an interview with Valerie Ryan in *Publishers Weekly*. "Out of consideration for them, I often leave out as much as I include."

Works by the Author

Beautiful Seattle (1979), reprinted as *Beautiful America's Seattle* (1989)
Beautiful San Juan Island and Puget Sound (1980)
The Stranger Beside Me (1980/revised 2001)
Mind Games (1984)

Small Sacrifices (1987)

If You Really Loved Me: A True Story of Obsessive Love, Murder, and Betrayal (1991)

Everything She Ever Wanted (1992)

Dead by Sunset: Perfect Husband, Perfect Killer? (1995)

Bitter Harvest: A Woman's Fury, a Mother's Sacrifice (1998)

Jerry Harris Case (1999)

… And Never Let Her Go: Thomas Capano, the Deadly Seducer (1999)

Every Breath You Take: A True Story of Obsessive Revenge and Murder (2001)

Without Pity: Ann Rule's Most Dangerous Killers (2003)

Heart Full of Lies: A True Story of Desire and Death (2003)

Green River, Running Red: The Real Story of the Green River Killer—America's Deadliest Serial Murderer (2004)

Too Late to Say Goodbye: A True Story of Murder and Betrayal (2007)

Ann Rule's Crime Files

A Rose for Her Grave and Other True Cases (1993)

You Belong to Me and Other True Cases (1994)

A Fever in the Heart and Other True Cases (1996)

Ann Rule's Omnibus (1997), with *A Rose for Her Grave, You Belong to Me,* and *A Fever in the Heart*

In the Name of Love and Other True Cases (1998)

The End of the Dream: The Golden Boy Who Never Grew Up and Other True Cases (1999)

A Rage to Kill and Other True Cases (1999)

Empty Promises and Other True Cases (2001)

Last Dance, Last Chance and Other True Cases (2003)

Kiss Me, Kill Me (2004)

Worth More Dead and Other True Cases (2005)

No Regrets (2006)

True Crime Annals Written as Andy Stack

The I-5 Killer (1983)

Lust Killer (1983)

The Want-Ad Killer (1983)

Fiction written as Ann Rule

Possession (1983)

Television Adaptations

Small Sacrifices: A True Story of Passion and Murder (ABC, 1989)

Dead by Sunset (NBC 1995)

… And Never Let Her Go (CBS, 2001)

Ann Rule Presents: The Stranger Beside Me (USA, 2003)

For Further Information

"Ann Rule Answers Seven Deadly Questions," *Annabelle* magazine. http://www.annabellemagazine.com/annabelle%20issue%203/AnnRule.html (viewed September 20, 2006).

Ann Rule entry, Contemporary Authors Online. Reproduced in Biography Resource Center. Farmington Hills, MI: Thomson Gale, 2005. http://galenet.galegroup.com/servlet/BioRC.

Ann Rule Web site. http://www.annrules.com/bio.htm (viewed September 20, 2006).

Blackwell, Gordon, *Every Breath You Take* review, *Library Journal,* May 15, 2002.

Dead by Sunset review, *Publishers Weekly,* September 4, 1995.

Dellasega, Cheryl, "Mothers Who Write: Ann Rule," *Writers Write,* 2001. http://www.writerswrite.com/journal/mar01/rule.htm (viewed September 20, 2006).

Moorers, Alan, *Green River, Running Red* review, *Booklist,* September 15, 2004.

Morris, Edward, "Ann Rule Writes to Give Crime Victims a Voice," *BookPage.* http://www.bookpage.com/0110bp/ann_rule.html (viewed September 20, 2006).

Pitt, David, *Empty Promises* review, *Booklist*, December 15, 2000.

Rule, Ann, "How I Write," *The Writer,* December 2001.

Ryan, Valerie, "Ann Rule: Psychopathic Killers Are Her Specialty in the True-Crime Genre," *Publishers Weekly*, May 3, 1991.

Sachs, Andrea, "The Rule of Law: Crime Author Ann Rule Locks Up the Best-Seller Lists," *Time,* June 28, 2004.

Carl Sagan

Science

Benchmark Title: *Cosmos*

New York, New York

1934–1996

Photo courtesy Penguin Group

About the Author and the Author's Writing

Astronomer Carl Sagan made his first appearance on Johnny Carson's *Tonight Show* on November 30, 1973. He was such a congenial, articulate, and knowledgeable match for the witty, exuberant entertainer and talk-show host—they discussed what the first question should be to a representative of an alien civilization, once contact was made—that he came back to the show twenty-six times over the next thirteen years. He then went on to further popularize science on thirteen episodes of *Cosmos* on PBS beginning in 1980, reaching an audience of some 400 million and surpassed in popularity only by Ken Burns's documentary *Civil War*.

A multidisciplined scientist, Sagan worked tirelessly to explain the inexplicable to the general public. If the truth was inadequate, he couched his theories in fiction; his novel *Contact* was adapted as a motion picture starring Jodie Foster and won a 1998 Hugo Award for the best science fiction novel of the year.

The author's *Shadows of Forgotten Ancestors* (1992) examines the origins of human life forms, through natural selection and serendipity, on Earth; *Pale Blue Dot* (1997) considers the vast potential of space exploration.

Sagan was particularly intrigued with the prospect of alien beings. "The significance of a finding that there are other beings who share this universe with us would be absolutely phenomenal, it would be an epochal event in human history," he is quoted in his obituary on CNN Interactive. He put his thoughts into print in such works as *Cosmic Connection: An Extraterrestrial Perspective,* first published in 1973. In reviewing the book, *Library Journal*'s Michael Rogers observed the author "possessed a particular talent for taking something very complicated and explaining it in terms that the average person could easily understand."

Sagan's infectious persona does not undermine his genius; he made enormous contributions, beginning as a graduate student, to our understanding of the planets Mars and Venus, for example. He was the first to put forward the theory that color variations on Mars are due to dust storms—as was confirmed in the early 1970s by *Mariner 9*. He was also the first to suggest Venus' atmosphere of carbon dioxide and water vapor retained the sun's heat, creating a greenhouse effect—something the Soviet probe *Venera IV* verified, according to Ted A. Nichols II, writing for the Astronomical Society of Harrisburg, Pennsylvania. In 1970, he received NASA's Medal for Exceptional Scientific Achievement and twice earned its Medal for Distinguished Public Service.

Sagan's experiments, funded by NASA and based on Stanley and Harold Urey's work in the creation of organic molecules in an artificial atmosphere—the same atmosphere that was present on Earth—led to his securing a patent on the process. Patent 3,756,934, issued September 4, 1973, is for "Production of Amino Acids from Gaseous Mixtures Using Ultraviolet Light."

Sagan was a doubter and had frequent arguments with his mother over his apparent lack of faith. "Sagan's loss of faith intersected neatly with his growing fascination with extraterrestrial life," commented Keay Davidson in an appreciation in *Skeptical Inquirer*. "He had rejected a supernatural explanation of the origin of life (and everything else); therefore he needed to find a scientific one." More than a decade after his death, Sagan's religion dialogue—expressed in a series of lectures in Glasgow in 1985—were collected by his wife and editor, Ann Druyan, and published in a new 2007 book.

Sagan was born in 1934 in New York City and grew up in Brooklyn. His parents were factory manager Samuel Sagan and Rachel Gruber Sagan. He received four degrees from the University of Chicago: an A.B. with honors in 1954; a B.S. in 1955 and an M.A. in 1956, both in physics; and a Ph.D. in 1960 in astronomy and astrophysics. He was married three times and had six children. His third wife, Ann Druyan, was a collaborator in writing *Comet* and *Shadows of Forgotten Ancestors,* as well as the *Cosmos* television series, and she produced the movie *Contact*.

As a scientist, educator, and writer, Sagan had a varied life. His university and other affiliations include University of California, Berkeley; Harvard University; and the Smithsonian Institution. He was at Cornell University from 1970 and had been designated David Duncan Professor of Astronomy and Space Sciences at Cornell University before his death in 1996 of pneumonia, a complication of bone marrow disease.

Always an optimist, Sagan remarked in *U.S. News & World Report* in 1985, "Our strengths [as a human race] are a kind of intelligence and adaptability. In the last few thousand years, we've made astonishing cultural and technical advances. In other areas, we've not made so much progress. For example, we are still bound up in sectarian and national rivalries." At the same time he decried our continued reliance on fossil fuels. Decades later, our problems persist.

Sagan was a persuasive writer, a riveting public speaker, an ardent debunker of scientific myth. Many of his books were bestsellers, and *The Dragons of Eden* brought him a Pulitzer Prize in 1978. The book described the evolution of human intelligence. As *Time* quoted him in 1996, "We make our world significant by the courage of our questions and by the depth of our answers." Sagan never balked at posing the toughest of questions—and striving to find their answers.

Works by the Author

The Atmospheres of Mars and Venus, with W. W. Kellogg (1961)
Organic Matter and the Moon (1961)
Intelligent Life in the Universe, with I. S. Shklovski (1963)
Planets, with Jonathan Norton (1966)
Planetary Exploration: The Condon Lectures (1970)
The Air War in Indochina, with R. Littauer and others (1971)
Mars and the Mind of Man, with Ray Bradbury, Arthur Clarke, Bruce Murray,
   and Walter Sullivan (1973)
Life Beyond Earth and the Mind of Man, with others (1973)
The Cosmic Connection: An Extraterrestrial Perspective (1973), expanded as
   Carl Sagan's Cosmic Connection: An Extraterrestrial Perspective (2000)
Other Worlds (1975)
The Dragons of Eden: Speculations on the Evolution of Human Intelligence
   (1977)
Murmurs of Earth: The Voyager Interstellar Record (1978)
Broca's Brain: Reflections on the Romance of Science (1979)
Cosmos (1980)
The Fallacy of Star Wars, with R. Garwin and others (1984)
The Cold and the Dark, with Paul R. Ehrlich, Donald Kennedy, and Walter Orr
   Roberts (1984)
Comet, with Ann Druyan (1985)
A Path Where No Man Thought: Nuclear Winter and the End of the Arms Race,
   with Richard Turco (1989)
Shadows of Forgotten Ancestors: A Search for Who We Are, with Ann Druyan
   (1992)
Pale Blue Dot: A Vision of the Human Future in Space (1994)
The Demon-Haunted World: Science as a Candle in the Dark (1995)
Billions and Billions: Thoughts on Life and Death at the Brink of the Millennium
   (1997)
The Varieties of Scientific Experience: A Personal View of the Search for God,
   (2007) edited by Ann Druyan

Editor

Planetary Atmosphere, with Tobias C. Owen and Harlan J. Smith (1971)
Space Research XI, 2 vols., with K. Y. Kondratyev and M. Roycroft (1971)
UFOs: A Scientific Debate, with Thornton Page (1972)
*Soviet-American Conference on the Problems of Communication with Extrater-
   restrial Intelligence* (1973)

Television and Radio Scripts

Cosmos (PBS, 1980), with Ann Druyan and Steven Soter
American Chemical Society series for Voice of America

Fiction

Contact (1985)

For Further Information

Ansen, David, "Contact," *Newsweek,* July 21, 1997.

"Carl Sagan, Cornell Astronomer, Dies Today," Cornell News. http://www. news.cornell.edu/releases/Dec96/saganobit.ltb.html (viewed March 30, 2007).

Carl Sagan entry, Contemporary Authors Online. Reproduced in Biography Resource Center. Farmington Hills, MI: Thomson Gale, 2005. http:// galenet.galegroup.com/servlet/BioRC.

Davidson, Keay, "The Universe and Carl Sagan," *Skeptical Inquirer,* November 1999.

Eicher, Dave, "Carl Sagan, 1934–1996," *Astronomy*, March 1997.

Head, Tom, editor. *Conversations with Carl Sagan.* Jackson: University Press of Mississippi, 2006.

Nichols, Ted A. II, "The Life of Doctor Carl E. Sagan, the People's Astronomer," Astronomical Society of Harrisburg, Pennsylvania. http://www.astrohbg. org/carl_sagan.php (viewed March 30, 2007).

Quarles, Norma, "Carl Sagan Dies at 62," CNN Interactive. http://www. cnn.com/US/9612/20/sagan/ (viewed May 7, 2006).

Rogers, Michael, *Carl Sagan's Cosmic Connection* review, *Library Journal,* November 15, 2000.

"Today's Technology May Find E.T. If He's Out There," *U.S. News & World Report*, October 21, 1985.

David Sedaris

Autobiography, Humor, Memoir

Benchmark Title: *Me Talk Pretty One Day*

Raleigh, North Carolina

1957–

About the Author and the Author's Writing

The woman spoke with a heavy western North Carolina accent, which I used to discredit her authority. Here was a person for whom the word pen *had two syllables. Her people undoubtedly drank from clay jugs and hollered for Paw when the vittles were ready—so who was she to advise me on anything?*

—David Sedaris, describing his speech therapist in *Me Talk Pretty One Day*

The Obie Award–winning (for the play *One Woman Shoe*) David Sedaris pokes fun at himself, his family, his friends, his acquaintances—anyone within reach in his essays read on National Public Radio or collected in one of his several best-selling books. "While it's easy to think of Dave Barry as an especially funny version of a guy you might know," suggested Kim Walter in *Time* magazine, "it's hard to imagine knowing anyone like David Sedaris."

Sedaris was one of six children of Lou and Sharon Sedaris. He grew up in Raleigh, North Carolina, then attended Kent State University and the School of the Art Institute of Chicago.

"I didn't read when I was a kid," Sedaris confessed in an interview with Seth Rogovoy for BerkshireWeb. "I started reading when I was about twenty. I just turned into a reader one day after I dropped out of college. I started reading everything I could get my hands on, all those books that people were supposed to read. And I started reading a lot of contemporary fiction."

Picking up the story in another interview, on the Barnes & Noble Web site, he said, "I started writing when I was twenty, and my first book came out seventeen years later.... After graduating, I started reading out loud. There used to be this little club in Chicago, Lower Links it was called, and my friends and I would often perform there. One night, Ira Glass [host of NPR's *This American Life*] heard me read, and he called me a few years later [after Sedaris had moved to New York] asking if I would like to be on the radio. That pretty much changed everything for me."

When Glass invited Sedaris to submit material for *This American Life*, Sedaris offered "Santaland Diaries"—delivered in his distinctive, quavering voice. After that,

Sedaris's monologues became a regular radio feature. He made three recordings, and his written essays and short stories formed the basis of his first book, *Barrel Fever* (1994), which picks on chain smokers and siblings named Hope or Faith. He has also written several satiric plays with his sister, Amy Sedaris.

His writing career was not an instant one; he also worked as a performance artist, moved furniture, dressed as an elf in Macy's department store (the inspiration for "Santaland Diaries"), painted houses, picked apples, and cleaned apartments. All of these temporary avocations, of course, provided material for his later writings.

"It doesn't really matter what your life was like, you can write about anything," he said in an interview with Linda Richards of *January Magazine*. "I felt sorry for these kids [middle-class students he taught in Chicago], that they thought that their whole past was absolutely worthless because it was less than remarkable."

The author makes the unordinary seem ordinary. "While Sedaris's essays give the sense of ordinary reality, they are unquestionably reflected through the distorting mirror of his outlook," suggests journalist Michael Sims of Bookpage.com.

Dress Your Family in Corduroy and Denim (2004) includes, among other essays, one about the supreme embarrassment of going with his father to confront the parents of a boy who struck David in the mouth with a rock, necessitating a root canal.

"My family isn't really all that different from anyone else's," the author told *BookPage*'s Allison Block recently. "Well, maybe they're a bit more *entertaining*."

He urges young people to consider writing as a career. "I tell them with complete conviction that if I can write books, anyone can," he said in a conversation with *Instructor*'s Gary Drevitch. "They cannot, however, be as rich as me."

How rich Sedaris is, we don't know. But he is recognizable. So much so, he left New York for Paris. And when people there began to notice him, he and his partner, Hugh Hamrick, moved to London. Sedaris is open about being gay, although he thinks the decision to make one's preferences known is a private one. "I write that I live in France with my boyfriend because it's true," he told Robert L. Pela for *The Advocate* in 2000. "We should have reached a time by now where that reads the same as 'I live in France with my wife.' "

> *While my mother grocery-shopped, I would often loiter near the front of the store. It was my hope that some wealthy couple would stuff me into the trunk of their car. They might torture me for an hour or two, but after learning that I was good with an iron, surely they would remove my shackles and embrace me as one of their own.*
>
> —David Sedaris's exaggerated description of his family strife, from *Holidays on Ice*

◆ Works by the Author

Origins of the Underclass, and Other Stories (1992)
Barrel Fever: Stories and Essays (1994)
Holidays on Ice (1997)
Naked (1997)
Me Talk Pretty One Day (2000)
Dress Your Family in Corduroy and Denim (2004)

Editor

Children Playing before a Statue of Hercules (2005)

Drama

Jamboree (1991)

Stump the Host (1993)

One Woman Shoe, with Amy Sedaris as The Talent Family (1995)

The Santaland Diaries, with Joe Nantello (1996), published as *Santaland Diaries and Seasons Greetings: Two Plays* (1998)

Little Freida Mysteries, with Amy Sedaris as The Talent Family (1997)

Incident at Cobbler's Knob, with Amy Sedaris as The Talent Family (1997)

The Book of Liz, with Amy Sedaris as The Talent Family (2001)

Recorded Comedy Albums

Barrel Fever and Other Stories (2001)

The David Sedaris Box Set, with Amy Sedaris and Ann Magnuson (2002)

David Sedaris Live at Carnegie Hall (2003)

The Ultimate David Sedaris (2006)

For Further Information

Bergquist, Kathie, "David Sedaris La Maison de Mes Dents," *Publishers Weekly,* June 19, 2000.

Block, Allison, "Material Witness: Sedaris Finds Seam-Splitting Humor in the Fabric of Life," *BookPage,* June 2004. http://www.bookpage. com/0406bp/david_sedaris.html (viewed September 20, 2006).

David Sedaris entry, Contemporary Authors Online. Reproduced in Biography Resource Center. Farmington Hills, MI: Thomson Gale, 2006. http:// galenet.galegroup.com/servlet/BioRC.

David Sedaris profile, Barnes & Noble. http://www.barnesandnoble.com/writers/ writer.asp?cid=881776 (viewed September 20, 2006).

Drevitch, Gary, "David Sedaris: The Hilarious Best-Selling Author and NPR Humorist Talks about Great Teachers and Other American Heroes," *Instructor,* December 2005.

Kim, Walter, "Wry Slicer; Neurotic, Self-Absorbed and Laugh-Out-Loud Funny, David Sedaris Takes Readers on a Wild Ride through His Improbable Life," *Time,* September 17, 2001.

Maryles, Daisy, and Dick Donahue, "Talk Funny, Make Money," *Publishers Weekly,* June 26, 2000.

Moffett, Matthew L., *Dress Your Family in Corduroy and Denim* review, *School Library Journal,* January 2005.

Pela, Robert L., "Pretty Witty," *The Advocate,* June 20, 2000.

Richards, Linda, David Sedaris interview, *January Magazine.* http://www. januarymagazine.com/profiles/sedaris.html (viewed September 22, 2007).

Rogovoy, Seth, "David Sedaris: Just a Writer." http://www.berkshireweb. com/rogovoy/interviews/sedaris.html (viewed September 20, 2006).

Sims, Michael, "Talking Pretty with David Sedaris," *BookPage,* June 2000. http:// www.bookpage.com/0006bp/david_sedaris.html (viewed September 20, 2006).

Tim Severin

Courtesy Macmillan Publishing

Adventure, History, Travel

Benchmark Title: *The Brendan Voyage*

Jorhat, Assam, India

1940–

About the Author and the Author's Writing

When the bull killer whale dove, "There was a flash of the black-and-white flanks where the water sucked back from the massive body pushing through the sea; and the ripples came across and lapped gently against the leather hull. The killer whale had slid right under the boat, all eight or ten tons of him, curious, intelligent, and completely in control."

That experience in the Atlantic Ocean in 1976, would be thrilling even if it were in a modern craft. It was all the more so for Tim Severin and his four crewmen in the leather craft, a replica of one used by Saint Brendan to sail from Ireland to Newfoundland 1,400 years ago. Brendan wrote about it in *Navigatio Sancti Brendan Abbatis* in the sixth century. In 1978, Severin wrote about it in *The Brendan Voyage*.

Severin went on to make a specialty of authentically recreating the adventurous voyages of others—and writing of them.

"There's no question that the Brendan voyage was my most dangerous journey," the author said in an interview with *Outside* magazine's Mark Jenkins in 2004. "The margins were very slim. It set the threshold for fear. Once you've been really, really scared and then you come through and everything's fine at the end, it's very difficult to get as frightened again."

And that's not for lack of trying. Severin, whose land home is in the hills of County Cork, Ireland, has repeatedly faced the dangers of old in recreating the water trails of Genghis Khan, Sinbad, and Jason. His *The Spice Islands Voyage* follows the sailing route of Alfred Wallace, the little-remembered nineteenth-century British naturalist whose writings of birds of paradise and blue-capped maleos found in Indonesia (in a book titled *The Malay Archipelago*) predated Charles Darwin's.

Severin was born in Jorhat, Assam, India, the son of Maurice Rimington Watkins Severin and Inge Severin. His father was a second-generation tea planter, his mother a writer. In 1966, he married Dorothy Sherman, and they had one child; they divorced in 1979. In addition to his adventures and his writing, lecturing, and filmmaking, Severin headed the Oxford Marco Polo Route Project in 1961. He attended Oxford University, receiving a B.A. in 1962, an M.A. and a separate bachelor of literature degree in 1968. In 1966, he received an honorary doctorate in letters degree from Trinity College. His numerous awards include a Christopher Prize, Royal Geographical Society's Gold Medal, Royal Scottish Geographical Society's Livingstone Medal, and Académie de la Marine's literary medal.

Severin was never satisfied with book research. While still a student at Oxford, he motorcycled part of Marco Polo's land route. The trip resulted in his first book, *Tracking Marco Polo,* in 1964. Reviewer Ronald Varney said it "proves an entrancing blend of hilarity and high adventure, chaos and revelation. From the start the project is woefully under-budgeted and ill-prepared.… Among the numerous, ignominious crashes suffered along the way is one in which the author breaks his foot, nearly ending the trip."

Soon Severin's interests drew him to the sea—although not in a confrontational way. As *Geographical*'s Claire Hutchings remarked of the Brendan recreation, "You begin to wonder whether Severin really is out of his mind. Few modern yachts would attempt this route, so how on earth would a boat made out of medieval materials and using medieval technology complete the journey?"

"I have exactly the same attitude towards the sea as historic—or, if you like, aboriginal sailors—would have had, which is that you've great respect for the sea and what you want is perfect conditions. Not this notion of going out and challenging the sea," he said in an interview with Joanne Hayden for the *Sunday Business Post.*

When he begins a project, the adventurer explained to *Geographical* in 1997, he does extensive research to eliminate the embellishments and get at the heart of the original feat. His replications are homage to the real thing. "I prefer that low-tech, slower pace of travel," he said, describing the Spice Islands expedition of naturalist Alfred Russel Wallace. "These are historical projects and it is about finding out whether a particular type of boat [in this case a native sailing boat called a *prahu*] will do the journey and also to see what it is like living and working on them."

In 1999, Severin explored the sources of the legendary great white whale that Herman Melville incorporated in his classic tale *Moby Dick.* As with his other books, the author's *In Search of Moby Dick* (2000) works "on two levels," *Geographical*'s reviewer Sophie Ransom said. "It is a quest for the white whale, but also an exploration of the social and cultural history of the communities Severin visits. In meeting the islanders he learns about their superstitions and their beliefs. Legend surrounds the white whale in particular."

The author's occasional land forays are no less challenging. Eamon Delaney in *Publishers Weekly* commented on Severin's 1987 "eight-month horseback ride from Belgium, retracing the route of the First Crusade to Jerusalem as traveled by Duke Godfrey de Bouillon. But surely, in emulating the assault on the infidel, he must have been the target of every Islamic militant around?"

Severin's latest works have been teen fiction: a trilogy depicts Thorgils, the son of Norse chieftain Leif the Lucky, who inherited second sight from his Celtic mother

Thorgunna, as he seeks his destiny. These young adult novels are, of course, true to their sources.

"Fiction is more seductive and more dangerous," the author said in an interview on the Pan Macmillan Web site. "It requires more discipline at the keyboard—those hours of facing the computer screen half filled with words—yet there's also the chance to let imagination roam. My happy discovery, as I've ventured into writing fiction, is to discover that the story occasionally takes on a life of its own."

Works by the Author

Tracking Marco Polo (1964)

Explorers of the Mississippi (1967)

The Golden Antilles (1970)

The African Adventure: Four Hundred Years of Exploration in the Dangerous Continent (1973)

The Horizon Book of Vanishing Primitive Man (1973), published in Great Britain as *Vanishing Primitive Man* (1973)

The Oriental Adventure: Explorers of the East (1976)

The Brendan Voyage (1978)

The Sinbad Voyage (1982)

The Jason Voyage: The Quest for the Golden Fleece (1985)

The Ulysses Voyage: Sea Search for the Odyssey (1987)

Crusader: By Horse to Jerusalem (1989)

In Search of Genghis Khan (1991)

The China Voyage: A Pacific Quest by Bamboo Raft (1994)

The Spice Islands Voyage: The Quest for Alfred Wallace, the Man Who Shared Darwin's Discovery of Evolution (1997)

In Search of Moby Dick: Quest for the White Whale (2000)

In Search of Robinson Crusoe (2002)

Television Scripts

The Brendan Voyage (1978)

The Sinbad Voyage (1981)

Crusader (1989)

In Search of Genghis Kahn (1991)

The China Voyage (1995)

The Spice Islands Voyage (1997)

Fiction for Young Adult Readers

Viking Trilogy

Odinn's Child (2005)

King's Man (2006)

Sworn Brother (2006)

For Further Information

Delaney, Eamon, "Tim Severin: Meeting with an Explorer," *Publishers Weekly,* June 26, 2000.

Flanagan, Margaret, *Odinn's Child* review, *Booklist,* July 1, 2006.

(Giles) Timothy Severin entry, Contemporary Authors Online. Reproduced in Biography Resource Center. Farmington Hills, MI: Thomson Gale, 2002. http://galenet.galegroup.com/servlet/BioRC.

Hayden, Joanne, "Reluctant Adventurer Has Nerves of Steel: an Interview with Tim Severin," *The Sunday Business Post* [online], July 7, 2002. http:// archives.tcm.ie/businesspost/2002/07/07/story348303628.asp (viewed May 3, 2006).

Hutchings, Claire, *The Brendan Voyage* review, *Geographical,* March 1996.

Jenkins, Mark, "Captain Retro," *Outside,* June 2004.

Ransom, Sophie, *In Search of Moby Dick* review, *Geographical,* December 1999.

Sykes, Lisa, "A Spice Island Adventure," *Geographical,* November 1997.

Tim Severin interview, Pan Macmillan, 2005. http://www.panmacmillan. com/interviews/displayPage.asp?PageID=3883 (viewed September 22, 2007).

Tim Severin Web site. http://www.timseverin.net (viewed May 3, 2006).

Varney, Ronald, "Tracking Marco Polo," *Smithsonian,* July 1986.

Dava Sobel

History, Science

Benchmark Title: *Galileo's Daughter*

New York, New York

1947–

Photo by Jerry Bauer

About the Author and the Author's Writing

Dava Sobel, a self-described nerd, studied science in high school and biochemistry in college but later decided she didn't have what it took to become a laboratory scientist. She always liked to write, and that's where she was eventually drawn for a career.

"What John Grisham is to the legal thriller," suggested John F. Baker in *Publishers Weekly,* "Dava Sobel has become to a hot new genre that can only be described as historical narrative about offbeat but significant figures. The books it encompasses are difficult to define but instantly recognizable, and, happily for their publishers, seem to appeal to large numbers of readers."

Born in the Bronx, New York, in 1947, she was the daughter of Samuel H. Sobel and Betty Gruber Sobel. Her father was a physician, her mother a chemist. She attended the Bronx High School of Science and State University of New York at Binghamton. "I had a really hard time in college because I couldn't make up my mind," Sobel told Sara F. Gold of *Publishers Weekly.* "I changed my major five times. I changed schools three times."

One facet of Sobel's studies always appealed to her: writing. "Someone once said to me, 'I would hate your job, because it's like writing one long research paper after another.' It is indeed just like that, which is why I love it so much," the author told *American Scientist* online.

Sobel worked at a variety of jobs before settling into full-time writing. She was a technical manual writer for IBM and a cohost of a medical program at a Maine television station. While working at Ithaca College as public relations staff, she heard a program by astronomer Carl Sagan and fell in love with the solar system. She grabbed the opportunity (and the $5 fee) to interview the scientist for an underground student newspaper. From there, she made the leap to becoming a science writer for the *New York Times.*

She married Arthur C. Klein, a marketing and direct mail consultant, and they have two children. Her husband, who suffered chronic back pain, sought out physicians who used nontraditional approaches. In 1985, Klein and Sobel compiled a book, *Backache Relief.* They followed with *Arthritis: What Works* in 1989 and two exercise books.

After she and her husband had divorced, Sobel collaborated with radio astronomer Frank Drake of the University of California at Santa Anna, at the suggestion of Dick Teresi, former editor of *OMNI* magazine, on a book about the possibilities of extraterrestrial life forms. *Is Anyone Out There?* came out in 1992. Drake was a pioneer of SETI—the search for extraterrestrial intelligence. "Our book was about the serious scientific side of searching for extraterrestrial intelligence, including the efforts that had been made to date at publication time (1992), which included the NASA-SETI Microwave Observing Project," the author said in an e-mail.

As a freelance writer, Sobel crafted essays and news stories for *Audubon, Omni, Science Digest, Discover, Life,* and the *New Yorker.* Assignments took her to space shuttle launches and to the Jet Propulsion Laboratory in Pasadena. In 1980, she became a subject in Circadian rhythm sleep experiments, and she wrote about them for the *New York Times.*

Harvard Magazine was the only periodical willing to take a chance on an idea she pitched to report on a symposium organized by Will Andrews and held at university in 1993. The program was "the best scientific meeting" she had ever attended, she told *Sky & Telescope*'s David H. Levy. "There were experts in cartography, navigation, the history of science, horology, materials science, shipping, and economics. I had no idea how much was involved in solving the problem of determining one's longitude at sea during the eighteenth century. It was a life-and-death issue." Seasoned navigators at sea could determine latitude from observations of the midday sun. But longitude was anyone's guess.

Her article caught the eye of an editor at the Walker publishing house, George Gibson, who commissioned her to write the book *Longitude.* The focus of her book is John Harrison, an obscure watchmaker from Yorkshire who ultimately solved the problem of longitude; although he struggled for years to claim a £20,000 sterling prize from the British Parliament's Board of Longitude. When her agent sought a British publisher for the book, after the American edition came out, there were a dozen rejections before Fourth Estate eventually brought out an edition, which sold even better than the U.S. title.

In the course of her research on another topic, Sobel's discovery of a letter to Galileo from an offspring led to another popular book, *Galileo's Daughter,* published in 1999. In Galileo's day, scientists were not expected to marry. But with his mistress of nearly twelve years, he had two daughters and a son. One daughter, Virginia (later Suor Maria Celeste), kept in touch with her father. Sobel, who had studied Italian while in college, examined and translated some 124 letters from several sources.

Sobel struggled with the content of her book—alternating letters with background about Galileo—and at her editor's urging, ultimately printed only twenty of the letters in the book. (All appeared online and in a subsequent book, *Letters to Father,* published in 2001.)

Galileo's Daughter, said salon.com reviewer Casey Greenfield, "is most remarkable for its graceful combination of scholarly integrity and rhapsodic tone. Sobel imbues this potentially dry, academic story with the language and cadence of oral storytelling, and she gives it all the dramatic suspense that narrative demands."

"My planet fetish began, as best I can recall, in third grade, at age eight—right around the time I learned that Earth had siblings in space, just as I had older brothers in high school and college," the author explains in her 2005 publication, *The Planets,* which devotes its chapters to the history and lore of each of the orbs in our solar system. "The presence of the neighboring worlds was a revelation at once specific and mysterious in 1955, for although each planet bore a name and held a place in the Sun's family, very little was known about any of them. Pluto and Mercury, like Paris and Moscow, only better, beckoned a childish imagination to ultra-exotic utopias."

Sobel struggled to find a structure for her 2005 book, rejecting the idea of featuring a particular astronomer with each orb. "I looked for non-scientific connections," she explained to Dave Weich of Powells.com, "and there were more than I'd thought: mythology, science fiction, astrology…. That's what gave me the idea. There were enough themes to match with the planets."

Today Sobel is strongly aligned with the planets. "I now mostly write about astronomy and the history of science," she said in an interview with *Chicago Maroon,* the University of Chicago's student newspaper, following her appointment in 2005 as the University of Chicago's Vare Nonfiction Writer-in-Residence. "What I get to do in these books is try to approach the material from a personal take on it and find out the facts, but then arrange them in a way that I think will appeal to people who are not geeks or who actually avoid reading about science."

Works by the Author

Backache Relief: The Ultimate Second Opinion from Back-Pain Sufferers Nationwide Who Share Their Successful Healing Experiences, with Arthur C. Klein (1985)

Arthritis: What Works, with Arthur C. Klein (1989)

Is Anyone Out There? The Scientific Search for Extraterrestrial Intelligence, with Frank D. Drake (1992)

Arthritis: What Exercises Work, with Arthur C. Klein (1993)

Backache: What Exercises Work, with Arthur C. Klein (1994)

Longitude: The True Story of a Lone Genius Who Solved the Greatest Scientific Problem of His Time (1995)

Galileo's Daughter: A Historical Memoir of Science, Faith, and Love (1999)

The Planets (2005)

Translator and Annotator

Letters to Father: Suor Maria Celeste to Galileo, 1623–1633 by Suor Maria Celeste Galilei (2001)

Editor

The Best American Science Writing 2004 (2004)

Contributor

Haven: The Dramatic Story of 1,000 World War II Refugees and How They Came to America, by Ruth Gruber (2000)

For Further Information

Baker, John F., "Dava Sobel: Matters of Science and Faith," *Publishers Weekly,* October 4, 1999.

Dava Sobel entry, Contemporary Authors Online. Reproduced in Biography Resource Center. Farmington Hills, MI: Thomson Gale, 2005. http://galenet. galegroup.com/servlet/BioRC.

Dava Sobel interview, *American Scientist* [online]. http://www.americanscientist. org/template/ScientistNightstandTypeDetail/assetid/48489;jsessionid= aaa5LVF0 (viewed October 13, 2006).

Dava Sobel Web page, http://www.davasobel.com (viewed November 30, 2006).

Easterbrook, Gregg, *Longitude* review, *Washington Monthly,* January-February 1996.

Freund, Sandy, *Planets* review, *School Library Journal,* February 2006.

Glickel, Jen, "The Uncommon Interview; Dava Sobel," *Chicago Maroon,* Nov. 29, 2005. http://maroon.uchicago.edu./news/articles/2005/11/29/the_uncommon _intervi.php (viewed May 23, 2006).

Gold, Sarah F., "She Can Thank Her Lucky Stars," *Publishers Weekly,* October 10, 2005.

Greenfield, Casey, *Galileo's Daughter* review, salon.com. http://www.salon. com/books/review/1999/11/11/sobel/index.html (viewed May 23, 2006).

Jones, Malcolm, "When the Earth Moved: Dava Sobel Pairs Galileo's Story with His Daughter's to Give Us 17th-Century Italian Life in the Round," *Newsweek,* October 11, 1999.

Letters to Father review, *Publishers Weekly,* August 27, 2001.

Levy, David H., "A Master Storyteller: An Acclaimed Writer Brings Science History Vividly and Lovingly to Life," *Sky & Telescope,* October 2005.

Scott, Whitney, *Galileo's Daughter* review, *Booklist,* March 15, 2000.

Sinnot, Roger W., *Longitude* review, *Sky & Telescope,* July 1996.

Weich, Dave, "From Florence to Pluto with Dava Sobel," Powells.com. http://www.powells.com/authors/sobel.html (viewed April 20, 2006).

Art Spiegelman

Biography, History, Memoir

Benchmark Title: *Maus*

Stockholm, Sweden

1948–

About the Author and the Author's Writing

Stories can be powerfully told with images. In the aftermath of the destruction of the World Trade Center in 2001, Art Spiegelman had an assignment both enviable and daunting: create a cover for the next issue of the *New Yorker*. It was not an assignment he could walk away from; it was an unprecedented opportunity to make an artistic statement. And his wife, Françoise Mouly, was the magazine's cover editor.

Spiegelman's cover for the September 24 issue was the haunting depiction of the now-gone twin towers, black images on a black background. The Manhattanite explained how the tragedy affected him in a report posted at *New Yorker* online October 3, 2001: "Whenever I've walked north in the hours and days that have followed, I've turned back—as if toward Mecca—to see if my buildings were still missing. Not especially well equipped to help in the search for survivors, I applied myself to searching for an image of the calamity. Despite what felt like the irrelevancy of the task, it gave me a way to fend off trauma and focus on something."

Spiegelman hadn't yet cleansed himself of the subject; he crafted a graphic novel, *In the Shadow of No Towers,* published in 2004. "It was a lifesaver, because when I started off, I wasn't making a book. I was making pages while waiting for the world to end," he told journalist Kenneth Terrell. "But it wasn't. Or if it was, it was taking its time."

Spiegelman has been an innovator as a memoirist and social commentator, and as a comic book artist. He pioneered use of the graphic novel format for memoir and nonfiction in the United States. Born in Stockholm, Sweden, in 1948, he was the son of Vladek and Anja Zylbergerg Spiegelman. The family immigrated to Queens. From 1965 to 1968, Spiegelman studied philosophy and art at Harpur College (now State University of New York at Binghamton). He became a naturalized citizen and married Paris native Mouly in 1977; they have two children.

From 1966 to 1989, he worked as a creative consultant, designer, artist, editor, and writer for Topps Chewing Gum, his projects including Wacky Packages and Garbage Pail Kids. He also taught at the San Francisco Academy of Art in 1974–1975 and at the New York School of Visual Arts from 1979 to 1987. From 1991 to 2003, he was staff artist and writer for the *New Yorker*, during Tina Brown's editorship, and is now a freelance artist and writer.

As a youth, Art devoured the Disney comic book adventures of Donald Duck and Uncle Scrooge, as engrossingly told by Carl Barks, and the Dell illustrated adventures of Little Lulu and Tubby. He consumed the satiric *Mad* magazine (whose message, he said in an NPR interview "was basically … 'Think for yourselves, kids.' "). In later years, he said in a *Booksense* interview, he read Kafka. "That was important to me. Faulker. See, I can't tell how things influenced me. I can tell I read these things and they stayed with me. Vladimir Nabokov stayed with me, Gertrude Stein stayed with me. Dashiell Hammett and Raymond Chandler and James M. Cain stayed with me."

He was drawn to the underground comics medium of the 1960s, with Zap comix, R. Crumb, and S. Clay Wilson. He and Mouly established and edited *Raw,* an annual published beginning in 1980. While he toyed with his panel presentations, he ultimately "decided that what people really want from comics is narrative," he told Nina Siegal of the *Progressive.* "To tell the story of Maus "involved using all the specific discoveries I'd made about how comics work formally and using those formal elements not to jump or undercut the narrative but to allow the narrative to happen more seamlessly."

Spiegelman completed his first chapter of Maus in 1972, wrote comics historian Ron Goulart, and it appeared in the underground publication *Funny Animals.* It began the story of his parents, Polish Jews who attempted to flee the Nazis. "The story of his parents and his own complex and ambivalent relationship with them was expanded and presented in numbers two through eight of *Raw,"* according to Goulart. Issued as a book in 1986, *Maus* secured Spiegelman a Pulitzer Prize. *Maus* was not without its controversy, however. Some complained of its anthropomorphism, depicting Jews and Germans as mice and cats, and Poles as pigs.

Spiegelman brushed off the matter in a *Comics Journal* interview. "Ultimately, what the book is about is the commonality of human beings. It's crazy to divide things down the nationalistic or racial or religious lines.… These metaphors, which are meant to self-destruct in my book—and I think they do self-destruct—still have a residual force that allows them to work as metaphors, and still get people worked up over them."

Critic Adam Gropnik, writing in the *New Republic,* observed that the work's drama came, "from the tension between its words and pictures, between the detail of its narration and dialogue and the hallucinatory fantasy of its images. At the heart of our understanding (or our lack of understanding) of the Holocaust is our sense that this is both a human and an inhuman experience."

The author crafted a sequel to *Maus,* which reunited his parents after their concentration camp experiences and brought them to America's Catskills. "There are moments of quirky, uneasy, liberating humor, but make no mistake, *Maus II* is deadly serious," *Publishers Weekly*'s reviewer said. "A timeless book, it burns into the mind."

A variety of projects keep the author/artist busy. Spiegelman spun a *New Yorker* profile of innovative Plastic Man creator/artist Jack Cole into a book (with art design by Chip Kidd). And he and Mouly went on to produce three (so far) volumes of Little Lit books, compilations of folk tales in comic book format. Spiegelman in 1999 illustrated a jazz age poem by early *New Yorker* editor Joseph Moncure March, *The Wild Party,* a racy tale of a vaudeville dancer and murderer.

The *New York Times Magazine* praised Spiegelman, saying that "to the comics world is a Michelangelo and a Medici both, an influential artist who is also an impresario and an enabler of others.... It would be almost impossible to overstate the influence of *Maus* among other artists."

Works by the Author

The Complete Mr. Infinity (1970)
The Viper Vicar of Vice, Villainy, and Vickedness (1972)
Zip-a-Tune and More Melodies (1972)
Ace Hole, Midget Detective (1974)
Language of Comics (1974)
Breakdowns: From "Maus" to Now: An Anthology of Strips (1977)
Every Day Has Its Dog (1979)
Work and Turn (1979)
Two-Fisted Painters Action Adventure (1980)
Maus: A Survivor's Tale, Volume 1, My Father Bleeds History (1986)
Raw: Open Wounds from the Cutting Edge of Commix, No. 1 (1989)
Raw No. 2, edited by Françoise Mouly (1990)
Maus: A Survivor's Tale, Volume 2, And Here My Troubles Began (1991)
Complete Maus (1994)
Jack Cole and Plastic Man: Forms Stretched to Their Limits, with Chip Kidd (2001)
In the Shadow of No Towers (2004)

Editor

Whole Grains: A Book of Quotations, with Bob Schneider (1972)
Raw: The Graphic Aspirin for War Fever, by Françoise Mouly (1986)
Read Yourself Raw: Comix Anthology for Damned Intellectuals, with Françoise Mouly (1987)
Jimbo: Adventures in Paradise, by Gary Panter, editor with Françoise Mouly and contributor (1988)
Skin Deep: Tales of Doomed Romance, by Charles Burns, editor with R. Sikoryak (1992)
The Narrative Corpse, with R. Sikoryak (1995)
It Was a Dark and Silly Night ..., with Françoise Mouly (2003)

Contributor

The Apex Treasury of Underground Comics, edited by Don Donahue and Susan Goodrich (1974)
Drawn Together: Relationships Lampooned, Harpooned, and Cartooned, edited by Nicole Hollander, Skip Morrow, and Ron Wolin (1983)
The Complete Color Polly and Her Pals, Volume 1: The Surrealist Period, 1926–1927 (1990)

Tijuana Bibles: Art and Wit in America's Forbidden Funnies, 1930s–1950s, edited by Bob Adelman (1997)

* *Little Lit: Folklore and Fairy Tale Funnies,* with Françoise Mouly (2000)

Little Lit 2: Strange Stories for Strange Kids, with Françoise Mouly (2001)

City of Glass: The Graphic Novel, by Paul Auster (2004)

Illustrator

The Wild Party: The Lost Classic, by Joseph Moncure March (1994)

For Juvenile Readers

I'm a Dog (1997)

For Further Information

Art Spiegelman entry, Contemporary Authors Online. Reproduced in Biography Resource Center. Farmington Hills, MI: Thomson Gale, 2004. http://galenet.galegroup.com/servlet/BioRC.

Bird, Alan, "Comic Books Come of Age," *BookPage.* http://www.bookpage.com/0308bp/spiegelman_mouly.html (viewed September 26, 2006).

Bolhafner, J. Stephen, "Art for Art's Sake: Spiegelman Speaks on RAW's Past, Present and Future," *Comics Journal,* October 1991.

Gopnik, Adam, *Maus* review, *New Republic,* June 22, 1987.

Goulart, Ron, editor. *The Encyclopedia of American Comics from 1897 to the Present.* New York: Facts on File, 1990.

"Intersections: Of 'Maus' and Spiegelman," NPR, January 26, 2004. http://www.npr.org/templates/story/story.phpo?storyId=1611731 (viewed September 26, 2006).

Jack Cole and Plastic Man review, *Publishers Weekly,* September 3, 2001.

Maus II review, *Publishers Weekly,* September 27, 1991.

McGrath, Charles, "Not Funnies," *New York Times Magazine,* July 11, 2004.

Siegel, Nina, Art Spiegelman interview, *The Progressive,* January 2005.

Smith, Christopher Monte, +Art Spiegelman interview, BookSense.com. http://www.booksense.com/people/archive/spiegelmanart.jsp (viewed September 26, 2006).

Spiegelman, Art, "Drawing Blood," *Harper's,* June 2006.

Terrell, Kenneth, "9/11: The Comic Book," *U.S. News & World Report,* September 13, 2004.

Robert Sullivan

Investigative Reporting, Nature, Travel

Benchmark Title: *Rats*

New York, New York

1962–

Photo courtesy Bloomsbury USA

About the Author and the Author's Writing

Robert Sullivan isn't sure he wants to be categorized a nature writer. "My books often get shelved in nature sections," he said in an interview with Dave Weich. "I don't think that's what I've been doing. If you're from New York or New Jersey, I didn't think you were allowed to be a nature writer. So I thought, 'If I'm getting put in the nature section, I'm going to try to write a nature book about something that nobody thinks of as natural. I'll write about rats'."

We'll get to rats, and *Rats,* later. First, we have to get through the Great Swamp. In the early 1980s, Sullivan was a reporter with the *Herald and News.* He went on to become a frequent contributor to *Rolling Stone, Condé Nast Traveler,* the *New York Times Magazine,* and the *New Yorker.* He is an associate editor of *Vogue.*

Sullivan's first nonfiction book, *The Meadowlands,* published in 1998 (following a children's book about reindeer), was an affectionate investigation of the New Jersey Meadowlands that he so often drove through as a teen. Although born in Queens, Manhattan, in 1962, he grew up on Long Island, and his family eventually moved to New Jersey's Morris County. He frequently traveled to and through the Great Swamp. "When you drive to the Yes concert [in Manhattan] or to watch the Rangers play, you go over the Meadowlands. You go over this horrible place that's really smelly and disgusting. Every joke about New Jersey is really a joke about the Meadowlands." Yet after Sullivan had married and moved to Portland, Oregon, he missed the Meadowlands. He came back.

"Some people climb Mount Everest and write about it," Sullivan told reporter Tina Traster of the *Bergen Record.* "I wrote about the Meadowlands." He described the blighted landscape's trash mounds and long-ago crimes, its inventors and mosquito trappers. He emphasized that it was really the occupants of the Meadowlands that interested him. "Everybody's got great stories, and if I can get paid to write about other people's stories, well, then, that's just a consolation."

"*The Meadowlands* is everything a creative nonfiction book should be: carefully researched, chock full of fascinating details and historical facts, and rife with life's ironies," said Susan Wickstrom of *Williamette Week*. "It captures the surreality of a place where the worst and best that humankind can spew battle the power of the natural world."

"Great Swamp taught me how to really love a specific area in a very particular way," he said in a conversation with Fiona Somers. "I can still remember the first pictures I took with my first camera, and I remember the colors of the grasses and the reeds; I remember thinking how beautiful they looked. I love Great Swamp."

Sullivan didn't particularly love whales, but they became his next topic, thanks to a *New York Times* editor who assigned him to write a three-thousand-word article about plans of the Makah tribe to hunt whales. He spent two years getting to know his subjects. The week the hunt was scheduled, Neah Bay was a media circus, and the Native Americans called it all off. "With cameras poised on them, they did not hunt a whale," Sullivan told an audience at New York University's Center for Humans and Nature in 2004. "I would argue that to not do something in front of cameras in the United States of America today is one of the most amazing triumphs you could ever come up with. They did not hunt a whale." Sullivan wrote about it in *A Whale Hunt,* published in 2002. Reviewer Kurt Kamin remarked on "Sullivan's conversational tone and detailed observations, and his ability to present the ironies and absurdities in this remarkable story of man versus man and man versus nature."

After eight years on the West Coast, the author brought his family back to New York. And rats. "Though the idea of chronicling an entire year and a half of chasing rats is intriguing enough to create a good book, Sullivan took it about seven steps further," said a *ContemporaryLit* (About.com) reviewer. "Not only did he follow the rats, but he traced their history down to miniscule details not even a Ph.D. student writing a thesis would have explored."

How Not to Get Rich, Sullivan's 2005 book, is a tongue-in-cheek (yet factual) examination of educational, vocational, and social opportunities that are sure to leave one in the poorhouse.

Sullivan's research took him on the road. In *Cross Country,* "He writes relentlessly about the origins of the Interstate Highway System, the first automobiles, the first gas stations, the first motels, the rise of fast food, and even the nascence of coffee cup lids or 'drink-through lids,' " said a *ContemporaryLit* reviewer.

"People remember their cross-country trips," Sullivan wrote in *Cross Country,* "emotionally speaking, crossing the country is a big deal." He should know; with parents and in-laws on opposite coasts, he's made the trek—ninety thousand miles worth—more than two dozen times.

Concluding that "travel by couch beats coach," *USA Today* reviewer Bob Minzesheimer praised Sullivan as "sensitive, witty and well-read, which is why it's so much fun to have him along for the ride."

 Works by the Author

The Meadowlands: Wilderness Adventures on the Edge of a City (1998)

A Whale Hunt: How a Native-American Village Did What No One Thought It Could (2002)

How Not to Get Rich: Or Why Being Bad Off Isn't So Bad, with Scott Menchin (2005)

Rats: Observations on the History and Habitat of the City's Most Unwanted Inhabitants (2005)

Cross Country: Fifteen Years and Ninety Thousand Miles on the Roads and Interstates of America with Lewis and Clark, a Lot of Bad Motels, a Moving Van, Emily Post, ... Kids, and Enough Coffee to Kill an Elephant (2006)

Fiction for Juvenile Readers

Flight of the Reindeer; The True Story of Santa Claus and His Christmas Mission (1996)

For Further Information

Barcott, Bruce, *Cross Country* review, *New York Times Book Review,* July 2, 2006.

Flanagan, Mark, *Cross Country* review, About.com. http://contemporarylit. about.com/od/memoir/fr/crossCountry.htm (viewed September 27, 2006).

Kamin, Kurt, *A Whale Hunt* review, *Etude: New Voices in Literary Nonfiction.* http://etude.uorgeon.edu/autumn2002/books/whale.html (viewed September 27, 2006).

Minzesheimer, Bob, "Travel by Couch Beats Coach," *USA Today,* July 19, 2006.

Robert Sullivan interview, "Musings on Swamps, Whales, and Rats," New York University, May 25, 2004. http://www.cceia.org/resources/transcripts/ 4983.html (viewed September 22, 2007).

Somers, Fiona, "Meet Robert Sullivan," Great Swamp Watershed Association. http://www.greatswamp.org/Newsletter/atw004/news004.htm (viewed September 27, 2006).

Traster, Tina, "Author Finds His Everest in North Jersey," *Bergen Record,* April 15, 1998.

Venable, Colleen, *Rats* review, About.com. http://contemporarylit.about.com/ od/history/fr/rats.htm (viewed October 15, 2006).

Weich, Dave, "Walled in with Robert Sullivan," Powells.com. http://www. powells.com/authors/sullivan.html (viewed September 27, 2006).

Wickstrom, Susan, "The Unnaturalist," *Willamette Week,* April 15, 1998.

Gay Talese

Investigative Reporting, Memoir, Sports, True Crime

Benchmark Title: *Honor Thy Father*

Ocean City, New Jersey

1932–

Photo by Joyce Tenneson

About the Author and the Author's Writing

Gay Talese would have turned in a fascinating story, even if Frank Sinatra had been healthy. But the fact the singer brushed off an interview because of a cold gave the capable journalist just the hook he needed for a piece widely acclaimed as the acme of biographical reportage.

"Frank Sinatra, holding a glass of bourbon in one hand and a cigarette in the other, stood in a dark corner of the bar between two attractive but fading blondes who sat waiting for him to say something," Talese began his essay for *Esquire*'s April 1966 issue. "But he said nothing: he had been silent during much of the evening." Talese wrote his profile from observation, research, and interviews with others. It's as fascinating a portrayal of the singer as you'll find.

"It takes the imagination to see the story that's not necessarily the story you thought," the author said in a *Writer's Digest* interview in 2006. "Talk about fame—here was a guy who was so famous, even he didn't know who he was, he's so drenched in fame.... If I would've talked to him, I wouldn't even have made a dent in his consciousness."

Gay Talese was never satisfied with simple question-and-answer interviews. "I like to move beyond the words and get into the actions of people," he told University of Southern California interviewer Irwin R. Lewis. "I like to be outdoors and moving from place to place with people.... I like to come to know people by watching them as they go through, in a rather ordinary way, what is their daily life, what is their daily routine."

The writer never knocks off a piece hurriedly; he takes what time is necessary —he followed Sinatra around for three or four weeks, for example, from a Las Vegas club to a Burbank television studio. He ran up an expense account of $7,000. The magazine paid it, although as Talese later lamented, those days, and those budgets, have changed enormously.

Scoffing at being called a "new journalist," Talese calls his technique "hanging around," and he's done it through a dozen books. It involves legwork, telephone diligence, knowing people, being there, and watching.

Born Gaetano Talese in 1932, he was the son of Joseph F. Talese and Catherine DePaolo Talese of Ocean City, New Jersey, an island community just south of Atlantic City. His father was an Italian immigrant, a tailor. His mother was a department store buyer and clothing store proprietor. While in high school, he wrote articles and columns for the weekly *Ocean City Sentinel-Ledger*. In 1953, he received a Bachelor of Arts degree from the University of Alabama and subsequently served in the U.S. Army for two years, reaching the rank of lieutenant. In 1959, he married editor Nan Ahearn, and they raised two daughters. They live on New York's Upper East Side.

For more than a decade, the author worked at the *New York Times* (with several months' military service with the Tank Corps in Kentucky, to fulfill ROTC obligations), first as copy boy, then a reporter.

Looking to get noticed at the *Times,* Talese was "drawn to the kind of story that is present, yet ignored by everyone because they are following 'the big story,' " Barbara Lounsberry observed in a portrait of the author that appears on Talese's Web site. "In November 1953, his curiosity led him to climb the stairs to the attic of the Times Square building to interview and write about the man behind the famous five-foot headlines that revolve glitteringly around Times Square. Only Talese thought to look beyond the façade."

Talese wrote a dozen articles for the *New York Times Magazine*. When he left the newspaper in 1965 to freelance full time, he took with him a book's worth of experiences. He wrote first *Esquire* articles, then an entire book, *The Kingdom and the Power* (1969), about the inner workings of the *New York Times*.

"I did not ever want to be a traditional journalist," the author said in *Pages* in 2006. "I did not want to write 'news.' My definition of a story idea was more the story of private life, of people who were not necessarily making 'news' but making their way through private adventures and trying to make sense of their daily lives and also discovering ways to endure or overcome obstacles."

Pick any Talese book, and it will bear his exemplary odd angles, depth, and assured writing. *Fame and Obscurity* (1970) contains his stories about entertainer Frank Sinatra, baseball star Joe DiMaggio, and boxer Floyd Patterson. *Honor Thy Father,* published a year later, is about the feuds and fury of the Bonanno organized crime family. *Thy Neighbor's Wife* (1980) opens the doors on the 1950s sexual revolution. *Unto the Sons* (1992) describes the immigrant experience in the decades between the World Wars.

"I suppose there's a part of me that resists taking the easy way," Talese told Charles McGrath. "As an old self-flagellating Catholic, I need to suffer, and something has to be hard to be worthy."

He continues to surprise readers even with his recent memoir, *A Writer's Life,* published in 2006. He apparently did not have a happy childhood. "Contrary to Italian-American stereotype," reviewer Kurt Andersen noted, "he remembers no jolly home-cooked meals.... He did poorly in school, and was rejected by every one of the 20-odd Northeastern colleges to which he applied."

Even with his reputation, Talese had to shop his article "Ali in Havana"—about the champ's visit to Fidel Castro, apparently a not-hot topic—to a dozen periodicals before *Esquire* published it in 1996. The essay ended up in *The Best American Essays 1997.*

Talese never takes his writing less than absolutely seriously. As he said in *The Writer,* "I don't do hatchet jobs. I've done a lot of pieces on a lot of people, and with all my years on the *New York Times* and *Esquire* and the books, no one ever refuses to see me after I write about them."

Works by the Author

New York: A Serendipiter's Journey (1961)

The Bridge: The Building of the Verrazano-Narrows Bridge (1964)

The Overreachers (1965)

The Kingdom and the Power: Behind the Scenes at the New York Times, The Institution That Influences the World (1969)

Fame and Obscurity (1970)

Honor Thy Father (1971)

Thy Neighbor's Wife (1980)

Unto the Sons (1992)

Writing Creative Nonfiction: The Literature of Reality, with Barbara Lounsberry (1995)

The Gay Talese Reader: Portraits and Encounters, with introduction by Barbara Lounsberry (2003)

A Writer's Life (2006)

Editor

The Best American Essays 1987, with Robert Atway (1987)

Contributor

The Best American Essays 1997 (1997)

For Further Information

Andersen, Kurt, "A Reporter's Reporter," *New York Times Book Review,* April 20, 2006.

Gay Talese Web site. http://www.gaytalese.com (viewed April 24, 2006).

Hirschman, David S., "So What Do You Do, Gay Talese?" MediaBistro Web site, April 27, 2004. http://www.mediabistro.com/articles/cache/a1498.asp (viewed May 29, 2006).

Kovach, Ronald, "A Writer & a Gentleman," *The Writer,* two parts, January and February, 2005.

Lewis, Irwin R., "An Interview with Gay Talese," University of Southern California College of Letters, Arts & Sciences. http://www.usc.edu/dept/LAS/mpw/faculty/talese.php (viewed April 24, 2006).

McGrath, Charles, "Gay Talese's New Memoir Emerges after 14 Tortured Years," *New York Times,* April 18, 2006.

Rattini, Kristin Baird, "The Goal," *Pages,* May-June 2006.

Schneider, Maria, "A Writer of Uncommon Character," *Writer's Digest,* August 2006.

Talese, Gay, "Frank Sinatra Has a Cold," *Esquire*, April 1966.

Deborah Tannen

Investigative Reporting

Benchmark Title: *You Just Don't Understand*

Brooklyn, New York

1945–

Deborah Tannen by farwellphotography.com

About the Author and the Author's Writing

Never a false word comes from Deborah Tannen. Language and linguistics, after all, are her specialty. Her book *You Just Don't Understand*, published in 1990, was on the *New York Times* bestseller list for nearly four years, and it has been popular in other nations from Brazil to Hong Kong, having been translated into twenty-nine languages.

You Just Don't Understand looks at how a man and a woman can leave a conversation with very different perspectives on what was just said or meant. To women, conversation is often a negotiation, she says. To men, it is often more like reporting on the status quo, an exchange of information. "Calling on her research into the workings of dialogue, Tannen examines the functioning of argument and interruption, and convincingly supports her case for the existence of 'genderlect,' " *Publishers Weekly* said in its review—in other words, a not insignificant communications gap.

Tannen, who has taken her message to such television programs as *Good Morning America* and *48 Hours* and has conversed with television talk-show hosts from Oprah Winfrey to Larry King, has stellar academic credentials. She is a university professor in the linguistics department at Georgetown University. In addition to twenty books, she has written one hundred scholarly articles. She is a member of the PEN/Faulkner Foundation Board.

Born in 1945 in Brooklyn, New York, she was the daughter of attorney Eli S. Tannen and his wife, Dorothy Rosen Tannen, an electrologist. She received a B.A. from the State University of New York at Binghamton in 1966, and an M.A. in English literature from Wayne State University in 1970. After receiving a second M.A., in linguistics, from the University of California at Berkeley in 1976, she earned her Ph.D. from the same school in 1979. In 1988, she married Michael Macovski, a college professor.

345

Before her present position at Georgetown, the author taught at several colleges including Detroit Institute of Technology. Her writing began with contributions to scholarly works edited by others. In 1983, she wrote a biography of Greek novelist Kilika Nakos; with *Conversational Style* (1984), she began writing for a general audience. *Conversational Style* offers readers tips on analyzing exactly what was said in an emblematic conversation over Thanksgiving dinner—and sows the seeds of her later books, such as *That's Not What I Meant. You Just Don't Understand,* which came out in 1990, narrows in on gender.

Looking specifically at the workplace, Tannen in *Talking from 9 to 5* identifies some of the differences between men and women in an office environment. Just one of the points she makes: "It's very common in a workplace setting that women—even women in positions of authority: managers, bosses—will tell subordinates what to do in a way that you could describe as indirect," the author told interviewer Tom Peters. She might, the author went on, say " 'You know what you might do?' or 'Could you do me a favor and type this?' " A male, on the other hand, is much more likely to give a direct command.

Tannen's *The Argument Culture* (1998) looks at a fondness, particularly in American media, to debate things ceaselessly. In this book, she suggests that "our spirits are corroded by living in an atmosphere of unrelenting contention." She upbraids the American legal system for pitting parties against each other, the stronger (and not necessarily the innocent) coming out the victor. "Tannen's obvious passion for helping people understand one another is well served here by her clear, direct writing," a *Publishers Weekly* reviewer said.

Tannen dates our desire to argue to Aristotle's time, "the idea that opposition is the best way to think about anything," she told interviewer David Gergen. "But it has certainly gotten worse, where we feel that only debate is acceptable as a form of discourse, that only war metaphors work; otherwise, everybody will be bored and go away."

The author makes a strong case for better dialogues with family members and particularly teenagers in *I Only Say This Because I Love You,* published in 2001.

Of course, Tannen herself can get away with little. She related in *Good Housekeeping* a recent greeting of her twenty-one-year-old daughter. " 'Hi, honey,' I said, giving her a hug as she walked through the door—to which she replied, 'Why aren't you happier to see me?' I thought to myself, How did she pick up on the fact that I'm distracted? What I also thought was, Can't I get away with anything?"

Works by the Author

Lilika Nakos (1983)

Conversational Style: Analyzing Talk among Friends (1984), revised (2005)

That's Not What I Meant: How Conversational Style Makes or Breaks Relationships (1986)

Talking Voices: Repetition, Dialogue, and Imagery in Conversational Discourse (1989)

You Just Don't Understand: Women and Men in Conversation (1990), reprinted as *You Just Don't Understand: Talk between the Sexes* (1991)

Gender and Discourse (1994)

Talking from 9 to 5: How Women's and Men's Conversational Styles Affect Who Gets Heard, Who Gets Credit, and What Gets Done at Work (1994)

The Argument Culture: Moving from Debate to Dialogue (1998), reprinted as *The Argument Culture: Stopping America's War of Words* (1999)

I Only Say This Because I Love You: How the Way We Talk Can Make or Break Family Relationships throughout Our Lives (2001), reprinted as *I Only Say This Because I Love You: Talking to Your Parents, Partner, Sibs, and Kids When You're All Adults* (2002)

Different Games, Different Rules: Why Americans and Japanese Misunderstand Each Other, with Haru Yamada (2002)

You're Wearing That? Understanding Mothers and Daughters in Conversation (2005)

Family Talk, with Shari Kendall and Cynthia Gordon (2007)

Editor

Analyzing Discourse: Text and Talk (1982)

Spoken and Written Language: Exploring Orality and Literacy (1982)

Coherence in Spoken and Written Discourse, with Muriel Saville-Troika(1984)

Language and Linguistics: The Interdependence of Theory (1986)

Linguistics in Context: Connecting Observation and Understanding (1988)

Gender and Conversational Interaction (1993)

Framing in Discourse (1993)

The Handbook of Discourse Analysis, with Deborah Schiffrin (2001)

Linguistics, Language, and the Real World: Discourse and Beyond, with James E. Alatis (2001)

Contributor

Individual Differences in Language Ability and Language Behavior, edited by Charles Filmore (1979)

New Directions in Discourse Processing, edited by Roy Freedle (1979)

The Pear Stories: Cognitive, Cultural, and Linguistic Aspects of Narrative Production, edited by Wallace Chazfe (1980)

Current Issues in Bilingualism, edited by James E. Alatis (1980)

Istoria tis Parthenias tis Despoinidas Tade, by Lilka Nakos (introduction) (1981)

Conversational Routine, edited by Florian Courlas (1981)

Linguistics and the Professions, edited by Robert Di Pietro (1982)

Linguistics and Literacy, edited by William Frawley (1982)

Language and Social Identity, edited by John Gumperz (1982)

The Social Organization of Doctor/Patient Communication, edited by Sue Fisher and Alexandra Dundas Todd (1983)

Literacy for Life: The Demand for Reading and Writing, edited by Richard W. Bailey and Robin Melanie Fosheim (1983)

Discovered Tongues: Poems by Linguists, edited by William Bright (1983)

Meliglossa, edited by Donna Jo Napoli and Emily Rando (1984)

Literacy, Language, and Learning: The Nature and Consequences of Reading and Writing, edited by David Olson, Nancy Torrance, and Angela Hildyard (1985)

Best American Short Plays 1993–1994 (1994)

For Further Information

Allen, Jennifer, "Why Can't We Just Get Along?," *Good Housekeeping,* March 2006.

"Argument Culture: Moving from Debate to Dialogue," *Publishers Weekly,* February 16, 1998.

Deborah Tannen entry, Contemporary Authors Online. Reproduced in Biography Resource Center. Farmington Hills, MI: Thomson Gale, 2007. http://galenet.galegroup.com/servlet/BioRC.

Deborah Tannen Web page. http://www9.georgetown.edu/faculty/tannend/bio.htm (viewed April 2, 2007).

Gergen, David, Deborah Tannen interview, *NewsHour* with Jim Lehrer. http://www.pbs.org/newshour/gergen/march98/tannen_3-27.html (viewed September 22, 2007).

Peters, Tom, Deborah Tannen interview, Tom Peters Management Consulting. http://www.tompeters.com/cool_friends/content.php?notes=005918.pho (viewed April 2, 2007).

Stuttaford, Genevieve, *You Just Don't Understand* review, *Publishers Weekly,* May 11, 1990.

Paul Theroux

Travel

Benchmark Title: *The Great Railway Bazaar*

Medford, Massachusetts

1941–

Photo by Greg Martin

About the Author and the Author's Writing

"In general, travel is awful," Paul Theroux said in a salon.com interview in 1999. "It's uncomfortable. It's tedious. It's repetitive. And in order to achieve the epiphanies of travel—the vistas, the experience—you have to go through an awful lot of hell and high water."

Theroux's legion of readers is a mixture of armchair travelers who are satisfied to let him experience the rigors of China or South Africa or the Mediterranean while they relax with the written report and adventurers who have not only sought out Theroux's destinations but found other exotic places—to the point there are few spots on the globe today without visitors. Algeria, the author points out, is certainly one exception.

Paul Theroux was born in Medford, Massachusetts, in 1941, one of nine children of salesman Albert E. Theroux and Anne Dittami Theroux. He attended the University of Maine for a year, then transferred to the University of Massachusetts, where he declared himself a pacifist and resisted joining the then-mandatory ROTC. During a Vietnam War protest, he was arrested. After earning a bachelor of arts degree in 1963, he began postgraduate study at Syracuse University, then joined the Peace Corps. Assigned to a school in Malawi, South Central Africa, he taught English. During this time, *The Christian Science Monitor* published his "Letter from Africa" (1964), *Central African Examiner* printed his first poem the same year, and he completed a novel, *Waldo,* which was published in 1967. His political articles criticized the regime in that country—and they drew the ire of the German secret service. As a result, he was deported from the country and thrown out of the Peace Corps.

A writing career beckoned the peripatetic Theroux. "Writing was in my mind from the time I was in high school," the author said in an interview with Dave Weich, "but more, the idea that I would be a doctor. I really wanted to be a medical doctor, and

I had various schemes: one was to be a psychiatrist, another was tropical medicine. I thought tropical medicine would be a way of getting me to another country."

Theroux quickly returned to Africa, however, and lectured in English at Makerere University in Kampala, Uganda. He and his first wife—he met and married Anne Castle at the school—left during civil unrest in the country. While at Makerere, Theroux became friends with author V. S. Naipaul. As Theroux later remembered in *Sunrise with Seamonsters* (1985), the relationship with the renowned author was a deep inspiration. "With me he was a generous, rational teacher." At Naipaul's encouraging, Theroux began *Fong and the Indians* (1968), the first of three novels set in Africa. He also wrote a critical overview of Naipaul's writing, *V. S. Naipaul: An Introduction to His Works*, published in 1972.

Theroux next taught at the University of Singapore, leaving in 1971 to become a full-time professional writer. He wrote popular and critically acclaimed fiction, often set in exotic locales, such as The *Mosquito Coast,* about a man who uproots from his middle-class drudgery in Massachusetts, taking his family to what he thinks of as a Honduran Eden, called Jeronimo. His wife and children think otherwise.

Theroux was equally popular with nonfiction, beginning with *The Great Railway Bazaar* in 1975. That book was based on journals the author kept during a four-month rail sojourn through Asia, the Far East and what was then the Soviet Union. Theroux insists that travel by rail, tire, or foot, and preferably crossing borders, is the only way to truly experience a country. *Washington Post Book World* reviewer David Roberts hailed the book as "travel writing at its very best—almost the best, one is tempted to say, that it can attain. Paul Theroux … here transforms what was clearly a long, ultimately tedious journey by train … into a singularly entertaining book."

As much as the places through which he travels, the author marvels at his transport —trains with such exotic names as the *Khyber Mail,* the *Mandalay Express,* and the *Trans-Siberian Express.* "The human contact is one of the most appealing aspects of the book," noted a TravelLiterature.org reviewer. "Where other travel writers indulge in historical or geographical detail, Theroux enthuses about his fellow passengers. Thus we meet Duffill, who is abandoned (without luggage) in Italy, we meet tycoons and drug addicts, we meet the U.S. military in Vietnam, and Chinese dentists in Sri Lanka."

The manner in which Theroux reports appeals to his readers. His prose is rich in detail, keen on irony. Critics have characterized Theroux as prickly or irascible. He responds that he's actually being ironic—and irony can at times be mistaken for dyspepsia or sarcasm. And so what if he is prickly? "Paul Theroux has produced some of the most wicked, funny, sad, bitter, readable, knowledgeable, rude, contemptuous, ruthless, arrogant, moving, brilliant and quotable books ever written," asserted John Coyne on the Peace Corps Writers Web site.

For *The Old Patagonian Express* (1979), he traveled the Americas, north and south. For *Riding the Iron Rooster* (1989), the writer spent an entire year exploring one country—China. He was off the rails, but in familiar territory, in *Dark Star Safari* (2003), looking at the ivory trade in Ethiopia and the land seizures in Zimbabwe. Two books collect his shorter travel writings: *Sunrise with Seamonsters* (1985) and *Fresh Air Fiend* (2000). Of the second book, the *Publishers Weekly* reviewer remarked, "A solitary experience that requires self-imposed exile, optimism and a fair amount of 'self-delusion,' travel is also as Theroux notes, 'almost entirely an inner experience.' "

Paul and Anne Theroux had two children together. The couple divorced in 1993. Theroux married Sheila Donnely in 1995. They live on Cape Cod and in Hawaii.

Travel—and Africa—will forever beckon Theroux. As he said on the Wanderlust Web site, "We live in a world where anyone can find you at anytime.… In Africa you find solitude, and can be inaccessible in an invasive world."

Perhaps seeking a locale even more remote, Theroux says on his Web site that his next book will be about the polar regions.

 ## Works by the Author

V. S. Naipaul: An Introduction to His Works (1972)
The Great Railway Bazaar: By Train through Asia (1975)
The Old Patagonian Express: By Train through the Americas (1979)
Sailing through China (1984), published in England as *Down the Yangtze* (1995)
The Kingdom by the Sea: A Journey around Great Britain (1985)
The Imperial Way: By Rail from Peshawar to Chittagong, with Steve McCurry (1985)
Sunrise with Seamonsters: Travels and Discoveries 1964–1984 (1985)
Patagonia Revisited, with Bruce Chatwin (1986)
Riding the Iron Rooster: By Train through China (1989)
To the Ends of the Earth: The Selected Travels of Paul Theroux (1990)
Traveling the World; The Illustrated Travels of Paul Theroux (1990)
The Happy Isles of Oceania: Paddling the Pacific (1992)
The Pillars of Hercules: A Grand Tour of the Mediterranean (1995)
Sir Vidia's Shadow: A Friendship across Five Continents (1998)
Fresh Air Fiend: Travel Writings, 1985–2000 (2000)
Nurse Wolf and Doctor Sacks (2001)
Dark Star Safari: Overland from Cairo to Cape Town (2003)
Vineyard Days, Vineyard Nights (2004)
The Cold World (2009), announced

Fiction

Waldo (1967)
Fong and the Indians (1968)
Girls at Play (1969)
Murder in Mount Holly (1969)
Jungle Lovers (1971)
Sinning with Annie and Other Stories (1972)
Saint Jack (1973)
The Black House (1974)
The Family Arsenal (1976)
The Consul's File (1977), short stories
Picture Palace (1979)
World's End and Other Stories (1980)

The Mosquito Coast (1982)

The London Embassy (1982), short stories

Doctor Slaughter (1984)

Half Moon Street; Two Short Novels (1984), includes *Doctor Slaughter* and *Doctor DeMarr*

O-Zone (1986)

My Secret History (1989)

Doctor DeMarr (1990), published in Great Britain

Chicago Loop (1991)

Millroy the Magician (1994)

My Other Life (1996)

On the Edge of the Great Rift: Three Novels of Africa (1996), includes *Fong and the Indians, Girls at Play,* and *Jungle Lovers*

Kowloon Tong (1997)

The Collected Stories (1997)

The Collected Short Novels (1999)

Hotel Honolulu (2001)

The Stranger at the Palazzo d'Oro and Other Stories (2004)

Blinding Light (2005)

Mother (2007)

The Elephanta Suite: Three Novellas (2007)

Drama

Saint Jack (screenplay), with Peter Bogdanovich and Howard Sackler (1979)

The White Man's Burden: A Play in Two Acts (1987)

For Juvenile Readers

A Christmas Card (1978)

London Snow: A Christmas Story (1979)

For Further Information

Coyne, John, "Talking with … Paul Theroux," Peace Corps Writers. http://www.peacecorpswriters.org/pages/2003/0303/303talkthero.html (viewed September 29, 2006).

Fresh Air Fiend review, *Publishers Weekly,* April 3, 2000.

Garner, Dwight, "Paul Theroux: His Secret Life," salon.com., 1999. http://www.salon.com/weekly/interview960902.html (viewed September 29, 2006).

Great Railway Bazaar review, Travel Literature Web site. http://www.travelliterature.org/reviews/bazaar.shtml (viewed October 23, 2006).

Keir, Graff, *Dark Star Safari* review, *Booklist,* February 1, 2003.

Paul (Edward) Theroux entry, Contemporary Authors Online. Reproduced in Biography Resource Center. Farmington Hills, MI: Thomson Gale, 2005. http://galenet.galegroup.com/servlet/BioRC.

Paul Theroux interview, Wanderlust Web site. http://wanderlust.co.uk/features/ feat55b.html (viewed September 29, 2006).

Roberts, David, *The Great Railway Bazaar* review, *Washington Post Book World,* September 7, 1975.

Weich, Dave, "The World According to Paul Theroux," Powells.com. http:// www.powells.com/authors/theroux.html (viewed September 23, 2007).

Hunter S. Thompson

Adventure, Investigative Reporting, Memoir, Sports

Benchmark Title: *Fear and Loathing in Las Vegas*

Louisville, Kentucky

1937–2005

About the Author and the Author's Writing

With a popular book added to his credentials—about his escapades with a deadly motorcycle gang—Hunter S. Thompson accepted a *Playboy* assignment to profile Jean-Claude Killy, the Olympic skier. He "turned in a lengthy piece in which he suggested that, 'on balance, it seems unfair to dismiss him as a witless greedhead, despite all the evidence'," according to Louis Menand in a *New Yorker* remembrance. *Playboy* dumped the story. It would take a few more tries in the alternative media (in low-circulation periodicals and underground publications) before Thompson found his pace, and his "gonzo journalism" was born. His story "The Kentucky Derby Is Decadent and Depraved," which ran in *Scanlan's Monthly* in 1970, is generally considered his first off-the-wall (i.e., "gonzo") piece.

Thompson had missed his deadline. He forwarded pages from his notebook to the printer so that the story could run. The article proved unusually popular with readers. "If I can write like this and get away with it," the author is quoted in the *New York Times* obituary, "why should I keep trying to write like *The New York Times*?" Thus, gonzo writing—some call it an offshoot of the New Journalism movement, others say it is just drug-induced, wacky, witless writing—is characterized by little or no editing, freeform interviews, exaggeration, subjectivity (the reporter is part of the story), and editorializing. As Thompson would say, why let facts get in the way, if the story is essentially the truth?

"You can't be objective when you're dealing with passionate situations, politics and so forth," Thompson explained in a *Freezerbox Magazine* interview. "For instance if you were objective about Richard Nixon, you would never get him or understand him. You had to be subjective to understand Nixon. You have to be subjective to understand the Hells Angels."

The writer found a relatively stable home for his work with *Rolling Stone* magazine, where many of his articles were illustrated by a Welshman named Ralph Steadman. In later years, Thompson wrote a sports column for ESPN.

Thompson was born in 1937 in Louisville, Kentucky, the son of insurance agent Jack Thompson and Virginia Ray Thompson. He graduated from high school, although he couldn't attend the ceremony because he was serving a six-week jail sentence following a robbery conviction. From 1956 to 1958, he served in the U.S. Air Force, assigned to Elgin Air Force Base in Florida, and he wrote sports stories for the base newspaper. Again a civilian, he began to write freelance articles, including one about the Hells Angels for the *Nation* in 1965 that led to a book contract. He studied journalism at Columbia University. He was twice married, to Sandra Dawn in 1963 and, after a divorce, to Anita Beymuk in 2003. He had one child.

Thompson made his mark with *Fear and Loathing in Las Vegas,* his account of the annual Mint 400 motorcycle race and the National District Attorneys Association's Convention on Narcotics and Dangerous Drugs in Las Vegas in 1971—experienced and probably written while under the influence of a range of narcotics. "We were somewhere around Barstow," he writes in the book, "on the edge of the desert when the drugs began to take hold. I remember saying something like 'I feel a bit light-headed; maybe you should drive….' And suddenly there was a terrible roar all around us and the sky was full of what looked like huge bats." Through the LSD haze emerged a clarity of vision that had enormous appeal to an establishment-weary readership. Thompson polished his in-your-face "truth"-telling in *Fear and Loathing on the Campaign Trail*, about the 1972 presidential race. "The people loved it, and Thompson rather quickly jetted to the lofty heights of cult figure status," Susan Campbell said in the *Hartford Courant.*

As he wrote more than a dozen books, some of which collected his magazine articles, Thompson grew into a new image. "He built a public persona as a drug-fueled risk-taker," Ed Andrieski wrote, "but friends and family say that masked the Kentucky-born writer's true nature—a Southern gentleman and meticulous craftsman who lived and wrote at Owl Farm [in Woody Creek, Colorado] from the late 1960s until his death."

Thompson's drug haze didn't make it easy for his editors. Robert Love, writing in *Columbia Journalism Review,* worked on a dozen Thompson pieces for three magazines. "Fact-checking Hunter Thompson was one of the sketchiest occupations ever created in the publishing world," he said. "For the first-timer, it was a trip through a journalistic fun house, where you didn't know what was real and what wasn't. You knew you had better learn enough about the subject at hand to know when the riff began and reality ended. Hunter was a stickler for numbers, for details like gross weight and model numbers, for lyrics and caliber, and there was no faking it."

Thompson eventually found himself an anachronism; his audience had matured. His rants were old-hat to a generation now more concerned about home values, college tuition and pensions. *Hey Rube* (2005), one of his last books, evidenced a return to his edgy humor and frequent insights in the world of professional sports. A typical essay is his suggestion for improving baseball: "Eliminate the Pitcher."

Thompson's frequent illustrator Ralph Steadman believes the author's work will endure. He told *The Boston Globe,* "He was a kind of Mark Twain as well. I think we'll look wistfully back on his work and say what a great time that was: People were still smoking and drinking; there was a freedom we'd all fought for in the '60s; we were on the road, fearlessly."

The gonzo writer committed suicide in early 2005. Among those attending a funeral for Thompson in August 2005, five months later, were actors Sean Penn and Johnny Depp, who helped fire his ashes from a cannon onto the grounds behind his home: one last act of protest.

The message on the refrigerator in Thompson's kitchen the day he died read, "Never call 911/Never/This means you/HST."

 Works by the Author

Hell's Angels: A Strange and Terrible Saga (1966)

Fear and Loathing in Las Vegas: A Savage Journey to the Heart of the American Dream (1972), reprinted as *Fear and Loathing in Las Vegas and Other American Stories* (1996)

Fear and Loathing on the Campaign Trail '72 (1973)

The Great Shark Hunt: Strange Tales from a Strange Time, Gonzo Papers, vol. 1 (1979)

The Curse of Lono (1983)

Generation of Swine: Tales of Shame and Degradation in the '80s, Gonzo Papers, vol. 2 (1988)

Songs of the Doomed: More Notes on the Death of the American Dream, Gonzo Papers, vol. 3 (1990)

Silk Road: Thirty-Three Years in the Passing Lane (1990)

Better Thank Sex: Confessions of a Political Junkie, Gonzo Papers, vol. 4 (1993)

The Proud Highway: The Saga of a Desperate Southern Gentleman, 1955–1967, edited by Douglas Brinkley (1997)

Fear and Loathing in America: Brutal Odyssey of an Outlaw Journalist, 1968–1976 (2000)

The Kingdom of Fear: Loathsome Secrets of a Star-Crossed Child in the Final Days of the American Century (2003)

Hey Rube: Blood Sport, the Bush Doctrine, and the Downward Spiral of Dumbness: Modern History from the Sports Desk (2004)

The Mutineer: Rants, Ravings, and Missives from the Mountaintop, 1977–2005 (2007)

Contributor

America, by Ralph Steadman (1989)

Gonzo: The Art, by Ralph Steadman (1998)

The Gospel According to ESPN: Saints, Saviors and Sinners, by Jay Lovinger (2002)

Fiction

The Rum Diary: The Long Lost Novel (1998)

Screwjack: A Short Story (2000)

Film Adaptations

Where the Buffalo Roam (1980)

Fear and Loathing in Las Vegas (1998)

The Rum Diary (announced)

For Further Information

Andrieski, Ed, "Hunter Thompson Widow Talks about Send-Off," *USA Today*, August 17, 2005.

Bulger, Adam, "The Hunter S. Thompson Interview," *Freezerbox*. http://www.freezerbox.com/archive/article.php?id=287 (viewed September 23, 2007).

Campbell, Susan, "The End of Gonzo: Thompson's Stories 'Least Accurate Yet Most Truthful'," *Hartford Courant*, February 22, 2005.

Higgins, Matt, "The Gonzo King: An Interview with Hunter S. Thompson," *High Times,* September 2, 2003. http://www.hightimes.com/ht/entertainment/content.php?bid=228&aid=2 (viewed September 29, 2006).

Hinckle, Robert, editor, "Who Killed Hunter Thompson? An Inquiry into the Life & Death of the Master of Gonzo." San Francisco: Last Gasp, 2007.

Hunter S(tockton) Thompson entry, Contemporary Authors Online. Reproduced in Biography Resource Center. Farmington Hills, MI: Thomson Gale, 2005. http://galenet.galegroup.com/servlet/BioRC.

Love, Robert, "A Technical Guide for Editing Gonzo; Hunter S. Thompson from the Other End of the Mojo Wire," *Columbia Journalism Review*, May-June 2005.

MacDonald, Jay, "Hunter S. Thompson: Surprised He's Still Here," Bankrate.com. http://www.bankrate.com/brm/news/investing/20041101a1.asp (viewed September 29, 2006).

Marin, Cheech, "The Doctor Is Still In: Hunter S. Thomson Joins the Ranks of the Classics," *Newsweek,* November 25, 1996.

Menand, Louis, "Believer," *New Yorker,* March 7, 2005.

Mundow, Anna, "Gonzo, but Not Forgotten," *Boston Globe,* November 5, 2006.

Seymour, Corey, *Gonzo: The Oral History of Hunter S. Thompson.* New York: Wenner Books, 2007.

Slackman, Michael, "Hunter S. Thompson, Outlaw Journalist, Is Dead at 67," *New York Times,* February 22, 2005.

Steadman, Ralph, *The Joke's Over: Bruised Memories: Gonzo, Hunter S. Thompson and Me.* New York: Harcourt, 2006.

Taylor, Michael, "Thompson's Career Was More than Just a Party; His Gonzo Legacy Began with Writing, Transcended Persona," *San Francisco Chronicle*, February 22, 2005.

Weingarten, Marc, *The Gang That Wouldn't Write Straight: Wolfe, Thompson, Didion, and the New Journalism Revolution.* New York: Crown, 2006.

Whitmer, Peter O., *When the Going Gets Weird: The Twisted Life and Times of Hunter S. Thompson: A Very Unauthorized Biography.* POW: 1999.

Woodward, Joe, "The End of the Story," *Poets & Writers,* May-June 2005.

Henry David Thoreau

Environment, Memoir, Travel

Benchmark Title: *Walden*

Concord, Massachusetts

1817–1862

Photo 1856 Maxham Daguerreotype (detail)
from *The Writings of Henry David Thoreau* (1906),
courtesy the Thoreau Institute at Walden Woods

About the Author and the Author's Writing

Grasping the 6 × 6 pine timbers, the students and staff volunteers at Berkshire School in Sheffield, Massachusetts, on a brisk autumn day in 2003, raised the frame wall upright, holding it stable as swift hands wedged bridging and braces into mortised holes. A whack of a mallet. A jiggle of a post. White oak pins driven into place. The skeleton of the small house stood proud by afternoon's end: a replica of Thoreau's house, a literary symbol, a refuge and tool for students at the preparatory school.

In spring 1845, Henry David Thoreau borrowed an ax and cut and hewed all the timbers and shaped their notches and tenons when he built his remote dwelling in Concord, Massachusetts. "At length, in the beginning of May, with the help of some of my acquaintances, rather to improve so good an occasion for neighborliness than from any necessity, I set up the frame of my house," he wrote in his 1854 memoir, *Walden*. "No man was ever more honored in the character of his raisers than I. They are destined, I trust, to assist at the raising of loftier structures one day."

Many a house has been modeled on Thoreau's, many a river excursion or mountain hike taken with his example in mind, many an essay and book written from his prototype. Consider some of the authors profiled in this book: Michael Pollen built a Thoreau-esque backyard study in Connecticut; John McPhee retraced Thoreau's voyage down the Concord River; and Beth Powning attempted self-sufficiency at a rural Canadian farmstead. Edward Abbey mused on Transcendentalism as he rafted down the Colorado River. Cornel West in his book *Democracy Matters* recalled Thoreau's sitting for a night in jail for refusing to pay a tax in support of the Mexican War.

All this is to say, Thoreau is one of America's most influential nonfiction writers. He was a keen observer of nature. He wrote joyously of his trips to Cape Cod or Quebec or to the top of Mount Katahdin. He became a character in his own books, such as *Walden*, a technique since adopted by a generation of creative nonfictionists. He was not afraid to take a political stand, as in his support for abolitionist John Brown. Modern-day writers aspire to his independence and spirit.

Henry David Thoreau, the son of pencil-maker John Thoreau and his wife, Cynthia, was born and died in Concord. He never married, although he was once in love with a young woman, Anna Sewell, who rejected his proposal of marriage.

"In height, he was about the average; in his build, spare, with limbs that were rather longer than usual, or of which he made a longer use," said his frequent hiking companion William Ellery Channing in his biography of the writer. "His face, once seen, could not be forgotten. The features were quite marked: the nose aquiline or very Roman, like one of the portraits of Caesar (more like a beak, it was said); large, overhanging brows above the deepest set blue eyes that could be seen, in certain lights, and in others gray,—eyes expressive of all shades of feeling, but never weak or near-sighted."

A graduate with Harvard's class of 1837, Thoreau briefly taught in public school, co-owned a private school with his brother John and taught there, and privately tutored students. But mostly he helped his father make pencils and, later, graphite. Ralph Waldo Emerson mentored Thoreau and in an 1862 eulogy wrote that his friend "declined to give up his large ambition of knowledge and action for any narrow craft or profession, aiming at a much more comprehensive calling, the art of living well."

Thoreau thrived in Concord's rich literary community. He planted a garden for newlyweds Nathaniel and Sophia Hawthorne. Young Louisa May Alcott was among the doting visitors to his pondside retreat, where he maintained three chairs, as he wrote: "one for solitude, two for friendship, three for society." He lectured, although was not acclaimed for his talents in public speaking, and was in demand as a land surveyor. "I had never thought of knowing a man so thoroughly of the country as this friend of mine, and so purely a son of Nature," Amos Bronson Alcott wrote of his friend in 1862. "Perhaps he has the profoundest passion for it of any one living; and had the human sentiment been as tender from the first, and as pervading, we might have had pastorals of which Virgil and Theocritus would have envied him the authorship, had they chanced to be his contemporaries."

Only two of his books came out during Thoreau's lifetime, *A Week on the Concord and Merrimack Rivers,* in 1849, and *Walden,* five years later; neither was a bestseller. Thoreau crafted both books from his decades-long journal during a quasi-solitary sojourn to a cabin he built near Walden Pond, on land owned by Emerson. An abolitionist, he was among the few to hail John Brown's raid on Harper's Ferry: "I see now that it was necessary that the bravest and humanest man in all the country should be hung," he told those who came to hear him speak in October 1859. He refused to pay a poll tax because he believed the money would support a war with Mexico. His essay "Civil Disobedience"—in which he wrote "Under a government which imprisons any unjustly, the true place for a just man is also a prison"—inspired Mahatma Gandhi and Dr. Martin Luther King Jr. An inveterate observer, he was among the first to write of the forest's natural succession. He opposed materialism, urging simplicity.

"Mr. Thoreau dined with us yesterday," Hawthorne wrote in his notebook for September 1, 1842. "He is a singular character—a young man with much of wild original nature still remaining in him; and so far as he is sophisticated, it is in a way and method of his own."

Thoreau is often quoted, and justly so. Here's a favorite: "Many go fishing all their lives without knowing that it is not fish they are after."

Works by the Author

A Week on the Concord and Merrimack Rivers (1849)

Walden; or, Life in the Woods (1854)

Excursions, edited by Sophia Thoreau and Ellery Channing (1864)

The Maine Woods, edited by Sophia Thoreau and Ellery Channing (1864)

Cape Cod, edited by Sophia Thoreau and Ellery Channing (1865)

Letters to Various Persons, edited by Ralph Waldo Emerson (1865)

A Yankee in Canada, with Anti-Slavery and Reform Papers (1866), revised as *Anti-Slavery and Reform Papers,* edited by H. S. Salt (1890); revised and enlarged as *Essays and Other Writings of Henry David Thoreau,* edited by Will H. Dircks (1891)

Early Spring in Massachusetts: From the Journal of Henry D. Thoreau, edited by H. G. O. Blake (1881)

Summer: From the Journal of Henry D. Thoreau, edited by H.G.O. Blake (1884)

Winter: From the Journal of Henry D. Thoreau, edited by H.G.O. Blake (1888)

Autumn: From the Journal of Henry D. Thoreau, edited by H.G.O. Blake (1892)

Familiar Letters of Henry David Thoreau, edited by F. B. Sanborn (1894)

Miscellanies, edited by Horace E. Scudder (1894)

Some Unpublished Letters of Henry D. and Sophia E. Thoreau, edited by Samuel Arthur Jones (1899)

Life without Principle (1902)

On the Duty of Civil Disobedience (1903)

Journal, 14 volumes, edited by Bradford Torrey (1906)

The Writings of Henry David Thoreau, 20 volumes, edited by Bradford Torrey and Francis H. Allen (1906)

The Heart of Thoreau's Journals, edited by Odell Shepard (1927)

A Pig Tale (1947)

Consciousness in Concord: The Text of Thoreau's Hitherto Lost Journal (1840–1841), edited by Perry Miller (1958)

The Correspondence of Henry David Thoreau, edited by Walter Harding and Carl Bode (1958)

Thoreau's Minnesota Journey: Two Documents, edited by Walter Harding (1962)

The Thoughts of Thoreau, edited by Edwin Way Teale (1962)

Transcendental Climate (1963), includes "Thoreau's Reading on Canada" and "Field Notes of Surveys Made by Henry D. Thoreau since November 1849"

Thoreau's Literary Notebook 1840–1848, edited by Kenneth Walter Cameron (1964)

Over Thoreau's Desk: New Correspondence (1965)

The Writings of Henry D. Thoreau (including *Journal*), various editors (since 1971)

The Literary Manuscripts of Henry David Thoreau, edited by William L. Howarth (1974)

Faith in a Seed: The Dispersion of Seeds and Other Late Natural History Writings, edited by Bradley P. Dean (1993)

Wild Fruits: Thoreau's Rediscovered Last Manuscript, edited by Bradley P. Dean (1999)

Letters to a Spiritual Seeker, edited by Bradley P. Dean (2004)

Poetry

Poems of Nature, edited by H. S. Salt and Frank B. Sanborn (1895)

Collected Poems of Henry Thoreau, edited by Carl Bode (1943), enlarged edition (1964)

For Further Information

Alcott, Amos Bronson, "The Forester," *Atlantic Monthly,* April 1862.

Barksdale, Maynard W., "Thoreau's House at Walden, "*Art Bulletin,* June 1999.

Borst, Raymond R., *The Thoreau Log: A Documentary Life of Henry David Thoreau 1817–1862.* New York: G.K. Hall, 1992.

Canby, Henry Seidel, *Thoreau.* Boston: Beacon Pres, 1939.

Channing, William Ellery, *Thoreau the Poet-Naturalist with Memorial Verses, New Edition, Enlarged,* edited by F. B. Sanborn. Boston: Charles E. Goodspeed, 1902.

Drew, Bernard A., "Thoreau's Tarn Identified: Gilder Pond," *The Concord Saunterer, New Series,* Vol. 9, 2001.

Ebbert, Stephanie, "Milestone for Walden Woods," *Boston Globe,* May 15, 2006.

Emerson, Ralph Waldo, "Eulogy for Henry David Thoreau," *Atlantic Monthly,* August 1862.

Hamlin, Suzanne, "After 150 Years, 'Walden' Is Still Yielding Secrets," *New York Times,* July 5, 1995.

Harding, Walter, *The Days of Henry Thoreau: A Biography.* Princeton, NJ: Princeton University Press, 1982.

Hawthorne, Sophia, editor. *American Notebooks,* by Nathaniel Hawthorne. Boston: Houghton, Mifflin, 1883.

Henry David Thoreau entry, *Authors and Artists for Young Adults,* Vol. 42. Detroit, MI: Gale, 2002.

Johnson, Linck C., *Thoreau's Complex Weave: The Writing of "A Week on the Concord and Merrimack Rivers."* Charlottesville, VA: Bibliographical Society of the University of Virginia/University of Virginia Press, 1986.

Maynard, W. Barksdale, *Walden Pond.* New York: Oxford University Press, 2004.

McPhee, John, "1839/2003," *New Yorker,* December 15, 2003.

Richardson, Robert D. Jr., *Henry Thoreau: A Life of the Mind.* Berkeley: University of California Press, 1986.

Richardson, Robert D., "Walden's Ripple Effect; One Hundred Fifty Years after Its Publication, Henry David Thoreau's Meditation Remains the Ultimate Self-Help Book," *Smithsonian,* August 2004.

Sanborn, F. B., *Henry D. Thoreau.* Boston: Houghton, Mifflin, 1882.

Sattelmeyer, Robert. *Thoreau's Reading: A Study in Intellectual History with Bibliographical Catalogue.* Princeton, NJ: Princeton University Press, 1988.

Schreiner, Samuel A. Jr., *The Concord Quartet: Alcott, Emerson, Hawthorne, Thoreau, and the Friendship That Freed the American Mind.* New York: John Wiley & Sons, 2006.

Shanley, J. Lyndon, *The Making of "Walden" with the Text of the First Version.* Chicago: University of Chicago Press, 1957.

Sims, David, "Building to a Different Drummer," *Smithsonian,* April 2002.

Thoreau Institute Web site. http://www.walden.org/institute (viewed November 13, 2006).

Calvin Trillin

Food, Investigative Reporting, Memoir, Travel

Benchmark Title: *American Fried*

Kansas City, Missouri

1935–

Photo by Josi Jowell

About the Author and the Author's Writing

> *My capacity to take in the splendors visible from the car was hampered, of course, by the concentration required to defend half of the backseat from Sukey's incursions, the imaginary line down the seat having created a situation that I later compared to the border tension between Finland and the Soviet Union. In this comparison I thought of myself as Finland....*
>
> —*Messages from My Father*

Calvin Trillin is known for his humorous take on everything from food (he once said health food made him ill) to the state of Nebraska to the American presidency.

Food and politics, maybe. But Nebraska? "Trillin knows where all the old chicken a la king has gone: stored in silos in Kansas right next to the ones filled with old Nehru jackets," we learn on the Calvin Trillin Web page at Chelsea Forum, which continues with, "He personally has revised the mottoes that appear on state automobile license plates: Nebraska, for example, is 'a long way across,' and Arkansas on his first try was a little verbose: 'Not as Bad as You Might Imagine'."

Trillin knows Kansas because he's from that part of the country. His father, Abe Trillin, ran a grocery in Kansas City, collected Yiddish curses and yellow neckties —and provided a rich character for the author's popular memoir, *Messages from My Father*.

Calvin Trillin was born in 1935 and, fulfilling his dad's long-held dream, graduated from Yale University with a bachelor of arts degree in 1957. After that, he served in the U.S. Army. He married English teacher Alice Stewart, and they raised two daughters. From 1960 to 1963, he wrote for *Time* magazine (mostly about medicine and religion)—which became the basis of a later comic novel called *Floater* (1980). It tells the story of a reporter who moves from one department to another, week to week.

Trillin in 1963 settled in with the *New Yorker*, where he wrote essays as a peripatetic cross-country traveler for a decade and a half. Trillin said he came to enjoy a three-week rotation: one week to research a story, another week to write it, a third week to think about a new topic—and compose an essay for the *Nation*. The author also wrote a syndicated column ("Uncivil Liberties") for King Features and rejoined *Time* as a columnist in 1996.

Trillin thrives on a diversity of subjects. "The other way of looking at it," he told interviewer Dave Weich, "is that I've never gotten my act together and decided what I want to concentrate on. Maybe I have a short attention span."

He began writing poetry by accident, taken by the name of a particular New Hampshire senator to scratch out a poem "If You Knew What Sununu in 1990." Three collections of his verses with political twists have been published.

He continued to write fiction from time to time. His 2002 novel *Tepper Isn't Going Out* is about an everyman's assault on the establishment; mailing-list broker Murray Tepper becomes a folk hero when he stuffs blanks in a parking meter and sits in his car all day, reading a newspaper, protesting the difficulty of finding a parking space in New York.

His memoir *Remembering Denny* (1993), about a university friend who took his own life, nudged Trillin onto the best-seller list. Trillin continued to collect his essays (*Enough Is Enough* includes seventy-seven "Uncivil Liberties" pieces on topics ranging from computer spell checkers to telephone solicitations). And his food essays took on a life of their own, delightful jaunts on the far side, revealing unexpected facts of the trade. "To Kenny's way of thinking a complimentary mention is worse than a knock," he wrote in the *New Yorker* of Kenny Shopsin, co-owner of the thirty-four-seat Greenwich Village café, Shopsin's General Store. "It brings review-trotters—the sort of people who go to a restaurant because somebody told them to. Kenny finds that review-trotters are often 'petulent and demanding."

Of course, Shopsin's is only a couple of blocks from Trillin's home. How does he find a good restaurant when traveling? "Eat only ethnic food if the local ethnic group is populous enough to have at least two aldermen.' "

Trillin once, in a salon.com interview, likened his self-mocking style to "the sort of deflating humor of the Eastern European shtetl … the same as Midwestern humor. Midwesterners are always knocking down the big shot and talking about people who got too big for their britches."

That's not the only asset of growing up Jewish in the Midwest. "It's the Kansas City kid in me that can write with passion and knowledge about Barbecue and Bubb's Daddy. But endless hours in Chinatown made me the writer I am today. For instance, I pitched a tent on Mott Street for a week just to find the right kind of dumpling for a write-up in the *New Yorker*," he said in an interview with Diane Grove.

In 2006, Trillin finally wrote *About Alice,* about his frequent travel companion, his wife, Alice, whom, he reveals, had "a weird predilection for limiting our family to three meals a day" and insisted on attending each child's grammar school play, lest "the country would come and take the child" but who ultimately "managed to navigate the tricky waters between living a life you could be proud of and still delighting in the many things there are to take pleasure in."

In other words, it's a love story.

Works by the Author

An Education in Georgia: Charlayne Hunter, Hamilton Holmes, and the Integration of the University of Georgia (1964)

U.S. Journal (1971)

American Fried: Adventures of a Happy Eater (1974)

Alice, Let's Eat: Further Adventures of a Happy Eater (1978)

Uncivil Liberties (1982)

Third Helpings (1983)

Killings (1984)

With All Disprespect: More Uncivil Liberties (1985)

If You Can't Say Something Nice (1987)

Travels with Alice (1989)

Enough's Enough (and Other Rules of Life) (1990)

Remembering Denny (1993)

The Tummy Trilogy (1994), includes *American Fried, Let's Eat*, and *Third Helpings*

Deadline Poet; or, My Life as a Doggerelist (1994)

Messages from My Father (1996)

Family Man (1998)

Feeding a Yen: Savoring Local Specialties, from Kansas City to Cuzco (2003)

Obliviously On He Sails: The Bush Administration in Rhyme (2004)

A Heckuva Job: More of the Bush Administration in Rhyme (2006)

About Alice (2006)

Fiction

Barnett Frummer Is an Unbloomed Flower and Other Adventures of Barnett Frummer, Rosalie Mondie, Roland Magruder, and Their Friends (1969)

Runestruck (1977)

Floater (1980)

American Stories (1991)

Tepper Isn't Going Out: A Novel (2002)

Stage Adaptations

Calvin Trillin's Uncle Sam (1988)

Calvin Trillin's Words, No Music (1990)

For Further Information

Calvin Trillin biography, the *Nation.* http://www.thenation.com/directory/bios/calvin_trillin (viewed October 10, 2006).

Calvin Trillin entry, Contemporary Authors Online. Reproduced in Biography Resource Center. Farmington Hills, MI: Thomson Gale, 2006. http://galenet.galegroup.com/servlet/BioRC.

Calvin Trillin page, Chelsea Forum. http://www.chelseaforum.com/speakers/Trillin.htm (viewed October 27, 2006).

Grove, Diana, "An Interview with American Humorist, Calvin Trillin," *Opium Magazine,* June 13, 2005. http://www.opiummagazine.com/entry.asp?PageID=119 (viewed October 10, 2006).

Knoblauch, Mark, *Feeding a Yen* review, *Booklist,* March 15, 2003.

Messages from My Father review, *Publishers Weekly,* March 25, 1996.

Miller, Laura, "Calvin Trillin: The Food Writer and Humorist Gets Serious about Fathers and Sons," salon.com. http://www.salon.com/weekly/interview960624.html (viewed October 10, 2006).

Popkin, James, "On the Road with Calvin and Alice," *U.S. News & World Report,* January 22, 1990.

Trillin, Calvin, "Annals of Gastronomy: Don't Mention It—The Hidden Life and Times of a Greenwich Village Restaurant," the *New Yorker,* April 15, 2002.

Weich, Dave, "Calvin Trilliln Is Going Out—to Eat (Again)," Powells.com. http://www.powells.com/authors/trlilin.html (viewed October 10, 2006).

Barbara Tuchman

Biography, History

Benchmark Title: *The Guns of August*

New York, New York

1912–1989

About the Author and the Author's Writing

In 1963, two-time Pulitzer Prize winner Barbara Tuchman told an audience at Radcliffe College that she was fascinated with history ever since as a child she read Lucy Fitch Perkins' children's series—adventures of American Twins during the 1770s or Belgian Twins in the years before World War I. She also read G. A. Henry's tales of Wolfe in Canada and Alexandre Dumas's romances of intrigue in French palaces.

Tuchman's real world complemented her imaginary one. Born Barbara Wertheim in 1912, the daughter of Maurice Wertheim and Alma Morgenthau Wertheim, she grew up in New York City. Her father was a banker, publisher, founder of the Theatre Guild, and president of the American Jewish Committee. Her grandfather, Henry Morgenthau Sr., was ambassador to Turkey in Woodrow Wilson's administration, and her uncle, Henry Morgenthau Jr., was secretary of the treasury for President Franklin D. Roosevelt. Through her family, she was exposed to politics and public affairs at a young age.

She majored at Radcliffe in history and literature, earning a bachelor of arts in 1933. Her honors thesis was titled "The Moral Justification for the British Empire." She became a research assistant at the Institute of Pacific Relations. She became an editorial assistant at the *Nation* and went to Madrid to cover the war in Spain; she then became a staff writer for a Spanish government publication issued from London. She continued writing for *New Statesman* and *Nation* for another year, then returned to New York. Her first book, *The Lost British Policy* (1938), described what she saw as the end of liberalism with the defeat of the Loyalists in the Spanish Civil War.

She married internist Lester R. Tuchman in 1940, and they raised three daughters. From 1943 to 1945, she worked for the Office of War Information while he was overseas.

Tuchman became a highly respected historian and one of the few of her gender working in the field. Her key books remain in print, two decades after her death.

In 1948, she began to compile *Bible and Sword,* an ambitious examination of the relationship between England and Israel which was published in 1956. Her next book, *The Zimmerman Telegram* (1958), took a detailed look at the circumstances surrounding the intercepted German message that prodded America to enter the First World War.

From the start, Tuchman was determined to be a popular—rather than academic—historian. Her work had to tell a story, to draw in readers. She became known for a strong storytelling style and lucid writing supported by solid research, fact building on fact to establish patterns. "One of the difficulties in writing history is the problem of how to keep up suspense in a narrative whose outcome is known," she admitted in an essay in her 1981 collection, *Practicing History*. "I found that if one writes as of the time, without using the benefit of hindsight, resisting always the temptation to refer to events still ahead, the suspense will build itself up naturally."

Research and handling of huge amounts of material were Tuchman's strengths. Whenever possible, she visited sites she was writing about. "Prior to writing *The Guns of August,* she went to Europe for an on-the-spot survey of the areas where the early land battles of World War I had taken place," commented Seymour Brody in a biographical essay. "She followed the routes that the German armies had taken through Luxembourg, Belgium, and northern France in their attempt to reach Paris. She tried to personally familiarize herself with the history that she was writing."

The Guns of August, published in 1962, examined the intrigue that led to World War I and brought Tuchman her first Pulitzer Prize. Discussing the historian's craft in an essay for *Harper's* in 1965, the author wrote, "It is more rewarding … to assemble the facts first and, in the process of arranging them in narrative form, to discover a theory or a historical generalization emerging of its own accord."

Stepping back from the world of politics, Tuchman examined the social forces during the same time period in *The Proud Tower* (1966). Her next book, *Stilwell and the American Experience in China,* published in 1971, focused on the career of one American military leader, General Joseph "Vinegar Joe" Stilwell, as reflected against China's evolution from a feudal kingdom to a Communist regime. It, too, won the author a Pulitzer Prize.

Tuchman mustered her impressions of war in *The March of Folly* (1984), an examination of four conflicts, the latest the Vietnam War. Among her conclusions: humans do not excel in governing. "In this sphere, wisdom, which may be defended as the exercise of judgment acting on experience, common sense and available information, is less operative and more frustrated than it should be," she wrote. "Why does intelligent mental process seem so often not to function?"

In one of her last works, *The First Salute* (1988), the author examined the American Revolution in the context of the generations-long conflict between England and France. Barbara Tuchman died in Greenwich, Connecticut, in 1989, of complications from a stroke.

Works by the Author

The Lost British Policy: Britain and Spain Since 1700 (1938)
Bible and Sword: England and Palestine from the Bronze Age to Balfour (1956)
The Zimmermann Telegram (1958/revised 1966)
The Guns of August (1962), published in England as *August 1914* (1962)
The Proud Tower: A Portrait of the World before the War, 1890–1914 (1966)

Stilwell and the American Experience in China, 1911–1945 (1971), in England as *Sand against the Wind: Stilwell and the American Experience in China, 1911–1945* (1971)

Notes from China (1972)

A Distant Mirror: The Calamitous 14th Century (1978)

Practicing History: Selected Essays (1981)

The March of Folly: From Troy to Vietnam (1984)

Tuchman Set of Three (1984), includes *Guns of August, Proud Tower,* and *March of Folly*

The First Salute: A View of the American Revolution (1988)

The Book: A Lecture Sponsored by the Center for the Book in the Library of Congress and the Authors League of America, Presented at the Library of Congress, October 17, 1979 (1988)

For Further Information

Barbara Tuchman entry, Books and Writers. http://www.kirjasto.sci.fi/tuchman.htm (viewed October 10, 2006).

Barbara Tuchman entry, *Encyclopedia of World Biography.* Detroit, MI: Thompson-Gale, 1998.

Barbara Tuchman entry, Everything2.com. http://www.everything2.com/index.pl?node_id=1115176 (viewed September 24, 2007).

Barbara W(ertheim) Tuchman entry, Contemporary Authors Online. Reproduced in Biography Resource Center. Farmington Hills, MI: Thomson Gale, 2004. http://galenet.galegroup.com/servlet/BioRC.

Brody, Seymour "Sy," Barbara Wertheim Tuchman entry, Jewish Virtual Library. http://www.jewishvirtuallibrary.org/jsource/biography/tuchman.html (viewed October 10, 2006).

Kidder, Rushworth M., "How Good People Make Tough Choices: Resolving the Dilemmas of Ethical Living." http://mgv.mim.edu.my/books/bookpref/12127.htm (viewed September 24, 2007).

Seaman, Donna, *Stilwell and the American Experience in China* review, *Booklist,* March 1, 2002.

Tuchman, Barbara, "History by the Ounce," *Harper's,* July 1965.

Sarah Vowell

History, Investigative Reporting, Memoir

Benchmark Title: *Assassination Vacation*

Muskogee, Oklahoma

1969–

About the Author and the Author's Writing

"There's something educational about trying to see the good in things, holding some old picture in your hands and telling another person why it's significant and excellent, special," Sarah Vowell writes in one of her essays in *The Partly Cloudy Patriot*. The sentence sums up her writing—both on page and over radio—if you add in her natural sense of humor and penchant for taking the road less traveled.

Of Cherokee ancestry, Sarah Vowell was born in Muskogee, Oklahoma, in 1969 and grew up in rural Oklahoma, where she says female role models were a rarity, at least those with careers. "Other than my first-grade teacher, every woman of my small-town acquaintance was a housewife or a widowed housewife," she wrote in a *Time* essay in 2000. So she latched onto television's "Charlie's Angels"—women with real jobs and real purpose. After working at her college radio station and spending a college semester in the Netherlands, then graduating with a B.A. from Montana State University in 1993, she earned an M.A. from the School of the Art Institute in Chicago. She also taught there for a time. She became a contributing editor to *This American Life* on National Public Radio. She has written for *Esquire, McSweeney's, The Village Voice,* salon.com, *Spin,* and the *Los Angeles Times*.

One of her first productions for the Ira Glass–hosted radio show *This American Life* was about the Trail of Tears—and it got a startlingly strong response from people who wanted to hear more about the past. She found a real thirst for richer history than many received in social studies class.

History figures in a lot of Vowell's writing for that and another reason. "When my [twin] sister and I were children," she told interviewer Robert Birnbaum, "we were constantly being dragged around to Civil War battlegrounds. And mainly western history sites, things having to do with Buffalo Bill or, 'Okay kids, pile in the car, we're going to see Sequoia's cabin.' So there are lots of photos of my sister and me perched on top of cannons and things like that."

Vowell went past her production role and onto an on-air role in radio; the dual role of writer and performer had an impact on her essay writing. She reads aloud everything that she writes, listening to the rhythm. On the other hand, writing for print means she needs to compose less conversational prose—to use complete sentences.

Ultimately, she told interviewer Birnbaum, she prefers print because the writer can present more information in that medium.

Vowell's first book is about the current condition of radio, AM and FM, concentrating on the Chicago area. She yawns at Garrison Keillor and thinks Rush Limbaugh is over the top. "If you worship at the altar of the media god Alternative and take radio really, really seriously," *Booklist*'s Mike Tribby wrote, noting the author's disdain for the mainstream, "Vowell's rant is just the thing. If you don't, it is still stimulating."

Take the Cannoli, published in 2000, collects a variety of pieces, some originally written for radio. *Library Journal*'s reviewer said it "explains her journey from natural-born liberal to understanding the differences between herself and her conservative family." It includes the story of the trip she and her sister Amy made, following the Trail of Tears in search of their Native American heritage.

Her next book, *The Partly Cloudy Patriot* (2003), "mines history and current events for insights into American life," reviewer Antoinette Brinkman said, noting the author's "Gen-X frame." Topics range from arcade games to post–September 11 patriotism. "Interspersed are musings on presidential libraries, U.S./Canadian differences, and being a twin, as well as a history buff's view of why the field is significant."

Vowell reached her stride with her 2005 release *Assassination Vacation,* an examination both riotous and reassuring, to sites associated with three presidential assassinations. An amazing link to the killings of Lincoln, Garfield, and McKinley, she found, was Robert Todd Lincoln, "a.k.a. Jinxy McDeath," who was on the scene all three times. "There are family anecdotes and real scholarship in this quirky road trip," commented *School Library Journal*'s reviewer.

The author shows skill in finding unusual angles and in researching them thoroughly. She "can from time to time turn a phrase (the McKinley National Monument in Ohio looks like 'a gray granite nipple on a fresh green breast of grass') and has a nice sense of humor both about herself and the scenes she encounters," Jamie Malanowski wrote in *Washington Monthly*.

Indeed, her description of her uncomfortable stay at a bed-and-breakfast in the Massachusetts Berkshires while making a visit to the home and studio of Lincoln sculptor Daniel Chester French is priceless. At breakfast with a middle-aged Englishman and an older couple from Greenwich, Connecticut, she describes the scene in which she can think of nothing to say. "Seated at the head of the table, I am the black hole of breakfast, a silent void of gloom sucking the sunshine out of their neighborly New England day."

Vowell is confident in her writing. In an interview with Dave Weich of Powells.com, she describes being on a panel at the Sydney Writer's Festival. "A very scholarly, upstanding, Australian writer was beating up this poor German guy who had written a fictionalization of the Holocaust," she said. "I remember she said, 'We must avoid easy entertainments.' And I was just sitting there thinking, *Lady, entertaining is hard*. Anybody can bore something up, but making some of this stuff entertaining is the hardest thing there is."

Works by the Author

Radio On: A Listener's Diary (1997)
Take the Cannoli: Stories from the New World (2000)
The Partly Cloudy Patriot (2003)
Assassination Vacation (2005)

Contributor

McSweeney's Quarterly Concern No. 1 (1998), edited by David Foster Wallace
Family Ties: A Contemporary Perspective, compiled by Peabody Essex Museum (2005)

Audio Recording

This American Life: Lies, Sissies and Fiascos (1999), with Dishwasher Pete, Scott Carier, Ira Glass, Jack Hitt, David Sedaris, and Sandra Tsing Loh

For Further Information

Birnbaum, Robert, Sarah Vowell interview, *Identity Theory.* http://www. identitytheory.com/people/birnbaum66.html (viewed October 10, 2006).

Brinkman, Antoinette, *Partly Cloudy Patriot* review, *Library Journal,* August 2002.

Kingsbury, Pam, *Take the Cannoli* review, *Library Journal,* March 1, 2000.

Malanowski, Jamie, "What a Way to Go: Sarah Vowell's Morbidly Funny Tour of Presidential Assassination Sites," *Washington Monthly*, April 2005.

"Sarah Vowell: Death Takes a Holiday," NPR. http://www.npr.org/templates/ story/story.php?storyId=4646283 (viewed September 24, 2007).

Sarah Vowell entry, Contemporary Authors Online. Reproduced in Biography Resource Center. Farmington Hills, MI: Thomson Gale, 2005. http:// galenet.galegroup.com/servlet/BioRC.

Tribby, Mike, *Radio On* review, *Booklist,* December 1, 1996.

Vowell, Sarah, "Those Liberated Angels: How Farrah and Her Friends Made Me a Feminist," *Time,* November 6, 2000.

Weich, Dave, "The Incredible, Entertaining Sarah Vowell," Powells.com. http://www.powells.com/authors/vowell.html (viewed October 10, 2006).

Woodcock, Susan H., *Assassination Vacation* review, *School Library Journal*, November 2005.

Andrew Weil

Health, Investigative Reporting

Benchmark Title: *Spontaneous Healing*

Philadelphia, Pennsylvania

1942–

About the Author and the Author's Writing

What do people think of when they hear the name Andrew Weil? Holistic healing or alternative medicine? Healthy aging or anti-inflammatory diet? All of these terms describe the well-known doctor.

Dr. Andrew Weil is a proponent of taking control of personal health issues. Some call him a guru; he prefers the term "godfather." He sees himself as a dispenser of vital information.

Born in Philadelphia in 1942, he was the son of merchant Daniel P. Weil and clothing designer Jenny Silverstein Weil. In 1964, he received his undergraduate degree from Harvard University. Weil then entered medical school, and in his last year at Harvard he published a study of marijuana use—among its conclusions, that novice users did not necessarily get intoxicated—nearly jeopardizing his graduation. Weil did receive his M.D. in 1968—and he went on to become one of the university's best-known physician graduates.

From 1969 to 1970, he served with the U.S. Public Health Service. He has one child from his marriage to Sabine Charlotte Kremp (they are now divorced). He is a gardener, cook, and wilderness explorer by avocation.

Weil began his career as a research associate (he studied the medicinal value of plants) at the Botanical Museum of Harvard University. Since 1976, he has specialized in holistic medicine in private practice in Tucson, Arizona. In addition, he has lectured in medicine at the University of Arizona's College of Medicine and established and directs its Program in Integrative Medicine. He has also served as a fellow with the Institute of Current World Affairs in New York.

I was always interested in things biological," the physician said in an interview on David Redwood's Web site. "I became very disillusioned with the kind of medicine that I was being taught, so when I finished my basic clinical training, I really dropped out of that world, and found ways to travel around. I was mostly living as a writer, and observing other kinds of healing practices. It was only after some time that very gradually I was drawn into practicing."

Weil has a string of best-selling books, including *Natural Healing Power* and *Healthy Aging,* as well as spoken-word and musical recordings, newsletters, and a

Web site. He has achieved great celebrity, as Sanjay Gupta wrote in *Time,* with his recipe of sound traditional medicine, herbal remedies, and changes in lifestyle. "If you have an inflamed appendix, he advises, go see a surgeon; black cohosh won't work. But if you want to fight your acne with diet or get the real skinny on vitamin E, a quick trip to drweilselfhealing.com will get you what you need."

Weil's early writings were about consciousness and attempts by men and women to alter their minds. He soon moved on to look at aspects of healing and of healthy eating—aspects of an overall approach he calls integrative medicine.

About healing, Weil in *Spontaneous Healing* (1995) looks to Eastern medicine for thoughts on strengthening the body to deal on its own with ailments, as opposed to the Western approach of treating symptoms. "At every level of biological organization, from DNA up, the mechanics of self-diagnosis, self-repair and regeneration exist in us," he writes.

"Health is a state of balance," Weil told Anna B. Alexander of *Prevention* magazine. "It is the balance between the body's healing system and whatever outside stresses we come across. On a day-to-day basis, optimum health is that inner resilience that allows you to come into contact with millions of germs every day and not get an infection or to be exposed to carcinogens and not get cancer."

About eating, Weil in *The Healthy Kitchen,* a cookbook published in 2002, treats the habit of eating three-times-a-day as not necessarily a pleasurable activity, just a necessary one. "According to Weil, eating has become yet another stressful activity that must be fit into jam-packed days," *Publishers Weekly* said. As a remedy, Weil and his coauthor Rosie Daley offer suggestions both classic and adventurous, from eggs or pasta to broccoli pancakes.

"I think it is more important to eat some carbohydrates at breakfast, because the brain needs fuel right away," he said in an interview on the Web site Share Guide, "and carbohydrate is the bet source. But it is a good idea to eat a combination of carbohydrates and protein at breakfast. Maybe some fruit, and whole grain bread and some protein, whether that's cheese, tofu, or something like that."

A recent turn for Weil is looking at aging. He explains in *Healthy Aging* (2005) that two chemical actions age the body: one has to do with the body's dealing with proteins and sugar, glycation. The other is oxidation in body cells, a spur to chronic disease. He suggests low-sugar, low-carbohydrates in the diet and intake of antioxidants and multivitamins to keep our bodies youthful.

Weil thrives on his role as a guide to his patients and his readers, and writing is a big part of that role.

"Writing has been my life, and it's brought me much satisfaction and reward," Weil told journalist Brad Wetzler of *Book* magazine. "I think I will always write."

◣ Works by the Author

> *The Natural Mind: A New Way of Looking at Drugs and Higher Consciousness* (1972), revised as *The Natural Mind: An Investigation of Drugs and the Higher Consciousness* (1986)
>
> *The Marriage of the Sun and Moon: A Quest for Unity in Consciousness* (1980)

Chocolate to Morphine: Understanding Mind-Active Drugs, with Winifred Rosen (1983), revised as *From Chocolate to Morphine: Everything You Need to Know about Mind-Altering Drugs* (1993)

Health and Healing: Understanding Conventional and Alternative Medicine (1983)

Natural Health, Natural Medicine: A Comprehensive Guide for Wellness and Self-Care (1990)

Spontaneous Healing (1995)

Eight Weeks to Optimum Health: A Proven Program for Taking Full Advantage of Your Body's Natural Healing Power (1997), revised (2006)

Roots of Healing: The New Medicine, with Michael Toms (1997)

Eating Well for Optimum Health: The Essential Guide to Food, Diet, and Nutrition (2000)

The Healthy Kitchen: Recipes for a Better Body, Life and Spirit (2002)

Healthy Aging: A Lifelong Guide to Your Physical and Spiritual Well-Being (2005)

The Healthy Brain Kit, with Gary Small (2007)

Ask Dr. Weil Series, edited by Steven Petrow

Vitamins and Minerals (1997)

Women's Health (1997)

Your Top Health Concerns (1997)

Common Illnesses (1997)

Healthy Living (1997)

Natural Remedies (1997)

Ask Dr. Weil (1998)

Audio CD Series

Breathing, The Masterkey to Self Healing (1999)

The Andrew Weil Audio Collection: Breathing, The Masterkey to Self Healing/ Meditation for Optimum Health (2001)

Eating Wisdom, with Michael Toms (2001)

Dr. Andrew Weil's Guide to Optimum Health: A Complete Course on How to Feel Better, Live Longer, and Enhance Your Health Naturally (2002)

Taking Care of Yourself: Strategies for Eating Well, Staying Fit, and Living in Balance (2002)

The Beginner's Guide to Healthy Eating (2003)

Self-Healing with Guided Imagery: How to Use the Power of Your Mind to Heal Your Body, with L. Martin and M. D. Rossman (2004)

Self-Healing with Sound & Music (2004)

Feel Better, Live Longer (2005)

Heal Yourself with Medical Hypnosis: The Most Immediate Way to Use Your Mind-Body Connection!, with Steven Gurgevich (2005)

Dr. Andrew Weil's Mindbody Toolkit: Experience Self Healing with Clinically Proven Techniques (2006)

Increase Vitality: Dr. Andrew Weil's Music for Self-Healing, with Joshua Leeds (2006)

Relax and De-stress: Rest, Re-balance, and Replenish with Classical Music for Healing, with Joshua Leeds (2006)

Walking: The Ultimate Exercise for Optimum Health, with Mark Fenton (2006)

For Further Information

Alexander, Anna B., "Ask Dr. Weil," *Prevention*, January 1998.

Andrew Weil entry, Contemporary Authors Online. Reproduced in Biography Resource Center. Farmington Hills, MI: Thomson Gale, 2006. http://galenet.galegroup.com/servlet/BioRC.

Andrew Weil Web site, http://www.drweilselfhealing.com/standard_pgs2.asp?iPageID=8 (viewed October 10, 2006).

Gupta, Sanjay, "Andrew Weil: The Guru of Self-Healing," *Time,* April 18, 2005.

Healthy Aging review, *Saturday Evening Post,* January-February 2006.

Healthy Kitchen review, *Publishers Weekly,* March 25, 2002.

Hughes, Dennis, "Interview with Dr. Andrew Weil," Share Guide. http://www.shareguide.com/Weil.html (viewed October 10, 2006).

Redwood, Daniel, "Andrew Weil, M.D. 'Integrative Medicine,' " DrRedwood.com. http://www.drredwood.com/interviews/weil.shtml (viewed September 24, 2007).

Spontaneous Healing review, *Publishers Weekly,* April 17, 1995.

Wetzler, Brad, "Dr. Midas: Andrew Weil Will Soon Turn His Golden Touch—and with It the Considerable Attention of His Followers—to the Aging Industry. Today, He's Just Home on the Ranch," *Book,* January-February 2003.

Cornel West

History, Investigative Reporting

Benchmark Title: *Race Matters*

Tulsa, Oklahoma

1953–

Photo by Brian Velenchenko

About the Author and the Author's Writing

Cornel West is an engaging classroom and public speaker, and his energy comes through in his many books on the African American experience and on religion and philosophy. "What is most rewarding about reading Cornel West is that he writes like he talks," Herb Boyd wrote in *Black Issues Book Review*. "As anyone who has been present at one of his speeches or lectures can tell you, there are few public intellectuals on the planet as spell-bindingly voluble."

West, professor of religion at Princeton University, has written for an academic audience, but he has also crafted accessible—and persuasive—works for a general readership. "His ease with ideas, his rat-a-tat-tat delivery and his impish grin have propelled the Oklahoma-born, Sacramento-raised grandson of a Baptist minister to his position as perhaps the best-known black scholar in America," CNN said in 2002.

His 2004 book *Democracy Matters* examines issues of freedom in America in the wake of the September 11 terrorist attacks on New York and Washington and he paints a grim picture of both leading political parties and of the press. Ultimately, as *Publishers Weekly* noted in its review, West "calls fiercely for an American Christianity that evokes the Christian ideals of love and justice, and that advocates deeper engagement with youth culture."

Cornel West was born in Tulsa, Oklahoma, in 1953, the son of Clifton L. West and Irene Bias West. His father was a civilian administrator with the U.S. Air Force, his mother a teacher. He graduated from Harvard in 1973 with an A.B. magna cum laude. In 1975, he earned his M.A. from Princeton, his Ph.D. in 1980.

From 1977 to 1983 he worked as assistant professor of philosophy of religion at Union Theological Seminary. He was affiliated with Yale University's Divinity School and with the University of Paris before he became professor of religion and director of African American studies at Princeton, 1988 to 1994. In 1994, he became professor of religion and Afro-American Studies at Harvard, and he was appointed as Alphonse Fletcher Jr. University Professor 1999 to 2002.

Drawn to the popular, he helped promote Louis Farrakhan's Million Man March and issued his hip-hop album as an effort at "danceable education." He resists labeling and pigeonholing. As he told interviewer Kendra Hamilton, "I think people should just be themselves—and by that I mean take seriously the Shakespearean imperative 'To thine own self be true.' And if in being true to oneself, you write popular books, that's fine; if you write academic books, that's fine, too.… This attempt to shape everyone into one mold is something that I just resist."

West didn't fit the Harvard mold. He left in 2002 in a widely publicized flap with then-President Lawrence Summers and returned to Princeton as University Professor of Religion. West and his third wife live in New Jersey.

West's disagreement with Harvard's administration—one issue was West's recording of a rap CD—in some ways echoes cultural travails in the United States. In three decades the country has seen growth in the black middle class. But that growth has come at a loss of unity. "We had a much deeper sense of community in '67 than we do in '97," he said in an interview with Henry Lewis Gates Jr. for *Frontline* in 1997. "This is important to say that not in a nostalgic way because it's not as if '67 was a time when things were so good. Materially speaking, we were much worse. But culturally speaking in terms of social connection, they were much better."

Expanding on that sentiment, West told Kenneth Meeks of *Black Enterprise,* "I think it's magnificent for black middle class and above, but it's a national disgrace for the black working poor and the very poor. There is a class difference that we have to acknowledge."

The September 11 terrorist attacks had one unexpected impact, he said in *Jet*: "Never before have Americans of all classes, colors, regions, religions, genders and sexual orientations felt unsafe, unprotected, subject to random violence and hatred."

One of his current messages to fellow blacks is introspection. "This is a difficult task given that Black culture and this society don't encourage emotional honesty, intimacy or self-love in men" he said in *Essence.* "So how do we begin to shift? How can brothers like you encourage more men to be who they truly are and be true to their emotional selves?"

Works by the Author

Prophesy Deliverance! An Afro-American Revolutionary Christianity (1982)
Prophetic Fragments (1988)
The American Evasion of Philosophy: A Genealogy of Pragmatism (1989)
Breaking Bread: Insurgent Black Intellectual Life, with bell hooks (1991)
Race Matters (1993)
Beyond Eurocentrism and Multiculturalism, Volume 1, Prophetic Thoughts in Postmodern Times; Volume 2, Prophetic Reflections, Notes on Race and Power in America (1993)
Keeping Faith: Philosophy and Race in America (1994)
Jews and Blacks; Let the Healing Begin, with Michael Lerner (1995)
Death Blossoms: Reflections from a Prisoner of Conscience, with Mumia Abu-Jamal (1996)

The Future of the Race, with Henry Louis Gates Jr. (1996)

Restoring Hope: Conversations on the Future of Black America, edited by Kevin Shawn Sealey (1997)

The Future of American Progressivism: An Initiative for Political and Economic Reform, with Roberto Mangabeira (1998)

The War against Parents; What We Can Do for America's Beleaguered Moms and Dads, with Sylvia Ann Hewlett (1998)

The Cornel West Reader (1999)

The African-American Century: How Black Americans Have Shaped Our Country (2000)

Democracy Matters: Winning the Fight against Imperialism (2004)

Audio CDs

Sketches of My Culture (2001)

Street Knowledge (2004)

Never Forget: A Journey of Revelations, with Black Men Who Mean Business (2007)

DVDs

Charlie Rose with Henry Louis Gates, Jr. and Cornel West (April 12, 1996) (2006)

Malcolm & Martin: Implications of Their Legacies for the Future, with Imam Zald Shakir (2006)

Editor

Theology in the Americas: Detroit II Conference Papers, with Caridad Guidote and Margaret Coakley (1982)

Post-Analytic Philosophy, with John Rajchman (1985)

White Screens, Black Images: Hollywood from the Dark Side, by John Snead, with Colin MacCabe (1994)

Encyclopedia of African-American Culture and History, with Jack Salzman and David Lionel Smith (1996)

Struggles in the Promised Land: Toward a History of Black-Jewish Relations in the United States, with Jack Salzman (1997)

The Courage to Hope: From Black Suffering to Human Redemption, with Quinton Hosford Dixie (1999)

The Other Malcolm, "Shorty" Jarvis: His Memoir, by Malcolm "Shorty" Jarvis with Paul D. Nichols (2001)

Taking Parenting Public; The Case for a New Social Movement, with Sylvia Ann Hewlett and Nancy Rankin (2002)

African American Religious Thought: An Anthology, with Eddie S. Glaude Jr. (2003)

Racist Traces and Other Writings: European Pedigrees/African Contagions, by James A. Snead with Kara Keeling and Colin MacCabe (2003)

For Further Information

Bombardieri, Marcella, "Some Seek a Scholar's Return," *Boston Globe,* June 6, 2006.

Cornel (Ronald) West entry, Contemporary Authors Online. Reproduced in Biography Resource Center. Farmington Hills, MI: Thomson Gale, 2004. http://galenet.galegroup.com/servlet/BioRC.

Democracy Matters review, *Black Issues Book Review*, September-October 2004.

Democracy Matters review, *Jet,* December 13, 2004.

Democracy Matters review, *Publishers Weekly,* June 7, 2004.

Gates, Henry Louis, Cornel West interview, *Frontline.* http://www.pbs.org/wgbh/pages/frontline/shows/race/interviews/west.html (viewed October 30, 2006).

Goodrich, Chris, *Race Matters* review, *Publishers Weekly,* November 2, 1992.

Hamilton, Kendra, "Dr. Cornel West, in His Own Words," *Black Issues in Higher Education,* May 23, 2002.

Meeks, Kenneth, "Backtalk with Scholar Dr. Cornel West," *Black Enterprise,* February 2005.

Morrison, John, *Cornel West.* New York: Chelsea House, 2003.

Naden, Corinne J., and Rose Blue. *Cornel West.* New York: Raintree, 2005.

"Prof. Cornel West Leaves Harvard Univ. for Princeton Univ.," *Jet,* April 29, 2002.

Taylor, Susan L., "Courage to Love with Cornel West," *Essence,* November 2005.

"West of Righteous—Interview with Author Cornel West," *Artforum,* February 1994.

"Who Is Cornel West?" CNN.com. http://archives.cnn.com/2002/fyi/teachers.ednews/01/10/west.harvard.ap/ (viewed September 24, 2007).

Wood, Mark David, *Cornel West and the Politics of Prophetic Pragmatism.* Chicago: University of Illinois Press, 2000.

Simon Winchester

Adventure, Biography, History, Travel

Benchmark Title: *The Professor and the Madman*

London, England

1944–

Courtesy HarperCollins

About the Author and the Author's Writing

The popularity of his books twice landed Simon Winchester an interview on Martha Stewart's syndicated television program, although the conversation was not quite what he may have expected. "She had me looking at the etymology of words like doily and antimacassar," he said in a conversation with Dave Weich of Powells.com, "and now she wants me back on the program to talk about fossils as home decorating items."

Of course, interesting stories lurk everywhere, and Winchester has a knack for discovering them. "History is full of forgotten characters. We tend to know about people who sign treaties and make the major inventions," the author said in a *Geographical* interview. He, on the other hand, has latched onto insane lexicographers (*The Professor and the Madman*, 1998) and onto shunned geologists (*The Map That Changed the World*, 2001).

Winchester was born in London, England, in 1944. He studied geology at St. Catherine's College, Oxford, receiving an M.A. in 1966. He worked on offshore oil rigs and worked in Uganda for a year. Then he read James Morris's *Coronation Everest*—about the 1953 Edmund Hillary-Tenzing Norgay expedition—and knew the career he wanted: writing. Morris (later to be Jan Morris) mentored Winchester, and they collaborated on one book.

From 1967 to 1970, Winchester reported for the Newcastle-upon-Tyne *Journal*. Early on he found an ability to compose interesting stories about uninteresting events. From 1970 to 1972, he was the Northern Ireland correspondent for the London *Guardian*. He served the same newspaper in Washington, D.C., from 1972 to 1976 and in New Delhi from 1977 to 1979. From 1979 to 1980, he served as chief U.S. correspondent for the *Daily Mail,* then became senior feature writer for the *Sunday Times*. In that role, he covered the Jonestown massacre and President Richard Nixon's resignation.

As a freelancer he has written for *Condé Nast Traveler, Smithsonian, National Geographic,* and other periodicals.

With homes in New York City, Scotland, and western Massachusetts, the author doesn't sit still for long. He has three children from two marriages, both of which ended in divorce.

While his later works are hybrid history-biography-adventure tales, Winchester began his book-writing career on a contemporary note, describing the ongoing unrest in Northern Ireland (*In Holy Terror*). He gravitated to travel books, describing his sojourns in Korea (*Korea: A Walk through a Land of Miracles*) or Hong Kong (*Hong Kong: Here There Be Dragons*) or China (*The River at the Center of the World*). This last book, said *Publishers Weekly*, shows the author as "Wryly humorous, gently skeptical, immensely knowledgeable as he wends his way along the 3900 miles of the great river."

In 1996, Winchester had a contract for a travel book. He planned to buy a second-hand tramp steamer in the Baltic and, with a friend who was a master mariner, set off on a yearlong world cruise. Making his preparations from his then home in upstate New York, he chanced to read a book during his morning bath. "There was a footnote in this book and it said readers will be familiar with the extraordinary story of W. C. Minor, the convicted American murderer who was such a prolific contributor to the *Oxford English Dictionary [OED]*. And I remember sitting up in the bath like sort of Archimedes must have done…. Eureka."

After hastily checking sources, Winchester found that Minor's files were still locked away at the British asylum where he had lived—and a book idea was born. When his publisher wanted the steamer book instead of something about a wordsmith, Winchester sought a new publisher, bought out his old contract, and set to investigating his new subject.

The result. *The Professor and the Madman* (1998) became a bestseller about the curious relationship between the institutionalized Minor and a dictionary editor, Professor James Murray.

Winchester attributed the book's success to a long rain the weekend the *New York Times Book Review* ran a praiseworthy review, and plenty of people had time to read it. Others such as Brad Hooper in *Booklist* attribute it to the author's ability: "The tale of their affiliation and friendship reads like a creatively conceived novel." Added *Library Journal*'s Gloria Maxwell, "Winchester does a superb job of weaving the historical facts of murder, madness, and scholarly pursuit into a fitting tribute to the remarkable OED."

Winchester told interviewer Debra Witt his strength is in shaping his presentation. "I learned that I'm a good story teller…. First of all, I know what makes a good story. But I also know when to stop, when the story's becoming boring."

Winchester followed his OED story with another obscure subject, William Smith, the engineer and canal digger who, in 1793, recognized the layered arrangement of rocks and fossils that make up the earth's crust. He created the world's first geological map—only to be skittered into oblivion and plagiarized by the cognoscenti of his day. That book was *The Map That Changed the World,* published in 2001. The author revisited the OED for a broader story in *The Meaning of Everything: The Story of the Oxford English Dictionary* (2003). Ever the geologist at heart, he surveyed two natural disasters, the Krakatoa explosion of 1883 for *Krakatoa: The Day the World Ex-*

ploded, August 27, 1883 (2003) and the San Francisco Earthquake of 1906 for *A Crack in the Edge of the World* (2005).

Winchester's opus has become so significant, Queen Elizabeth awarded him the Order of the British Empire for service to journalism and literature in 2006.

 Works by the Author

In Holy Terror: Reporting the Ulster Troubles (1974), published in the United States as *Northern Ireland in Crisis; Reporting the Ulster Troubles* (1975)

American Heartbeat: Notes from a Midwestern Journey (1976)

Their Noble Lordships; The Hereditary Peerage Today (1982), published in the United States as *Their Noble Lordships: Class and Power in Modern Britain* (1982)

Prison Diary, Argentina (1983)

Stones of Empire: The Building of the Raj, with Jan Morris (1983)

The Sun Never Sets: Travels to the Remaining Outposts of the British Empire (1985), published in England as *Outposts* (1985)

Korea; A Walk through the Land of Miracles (1988)

Pacific Rising: The Emergence of a New World Culture (1991)

Hong Kong: Here Be Dragons (1992)

Pacific Nightmare: How Japan Starts World War III: A Future History (1992)

Small World, with Martin Parr (1995)

The River at the Center of the World: A Journey up the Yangtze and Back in Chinese Time (1996)

The Professor and the Madman: A Tale of Murder, Insanity, and the Making of the Oxford English Dictionary (1998), published in England as *The Surgeon of Crowthorne* (1998)

The Fracture Zone: A Return to the Balkans (1999)

The Map That Changed the World: William Smith and the Birth of Modern Geology (2001), published in England as *The Map That Changed the World: The Tale of William Smith and the Birth of a Science*

Krakatoa: The Day the World Exploded, August 27, 1883 (2003)

The Meaning of Everything: The Story of the Oxford English Dictionary (2003)

A Crack in the Edge of the World: America and the Great California Earthquake of 1906 (2005)

For Further Information

Amodeo, Christian, Simon Winchester interview, *Geographical,* December 2003.

Burgess, Edwin B., *A Crack in the Edge of the World* review, *Library Journal,* September 15, 2005.

Davis, Clive, *The Meaning of Everything* review, *Wilson Quarterly,* autumn 2003.

Fabricant, Carolyn, "Splendidly Incongruous: The Fascinating Life of Sandisfield Author Simon Winchester," *Berkshire Eagle,* March 21, 2002.

Ferris, Henry, Simon Winchester interview, Simon Winchester Web site. http://www.simonwinchester.com/about/about_interview.html   (viewed October 30, 2006).

Harris, Karen, *The Map That Changed the World* review, *Booklist,* February 1, 2002.

Hooper, Brad, *The Professor and the Madman* review, *Booklist,* August 1998.

Krakatoa review, *Contemporary Review,* December 2003.

Maxwell, Gloria, *The Map That Changed the World* review, *Library Journal,* June 15, 2001.

Maxwell, Gloria, *The Professor and the Madman* review, *Library Journal,* January 2000.

Nelson, Matt, "An Explosion of Attention," *Publishers Weekly,* March 10, 2003.

The River at the Center of the World review, *Publishers Weekly,* September 16, 1996.

Simon Winchester entry, Contemporary Authors Online. Reproduced in Biography Resource Center. Farmington Hills, MI: Thomson Gale, 2004. http://galenet.galegroup.com/servlet/BioRC.

Todd, Alden, Simon Winchester interview, Commonwealth North Forum. http://www.commonwealthnorth.org/transcripts/winchester.html (viewed October 17, 2006).

Weich, Dave, "Simon Winchester Unearths Another Scholar," Powells.com. http://www.powells.com/authors/winchester.html (viewed October 10, 2006).

Witt, Debra, "Meet the Author: Simon Winchester," FashionPlanet.com. http://www.fashion-planet.com/sept98/columns/arts/book_winchester/winchester.html (viewed October 30, 2006).

Tom Wolfe

Adventure, Biography, Investigative Reporting, Memoir

Benchmark Title: *The Right Stuff*

Richmond, Virginia

1931–

About the Author and the Author's Writing

It was a departure, in the 1960s. A little radical. Social observers called it New Journalism. "What was new about it was the utilization of techniques in journalism that had previously been used only in fiction," Tom Wolfe told interviewer Steve Hammer. "Today, the techniques are very much known by writers for newspapers, and in magazine work." The techniques include presentation of a story in scenes, dialogue, depiction of character or scene through small details, and affording a perspective through one of the participants.

What separated Wolfe and other writers of his generation from earlier proponents of the literary style such as John Hersey and Ernest Hemingway and Truman Capote and Lillian Ross was, unquestionably, his intensity. He just knew *so much* about bootlegger-turned-stock-car-driver Junior Johnson or the Vegas slot machine addicts in their bikini-style shorts and Ken Kesey and his LSD-hazed Pranksters.

Thomas Kennerly Wolfe Jr. was born in 1931 in Richmond, Virginia, the son of business executive Thomas Kennerly and Helen Hughes Wolfe. In 1951, he received a bachelor of arts degree cum laude from Washington and Lee University; he earned a Ph.D. from Yale University in 1957. In 1978, he married Sheila Berger, art director for *Harper's* magazine; they have two children.

Wolfe joined the newsroom at the *Springfield* (Massachusetts) *Republican* in 1956, later moving to the *Washington Post*, where he was Latin American correspondent from 1959 to 1962. He then went to work for the New York *Herald Tribune* as a reporter and writer for its *New York Sunday* magazine—which eventually spun off as *New York*—from 1962 to 1966, returning as a contributing editor 1968 to 1976. In the interim, he was a writer for the *New York World Journal Tribune*. Since 1977, he has been a contributing editor to *Esquire* magazine. From 1978 to 1981, he was a contributing artist to *Harper's*.

Wolfe began using "New Journalism," according to Margo Harakas, when he struggled to write a story about a West Coast car customizer. He found "that standard journalistic techniques, those he had employed so successfully during his years of newspaper work, could not adequately describe the bizarre people and machines he had encountered in California." He relied on vernacular, on extensive dialogue, on character, on unusual language and punctuation.

In *The Kandy-Kolored Tangerine-Flake Streamline Baby,* Wolfe embraces the counterculture of the 1960s. In the book, we find Wolfe's colorful, evocative language in, for example, this description of Las Vegas: "He had been rolling up and down the incredible electric-sign gauntlet of Las Vegas' Strip, U.S. Route 91, where the neon and the par lamps—bubbling, spiraling, rocketing, and exploding in sunbursts ten stories high out in the middle of the desert—celebrate one-story casinos."

His 1968 novel, *The Electric Kool-Aid Acid Test,* brought out all of Wolfe's tricks, as befit the West Coast drug culture topic. "Wolfe rearranged his words in non-linear fashion and used punctuation as a graphic element, like E.E. Cummings on a mescaline bender," Marc Weingarten wrote in *The Gang That Wouldn't Write Straight.* "He was fond of ellipses, because his subjects talked in elliptical patterns, even thought in them.

He soared onto the bestseller lists in 1979 when he "completed a book he had been at work on for more than six years," according to a biography on his Web site, "an account of the rocket airplane experiments of the post World War II era and the early space program focusing on the psychology of the rocket pilots and the astronauts and the competition between them."

That book, *The Right Stuff,* won an American Book Award for nonfiction, a Columbia Journalism Award and a National Institute of Arts and Letters Harold Vursell Award for prose style. Wolfe contributed to our vocabulary such words as "radical chic" and "the Me Decade" and "good ol' boy." He also used an approach often criticized and occasionally abused by others. "Wolfe-like narrative stories are often told from the perspective of one or more of the main characters," explained Chris Harvey in *American Journalism Review.* "Readers become privy to a character's thoughts but are not told how the thoughts were discerned by the reporter."

Wolfe became a writer-celebrity. "Splendid in his trademark white suit, a blue-tending-toward-violet, high-collared shirt, and white tie with blue-tending-to-ward-violet polka dots, stepped from the jetway," journalist Thomas M. Gaughan described him in appropriate detail in an *American Libraries* profile. "He's slim, about five-feet-nine, almost delicate except for large, powerful-looking hands. In one he carried a leather satchel distressed by 50 years' use. His fine brown hair is graying around the rim and he regularly sweeps it off his forehead. When he smiles, crow's feet appear around his eyes."

In 1987, Wolfe brought his literary savvy to fiction with the critically acclaimed *The Bonfire of the Vanities*, a send-up of 1980s New York that was first serialized in *Rolling Stone.* Another multicharacter social novel, *A Man in Full,* headed the *New York Times* best-seller list for 10 weeks in 1998–1999.

Wolfe's recent *Hooking Up* (2000) collects his shorter pieces, including one about late *New Yorker* editor William Shawn's quirky sense of dress: "He always seems to have on about twenty layers of clothes," he wrote in the book, "about three button-up sweaters, four vests, a couple of shirts, two ties, it looks that way, a dark shapeless suit over the whole ensemble, and white cotton socks."

Wolfe is very much the rebel. "I see myself labeled a lot as a social conservative, and it doesn't bother me, particularly when I consider the alternative," he told *U.S. News & World Report.* "Usually what brings that characterization is going against the orthodoxy of the intellectual world. I use the term intellectual rather broadly to include the world of journalism as well as literature, theater, and so on."

 ## Works by the Author

The Kandy-Kolored Tangerine-Flake Streamline Baby (1965)
The Electric Kool-Aid Acid Test (1968)
The Pump House Gang (1968), published in England as The Mid-Atlantic Man and Other New Breeds in England and America (1969)
Radical Chic and Mau Mauing the Flake Catchers (1970)
The Painted Word (1975)
Mauve Gloves & Madmen, Clutter & Vine, and Other Short Stories (1976)
The Right Stuff (1979)
In Our Time (1980)
From Bauhaus to Our House (1981)
The Purple Decades: A Reader (1982)
Two Complete Books (1994), includes The Right Stuff and The Bonfire of the Vanities
Hooking Up (2000)

Editor

The New Journalism, with E. W. Johnson (1973)

Fiction

The Bonfire of the Vanities (1987)
A Man in Full (1998)
I Am Charlotte Simmons (2004)

Film Adaptations

The Last American Hero (1973), based on articles
The Right Stuff (1983)
The Bonfire of the Vanities (1990)
I Am Charlotte Simmons (announced)

For Further Information

Gaughan, Thomas M., "A Cab Ride with Tom Wolfe," American Libraries, July-August 1990.
Hammer, Steve, "Tom Wolfe Speaks His Mind," NUVO Newsweekly. http://www.nuvo.net/hammer.int/wolfe.html (viewed November 3, 2006).
Harakas, Margo, Tom Wolfe profile, Fort Lauderdale Sentinel, April 22, 1975.
Harvey, Chris, "Tom Wolfe's Revenge," American Journalism Review, October 1994.

Sanoff, Alvin P., "Tom Wolfe's Walk on the Wild Side," *U.S. News & World Report,* November 23, 1987.

Thomas Kennerly Wolfe Jr. entry, Contemporary Authors Online. Reproduced in Biography Resource Center. Farmington Hills, MI: Thomson Gale, 2004. http://galenet.galegroup.com/servlet/BioRC.

Tom Wolfe biography, Tom Wolfe Web page. http://www.tomwolfe.com/bio.html (viewed October 17, 2006).

Weingarten, Marc, *The Gang That Wouldn't Write Straight: Wolfe, Thompson, Didion, and the New Journalism Revolution.* New York: Crown, 2006.

Tobias Wolff

Memoir

Benchmark Title: *This Boy's Life*

Birmingham, Alabama

1945–

About the Author and the Author's Writing

Tobias Wolff had a miserable childhood. That in itself would be unremarkable, except that he decided to write about it—in *This Boy's Life,* published in 1989—and his memoir hit the mark with critics and readers, to the extent the book about a rebellious youth has become the nonfiction equivalent of J. D. Salinger's *The Catcher in the Rye*—required reading in many high school lit classes.

What *This Boy's Life* and a second work, *In Pharaoh's Army* (1994), which details his experiences in the Mekong Delta during the Vietnam War, show, the author said in a *Publishers Weekly* interview, "is someone who's unformed and trying to find a place in the world."

Both works are based on recollection; Wolff kept no journal. "I'm glad I didn't take notes," he continued in his dialogue with reporter Nicholas A. Basbanes, "because what is essential in that experience is exactly what would have stayed with me. I remembered what I needed to remember."

Some have challenged the validity of Wolff's memoirs, suggesting that they are too literarily shaped. Wolff responded that the source of the writing is memory, and, flawed or pure, there needs be no defense of that.

Tobias Jonathan Ansell Wolff was born in 1945 in Birmingham, Alabama, the son of aeronautical engineer Arthur S. Wolff and Rosemary Loftus Wolff. Arthur Wolff was a conman, forger, car thief, and deadbeat. He fabricated all sorts of tales—an ability that rubbed off on his son as a literary talent. Tobias Wolff's memoir is shaped as a series of stories, each well crafted, about him and his mother moving to Florida while Tobias's brother Geoffrey (who is also a writer) stayed with his father. Rosemary's new live-in boyfriend, Roy, was an abuser and stalked Rosemary to Utah. Roy tormented Toby, made him do meaningless household chores, and took his meager part-time job earnings. Toby learned to lie, cheat, and steal. He lied on his entrance exam to get into private Hill School, only to flounder in the rigid academic environment.

Wolff served in the army from 1964 to 1968 (including two years with Special Forces in Vietnam), reaching the rank of lieutenant. While his account of military service further enlightens his growth as an individual, the author insists there is no direct corollary between his two memoirs. He feels he was a much different person by the time he joined up than he had been as a troubled youth.

Upon his discharge, Wolff became determined to attend Oxford—and he did, with great dedication. In 1972, he received a B.A. with first class honors; in 1975, he received an M.A. from Oxford University, with a second master's from Stanford University in 1978. After graduating, he worked as a reporter for the *Washington Post* for six months. He was a waiter and a night security man and a high school teacher. From 1975 to 1978, he taught creative writing at Stanford University, then taught at Syracuse University from 1980 to 1997. In 1997, he returned to Stanford, also at times teaching at Goddard College in Vermont and Arizona State University at Tempe. He and his wife, Catherine Spohn, have three children. They live in California, where he teaches at Stanford University.

His first novel, *Ugly Rumours,* came out in 1975, but he has mostly concentrated on short stories, several collections of which have appeared since 1982.

Wolff enjoyed great powers of observation from his childhood. "I studied other people," he said in a salon.com interview. "I was watchful, but I don't know why. Memory is funny. Once you hit a vein the problem is not how to remember but how to control the flow.... When I was about 14 or 15 I decided to become a writer and never for a moment since have I wanted to do anything else."

That's not to say Wolff was always satisfied with his output. "You have an idea in mind of what you want to achieve when you sit down to write something," he told William Bradley of the *Missouri Review*. "It takes many years to accept that you will always fall short of that. Maybe now I can write the book that I might have had in mind five or twenty years ago. You're always lagging behind your best ideas."

Wolf could have thrived as a writer of fiction. "I was very reluctant to enter into the business of writing memoirs," he told interviewer David Schrieberg. "But whenever I started to invent around this autobiographical material, it would go flat, conventional. Whenever I'd go back and deal with the genuine experience, track it very closely, then it would come to life again."

"Just as his book is melancholy and hilarious by turns," *American Heritage* said of *Pharaoh's Army*, "so do the tales that make it up manage to seem at once surprising and inevitable—and thus nicely emblematic of a time that has yet to find an easy resting place in the national consciousness."

The author finds in his role as university instructor a comfortable dynamic for his writing. "A teaching community is ideal for a writer," he said in *Continuum Magazine*. "We're constantly trading books, talking about things, and it's a lot like the way that a knife gets sharpened by constant friction against a stone."

 # Works by the Author

This Boy's Life: A Memoir (1989)
In Pharaoh's Army: Memories of the Lost War (1994)

Fiction

Ugly Rumours (1975)
In the Garden of the North American Martyrs (1981), published in England as
   Hunters in the Snow (1982)

The Barracks Thief (1984), reprinted as *The Barracks Thief and Other Stories* (1984)

Back in the World (1985)

The Stories of Tobias Wolff (1988), includes *Hunters in the Snow, Back in the World*, and *The Barracks Thief*

Old School (2003)

Our Story Begins: New and Selected Stories (2008)

Editor

Matters of Life and Death: New American Stories (1982)

A Doctor's Visit: The Short Stories of Anton Chekhov (1987)

The Picador Book of Contemporary American Stories (1993)

Best American Short Stories (1994)

The Night in Question (1996)

Film Adaptation

This Boy's Life (1993)

For Further Information

"And Finally … Talking with Tobias Wolff," *Continuum Magazine,* summer 1998.

Basbanes, Nicholas A., "Tobias Wolff: 'This is … my last memoir,' " *Publishers Weekly,* October 24, 1994.

Bradley, William, "An Interview with Tobias Wolff," *The Missouri Review.* http://www.missourireview.com/index.php?genre=Interviews&title=An+Interview+with+Tobias+Wolff (viewed May 3, 2006).

In Pharaoh's Army review, *American Heritage,* November 1994.

Schrieberg, David, Tobias Wolff interview, *Stanford Today* Online September-October 1998. http://www.stanford.edu/dept/news/stanfordtoday/ed/9809/9809fea101.shtml (viewed May 3, 2006).

Smith, Joan, Tobias Wolff interview, salon.com. http://www.salon.com/dec96/interview961216.html (viewed May 3, 2006).

Tobias (Jonathan Anssell) Wolff entry, Contemporary Authors Online. Reproduced in Biography Resource Center. Farmington Hills, MI: Thomson Gale, 2004. http://galenet.galegroup.com/servlet/BioRC.

Tobias Wolff entry, *Newsmakers,* Vol. 1. Detroit: Thomson Gale, 2005.

Bob Woodward

Biography, Investigative Reporting

Benchmark Title: *All the President's Men*

Geneva, Illinois

1943–

About the Authors and the Authors' Writing

Journalist Bob Woodward emerged with the baby-boomer generation with the same intensity as Ida Tarbell's revelations about John D. Rockefeller and Standard Oil did with the pre–World War I population. With fellow *Washington Post* reporter Carl Bernstein, the author wrote an early 1970s newspaper series that became the book *All the President's Men*, and gave investigative reporting—to some, "muckracking"—a good name. Once he got his teeth into Washington, D.C.'s underbelly, he never let go. He has on his own written a dozen hard-hitting, and best-selling, nonfiction works in the decades since.

Robert "Bob" Upshur Woodward was born in 1943 in Geneva, Illinois, the son of Judge Alfred E. Woodward and Jane Upshur Woodard Barnes. He served in the U.S. Navy from 1965 to 1970. He received a bachelor of arts degree from Yale University in 1965. He was a reporter for the *Montgomery County Sentinel* in Maryland in 1970 and 1971, when he joined the *Washington Post* as a reporter. He became an editor from 1979 to 1981 and then was named assistant managing editor in 1981. He has two children from his marriage to Elsa Walsh; the marriage ended in divorce.

The *Washington Post* received a Pulitzer Prize for its coverage of the Watergate scandal, which brought down the Nixon presidency. Woodward was at the core of the paper's reportage—reportage that got off to the least auspicious of starts.

It was June 17, 1972. Woodward had been with the *Post* less than a year. Assigned to the police beat, he covered a Saturday morning arraignment of three men who had been nabbed breaking into the Watergate Hotel. The judge quizzed one of the men as to his employer: the CIA—Central Intelligence Agency. This was not your usual burglary story.

Woodward teamed with Bernstein, a copy boy who'd moved up to cover Virginia politics. As the connections fell together, as the story emerged, Woodward admitted he was concerned about the enormity and velocity of it all. "I was worried about the *Post*'s image of all of this, and that there would be a segment of society who said, you know, 'They were out to get him, those bastards, and they got him. ...' [W]e were just very careful. We had such good sources."

Investigative journalism entered a heyday. "In the dizzying wake of Nixon administration resignations, impeachment threats, and the celebrification of Woodward and Bernstein, newspapers all over the country tried to duplicate the *Washington Post*'s success on smaller scales," according to *Columbia Journalism Review*. "Everyone wanted to be on board the investigative bandwagon."

Woodward wrote one more book with Bernstein, *The Final Days,* about the demise of the Nixon presidency, before the two went their ways. (Woodward wrote an unexpected coda to the Nixon story in 2005, *The Secret Man,* when the man who, calling himself "Deep Throat," proved to be one of Woodward and Bernstein's critical administration sources, came forward with his story. He was W. Mark Felts, former second in command at the FBI.)

Woodward concentrated on books with an insider's view of Washington, the most recent a series of books about President George W. Bush and the war in Iraq: *Bush at War* (2002), *Plan of Attack* (2004), and *State of Denial* (2006). One conclusion from the last book mentioned is that the conflict was instigated to redeem the historical image of the Vietnam War quagmire. The old forces are still at work—Dick Cheney, Donald H. Rumsfeld, even Henry Kissinger—who each formulated foreign policy decades ago in earlier Republican administrations, Woodward insisted.

Woodward interviewed seventy-five administration and military officials—including Bush, twice, on the record—for the book.

With large-city newspapers increasingly part of multimedia conglomerates, the climate for investigative journalism isn't what it might be. "Newspapers that are truly independent, like the *Washington Post,* can still aggressively investigate anyone or anything with no holds barred," Woodward said in a *Washington Post* online forum. "Unfortunately, there is some evidence that some newspapers have a hands-off policy on favored politicians. But it's generally very small newspapers or local TV stations. If you interviewed 1,000 politicians and asked about whether the media's 'too soft' or 'too hard,' about 999 would say 'too hard.' "

◆ **Works by the Author**

All the President's Men, with Carl Bernstein (1974)
The Final Days, with Carl Bernstein (1976)
The Brethren: Inside the Supreme Court, with Scott Armstrong (1979)
Wired: The Short Life and Fast Times of John Belushi (1984)
Veil: The Secret Wars of the CIA, 1981–1987 (1987)
The Commanders (1991)
The Man Who Would Be President: Dan Quayle, with David S. Broder (1992)
The Agenda: Inside the Clinton White House (1994)
The Choice: November 5, 1996 (1996), revised as *The Choice: How Clinton Won* (2005)
Shadow: Five Presidents and the Legacy of Watergate (1999)
Maestro: Greenspan's Fed and the American Boom (2000)
Bush at War (2002)
Plan of Attack (2004)

The Secret Man: The Story of Watergate's Deep Throat, with Boyd Gaines (2005)

State of Denial: Bush at War, Part III (2006)

Contributor

The Fall of a President, with the staff of the *Washington Post* (1974)

Film Adaptation

All the President's Men (1976)

For Further Information

Bob Woodward and Ben Bradlee interview, Academy of Achievement, May 1, 2003. http://www.achievement.org/autodoc/page/woo1int-1 (viewed September 26, 2006).

Dennis, Brady, "Ex-Watergate Writer Laments 'Idiot Culture,' " *St. Petersburg Times,* March 19, 2004.

Feldstein, Mark, "Watergate Revisited: Thirty Years after President Nixon's Resignation, There's Little Agreement over Just How Important a Role Journalism Played in Bringing Him Down. But There's No Doubt the Episode Had a Significant Impact on the Profession," *American Journalism Review,* August-September 2004.

Forum with Bob Woodward, WashingtonPost.com. http://discuss.washingtonpost.com/zforum/97/woodward.htm (viewed November 6, 2006).

Havill, Adrian, *Deep Truth: The Lives of Bob Woodward and Carl Bernstein.* Secaucus, NJ: Carol, 1993.

McGeary, Johanna, "Inside Watergate's Last Chapter: After 33 Years of Secrecy, Deep Throat's Identity Is Revealed. But Questions Persist over His Motivations and How Valuable a Source He Really Was in the Scandal That Brought Down a President," *Time,* June 13, 2005.

Reeves, Richard, "Woodward and Bernstein," *Editor & Publisher,* October 30, 1999.

Robert Upshur Woodward entry, Contemporary Authors Online. Reproduced in Biography Resource Center. Farmington Hills, MI: Thomson Gale, 2005. http://galenet.galegroup.com/servlet/BioRC.

Rutten, Tim, "Wartime Quagmire," *Albany Times-Union,* October 8, 2006 (syndicated by the *Los Angeles Times*).

"Watergate: A Relentless Investigation Pays Off, and the Most Famous Journalistic Feat of Its Time Brings Down a President," *Columbia Journalism Review,* November-December 2001.

Genre Index

Author/Title Index

About the Author

BERNARD A. DREW is a freelance writer/editor and author of numerous articles and books, including *100 Most Popular Genre Authors* (Libraries Unlimited, 2005) and *100 Most Popular African American Authors* (Libraries Unlimited, 2006).